UNDERSTANDING
IQBAL'S
PHILOSOPHY

by

Dr. WAHEED ISHRAT

M.A (PHILOSOPHY), PH.D. (PHILOSOPHY)

SANG-E-MEEL PUBLICATIONS

LAHORE—PAKISTAN

910.01	Waheed Ishrat, Dr.
	Understanding Iqbal's Philosophy/ Dr. Waheed Ishrat.-Lahore: Sang-e-Meel Publications, 2007.
	325pp.
	1. Philosophy - Iqbal Studies.
I. Title.	

2007
Published by
Niaz Ahmad
Sang-e-Meel Publications,
Lahore.

ISBN 969-35-2073-4

SANG-E-MEEL PUBLICATIONS
Phones: 7220100 - 7228143   Fax: 7245101
http://www.sang-e-meel.com e-mail: smp@sang-e-meel.com
25 Shahrah-e-Pakistan (Lower Mall), P.O. Box 997 Lahore-54000 PAKISTAN
PRINTED AT: HAJI HANIF & SONS PRINTERS, LAHORE.

To my beloved wife,
Farida Waheed.

CONTENTS

1. The Origins and Sources of Iqbal's Philosophy 11
2. Methodology of Reconstruction of Religious Thought in Islam 49
3. Muslim Theory of Knowledge in the Perspective of Mulla Sadra and Iqbal 59
4. Iqbal and the Principle of Dynamism in Islam 74
5. Iqbal's Philosophy of Revolution 102
6. The Social Philosophy of Iqbal 123
7. The Reconstruction of Islamic Thought 141
8. Iqbal's Concept of Democracy 151
9. Iqbal and Ideology of Pakistan 200
10. The Pakistan Plan and the Role of Iqbal 226
11. Iqbal and Communism 259
12. Some rare Resemblances between Firdausi and Iqbal 272
13. Study of Iqbalics in Pakistan 292

INTRODUCTION

According to the Holy Qur'an, God created the universe with a purpose under a divine plan. In brief, the purpose was to manifest the attributes of His Essence. The plan was to create and operate all its components in unison where they operate together and move towards their betterment. All these components were subject to their predetermined destiny under God's command. At this stage He created Man for the purpose of appreciating the creation of God, striving to maintain it in its pristine beauty and to beautify it. God designated Man as His vicegerent on earth. For this purpose He endowed Man with a new attribute, not possessed by the previous components of creation. This was *Ruh* (soul) which enabled Man to have and use his intellect and perception, through which he got the awareness of ethical values and intuition which enabled him to select between good and evil acts.

Struggle between good and evil, between virtue and vice has been the saga of the human race since eternity. The fall of *Iblis* (Satan) from his high pedestal among *Jins* for disobeying God is not prostrating before the first Man towards evil. God endowed Man with His guidance through prophets and their divinely revealed books, philosophers, sages, mystics and leaders' right path. Thus, the struggle between virtue and vice started incumbent upon Man and is his duty and destiny as the vicegerent of God. It is more so on a *Mumin* because of his being endowed with the wisdom of all Divine revelations. This struggle is in material, spiritual, and intellectual fields. It requires cultivation and development of spiritual, intellectual as well as material strength. This strength can be acquired only by developing *Khudi,* so as to create appreciation of one's potential and develop spiritual and moral strength to face evil. The most important component of *Khudi* is an ardent and sincere Love of God. The Holy Qur'an provides recipes for developing *Khudi*.

Iqbal was a crusader against evil and the best one of his age. It is difficult to define his personality, and he is looked upon differently by different people. He had deep knowledge of and insight in philosophy, theology, history, *tasawwuf,* and literature - Urdu, Persian as well as English. In his early life Iqbal realized his duty to prepare the Muslim *Ummah* for this struggle to enable it to attain its rightful place from which it may be able to free all mankind from the yoke of evil. His approach and mission was to create an ideological revolution in the Muslim intelligentsia, as the first step. He has talked about revolution extensively in his works. This revolution does not consist of political sloganmongering and destructive activities for solving mundane and transient economic and political problems. His revolution is at the intellectual and philosophical level. It aims at freeing humanity in general and Muslims in particular from the slavery of the pessimistic and fatalistic Greek philosophy in the intellectual sphere and from the two mutually-contending extremist Western socio-economic philosophies of capitalism and communism. Thus, he set upon the task of restarting and completing the work initiated by previous fighters against evil, like Ibn-i-Taymiyyah, Imam Ghazali and Maulana Rumi. He was convinced that after attaining this freedom, humanity will gravitate towards the dynamic Islamic intellectualism and will be close to the middle path of the Islamic socio-economic system, which is closer to human nature than the two extreme systems of capitalism and communism. After much contemplation he decided to adopt Urdu and Persian verse as the media for his message to humanity. He produced eleven books of verse in Urdu or Persian, three books in English prose and one in Urdu prose together with innumerable articles in journals and lectures. The masterpiece of his prose is *The Reconstruction of Religious Thought in Islam*, which is the essence of his philosophy.

Since the death of Iqbal much work has been done on elucidating and popularizing different aspects of his books, by individuals as well as organizations in Pakistan and abroad. Among the many people engaged in this work Dr. Waheed Ishrat occupies a very prominent position. A glimpse at his background and his own struggle against the problems of life is necessary to understand and appreciate his work and contribution to convey Iqbal's message to the people.

Dr. Waheed Ishrat was born in February 1944 in Narowal near to Sialkot, in which respect he can claim being a neighbor of Iqbal. All his education was in Lahore, Pakistan, between 1960 and 1984. Throughout this period Islamics and Philosophy were his major fields of interest and study. He had Philosophy major in B.A., Philosophy in M.A. and completed his Ph.D. in the same subject. The subject of his Ph.D thesis was "Social Philosophy of Dr. Khalifah Abdul-Hakim", who was a friend and admirer of as well as writer on Iqbal. So his academic background brought him close to Iqbal. Soon after completion of his formal education

Introduction

Dr. Waheed Ishrat started attaining excellence in literary fields and obtained the Diplomas of Fazil in Punjabi and Persian by 1989 and Certificate in Management Systems. This education gave him the good grounding in literary writing which he has used very widely in his life. He gained a large amount of practical knowledge and experience in other relevant fields like journalism and producing academic literature in Urdu as well as English. He was Sub-Editor of *Waqf* and *Jumhoor* of Lahore (1972-73), Daily *Sadaqat* and *Nawa-i-Waqt* (1978-84). He worked as a Research Scholar, Department of Philosophy, Punjab University (1974-76), Research Assistant, Central Urdu Board (1976), and worked as Deputy Director (Research and Academic) in Iqbal Academy, Pakistan since 1984. He was also selected twice as Assistant Professor, Department of Iqbaliyat, Allama Iqbal Open University, Islamabad, Pakistan. In this capacity he gained experience in guiding and supervising original research. He has also started a journal called *Pakistani Falsafah* (Pakistani Philosophy).

Thus, Dr. Waheed Ishrat was amply equipped with academic and intellectual qualifications before joining the Iqbal Academy Pakistan where he is conducting original research on Iqbal, organizing publications of different types and is working as Editor of the two journals of the Academy, *Iqbaliyat* in Urdu and *Iqbal Review* in English. In addition to this intellectual and academic background he has been enriched by the experience of life. Not being the scion of any feudal elite family of Lahore he is not an ivory tower scholar. He started his life in penury instead of with a silver spoon, and rose to his present position by his own effort and initiatives. This gave him a pathos for the poor and unprivileged masses of Pakistan, which is reflected in his works.

He has worked very hard both in the field of his own publications and other work of the Academy. He is a prolific writer and has written a large number of books and papers, mostly in Urdu but some in Persian and Punjabi also. The field of his interest covers Philosophy, Iqbalics, new movements in politics and literature, Islamic Philosophy, Pakistan Movement, and poetic literature.

He shares the views of some scholars of Iqbalics that Iqbal's works should be translated into languages other than Urdu and Persian. Much work on this subject has been done and is proceeding at a fast speed in the Iqbal Academy, Pakistan. With his initiative I offered my services for preparing the English translation of ten papers written by him in Urdu. In

Understanding Iqbal's Philosophy

spite of my best efforts the work took longer than expected, due to unavoidable difficulties and my own preoccupation with the English translation and commentary of *Bang-i-Dara*. However, by the Grace of God this translation is ready and is presented to our esteemed readers. The book is named *Understanding Iqbal's Philosophy*. Perusal of the table of contents will show that the papers cover a good cross-section of Iqbal from esoteric to political subjects. If this translation is successful in conveying the message of Iqbal to the English-knowing lovers of Iqbal and his works I shall consider my labors well spent.

Dr. M.A.K. Khalil
106 Highland Drive.
Canada

Chapter 1

THE ORIGINS AND SOURCES OF IQBAL'S PHILOSOPHY

The search for the sources of thought of an eminent and multi-dimensional philosopher like Iqbal is the most difficult task, specially so as his thought is creative as well as harmonizing. It is creative in the sense that he showed a new direction to his period by his philosophy of *Khudi*[1] and theory of dynamism. It is harmonizing in the sense that, looking critically into the thoughts of the Eastern and Western philosophers in the light of his creative theory he established harmony between them and gave his own opinions. The history of philosophy has produced either those philosophers who presented their creative thought and the results of their creative thinking about life and the universe, or those who established harmony and relationship between the philosophers preceding them and reconciled the theories and thoughts of different thinkers. Iqbal is one of the few philosophers in the history of philosophy who themselves fixed the orbit of their creative thinking, established some basic premises of their thought and then tested the thoughts of different philosophers and sages on the basis of them and gave their own opinion after critical study. These are the dimensions of creative and harmonious thinking, overlooking which creates difficulties in grasping the sources of Iqbal's thought. Those who study Iqbal's philosophy superficially, sometimes ignore its ethical aspects, and sometimes consider Iqbal's philosophy as mere gleanings from different philosophers on account of faulty comprehension of his harmonizing aspect. In my opinion both these attitudes result from failure to distinguish between the creative and harmonizing aspects of Iqbal's thinking.

Perhaps nobody has so far claimed the existence of a complete system of thought in the creative aspect of Iqbal, or that Iqbal had developed a philosophic order from his thought. In fact, if Plato (430-347 B.C.) is the first link in the chain of European philosophical system then Ernst W. Kaufmann Hegel (1770-1831) is its last link. Nobody after Hegel attempted organizing his philosophical thoughts into a system. The system of Karl Marx (1818-1883), was not philosophical and we do not count it as a philosophical system. We see the best organization of a philosophical system in Iqbal, after Hegel, though Iqbal himself has never claimed it. In fact, like some eminent philosophers he has denied being a philosopher. For this reason perhaps it may appear unreasonable and an exaggeration, at first sight, but Iqbal has the components of a partially organized philosophical system in his concepts of the Truth, the universe, spiritual reality, the *Mard-i-Mumin*[2] or the *Fard-i-Musaddiqa*,[3] the *Khudi* and its political interpretation, and virtual democracy and its political interpretation. These should be researched just as the scattered pearls of wisdom of Socrates (469-399 B.C.) were researched and consolidated into a philosophical system by Plato. Perhaps nobody has looked upon Iqbal from this angle, because most of the work on Iqbal today has been of the nature of compilation, translation and explanation. Iqbal has not yet been researched and discovered in his entirety because, for this purpose, a creative and all-embracing mind was needed after Iqbal as was created in the person of Plato after Socrates.

I want to state a basic fact before dealing with the sources of Iqbal's philosophy. This is that no philosophy develops in a vacuum. Every philosophy needs a special soil, air and enviromnent for its cultivation and growth. If you want to witness this you can see that the Greek thought grew in a special sophisticated social and cultural environment of the second millennium before Christ. When this environment ceased to exist the Greek philosophy disappeared with it forever. Moreover, if you also look at the thoughts of Socrates and Plato they were not original in the sense that nobody had previously expressed such thoughts. A careful study and analysis of the thoughts of Socrates and Plato will reveal the echo of the thoughts of Socrates and Plato about God in Xenopheus (430-355 B.C.), a thinker of the period of the Illiad. In the same way the poems of Parmenides (d. 475 B.C.) "The Way of Truth" and "The Way of Syllogism" provide material for Plato's *Discourses* and the concept of *Wahdat-al-Wujud*[4] of Parmenides and Xenophius, which hypothesizes one existing entity is the basis of the main thought of Plato. In the same way the thoughts of philosophers such as Philatunis (204-7), Kindi (d. 870 C.E.), Farabi (870-956) and Hegel etc. have the elements of their preceding philosophers. In other words the existence of the effects of the thoughts and theories of preceding philosophers in the thinking of some philosophers is not a reflection on the originality of his thoughts. This is so because the study of the evolution of thought in the history of philosophy will clearly show that in the field of thinking the currents of thought run in a continuous stream and a philosopher draws inspiration only from the thoughts of his predecessor philosophers and after renovating their thinking with his originality presents them according to the objective

The Origins and Sources of Iqbal's Philosophy

conditions of his time. So it is not surprising to find some reflections of the thoughts of earlier philosophers in Iqbal's thinking and does not negate the originality of his thought. What is important to find out is whether Iqbal has read and presented the thoughts of philosophers preceding him in a historical and unquestioned manner or has critically reviewed them to organize his own thoughts. Serious study of Iqbal's *Lectures*[5] and other works gives strong impression of his critical approach to the works of earlier philosophers and will create the feeling that Iqbal has adopted an academic and critical approach in grasping and adopting them. Therefore, people who say that Iqbal's thinking is not original and that he has indulged in gleaning from such and such a philosopher appear to be ignorant of the history of human thought. The history of philosophy has no concept of any completely original thought, and the torch of thinking progresses through many hands. All this leads to the conclusion that Iqbal was an original thinker and grasped and adopted the earlier philosophies in a critical manner.

Basically, in its origin, Iqbal's philosophy is an extension of the tradition of Islamic thought alone. Iqbal's thought is organically linked to his own Muslim background. Iqbal's concept of the Truth, God, the universe, *Khudi* and *Mard-i-Mumin* themselves have roots in Islamic thinking. He himself traces the roots of each of his concepts to the history of Islamic philosophy, and when he finds the affirmation and support of his concepts in Western science and philosophy he cites them as additional support. He also criticises the philosopher whose thinking is not in conformity with the foundations of his thought. In this connection he criticises Plato, Aristotle (382-322 B.C.), Hegel, Marx and several other Western thinkers and even the Muslim writers of his own circle, such as Ibn-al-Arabi (d. 1240) and Hafiz Shirazi (d. 1389). In his creative thinking he first presents his own theories about the Truth, life and the universe and then tries to obtain further explanation and proof from Western learning and researches of Western philosophers. Dr. Annemarie Schimmel has unveiled this attitude of Iqbal in her famous book *Gabriel's Wing*. She says:

> "Iqbal continued to establish connection between Islamic traditions and new Western research by these comparative studies. His stand was that Muslims should learn Western knowledge and wisdom for, as the West has been indebted to Islamic civilization for learning and wisdom, Muslims would not lose anything by learning Western science and technology". (i)

Understanding Iqbal's Philosophy

Iqbal is not among the philosophers who get engulfed in abstract concepts and theories and engage themselves only in the superfineness of linguistic and logical excellence. Iqbal is a revolutionary philosopher, and in accordance with the saying of Marx that the much greater function of philosophy is to alter the normal conditions existing around it rather than subjective analysis of the universe. Iqbal also, with his original thinking, established a system of thought which aimed at revolutionizing the conditions existing in his time. The main aspect of his entire system of thought was practical, dynamic and revolutionary. He discarded, after criticism, every thought, concept and theory which preached inaction, and which was also a great obstacle to Iqbal in the task of changing and activating the existing conditions of Muslims. As Dr. Ishtiaque Hussain Quraishi explained, after detailed analysis, in his paper "The Psychological Sources of the Philosophy of Iqbal" (ii) that the centuries old static life of the Muslim *Ummah*, their declining preparedness, the destruction of the *khilafah*, the fall of Samarqand, Bukhara and Spain, the Hindu stratagem of absorbing the Muslims in, and the conditions militating against their organization as a political power, in the Indian sub-continent were movers for disturbing Iqbal and creating a storm within him. He criticised all those theories which were against the concept of dynamism in life and the universe. Iqbal's concept of life and the universe was that of having a soul in motion. Motion or dynamism is the basic component of his philosophy.

Motion or dynamism is the principle which moulded Iqbal's thought. He writes about dynamic thinking:

> "In its essential nature, then, thought is not static; it is dynamic and unfolds its internal infinitude in time like the seed which, from the very beginning, carries within itself the organic unity of the tree as a present fact. Thought is, therefore, the whole of its dynamic self-expression, appearing to the temporal vision as a series of definite specifications which cannot be understood except by a reciprocal reference". (iii)

The greatest opponent of Iqbal's dynamic philosophy of life and the universe was the belief of *Wahdat-al-Wujud*. This belief in *Wahdat-al-Wujud* whose rationale was based on Plato's theory of the universe, developed later in his system as a static monastic way as part of mysticism, diverted Muslims from the Islamic thinking of conquest and

The Origins and Sources of Iqbal's Philosophy

consolidation of the world towards the shame-ridden attitude of divorcing all worldly relations. As a result of this the Islamic world developed the monastic attitudes of inaction, pacifism and other worldliness, and the whole Islamic world was engulfed in a paralytic mystic state. Becoming estranged from the understanding of the universe, and from performing an active role in the reconstruction, shaping, conquest and organization of the world, it became progressively caught into slavery. The Arab writer Najla Izzuddin (1953) has analyzed this state of affairs as follows:

> "The decline of the internal creative power and expeditionary zeal of the Arab civilization was more devastating than the misfortunes and catastrophes that befell from outside. The ardent desire for intellectual inquiry and the pride of performance which were characteristic of the early times were throttled by the strong pressure of religious dogmas and centralization. Freedom of thought was banished and conservatism reigned supreme. Unbridled search for Truth was branded as atheism and irreligiousity. The fearless and bold people of the earlier times were relegated to obscurity. The brain trust engaged itself in preparing the explanations and abstracts of well-known subjects instead of using their intellect in discovering new avenues of knowledge." (iv)

This was the state of affairs which perturbed Iqbal. He revolted and rejected every theory which was against his dynamic concepts. This hit Aristotle most after Plato because Aristotle believed in the eternity of the universe. In the words of Dr. Schimmel:

> "Aristotle's concept of the eternity of the universe is antithetic to the Islamic concept of God, because according to this religion only the Living and Dynamic God is Eternal and not the universe. Iqbal considers life also as fleeting. Life is not only beauty and balance; it is also action and power." (v)

According to Dr. Schimmel the strongest reason for Iqbal's intellectual revolt against Greek thought was:

> "In Iqbal's view Greek philosophy is extremely abstract and conjectural and man cannot perform any productive work under its influence. It is an impractical philosophy and cannot even meet God through its concept devoid of Love." (vi)

Understanding Iqbal's Philosophy

See Iqbal's *Asrar-i-Khudi*, section VII titled "Exposition that Plato the Greek whose Thought greatly influenced the Mysticism and Literature of the Muslim Nations followed the Sheep's Doctrine and that We must beware of and eschew his Thought and Theories". The climax is reached in the last verse which says:

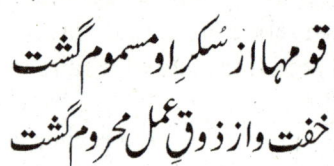

Full many a nation poisoned by his intoxication
Sank into deep sound slumber and lost the thrill of action's bliss.

The whole purpose of this detail is to lead you to the basic concepts of Iqbal's thought. What permeates the whole world of his philosophical organization like a principle is the concept of a Living and Dynamic God, who is not identical with the universe, but who is Unique, Unparallel, Unequal in His own Being and Essence. The universe and life are expositions of His Creativeness which are vibrant with life. Dr. Ishrat Hassan Enver in his book *The Metaphysics of Iqbal* has explained that to Iqbal God's *zat*[6] is dynamic and extremely creative. His words are:

"Consequently, the nature of God as revealed by intuition is, firstly, dynamic and highly active in its essence. Reality is one infinite life. It is a self-directing, self-conscious energy, continuously active. Every act of it is itself life which in turn is a self-directing energy. Looked at from outside these acts are spatial things and events. Some of the acts in the course of development have become self-conscious. These are 'I' and 'You'." (vii)

Detailing Iqbal's concept of the universe he writes:

"There is a gradual rising note of egohood in the whole universe. We are conscious of it firstly in our own self; secondly, in the objective nature before our eyes; and thirdly in the ultimate principle of all life, viz. God. Iqbal's philosophy is thus the Philosophy of Egohood. Egohood is for him the pivot of all reality." (viii)

The Origins and Sources of Iqbal's Philosophy

Khudi, which can also be called "Gnosis of self" or "Gnosis of *zat*" is found in Socrates' philosophy as "Know Thyself" and which also appears in the famous saying, "He who knows his Self knows his God". Iqbal himself writes in his 'Fourth Lecture':

"What then is matter? A colony of egos of low order out of which emerges the ego of a higher order, when their association and interaction reach a certain degree of co-ordination . ... The emergent, as the advocates of the Emergent Evolution teach us, is an unforeseeable and novel fact on its own plane of being, and cannot be explained mechanistically. ... We have seen that the ego is not something rigid. It organizes itself in time, and is formed and disciplined by its own experience:" (ix)

A well-known professor of philosophy, Dr. Absar Ahmad explains Iqbal's concept of *Khudi* thus:

"In Iqbal's thinking *Khudi* is that unit of intellect which is 'Self Knowing' and 'Self Cognizant' and is conscious of its *Zat* and its goals. *Khudi* here does not mean mind or discretion but is something which has to be kept well in mind or, on account of which man has mind and discretion. The same faculty in man calls himself 'I' on account of being self-knowing or self-cognizant. So Iqbal calls it '*ana*', or 'ego' or 'I'." (x)

In Iqbal's view this *Khudi* passes through three stages in its evolution which he has described thus in *Javid Namah*:

زندہ یا مردہ یا جاں بلب ازسہ شاہد کن شہادت را طلب
شاہدِ اوّل شعورِ خویشتن خویش را دیدن بہ نورِ خویشتن
شاہدِ ثانی شعورِ دیگرے خویش را دیدن بہ نورِ دیگرے
شاہدِ ثالث شعورِ ذاتِ حق خویش را دیدن بہ نورِ ذاتِ حق

"Whether thou be alive or dead, or on the verge of death
Depend on three things

A sense of one's own existence

Understanding Iqbal's Philosophy

One's own self to see with the help of one's own inner light

Then secondly,

A sense of existence of others; one's own self to see with the help of the light of others

And, thirdly, a sense of the existence of God,
And the power to see One's Self in the light vouchsafed by God".(xi)

This means that in the first stage Man requires a witness on himself through the intellect of his own existence, assays the limits of his own objectives, organizes his essence, sees himself in the light of his existence and shapes his faculties and potentialities. When he passes from this stage to the second one he tests himself with the intellect of others or with the eyes of history and makes history as a witness for his actions and character. In this way he fixes his place in the pages of history. In the third stage he makes the *Zat* of God a witness over his existence, presents himself to God and organizes his *Khudi* or his *Zat* within the premises of the purpose of submission to God. Iqbal states the following purpose of these stages of *Khudi*.

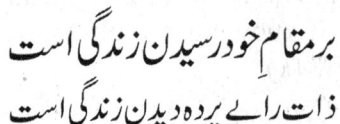

"Life lies in reaching one's own destined station
It lies in beholding the One Central Self without a veil." (xii)

That means that man reaches a stage where the *Zat* manifests itself to him with all its profundity. Surin Kierkegaard, the founder of the concept of *Wujudiyat*[7] has also described similar three stages in his philosophy which are beneficent, ethical and religious. However, S. Kierkegaard (1813-1855) could not reach the depths of thought traversed by Iqbal though his beneficent, ethical and religious periods also reflect the different stages of development of Man's personality (xiii).

In the process of explaining the sources of Iqbal's philosophy on the one hand we have to point out the internal sources which are subjective and are a part of his internal self without which Iqbal could not have been what he was and on the other hand we have to discover those objective

The Origins and Sources of Iqbal's Philosophy

sources which formed the basis for the formation of his thinking. Maulana Syed Abul Hasan Ali Nadvi in his book *Nuqush-i-Iqbal* has very beautifully referred to the creative elements which have played a very important role in the formation of Iqbal. During a lecture at the Cairo University in 1951 he said:

"In fact Iqbal acquired the creative elements which created and developed his personality in his own internal school. There are five creative components which made Iqbal's personality everlasting"(xiv).

Enumerating these five components he said:

'The first of these components which Iqbal acquired on the very first day of his entering his internal school is "Faith and Belief". This very belief is Iqbal's first patron and mentor and is the source of his power and strength and is the fountainhead of his wisdom and intelligence. The second component of Iqbal's personality is what is present today in every Muslim home, though alas the Muslims themselves are deprived of its light and have made themselves devoid of its knowledge and wisdom. I mean the Holy Qur'an. The third component which has greatly affected the development of Iqbal's personality is cognizance of his soul and *Khudi*. The fourth component which made and nourished Iqbal's personality is the early morning prayer and lamentation. It was Iqbal's rising in the small hours of the morning, prostrating before his Lord and lamenting and crying which continuously provided a new happiness to his soul, a new light to his heart and a new intellectual nourishment to him. Iqbal has himself highlighted the importance of early morning lamentations. For example he says:

عطار ہو، رومی ہو، رازی ہو، غزالی ہو

کچھ ہاتھ نہیں آتا بے آہ سحرگاہی

زمستانی ہوا میں گرچہ تھی شمشیر کی تیزی

نہ چھوٹے مجھ سے لندن میں بھی آدابِ سحرخیزی

"It may be Attar, or Rumi, or Razi, or Ghazali,[8]
Nothing is achieved without early morning lamentation (xv).

Understanding Iqbal's Philosophy

Though the winter air had the sword's sharpness
Even in London I did not lose the habit of early morning rising"(xvi).

And the fifth component which constituted the basis of Iqbal's thought was the study of Rumi's *Mathnavi*:

The three components stated by Maulana Abul Hasan Ali Nadvi are subjective whereas the Holy Qur'an and Rumi's *Mathnavi* are objective and are the fountainheads of his genius. In fact the deep study of and constant meditation on the Holy Qur'an was the criterion on which he tested all the old and new philosophies. Whatever he felt to be close to the teachings of the Holy Qur'an he regarded as the *Mumin*'s missing wisdom and accepted it. Similarly, he rejected after examination and criticism what he considered as remote from this current of thought. Iqbal dived into the Holy Qur'an and adopted it as the basis and standard of his entire thinking.

Regarding the study of the Holy Qur'an the anecdote which Iqbal himself stated is very important. According to this Iqbal's father had advised him to study the Holy Qur'an as if it had been revealed to him (xvii). This changed Iqbal's view of the Book of God,

تیرے ضمیر پہ جب تک نہ ہو نزولِ کتاب
گرہ کشا ہے نہ رازی نہ صاحبِ کشاف

"As long as the Book is not revealed to your heart
Neither Razi nor the author of *Kashshaf*[9] will clarify the meaning"(xviii).

The Holy Qur'an itself on being revealed to Iqbal's heart opened the hidden aspects of his thought. Therefore, he always considered his whole thought and poetry to be the *tafsir*[10] of the mystery of *Iman*.[11]

ولایت، پادشاہی، علمِ اشیا کی جہانگیری
یہ سب کیا ہیں؟ فقط اک نکتۂ ایماں کی تفسیریں

"*Walayat*[12], kingship, the universality of the knowledge of things
What are all these? Only *tafsirs* of the secret of *Iman*"(xix).

The Origins and Sources of Iqbal's Philosophy

He has prayed to God for a curse on himself in the sense that if he had included anything in his thinking and poetry outside the explanations of the Holy Qur'an he be deprived of the honour of paying the most humble homage to the Holy Prophet by kissing his feet on the Day of Judgement. This is a curse which no Muslim can impose on himself. On this basis alone it can be said that Iqbal himself, not only considers the Holy Qur'an to be the source of his thought and poetry, but calls his thought and poetry to be a *tafsir* of the Holy Qur'an. He says:

گر دلم آئینهٔ بے جوہر است   در بحر فم غیرِ قرآں مضمر است

اے فروغت صبحِ اعصار و دہور   چشم تو بینندهٔ فی ما فی الصدور

خشک گرداں بادہ در انگور من   زہر ریز اندر مئے کافور من

روزِ محشر خوار و رسوا کن مرا   بے نصیب از بوسۂ پا کن مرا

"If my heart is a mirror with no worth
And in my word if anything except the Holy Qur'an is concealed

O Thou who art the Light of the morning of time
Thy eye sees what is in our hearts

Dry up the wine in my grapes
Throw poison in my pure wine

Make me wretched and ignominious on the Judgement Day
Deprive me of kissing the feet (of the Holy Prophet)" (xx).

Syed Nazir Niazi, who has translated *The Reconstruction of Religious Thought in Islam* into Urdu, considers the Holy Qur'an to be the fountainhead of Iqbal's thought in his Introduction to the *Lectures*.

"In fact the real fountainhead of this thought is the Holy Qur'an, as stated earlier. And to the Holy Qur'an alone we will have to take recourse in solving all problems and difficulties which may appear in explaining it. If the author of *The Lectures* has used the present day terminology it is so for the sake of us Westernized people, because he is really addressing us and the rest of the world through us" (xxi).

Understanding Iqbal's Philosophy

Another pious researcher of Iqbal, Dr. Raziuddin Siddiqi, has written in the preface to Dr. Yusuf Husain Khan's book, *Ruh-i-lqbal*:

"In poetical aspects and in the light of modern knowledge Iqbal's works are a complete commentary of the Holy Qur'an. If the *Mathnavi* of Maulana Rumi was considered 'The Holy Qur'an in the Persian Language" eight hundred years ago, we can give the same status to Iqbal's works in this second millennium" (xxii).

Maulana Saeed Ahmad Akbarabadi in his *A View on Iqbal's Lectures* has attested similarly that:

'The high calibre of thought in "The Lectures" leaves no doubt that the Holy Qur'an is their real fountainhead" (xxiii).

Maulana Dr. Ghulam Mustapha Khan in his book *Iqbal and the Qur'an* (xxiv) has documented the encirclement of Iqbal's thought by the Holy Qur'an and a study of Muhammad Munawwar's book *The Reasoning of Iqbal* shows the sovereignty of the Holy Qur'an on Iqbal's thought. Though it is not possible to go into details, selections from Iqbal's verses, letters, speeches, statements and lectures give us the message of Iqbal that:

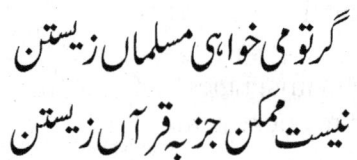

"If thou wantst to live as a Muslim
It is not possible except living by the Holy Qur'an" (xxv).

This is the all-pervading wisdom of his thought. This is so because he considers the Holy Qur'an to be a means of creating an exalted and elegant understanding of the varied innate relationships of Man and the surrounding universe. Iqbal got the greatest stimulation from the *Mathnavi* of Rumi in obtaining the philosophical understanding and depth of thought of the Holy Qur'an. Therefore, Maulana Jalaluddin Rumi's "Intellectual *Mathnavi*", which has been described as the Holy Qur'an in the Persian language, is the basic source of Iqbal's philosophy. Iqbal took Maulana's *Mathnavi* as a means of obtaining the insight into the Holy Qur'an:

The Origins and Sources of Iqbal's Philosophy

چو رومی در حرم دادم اذاں من
از و آموختم اسرارِ جاں من
بہ دورِ فتنہ ٔ عصرِ کہن ، ز و
بہ دورِ فتنہ ٔ عصرِ رواں ، من

"Like Rumi I am calling for prayer (*azan*) in the Haram[13]
I have learnt the secrets of life from him

He lived in the days of the mischief of the old
I live in the mischief of the current age" (xxvi).

In the seditious age in which beliefs and concepts were being destroyed and Muslims had become frustrated Maulana Rumi restored Man's beliefs and confidence and stabilized Faith and perceptions. This disunity, distress and helplessness of thought and insight was also the characteristic of Iqbal's times. The harmony and mature thinking, the affection and attachment to the Holy Qur'an were the meeting points for these eminent thinkers. The mysticism and mystics who had rendered knowledge to be a great veil had forgotten the Qur'anic edict that knowledge and science were the greatest virtues in its view. To Iqbal, Rumi is the opener of the secrets and wisdom of the Holy Qur'an. He goes more into the intrinsic rather than the extrinsic values of the Qur'anic injunctions. The wisdom of *Deen* is his special field. The doctrine of *Taqdir*[14] is the most important point of the companionship of Rumi and Iqbal. Iqbal got the theory of Will in his concept of *Khudi* from Rumi, that the *Khudi* on reaching its climax embraces God's Will. Iqbal and Rumi both think that the wrong understanding of Destiny has done much more harm to Man's *Khudi* and ethical life. Following Rumi, Iqbal gave a new meaning to human freedom and free will. Both believe in immortality and evolution, and are the philosophers who create the fervour for subjugation of the universe.

It is often stated in describing the influence of Rumi in shaping Iqbal's thought that Iqbal's concept of *Wahdat-al-Wujud* has been taken from Rumi. There is a long line of people who regard Maulana Rumi to be a believer in *Wahdat-al-Wujud*. But whether Maulana Rumi was really a believer in *Wahdat-al-Wujud* is no longer considered as fully proven.

Understanding Iqbal's Philosophy

There are several indications denying his belief in *Wahdat-al-Wujud*. R.A. Nicholson who is a researcher in Islamic learning, writes:

"Some people get the impression at first sight that Rumi believed in *Wahdat-al-Wujud*. I had the same belief earlier when I was not so well versed in the history of Islamic mysticism as I am now"(xxvii).

Actually Nicholson even denies that Mansur Hallaj was a believer in *Wahdat-al-Wujud*. Just as fixation of fundamentals of Iqbal's philosophy is the result of Maulana Rumi's influence the shaping of the aspects of Iqbal's thinking was done by Mujaddid Alf-i-Thani.[15] The concepts of *Wahdat-al-Wujud* which started creeping into Muslim society through Plato, Platonius and Ibn-al-Arabi[16] and brought the doctrine of *sukr*[17], which paralysed the entire Muslim society, met with strong opposition. Commenting on A. Schopenhauer's (1788-1860) theory of *Wahdat-al-Wujud*, a philosopher has said that this belief was veiled atheism. This veiled atheism sowed the seeds of withdrawal from the world, asceticism and inaction in Muslim society. This poison rendered Muslim minds unproductive and pushed Muslims into decline. The teachings of Mujaddid Alf-i-Thani are an important source for moulding Iqbal's thought:

"Junaid Baghdadi,[18] adopted the system of *sahv*[19] as opposed to *sukr*. Maulana Rumi taught *Khudi* in spite of being inclined towards *Wahdat-al-Wajud*, and Shaikh Ahmad Sirhindi, Mujaddid Alf-i-Thani criticized and rejected Shaikh Muhiyuddin Ibn-al-Arabi's theory of *Wahdat-al-Wajud* and presented the theory of *abdiyat*[20] in opposition to it strongly supported their efforts" (xxviii).

Iqbal's intellectual and cordial relationship with Mujaddid Alf-i-Thani can be judged from the fact that he said about Friedrich Nietzsche (d. 1900) that if he were alive in the time of Mujaddid and had been associated with him he would have been remunerated with eternal happiness:

کاش بودے در زمانِ احمدے
تا رسیدے بر سرورے سرمدے

"If God granted that he had lived in the time of Ahmad
He would have attained eternal happiness" (xxix).

The Origins and Sources of Iqbal's Philosophy

Iqbal got evidence from Mujaddid Alf-i-Thani against the theory of *Wahdat-al-Wujud.* Commenting on Ibn-al-Arabi's theory of *Wahdat-al-Wujud* Mujaddid said that the great Shaikh, Muhiyuddin Ibn-al-Arabi could not distinguish between *Wujud* and *Zat*.[21] He could not rise above *Wujud* to reach the *Zat* of God. He said the same thing about Plato, that he became besieged with *Wujud* and could not reach the *Zat*, because the *Zat* is higher than and separate from *Wujud*.[22] The *Zat* is Unequalled and Unique and Solitary. Mujaddid said:

"The glorious Shaikh (Ibn-al-Arabi) did not view their depravity, defects and discord, and fixed the truths of the possible as the cognitional forms of Allah, because these forms have assumed an external form after being reflected in the Eminent Allah's Mirror of Purity. This has been so because nothing existed outside it. He has not differentiated between these cognitional forms and the Attributes of Allah. So he asserted the positive opinion of *Wahdat-al-Wujud*. and he called the *Wujud* of the possible as identical with the *Wujud* of Allah" (xxx).

Dr. Burhanuddin Ahmad Faruqi in his *Mujaddid's Conception of Tawhid* has described Ibn-al-Arabi's concept of *Wahdat-ul-Wujud,* thus:

"Ibn-al-Arabi's position with regard to *Tawhid* is that Being is one, - it is that which exists. This Being is Allah. Everything else is His manifestations. Hence the world is identical with Allah" (xxxi).

This means that it would be correct to say that Ibn-al-Arabi considers Being and Allah or the universe and God as identical to each other. He writes:

"The identity of the world and Allah is conceived on the basis of the identity of His *Zat-o-Sifat* or Existence and Essence - substance and attributes; the world being only a *Tajalli*[23] or manifestation of His or Attributes" (xxxii).

Maulana Jami (1414-1492), while explaining the *Wahdat-al-Wujud* of his eminent Ibn-al-Arabi, said:

"The Being is indeterminate; it is the stage of *La-ta'ayyun* or Indeterminateness of the Unity. In its Determination it passes through five stages. The first two are *Ilmi* or Cognitive and the last three are *Khariji* or Existential. In the first Descent, the Unity becomes conscious of itself as pure Being, and the consciousness of *Sifat* is only *Ijmali*, i.e. general - it is implicit. In the second Descent, the Unity becomes conscious of itself as possessing the attributes; that is the stage of *Sifat-i-tafsili*, i.e., attributes in detail - it is explicit. These two Descents seem to be conceived in conceptual or logical rather than actual; for, they are out of time, and the distinction of *Zat* and *Sifat* or its attributes is only *Zahini* or logical. Then began the real actual Descents. The third Descent therefore is *Ta'ayyun-i-ruhi* or the determination as spirit or spirits, the Unity has broken itself up into so many spirits, for example angels. The fourth of its Descents is *Ta'ayyun-i-mithali* or ideal determination; thereby the world of Ideas comes into being. And the fifth Descent is *Ta'ayyun-i-jasadi* or physical determination; it yields the phenomenal or physical beings. These stages are only gradual realizations of the capacities that were already latent in the attributes" (xxxiii).

This means that this series of Descents or Determinations resembles the theory of Emanation of Plato, Platonius and Ibn-i-Sina (980-1050) (xxxiv). Ibn-i-Sina also, basing it on his rationality, believes in Emanation of the material universe from God and admits the universe and God to be each other's shadow and identical. But these philosophers seem to fail to visualize any *Zat* above and beyond the level of *Wujud*. That is so because *Wujud* is the *Shuhud*[24] of *Zat* and *Wujud* is contingent on *makan*[25] while *Zat* is *La makan*[26]. How can the *Wujud* contained in *makan* and the *La Makan Zat* be the same? Mujaddid Alf-i-Thani criticised the philosophers on this point and said:

"The Creator of the universe (*Subhanahu wa Ta'ala*) has none of the above relations proven to exist between Him and the universe. The comprehension of and approach to Allah is not of *Zat* but is one of *Ilm*[27] as has been accepted by the *Ahl-al-Haq*[28] and He is not united with anything and Allah is Allah and the universe is universe: That Unique and Indescribable. *Zat* cannot be identical with non-unique and the describable. The Eminent *Wajib*[29] cannot be said to be identical with the *Mumkin*.[30] The *Mumtana-al-Adam*[31] *Zat* cannot be identical with, *Ilmi* or Cognitive and the last three are *Khariji* or Existential" (xxxiv).

The Origins and Sources of Iqbal's Philosophy

The "Creator"[32] and the "created" have the relationship of the person reasoning and the article reasoned about. Mujaddid says:

"Though the universe is the theatre for the display of the reflections of the perfection of *Sifat* and appearance of Divine Names, but the view of the Real is not visible and the shadow of the Real is not the Real, is the religion of the people who believe in *Wahdat-al-Wujud*"(xxxv).

"The One who is identified by symbols (Allah) cannot be contained in the times and cannot exhibit His Self in the articles which only have the quality of *Mumkinat*. The *La makani Zat* cannot be contained in *makan*" (xxxvi).

Mujaddid also passed through the stage of *Wahdat-al-Wujud*. He says about this stage of his:

"If this *faqir*[33] had accepted *Wahdat-al-Wujud* it was on the basis of *Kashf*[34] and not through *taqleed*[35]. My denial of it now is also on the basis of *Ilham*[36] and *Ilham* does not have room for denial, although it is not an argument for others either". (xxxvii)

Here Mujaddid has stated three things which deserve consideration. One is that his belief in *Wahdat-al-Wujud* was not through *Taqleed* but through *Kashf*. This means that *Taqleed* is bad and *Kashf* is a stage of knowledge experienced by all believers in *Wahdat-al-Wujud*. The next higher stage is *Ilham* which is the most reliable way of attaining knowledge for those who are not prophets. The stage higher than *Ilham* is *Wahi*[37]. Being directly from God *Wahi* is an argument for those who are not prophets and obeying it is essential, whereas *Ilham is* for non-prophets and, through it does not have room for denial, obedience to it is not binding on others. However, one point is clear, that is *Ilham-i-Wahdat-al-Shuhud* is one stage higher than *Kashfi Wahdat-al-Wujud;* and Mujaddid's acceptance of the *Zat* of Allah as Unique and denial of the identity of the *makani* objects with the *La makani Zat* is a logical truth. The poetic romanticism presented in the *Wahdat-al-Wujud* has strengthened this concept so much in poetic tradition that our poetry has lost the potential of rising above the *Wujud* and reaching the *La makani Zat* and merging into the *Wahdat-al-Wujud* Being is considered to be the end all and the climax of poetry. The Eastern as well as the Western poetry is imprisoned in the *Wahdat-al-Wujud* and does not guide us to the highest level which is *Abudiyat* or *Abdiyat*. Mujaddid has explained this stage of *Abdiyat* thus:

"The stage of *Abdiyat* is the highest stage because it is the most perfect and complete in all respects. Only the loved ones are honoured with this stage and the lovers enjoy the pleasures of the vision. The pleasure in *Abdiyat* and affection for it is special for the loved ones. The lovers are attached to the vision of the beloved but the loved ones derive happiness from the *Abdiyat* of the beloved"(xxxviii).

یہ ایک سجدہ جسے تو گراں سمجھتا ہے
ہزار سجدے سے دیتا ہے آدمی کو نجات

"This one prostration before God which you consider difficult frees man from a thousand prostrations" (xxxix).

This very stage of *Adbiyat* echoes in Iqbal's philosophy of *Khudi*. Whereas Iqbal wants stability and immortality of *Khudi* and protection of its individuality he is not in favour of merging it with God but wants to see it elevated to the stage of *Adbiyat* as this is the same stage which God bestowed upon Man. In Mujaddid's view the only curtain between Man and God is his own *Nafs*[38]. This is so because Man desires his own *Nafs* and so, that really is the curtain. What is *Tajalli-i-Zati*[39] for Mujaddid Alf-i-Thani is the stage of *Khudi* according to Iqbal.

There are several other personalities, in addition to Maulana Rumi and Mujaddid Alf-i-Thani who have nourished Iqbal's thought, out of which three deserve special mention. They are Abdul Karim Al-Jili, Dawwani and Iraqi.

Jalaluddin Muhammad Ibn-al-Asad Dawwani. He was born in Dawwan, District of Gazrun. His father was a *qazi*, was educated in Shiraz and appointed *qazi* of Fars. He wrote treatises and annotations on philosophy and *Tasawwuf*. In Persian he wrote the well-known book, *Lavama-ul-Ishraq fi makarim-ul-Akhlaq*, which is also called, *Akhlaq-i-Jalali*. Iqbal has referred to his book *Zawwar* in the theory of time and has compared his theory of time with that of Professor Royce, according to which:

The Origins and Sources of Iqbal's Philosophy

"... if we take time to be a kind of span which makes possible the appearance of events as a moving procession and conceive this span to be a unity then we cannot describe it as an original stage of Divine activity, encompassing all the succeeding states of that activity. But the Mulla (Mulla Jalal-ud-Din Dawwani) takes good care to add that a deeper insight into the nature of succession reveals its relativity; so that it disappears in the case of God to Whom all events are present in a single act of perception" (xxxx).

In addition to Jalaluddin Dawwani, Iqbal also talked about the famous Sufi poet Fakhruddin Ibn-al-Ibrahim Iraqi (d. 1289) in connection with his concept of time. Iraqi was a Persian *Sufi* poet, a *hafiz*[40] and was brought up in Hamadan. He was a disciple of Shaikh Bahauddin Zakariyya of Multan, meditated at Multan and became *sahib-i-hal*[41] *Sufi*. He was married to the daughter of Khwaja Bahauddin Zakariyya, served his *Shaikh* for twenty-five years, travelled to Asia Minor (Qonia), Egypt and Syria (present day Syria and Iraq) and settled in Damascus. He is associated with the book titled, *Suluk-i-Iraqi* and *Kulliat-i-Lama'at* is his famous book (xxxxi). Iqbal has given great importance to Iraqi also in his concept of time. He writes:

"The Sufi poet Iraqi has a similar way of looking at the matter. He considers infinite varieties of time, relative to the varying grades of being intervening between materiality and pure spirituality. The time of gross bodies which arises from the revolution of the heavens is divisible into past, present and future; and its nature is such that as long as one day does not pass away the succeeding day does not come. The time of immaterial beings is also serial in character, but its passage is such that a whole year in the time of gross bodies is not more than a day in the time of an immaterial being. Rising higher and higher in the scale of immaterial beings we reach Divine time - time which is absolutely free from the quality of passage, and consequently does not admit of divisibility, sequence and change. It is above eternity; it has neither beginning nor end. The Eye of God sees all the visibles, and His ear hears all the audibles in one indivisible act of perception. The priority of God is not due to the priority of time; on the other hand, the priority of time is due to God's priority. Thus Divine time is what the Qur'an described as the 'Mother of Books' in which the whole of history, freed from the net of causal sequence, is gathered up in a single super-natural 'now,"(xxxxii).

Understanding Iqbal's Philosophy

The method of investigation of Iraqi in relation to time worked like a source for Iqbal's thought on the problem of time. Iqbal wrote an entire paper on Abdul Karim al-Jili (d. 1408), which explains his theory of "Absolute Unity". Al-Jili's concept of the *Insan-i-Kamil*[42] is the foundation of Iqbal's concept of *Mard-i-Mumin*[43] or *Insan-i-Kamil* of Iqbal himself. Iqbal himself has said about this "He combined in himself poetical imagination and philosophical genius" (xxxxiii).

A review of the influence of Abdul Karim al-Jili on Iqbal needs volumes. We have sampled only a few prominent and representative personalities of the tradition of Muslim thought, otherwise scores of Muslim thinkers are included in this vast study from whom Iqbal has nurtured his mind and after strengthening them with the study of modern knowledge and thought has presented them in a purified form.

The study of Western knowledge and wisdom has a key position as a representative source of Iqbal's thought, because the study of Islamic learning and its comparison with and verification and confirmation from Western learning is common in Iqbal's works. Iqbal considered Islamic civilization as the fore-runner of Western civilization, or considered the Western civilization as having evolved from Muslim civilizations. He thought that if the Islamic civilization had not become static and had grown in its natural way it would have been prosperous like the Western civilization. Moreover, the Islamic civilization, on account of its spiritual components would have been free from the evils which have appeared in the West due to relinquishing religion and compartmentalizing religion and politics.

جلالِ بادشاہی ہو یا جمہوری تماشا ہو
جدا ہو دیں سیاست سے تو رہ جاتی ہے چنگیزی

"It may be the majesty of kingship or the fun of democracy
If religion is separated from politics the latter becomes mere tyranny" (xxxxiv).

Iqbal appreciates the intellectual heights and scientific and technological achievements of the West but is vehemently critical of the confinement of the Western civilization to materialism and relegating religion and ethics to an unimportant position separating them from state-craft. He is not dazzled by the glamour of Western civilization, but

The Origins and Sources of Iqbal's Philosophy

descending into its interior he has pointed out the branch on which this civilization is standing and moving towards its end. Iqbal has viewed the fruits of Western knowledge and arts with open eyes and has adopted and accepted them after testing them on a special standard and has presented them as an argument and affirmation of the fruits of his thought. He has also traced he origins of the products of Western knowledge in the Islamic knowledge and arts and in the works of Islamic theologians, orators and philosophers. In the whole Eastern world Iqbal's philosophical evaluation of Western knowledge is distinct and unique. Iqbal has not adopted the attitude of the defeatist, apologist or blind follower, but one of criticism and creativity. Iqbal adopted this attitude during the period when the sun did not set on the Western civilization and the whole East, excepting a few countries, was under the political subjugation of the West. Under these conditions it was strange for a person to adopt towards the West a critical attitude at the intellectual level, to trace the origins of Western civilization and pronounce judgement on its merits and demerits. In the entire Islamic world Iqbal alone was thus favoured to reach this intellectual level.

However, in spite of all this it is not wrong that the acquisition of Western knowledge played an important role in moulding of Iqbal's thought. About benefitting from Western knowledge Dr. Ishrat Hassan Enver, describing the two stages of Iqbal's thought pre-Intuitional and Intuitional, says:

"The thought of Iqbal seems to have passed through two stages - the Pre-Intuitional and the Intuitional. In the first stage, Iqbal follows the traditional ways of thought which due to their affinity with Pantheism appealed most to the broken and tottering society of the Muslims of the time. But his visit to Europe energized his spirits, strengthened his will, and brought in its wake a political reaction in him. He began to emphasize action, activity and self-assertion, rather than passivity, indifference and self-negation. He gained strength for his thought from the study of Bergson, Friedrich Nietzsche and Mctaggart. This led him to accept the reality of the self and the force of the will as fundamental" (xxxxv).

It is not impossible to infer from this that Western knowledge had influenced Iqbal's thought to some extent. The study of Western learning helped him in arriving at and moulding the end results of this thinking. The evidence of benefitting from Western knowledge is amply available in his works. However, the benefits derived by Iqbal from the West are in the

Understanding Iqbal's Philosophy

detail and not in the principle. As far as principles are concerned his thoughts are not only Eastern but really an extension of Islamic thinking. Still his works show the trend of benefitting from Western knowledge in the organization, shaping and explanation of details... For example, Iqbal says:

> "A greater part of my life has been spent in the study of Western philosophy and this point of view has become second nature to some extent. Consciously or unconsciously I study the truths of Islam from this angle."

مے از میخانہءِ مغرب چشیدم
بہ جانِ من کہ دردِ سر خریدم
نشستم با نکویانِ فرنگی
ازاں بے سود تر روزے ندیدم

"I draw my wine from the tavern of the West
I purchase a headache for myself

I have sat with the good men of the West
But I have not seen a day with them without the longing for thee"(xxxxvi).

Here Iqbal has accepted the Western trend in his thinking and its influence on the study of Eastern and Islamic learning. The following letter indicates the extent of westernization in his thinking and philosophy. Hence, denying the influence of Western knowledge on Iqbal is neither factual nor realistic. Iqbal says:

> "I admit that I have benefitted from Hegel, Goethe, Mirza Ghalib Abdul Qadir Bedil and Wordsworth. Hegel and Goethe have guided me in penetrating the internal truth of things. Bedil and Ghalib taught me how to keep the spirit of the East alive in my feelings and their expression in spite of absorbing the values of Western poetry and Wordsworth helped in protecting me from materialism during my educational days" (xxxxvii).

The Origins and Sources of Iqbal's Philosophy

In the above extract whereas Iqbal has admitted that Wordsworth saved him from materialism and Hegel and Goethe guided him in reaching the internal truth of all matter. He has also said with reference to Mirza Ghalib and Abdul Qadir Bedil that in spite of absorbing the values of Western poetry the ambition and motivation of keeping alive the spirit of the East in his emotions and expressions was derived from them. Iqbal's entire thinking and manner of expression is represented by the conclusion that he absorbed the spirit of Western poetry and philosophy and benefitted from Western philosophy in the comprehension of the truth about matter, but at the same time he also retained orientalism together with the traditions of Muslim thought in a systematic way and reached their truth. These are the goals of the Holy Qur'an and Islam. He was impressed by Western thought, not because he had himself reached its Islamic origins, but because he considered Western civilization as only an extension of Islamic civilization. He points this out in his paper "Islam and the New Learning":

> Bacon, Descartes, and Mill are considered to be Europe's most eminent philosophers, whose philosophy is said to be based on experience, but the fact is that Descartes "Method" is present in Imam Ghazali's *Ihya-ul-Ulum* and they are so similar that an English historian has written that if Descartes knew Arabic we would have admitted that he committed plagiarism. Bacon himself was educated at an Islamic university. The objection raised by John Stuart Mill against the first hypothesis of logic is exactly the same as raised by Imam Fakhruddin Razi and all the fundamental principles of Mill's philosophy are present in the famous book of Shaikh Abu Ali Sina, *Shifa*. ... In fact I claim that not only with respect to modern learning but there is not one good aspect of human existence which has not been enlivened by Islam's extremely invigorating influence"(xxxxviii).

If Iqbal considered European civilization to be only an extension of Islamic civilization, the question arises as to why he did not content himself with the Islamic civilization and why he objected to Western knowledge and philosophy. There are three answers to this. First, Iqbal considered the European civilization to be an extension of the Islamic civilization and so considered benefitting from the thinking of European philosophers and thinkers as tantamount to retrieving the links of his own civilization. He considered it possible to create a stir in the centuries-old static condition of Islamic civilization by accepting the products of

Understanding Iqbal's Philosophy

Western learning in some measure. As this Western wisdom is not alien to Islamic wisdom its acceptance could bridge the gap which has occurred between the rise and present fall of Muslim civilization. Secondly, as his audience comprised of those who understood the language of Western learning it was necessary to talk in their own language. Thirdly, Iqbal knew that if the Islamic civilization had also continued to evolve, it would have positively produced the same results in science and technology as were produced by the West. Also, the products of many departments of learning have supported and confirmed Qur'anic concepts. So when the modern theories confirmed the truths of Islam Iqbal showed the world where their real source was.

Recently the Iqbal Academy has published a book by Dr. Muhammad Ma'ruf titled, *Iqbal and His Contemporary Western Thought*, in which the author has presented the study of the philosophers and schools of thought of the twentieth century whose influences are available in Iqbal's philosophy (xxxxix). According to Dr. Ma'ruf this book will open up many hidden niches and will help in fixing the position of Iqbal's thought in the world thought. In this book he has contradicted the thoughts of people like M.S. Raschid in the matter of comparison of Iqbal with Western philosophers that Iqbal's concept of God was borrowed from Hegel's concept of the Finite and has considered thoughts of such people as meaningless and prejudiced (L). This is so because Hegel's concept of the Finite cannot be concordant with Iqbal's *Al-Hayy al Qayyum*[44]. This book is very important in the study of Iqbal in which the concordance of Iqbal's thought with Western thought has been viewed on philosophical basis and includes a comparative study of Hegel, conceptualists, Immanuel Kant (1724-1804) naturalism, pragmatism and realism and other sociologists.

I will talk about four Western philosophers who are said to have influenced Iqbal much. I have Nietzsche, Bergson, Goethe and Sir Isaac Newton (1642-1723) in view, although each philosopher deserves a separate volume on account of his place and status. Kant and Dante (1265-1321) also deserve attention to some extent. This is so because it is said that Iqbal wrote his *Javid Namah* in the style of Dante's *Divine Comedy*. *Divine Comedy* was certainly in Iqbal's view but *Divine Comedy* itself was written in the style of *Mi'raj Namahs* written in Spain. There were several *Mi'raj Namahs* in Islamic literature apart from Dante's but the *Mi'raj*[45] of the Holy Prophet was the greatest source of inspiration for Iqbal. Iqbal took neither the style nor the happenings of the intellectual

The Origins and Sources of Iqbal's Philosophy

journey of *Divine Comedy*. Still a gap would have remained if Iqbal had ignored Dante at the time of writing the story of his intellectual journey. It is an accomplishment of Iqbal that in view of his acquaintance with Western literature in addition to the Eastern he did not ignore the *Divine Comedy* but in fact praised some of its literary styles. In the same way he used the products of Immanuel Kant's thought for affirmation of religion, because Kant tried hard to demolish the excessive power of intellect by fixing its limits in his book *A Critique of Pure Reason* and had freed Faith from the bondage of pure reason. He was talking about the "reason" which, while affirming the existence of the problem in a partial way, fails to see the Truth in its fullness.

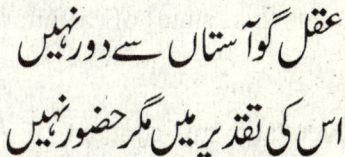

"Though reason is not far from the threshold
It is not fortunate enough to reach the Presence of God".
This means that while rationalism can guide Man to the *Wujud* of Allah it cannot comprehend and describe his *Zat*.

Analyzing the conditions of the eighteenth century Germany Iqbal says that at that time in Germany also reason was considered an ally of religion but when in a short period of time it became evident that dogmas could not be proved rationally the Germans had no alternative but to eliminate the portion of dogma from religion. But by relinquishing dogmas morality became pragmatic and so religiosity held sway under the influence of rationalism. This was the state of affairs of religious meditation and thinking when Kant appeared in Germany. When the limitations of human intellect became evident from *A Critique of Pure Reason* stratagem fabricated by rationalists about religion became a code of absurdity. Hence, it was correctly asserted that Kant was the highest favour bestowed by God on Germany. Iqbal compares Kant's doubts with those of Ghazali and obtains proof from him in the struggle between rationalism and religion. The products of the nature and limitations of rationalism in the works of Ghazali and Kant are echoed in Iqbal.

As regards Nietzsche asserting that his "Superman" is in any way connected with Iqbal's *Mard-i-Mumin* betrays ignorance of both Iqbal and Nietzsche. This is so because in calling Nietzsche *Majzub-i-Farangi*[46] and being unaware of God, Iqbal exposes the spiritual ineptness of Nietzsche.

35

Understanding Iqbal's Philosophy

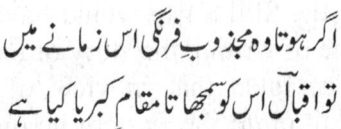

"If that *Majzub-i-Farangi* were alive at this time
Iqbal would have shown him the elegance of the Status of God."

Again when Iqbal says that would God grant Nietzsche to live during the period of Mujaddid and be associated with him he would have been rewarded with the truths of Eternal Happiness, it does not show even partial concordance and harmony between his and Nietzsche's thoughts. Iqbal has himself cleared this state of affairs in his letter to R.A. Nicholson. He says:

"He could not understand my concept of *Insan-i-Kamil* correctly and, confusing the issue, assumed my *Insan-i-Kamil* and the German thinker's "Superman" as the same. I had started writing about the *tasawwaf*'s belief of *Insan-i-Kamil* about twenty years ago, and this was the time when neither the sound of Nietzsche's beliefs had reached my ears nor had I read his books. Nietzsche is a thinker of the school of *Baqa-i-shakhsi*[47]. He asks all those who are anxious for acquiring subsistence whether they want to burden the earth permanently with their load. He has written like this because his concept of time was wrong. He never tried to understand the ethical side of the problem of time. On the contrary, in my view *baqa* is the highest longing of Man and is such a precious wealth on acquiring which Man concentrates all his powers. That is why I consider all forms and shapes of action, including conflict and war, to be necessary and, according to me, Man attains increased stability and firmness through them. Therefore, in pursuit of this thought, I have rejected the concept of a static being and similar *tasawwuf*, which is based on mere conjecture. I consider conflict necessary in ethical and not political ways, although on this subject the centre of Nietzsche's thought is perhaps politics". (Li)

Perhaps it will be ill-intentioned to say after this analysis by Iqbal himself that he has taken his concept of *Mard-i-Mumin* from Nietzsche. This is so because the "Superman" is blind, materialistic power, while the *Mard-i-Mumin* is adorned with *Wahi* and is a Godly man, whose climax is *Adbiyat*. In Iqbal's view the model *Mard-i-Mumin* in the applied world is the personality of the Holy Prophet, which is guided by *Wahi*, is master of

The Origins and Sources of Iqbal's Philosophy

ethical eminence and revolutionary and which resurrects new values of life with his actions, while Nietzsche's "Superman" in scholastic interpretation was Hitler, who was greedy for power and authority and was prepared to do anything to attain them. Iqbal's *Insan-i-Kamil* is a mercy to the human race, while Nietzsche's "Superman" is a destructive blind force which brings about destruction after tumult and oppression in the entire world. The late Abdur Rahman Tariq in his book, *Jahan-i-Iqbal* has very beautifully brought out the distance between Iqbal and Nietzsche comparing their works (Lii).

Dr. Annemarie Schimmel, being German, has very skilfully drawn parallels in the thoughts of Iqbal and Goethe. In her book, *Gabriel's Wing*, which has been translated into Urdu by Dr. Muhammad Riaz under the name *Shahpar-i-Jibrail* she has compared Iqbal and Goethe. She tries to harmonize Goethe's concept of God, "God, the Lord, Complete, Movement, in Eternal Endeavour and Action" with Iqbal's concept of God. Secondly, Goethe considers the existence of *Iblis* and Evil necessary for the evolution of life as does Iqbal shows his approval of the usefulness of *Iblis* and Evil. No doubt, Iqbal has praised Goethe as a visionary poet and a student of Eastern learning. But we have to realize that while the centre and orbit of Goethe's longing and the limits of his thought is in orientalism he is reduced to the position of a pointer at best, which guides Iqbal to his own real East. If so, why should Iqbal not be considered attached to the East through his thought and longings rather than through those of Goethe? (Liii)

Iqbal praised Goethe only because he loves orientalism. Goethe's disappointment with the West and his inclination to the East has been an important matter to Iqbal. Goethe's own *Divan*[48], titled *West-Oestlicher Divan* is known as "Movement of the East" in the history of German literature. In the words of Iqbal, "Apart from Hafiz, Goethe is indebted for his ideas to Shaikh Attar, Sa'di (d. 1292), Firdausi (d. 1020), and Islamic literature in general" (Liv).

Now, in the words of Iqbal, when Goethe tried to create Persian spirit in German literature, it is obvious that Iqbal was aware of the secret of the existence of Persian thinking in Goethe's thought. Schimmel is right to the extent of the existence of unlimited resemblance between the mode of thinking of German philosophers and Iqbal. Goethe is not related in any way with the sources of Iqbal's thought. By praising Goethe's literature Schimmel cannot prove it to be the source of Iqbal's thought. (Lv)

Understanding Iqbal's Philosophy

Bergson is given much importance as the source of Iqbal's thinking. Certainly the conclusions of Bergson's intellectual thought had greatly influenced the shaping of Iqbal's thought. Bergson strengthened Iqbal's thought by rejecting the materialistic interpretation of life, excessive emphasis on rationalism and the sameness of the body and the soul in the twentieth century. This is so because Bergson was intellectually a constructive and firm intellectual. In the words of the late Bashir Ahmad Dar:

> "What attracted Iqbal to Bergson was the fact that Bergson was a strong supporter of the deeper consciousness of human thought. In other words it can be said that he was a strong believer in the spiritual side of human existence and the function of intuition which creates the experience of motion" (Lvi).

> "Based on solid facts Bergson exposed the reality of the evolution which was considered the West to be the last nail in religion's coffin" (Lvii).

> "During the course of a meeting with Bergson Iqbal told him of the Hadith[49], "Do not curse time because I am myself time" he was astonished" (Lviii).

The front established by Bergson against science and materialism provided much strength to Iqbal's thought. Professor Jagannath Azad in his book, *The Intellectual Proximity and Remoteness of Iqbal and Bergson* has very well traced the movements which were common between Iqbal and Bergson and has also detailed their intellectual remoteness. The limitations of the mechanics of the length of life imposed by materialism and the non-permanence of time brought Iqbal close to Bergson because this was Iqbal's intellectual closeness to him. His intellectual distance from Bergson in Iqbal's own words was that:

> "For Bergson conscious experiences have merely the status of the past, the past, which running with the present, ultimately merges into it. Bergson ignores the fact that it is also an aspect of consciousness that it runs the future. Life is the practical realization of a thought and thought, assuming a practical form without any objective is inexplicable, irrespective of the practical form being conscious or sub-conscious. Not only this, but the fixation of the activity of our

perception and basic thought also is governed by our immediate objectives" (Lix).

In the same way the prolongation or permanence of time is purposeless in Bergson's view, while time is meaningful to Iqbal, because if evolution has no objective it is entirely meaningless in Iqbal's view.

The relationship between Einstein (1879-1955) and Iqbal is created by the theory of relativity. As the most important aspect of relativity is the discovery of time and space the prolongation of our life and the distance travelled by us in the vast field of time become absolutely unimportant. Appreciating the theory of relativity and fixing its usefulness Iqbal says:

"The philosophical value of the theory is twofold. First, it destroys, not the objectivity of Nature, but the view substance as simple location in space - a view which led to materialism in Classical Physics. 'Substance' for modern Relativity-Physics is not a persistent thing with variable states, but a system of inter-related events. In Whitehead's (1861-1947) presentation of the theory the notion of 'matter' is entirely replaced by the notion of 'organism'. Secondly, the theory makes space dependant on matter. The universe, according to Einstein, is not a kind of an island in an infinite space; it is finite but boundless; beyond it there is no empty space. In the absence of matter the universe would shrink to a point"(Lx).

Iqbal saw identity in Einstein's theory of relativity, which negated materialism. However, Iqbal had strong differences with Einstein in some matters. As Iqbal, like Bergson, is a believer in the reality of time he does not agree with the discovery of Einstein, which apparently denies time. This theory considers even the existence of time as unreal. At any rate Iqbal has praised the positive aspects of the theory of relativity and has criticized its negative ones.

The truth emanating from a detailed study of this subject is that Iqbal's mind was not imitative but creative, and was the one establishing connections between different thoughts. He established his theories and used the inferences drawn from the old and the new thinkers as his sources for the confirmation and elucidation of his own theories. Still he wanted religion to be defended in the present day world and had in view its explanation and interpretation in the language of the present age. Hence, he tried to benefit from the products of the thinking of the new thinkers with open eyes to explain the matter to the new minds in the new way and in doing so he did not allow the prejudices of the East and the West to blind him. He accepted everything good and criticized every faulty thought in the manner of a thinker endowed with enlightenment of the heart and the mind. In this way he brought into use his highest intellect in order to keep alight the torch of thinking of the human race. Still, if any single thing van be considered to be the source of his thought it is none other than the Holy Qur'an, because all the remaining products of Iqbal's intellect were explanations of this simple secret of Faith.

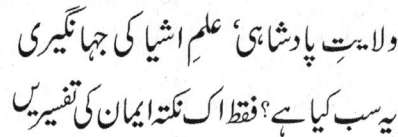

"*Walayat,* kingship, the universality of the knowledge of things
What are all these? Only *tafsirs* of the secret of *Iman*".

The Origins and Sources of Iqbal's Philosophy

References

(i) Schimmel, Annemarie (1987). *Gabriel's Wing*. Urdu Translation by Dr. Muhammad Riaz, titled, *Shahaipar-i-Jibreel*, Globe Publishers: p. 393

(ii) Quraishi, Ishtiaque Hussain (1966). *The Psychological Sources of Iqbal's Philosophy*. Annual Convocation Address, Punjab University, Lahore, Punjab, Pakistan.

(iii) Iqbal, Allama Dr. Sir Muhammad (1930). *Reconstruction of Religious Thought in Islam*; Shaikh Muhammad Ashraf, Lahore, Pakistan (1982): p. 6

(iv) Najla Izzuddin; *The Arab World*; Translated by Muhammad Hussain, Maktaba-i-Jadid, Lahore, 1960.

(v) Schimmel, ibid., p. 392

(vi) Ibid.

(vii) Hassan, Ishrat Enver (1944). *The Metaphysics of Iqbal*. pp. 7-8 Extracts from Presidential Remarks by Professor Dr. Syed Zafarul Hassan on *The Six Lectures*, delivered by Iqbal at the Muslim University, Aligarh, (1929): p. 7

(viii) Ibid: p. 8

(ix) Iqbal, ibid., pp. 106-107

(x) Ahmad, Absar (1973) "*Islami Ta'leem*", July-August.1973: p. 14

(xi) Iqbal, Allama Dr. Sir Muhammad (1932) *Javid Namah*. Versified English Rendering by A.Q. Niaz. Published by the Iqbal Academy, Lahore, Pakistan (1984): p. 22-23

(xii) Ibid., p. 23

(xiii) Qazi, Javid. (1973) *Wujudiat*. Published by Nigarishat, Lahore: p. 38

(xiv) Nadvi, Maulana Abul Hassan (1948). *Nuqush-i-Iqbal*. Idara-i-Nashriat-i-Islam, Karachi, Pakistan: p. 55

(xv) Iqbal, Allama Dr. Sir Muhammad (1975), *Kulliyat-i-Iqbal*, Urdu: p. 348

(xvi) Ibid. p. 332

(xvii) Syed, Nazir Niazi (1981). *Iqbal Ke Huzur*. Published by the Iqbal Academy. Lahore, Pakistan: pp. 60-61

(xviii) Iqbal, Allama Dr. Sir Muhammad (1975). *Kulliyat-i-Iqbal*, Urdu: p. 370

(xix) Ibid., p. 271

(xx) Iqbal, Allama Dr. Sir Muhammad (1975): *Kulliyat-i-Iqbal*, Persian: p. 20

(xxi) Iqbal, *Reconstruction, op. cit.* : Introduction

(xxii) Khan, Yusuf Hussain (1944) *Ruh-i-Iqbal* – Introduction

(xxiii) Akbarabadi, Maulana Saeed Ahmad (1987). *Khutbat-i-Iqbal Par ek Nazar*. Iqbal Academy, Lahore, Pakistan: p. 19

(xxiv) Khan, Ghulam Mustafa Khan (1988). *Iqbal awr Qur'an*, Iqbal Academy, Lahore, Pakistan. (This book is based on Iqbal's verses and Qur'anic verses). Muhammad Munawwar's *Burhan-i-Iqbal*, Published by Iqbal Academy, Lahore, Pakistan; see "Iqbal ba Huzur-i-Qur'an" and other papers.

(xxv) Iqbal, Allama Dr. Sir Muhammad (1975). *Kulliyat-i-Iqbal*, Persian: p. 123

(xxvi) Iqbal, Allama Dr. Sir Muhammad (1938). *Armaghan-i-Hijaz*. Published by Dr. Javid Iqbal, First Edition: p. 77

(xxvii) Nicholson, R.A. (1964*). The Idea of Personality in Sufism*.

(xxviii) Nadvi, Abdul Bari (1949). *Tajdeed-i-Tasawwuf awr Suluk*, First Edition: p. 160

(xxix) Iqbal, Allama Dr. Sir Muhammad (1975) *Kulliyat-i-Iqbal*. Persian: p. 741

(xxx) Mujaddid Alf-i-Thani (1984). *Maktubat-i-Imam-i-Rabbani*: p. 58

(xxxi) Faruqi, Burhan Ahmad (1940). *The Mujaddid's Conception of Tawhidd*. Published by Shaikh Muhammad Ashraf, Lahore, Pakistan: p. 58

(xxxii) Ibid., p. 58

(xxxiii) Ibid., p. 58

(xxxiv) Ishrat, Waheed. *Ibn-i-Sina ka Tasawwur-i-Hasti* (Unpublished Paper). Proceedings of Seminar, Department of Philosophy, Punjab University, Lahore, Pakistan

(xxxv) Mujaddid, Alf-i-Thani (1984). *Maktubat-i-Imam-i-Rabbani*: p. 111

(xxxvi) Ibid.,

(xxxvii) Ibid., p. 113

(xxxviii) Ibid., p. 114

(xxxix) Ibid., p. 58

(xxxx) Syed, Abdullah (1977) (Compiler) *Muta'alliqat-i-Khutbat-i-Iqbal*. Iqbal Academy, Lahore, Pakistan. p. 94

(xxxxi) Iqbal, p. 75

(xxxxii) Ibid., p. 114

(xxxxiii) Ibid., pp. 75-76

(xxxxiv) Sherwani, Latif Ahmad (1977). *Speeches, Writings and Statements of Iqbal*. Iqbal Academy, Lahore, Pakistan: p. 70

(xxxxv) Hassan, Enver Ishrat (1944). *The Metaphysics of Iqbal*; Published by Shaikh Muhammad Ashraf, p. viii.

(xxxxvi) Shaikh, Ataullah (1946) *Iqbal Nama*: Published by Shaikh Muhammad Ashraf, Vol. 1, p. 4

(xxxxvii) Iqbal, Allama Dr. Sir Muhammad (1985) *Kulliyat-i-Iqbal*, Persian: p. 929

(xxxxviii) Siddiqui, Iftikhar Ahmad (1923) (Translator). *Shazarat-i-Iqbal*: Bazm-i-Iqbal Lahore, Pakistan: p. 105

(xxxxix) Muinee, Syed Abdul Vahid (1963). *Maqalat-i-Iqbal*: Published by Shaikh Muhammad Ashraf, Lahore, Pakistan: pp. 239-240

(L) Ma'ruf, Muhammad (1987). *Iqbal and His Contemporary Western Religious Thought*: Published by Iqbal Academy, Lahore, Pakistan:

(Li) Ibid.,: Introduction

(Lii) Tariq, Abdur Rahman (1949). *Jahan-i-Iqbal*: Published by Malik Deen Muhammad, Lahore, Pakistan: pp. 19-20

(Liii) Ibid., See the paper titled, "*Iqbal awr Nietzsche*".

(Liv) Schimmel, op. cit. p. 406-407

(Lv) Iqbal, Allama Dr. Sir. Muhammad (1971). *Payam-i-Mashriq*, Thirteenth Edition 1971: Published by Shaikh Ghulam Ali & Sons Ltd., English Translation.

(Lvi) Dar, Bashir Ahmad (1956). *Iqbal awr Bergson*: Bazm-i-Iqbal, Lahore, Pakistan: p. 103

(Lvii) Ibid., p. 104

(Lviii) Iqbal, Justice Dr. Javid (1984). *Zinda Rud*. Vol. 3, Published by Shaikh Ghulam Ali & Sons Ltd., Lahore, Pakistan: p. 496

(Lix) *Shifa-i-Iqbal* (1987). Bazm-i-Iqbal, Lahore, Pakistan pp. 299-300

(Lx) Iqbal, op. cit. p. 38

The Origins and Sources of Iqbal's Philosophy

Foot Notes

(1). Self-Cognizance.

(2). The true believer.

(3). The authentic being.

(4). The belief that all Existence is one. Monism of *Wujud* (Being), Pantheism.

(5). *Six Lectures on the Reconstruction of Religious Thought In Islam* by Dr. Muhammad Iqbal delivered at the Muslim University, Aligarh, India In 1929 and at Madras in 1930.

(6). Essence.

(7). Pantheism.

(8). These are four of the most prominent and original Islamic thinkers, viz. Shaikh Fariduddin Attar (d. 1230), Maulana Jalaluddin Rumi (d. 1273), Fakhruddin Muhammad Razi (d.1228), and Abu Hamid Muhammad Ghazali (d. 1111).

(9). Abul Qasim Mahmud Zamakhshari of Khwarizm (d. 1160). The *tafsir* written by him known as the *Kashshaf* is very full in the explanation of words and idioms. The *tafsir* takes a decidedly rational and ethical view of doctrines. Numerous *tafsirs* have been written on it. Similarly *Tafsir-i-Kabir* by Fakhruddin Muhammad Razi is very comprehensive and strong in interpretation from a soil or spiritual point of view.

(10). Exegesis.

(11). Faith, Belief.

(12). Nearness to God involving His support and protection; Saintship.

(13). The Holy Sanctuary of the *Ka'ba*.

(14). Destiny.

(15). Shaikh Ahmed Sirhindi (1564-1624). He was a very eminent sufi and was born at Sirhind close to and northwest of Delhi, India. His main achievements are his *jihad* against the secularism and anti-Islamic practices of the Mughal Imperial court during the reign of Akbar and Jahangir, and his struggle to purify *tasawwuf* from all non-Islamic concepts and based it again on purely Qur'anic teachings. That is why he is called Mujaddid Alf-i-Thani or Revivalist of the Second Millennium.

(16). Muhyuddin lbn-al-Arabi (d. 1240). He is an eminent Muslim philosopher and was perhaps the first philosopher to introduce the philosophy of *Wahdat-al-Wujud,* from the Greek school into the Muslim world. In his own days he was opposed by other Muslim thinkers, the most prominent among whom is Ibn-i-Taymiyyah (d. 1327)

(17). Intoxication caused by a powerful spiritual experience.

(18). Abul Qasim al-Junaid Baghdadi (d. 909).

(19). Sobriety. The stage in the spiritual experience of a soil in which he has overcome intoxication.

(20). Servitude, or condition in which a person regards himself as a slave of God. In the Holy Quran the word '*abd* designates the nature, status and destiny of man that he is a slave of God, not a Divine Being, that he has no share in God's powers and rights and that he is to realize his '*ubudiyat* or slavehood and be a perfect servant or slave of God *('Abd*).

(21). Being and Essence respectively.

(22). The distinction of *Zat* and *Sifat* is very nearly the distinction of substance and attributes. At times it looks like that of Existence and Essence. It can be rendered as the distinction of Being and Nature, or It and Its Qualities. *Asma* (plural of *Ism)*, means divine names with reference to particular *Sifit* or *Zat* as they occur in the Holy Qur'an, for example *Ar-Rahim*, the Merciful, as they are the names of Allah in virtue of His Qualities or Activities, i.e. an *Ism* combines *Zat* and *Sifat.*

(23). *Tajalli* is really shining forth. The conception underlying is that God is Light and this Light shines forth as if bodily in many forms. Hence, it may be translated as Eradiation, Effluence, Emanation, Manifestation

The Origins and Sources of Iqbal's Philosophy

and in philosophical terminology as equivalent to Mode. When the Light shines forth on itself it is *Tajalli-ba-Nafsihi*. As the Light shines forth in various grades to the mystic, It is *Tajalli-i-Zati* or *Sifati* etc. with reference to the mystic it means the vision of the Light or Illumination by it. If this vision is that of the Being or *Zat* of Allah it is *Tajalli-i-Zati*.

(24). Vision; apparentism.

(25). Space.

(26). Independent of space.

(27). Cognition.

(28). Thinkers who follow the Truth.

(29). The one whose non-existence is inconceivable.

(30). The one whose neither the existence nor the non-existence is inconceivable.

(31). Immortal.

(32). Allah and the universe respectfully.

(33). A person who loves God to the extent of renunciation of his personal will in his affirmation of the Beloved's (God's) Will.

(34). Literally it means unveiling. It is apprehension of facts and events as well as truths, mundane as well as celestial by Inner sight or light. Generally the apprehension is symbolic.

(35). Blind and unquestioned following of some person or doctrine.

(36). *Ilham* is inspiration; technically is confined to mystics; it is reception of guidance or Inspiration from above. The guidance thus received is not absolutely infallible, hence it is not binding on all but only on the recipient of it, provided it is not contrary to any Injunction received through the Holy Prophet.

(37). *Wahi* is literally communication or command; technically it is communication imparted by God to a prophet, its highest form being communication through the agency of an angel. Guidance received through it is absolutely sure and binding on all.

(38). Carnal self.

(39). Appearance of the Divine Essence.

(40). One who knows the Holy Qur'an by heart.

(41). A sufi who is in a passing feeling expression, such as elation, suppression, hope, fear etc., contrasted to more durable or permanent states such as patience, gratitude, love and trust, which are called *Maqam* (station).

(42). Perfect Man.

(43). The true Believer.

(44). The living, Self-Subsisting, Eternal.

(45). Celestial Ascent of the Holy Prophet.

(46). *Majzub* is the one absorbed in God. *Majzub-i-Farangi* means one absorbed in the materialism of the West.

(47). The mystic experience of an Individual's subsistence or living by and in God after dying (*fana*) of the individual.

(48). Poetical collection.

(49). Traditions and sayings of the Holy Prophet.

Chapter 2

METHODOLOGY OF RECONSTRUCTION OF RELIGIOUS THOUGHT IN ISLAM

Reconstruction of Religious Thought in Islam stands as masterpiece in the thought of Muhammad Iqbal. He delivered these lectures in Lahore, Madras, Hyderabad Deccan and Aligarh, whereas seventh lecture entitled "Is Religion Possible?" was written at the invitation of Aristoletian Society of London.

Initially the book contained six lectures, whereas seventh lecture subsequently was added. Thus pretty attributes are very clear about these lectures. The first is that these were delivered by a prominent learned person who had deep observation of Eastern as well as Western knowledge of Indo-Pak sub-continent who was reported during his life time, and also afterwards at present. In these lectures, it has been tried to answer the questions on the social and civilization level faced by the Islamic world for its existence and revival.

I postpone detailed discussion for some other time, yet I would like to say that the challenges offered by the different results of the different types of knowledge of science and technology caused existence of religion, especially Islam subjected to danger, and rightly the question was raised as to what was the basic relation between the man's internal aspects and also between an individual person and society and in this respect what is the status of religion; and secondly, in this regard, it was also necessitated to search for the plausibility of religion in the light of old decaying beliefs about science and matter. Iqbal conceived these questions in time and formed them in different ways with the help of these lectures, and provided their answers. This was a great challenge, not only in the tradition of the subcontinent but also the Islamic world. This was a great challenge, out of which Iqbal came out victorious, and a scholar like him, possessing unlimited knowledge was suitable for this job.

The second importance of these lectures are seriousness of his writing, his learned method of reasoning, dignified thinking wherein he tries to carry the contents. The consciousness of Western as well as

Understanding Iqbal's Philosophy

Eastern traditions of knowledge appears to be more conspicuous when he talks about old thinkers and new philosophers, history experts and psychologists etc. in his criticism and observation in the vast background.

Thus these lectures have been mentioned in the light of vast background of the history of human thoughts. Therefore, there is great scope for a man to discuss these lectures according to his insight and capability.

My personal opinion is that some enormous works have not as yet come to light on the lectures of Iqbal whereas substantial work has been done on his poetry; and secondly the work which has been studied by me is explanatory; or else like the philosopher of Egypt, some people have totally rejected. Contrary to this Maulana Saeed Ahmed Akbarabadi in his book, entitled *Cursory Glance on the Lectures of Iqbal* is interpreted as a new Islamic scholastic philosophy. I do not mention the names of Muhammad Sharif Baqa, Dr. Khalifa Abdul Hakim, Prof. Muhammad Usman with relation to the book, entitled *Simplification of Lectures of Iqbal* because this book instead of criticizing Iqbal, comes under the title of elucidation and explanation.

According to me new formation of Islamic metaphysics is not a new thing with reference to its programme. This is the centuries-old effort to reconciliation and it was started by the Greek philosopher Philo who was the first to commence reconciliation of Judaism and philosophy. This tradition was fructified Philo's countryman, Christian philosopher of Alexandria, named Flatinos, by means of philosophy and religion. After the deterioration of Greek and Roman civilization, when Muslims exalted to peak of success of worldly life, and Baghdad acquired the position of Muslim intellectual centre, after the conquest of Iran, relations with Iranians and fire-worshippers and other civilizations came into existence. After the conquest of Egypt, Roman and Greek thoughts, and similarly after conquering Syria and Turkey Muslims came in contact with non-Muslim civilizations. Even prior to this when Muslims, Jews and Christians mutually came in contact with each other, then the simple and amicable intellectual teachings Islam had to face new questions and situation.

After the victory of Alexandria the flood of knowledge gushed out from its scholarly atmosphere and libraries, which caused all such questions which were under discussion in Jewish and Christian scholastic philosophy. The expansion of Muslim state gave rise to various

Methodology of Reconstruction of Religious Thought in Islam

metaphysical and linguistic problems about government management, language, dress, gathering and rising up and civilization. Jewish scholars translated these books in Arabic, as a result of which the thesis of "voluntary" and unvoluntary actions and rationalistic way of thinking, and thus the way of thinking which matured among Muslims was reconciliation between philosophy and science, which was in vogue earlier with Flatinos. Since Flatinos was also called the second Aristotle, and the Greek philosophy had reached Muslims through his mediation, and for a long time some of the Muslim scholars could not differentiate between Plato and Flatinos, and as such the influence of Platinos on the entire Muslim thought was very intense. Muslims could not set themselves free his thought and programme. Right from the beginning of first philosopher al-Kindi upto Farabi, Ibn-i-Sina, and Ibn-i-Arabi, the influence of Platinos is very deep upto implausible length, Plato's theory about examples similitude's emanation are changeable have been among Muslims through the mediation of Platinos. Here there is no scope for details. Even in Iqbal's thought about Allah correction of nature contains its echo.

The reconciliation between philosophy and religion, science and religion which strengthened and progressed among Muslims through al-Kandi, al-Farabi, Ibn-i-Sina, Ibn-i-Arabi, Imam Ghazali, Ibn-i-Rushd was owned by Sir Syed Ahmed in 1875 A.D. after our decline under the conception of Muslim revival. Sir Syed Ahmed Khan had Islamic knowledge to a certain extent but he had no access over Western learning. During the days of Sir Syed European mind and thought was clearly inclined towards Naturalism when Sir Syed, after having over-awed by European and Western civilization, adopted the way of reconciling religion with Nature, and when he observed religious beliefs in the light of Nature and Natural laws, he started explaining miracles and some other important and clear religious beliefs in ridiculous ways, due to which he was called a Naturalist and his thoughts about religion were not accepted. As a result of this Natural movement about religion, philosophy and poetry that school of poetic thought of Hali and Muhammad Hussain Azad came into existence which put into vogue Nature worship, natural scenes and patriotism.

Iqbal, being more cautious, philosophical and scholarly way, also used scientific and philosophical results to reconcile with and confirm religion which itself shows reconciliation and, its object with simplest words an apologizing difference to religion. The basis of entire philosophy of Iqbal is that modern science, nature, chemistry and all the results of other branches of knowledge are confirming basic conception and theories of religion. Here the question arises that if the results of science, philosophy and other branches of knowledge are confirming religion; are they acceptable to us and we accept their confirmation to be an argument in religion; but if the same theories of science and philosophy undergo a change in future or they contradict of their own selfs will we then cover these religions beliefs? Which were confirmed in the past? Or we will declare the new findings of science and philosophy to be false or else we will try to explain and interpret religious beliefs in their light, and then try a new reconciliation between religion and science. In this situation, whatever apparent form comes forth after repeated reconciliation of religion, what will be the form of the religion left and; as such who do we consider every new result of science to the final and categorical: only because they can be checked? From our this attitude whatever we prove is religion is without any colour or odour that it assurances the colour and shape of the utensil wherein it is put. It has no final and categorical identity of its own.

The reason of all this process as I observe is that an explicit process about progress of science and matter does exist. Its sketch is vertical which is drawn from under to upwards, whereas this process of evolution is missing from religious beliefs, and these are categorical and they are categorical like the days of eternity.

We are impressed by an evolving thing but we feel static position in a categorical and final thing: whereas if we observe deeply, we should testify knowledge about philosophy, science and matter on the criterion of categorical and final beliefs and facts. This is the job which Muslims have never performed. They have not testified knowledge and arts on the basis of the Holy Qur'an as their follower. Even Iqbal who drowned deep into Quranic knowledge and said that if he had offered anything in his teachings apart from the Holy Qur'an, he may not have the good fortune of kissing the feet of the Holy Prophet (p.b.u.h). He also remained deprived from this clear consciousness and he himself instead of treating the Holy Qur'an as the basis, be adopted the way of conforming Holy Qur'an with psychology, nature and other branches of knowledge which was entirely anti-Quranic and anti-Islamic, and through centuries Muslim philosophers and scholars had adopted.

According to me, the biggest problem of Muslims is not to reconcile religion with philosophy and science or any other types of beliefs or

Methodology of Reconstruction of Religious Thought in Islam

system. Whatever has even devoted as *Hikmat*, could not be evolved among Muslims. Instead of this they gathered metaphysics of Jews and Christians in the form of useless Islamic metaphysics from which Qur'an's own spirit was crushed and Qur'an's own beliefs and contents fell a pray to doubts. Instead of constructing their own basis of civilizations Muslims they invented an art of pasting their own labels in the results obtained by others tried to Islam use them. For example by pasting Islamic label on Greek system of medicine, they invented the art of making it Islamic and this resulted in preparation of prescriptions of sexual vitality for emperors, landlords and wealthy people. In this procedure no educational or research progress was visible. Therefore this came to an end in competition of medical system of the West after passing through death agony.

Now-a-days the Pakistani indigenous doctors mix European medicines in their ma'jun, and now they have much medicines. No one thought that should study whatever is mentioned in the Holy Qur'an and sacred Hadith (words and deeds of Holy Prophet about the nature of things and human structure and development). They should ponder as to whether thus any medical system comes or does not come into existence. The discussion is apt to becoming lengthy, but I wish to say friendly that *Lectures* represent Iqbal's deep thoughts: and these should be scrutinized with deeper thinking after passage of fifty years, because in the time initial lectures Iqbal for the possibility of religion, Iqbal has based knowledge on religious perception or religious experience, and he has termed it as science; just as there can be any other scientific experience but in these lectures Iqbal himself could not prove religious observation to be transferable. When religious experiences are not transferable, how can they become basis of any civilization? Observed, from this point of view, Iqbal's possibility of religion cannot initiate basis for any civilization or culture. This, in his lectures, Iqbal's conception of knowledge and religion, both are ambiguous, unscientific and unscholastic interpretations, and as such Iqbal's desire of revival of religion in new form is only an innocent desire and such mission.

Now concerning the definition of religion which Iqbal has mentioned in his first lecture that religion is the system of general facts which if accepted and understood as it deserves, then character and actions change.

Understanding Iqbal's Philosophy

I do not think that Iqbal has correctly understood this definition of religion by Whitehead or not because if a person accepts a system of facts only on the basis of amicable belief, it is not exceptional that his character and actions may be influenced. This is not a exceptional thing with reference to religion. The communists accepted Marx's theory and economics view point as a system of facts and its effects are also obvious. How can we now apply religion to it? Some fascist systems are accepted, and they form their positive effects. Should they be accepted as religion? The fact is that this definition of religion by Whitehead is not a plausible reasoning, nor is it a criterion for positive attitude of a religion. For example if a prophet after preaching for the whole of his life is not able to convince even a single person of the truth of Allah's existence, and also could not produce positive results of his views, then (God forbid) we will declare this as non-result producing and false. To apply results on religion is in itself a misunderstanding which Iqbal declared to be a standard of the truth of religion. Now when Iqbal says referring to Whitehead that time of a religion is that intellectual time, then why he declares the access to pure reality to be impossible and then according to the saying of a mystic, he says faith is like a bird which it itself finds out its own unmarked passage.

When Iqbal admits element of intellect along with sense of reeling in religion, and then to compare faith with a bird which only with the help of its intimation finds its way, deprived of intellect; it is to bring down faith on the lower level because instilment is animal attribute and intellect is human attribute. Only intellect is the basis of faith. The center system of man and religion can neither be understood, nor any verdict can be based on it in this way. Of course intellect does have different surfaces and stages. There is a difference between un-intellect of a child and Socrates. The intellect of a prophet or messenger of Allah which illuminated by the light of Allah is different from the intellect of an ordinary human being. *Iman* (Belief) is created only when we conceive full consciousness and understanding of fact. The stages of the faith of an ordinary person, a prophet and a scholar should also be differentiated. Therefore, Iqbal's theory of blaming intellect is not service for religion, because the commitment which produces intellect in us, cannot create any other thing, and the same commitment provides basic faith.

In history, a clear example is that of Socrates, whose knowledge and wisdom about commitment did not waver even by the fear of drinking person.

Methodology of Reconstruction of Religious Thought in Islam

Whatever distinctive features Iqbal has stated in his lecture on knowledge and religious observations are these:

1. Presence of mystic observations.
2. The comprehensive features of mystic perception.
3. The ecstasy of a mystic is only for a moment. It is unity with a personality which is beyond his self but despite this, it surrounding him.
4. Mystic perceptions are experiences directly. It is not possible to transfer them to others as original.
5. The mystic perceptions do not lose for a long time, whereas the echo of the mystic (Sufi) is personal and individual. The special features of a mystic as stated by Iqbal make the experience of a mystic (Sufi) vague, personal, individual and unable to be transferred. Therefore reaching results of which Iqbal speaks, that also is not final and correct because the religious and inner experience, that is also is not far-reaching as regards results.

Therefore religious experience is not transferable this does not provide basis of knowledge. This also cannot become the foundation of a large collective cultural and civil revolution. Instead of bearing knowledge with religious experience or observation of prophet or of a mystic (Sufi), should have based on the Holy Qur'an because only that is why word and speech of Allah, and that provides such a framework which guides human beings with collective system of life in every time for principles and basis. Religious experience is only an individual work, and this only can become the basis of personality and self. From this a collective system, civilization or culture cannot be evolved. The Holy Qur'an is not the personal religious experience of the Holy Prophet. This is the word and verdict of Allah which can become the basis of a man's personality and self. From this collective system of life or knowledge produced or evolved.

This is Allah's word which He has destined for man.

Iqbal cannot explain existence of knowledge with basis of religious experience. According to Berkeley, religious experience do lead us to understanding knowledge but cannot evolve or produce knowledge. Knowledge was taught to mankind by Allah Himself.

Understanding Iqbal's Philosophy

The Holy Qur'an is Allah's verdict which provides us such a framework by which we may be able to understand our circumstances and happenings with reference to which we may be able to evolve a system of life during every era and circumstances. Although religious conception is the basis of our individuality and spiritual maturity, yet the basis of knowledge and formation of the entire system of life can be based only is Allah's verdict, which means the Holy Qur'an and that is command for us. If religious experiences are treated as the basis of knowledge, then the priority of the Holy Qur'an will come under pressure, and every one will insist to make his religious experiences to be orders for others, which itself means to open a dangerous chapter.

In respect of religious conception Imam Ghazali's name is also respectable. In a book, entitled *Tahafat-al Filasafa* and *Munqiz min al-Zalal* he has censured and contempted and disgraced philosophers, and he has criticised philosophy intensely. Indeed not only in Islamic history but in the history of knowledge and wisdom of the world he is an exalted name and his thoughts and theories have great talent. Enormous is to be done on Imam Ghazali but his methods with which he attacks basic body and soul of philosophy, are not much effective because if under the view point of Ghazali the results and process of philosophy are brought under doubt, then the same objections will be levied on his mysticism and religious experience, then Imam Ghazali himself did not find any way to escape, instead of giving new intellectual theories, and formulating and proving a new system, he causes more confusions, and this criticism on philosophy and logic were confined to objections only which among Muslims because the cause of prevention growth of philosophy, but no new wisdom or insight could not emanate from it which we may call to be the wisdom of the Holy Qur'an or we may hear a good news or the light Quranic theories. We may hear about any new system based on the theories of the Holy Qur'an

The fact that Muslims memorized the Holy Qur'an with great beauty; understood research of its language and linguistic suspicious very respectedly decorated it in fine cloth with great adoration; touch it with eyes, translated it; wrote marginal notes and commentaries and explanations; wrote it in different types of calligraphy, and got them printed but in view of its unlimited respect did not study its programme, results and its contents and ways, and did not examine it with deep critical philosophical thought, and did not check it on scholastic, logical, scientific and critical level but after accepting un-Quranic scientific research and

Methodology of Reconstruction of Religious Thought in Islam

knowledge and they brought any verse in its support with great skill. I am of the opinion that if all scientific the Holy Qur'an cancels all the scientific research, its results and facts, then why should we not accept this cancellation instead of interpreting Qur'an and by taking system of Qur'an as the basis, a way of research, new way of scientific way of thinking of philosophy? What is its reason? Instead of words and contents of the Qur'an theories of science and philosophy are more active, moving and evolving. I do not accept this objection. Had we succeeded to form a new system of thinking, that would have remained evolving automatically due to its imperative attitude? The real fact is that our belief in the Holy Qur'an is limited to words and its language.

Internally and also mentally and intellectually, and we have more faith in results of science and philosophy because in the materialistic world they can be confirmed as "two and two makes four", whereas we do not have any criteria with us for confirming religious facts, apart from the Holy Qur'an itself. Human mind accepts natural facts more easily than metaphysical (after this world). Had we also formed our own scientific research and knowledge, then today we would have been able to control intellectual and mental leadership of the world, and instead of having been conquered, we would have conquered the West. My reasoning is that although in the Muslim scholastic world, with reference to Imam Ghazali, Ibn-i-Khaldun and Ibn-i-Taymiyyah, a weakling voice had been emanating, but no one has formulated such an enormous learning system and Iqbal who had independent opinion about the knowledge of East as well as of the West; he also could not take courage to fulfill this enormous work due to his poetic career, and therefore he limited his thinking only to down-trodden thoughts. Therefore, as Iqbal has said that new Western culture is the extension of Islamic civilization, we shall have to admit that Islamic civilization did not have its own specialities but they were the copies of Greek, Roman, Persian and Hindi civilization of the sub-continent, which Muslims always kept, covered with green cloth cover. Whereas on the basis of Qur'an we could form new civilization, a new culture, new attitude of life.

Iqbal in his preface of lectures said that our duty is that we should keep our observing eye on the evolution of human thought and in this respect we should be critical so that theories which may be better than the ones mentioned in lectures because the evolutions observed in various branches of knowledge, which will perhaps in future reveal harmony between religion and science which man is concealed.

Understanding Iqbal's Philosophy

Iqbal's this sentence limits that all his efforts of research is the research of harmony between religion and science, whereas I do not accept Iqbal's this apologizing attitude.

According to me religion in itself is a reality. Science is a chain of facts which is changing every moment. Therefore, religion cannot be changed according to every revelation.

We should study the Holy Qur'an according to its own framework and in the light of its own background, and we should examine as to how the worldly fact can be harmonized with these facts. Concerning lectures our future criticism will depend on this basis so that we may have guidance to proceed ourselves towards plausible framework of knowledge and advance revolutionary message of the Holy Qur'an towards correct direction.

Chapter 3

MUSLIM THEORY OF KNOWLEDGE IN THE PHILOSOPHICAL PERSPECTIVE OF MULLA SADRA AND IQBAL

Despite my confession that I did not have the opportunity of studying Mulla Sadra thoroughly because most of Mulla Sadra's thoughts are expressed in Arabic and secondly I did not have access to all the books of Mulla Sadra. Inspite of this, whatever I have to say about him, it is the methodology of his philosophy, which he had used to formulating his religious learning, thought and philosophy as that used by the other theologians of Islam, Christianity and Judaism. Here I shall be able to discuss his point of philosophizing the faith and discipline of Islamic thought which is not even slightly different from the one which had been popular among Muslims from the time of prevailing of philosophy and wisdom and which is common among all the philosophers like Mulla Sadra, Iqbal's thought is also based on these two things. One of these is that for basis of certainty of reality only intelligence and argument are not enough but it is essential that these should be accompanied with eye-witness and evidence. This is same view which was expressed by Imam Ghazali that we cannot know the reality of the words that he came on the heavenly throne, and in our times Kant has also emphasized that the acquiring the knowledge of the unseen is not possible which means the reality of things as they are, are beyond our knowledge. The world of knowledge we have built up is based on personal thoughts and principles of artificial mental sayings. This means that like Mulla Sadra, Kant is also convinced of the limitations of our understanding. In his lectures Iqbal also divided wisdom in partial and perfect wisdom, and following Maulana Rumi he insisted on the unaccessibility of knowledge alone. With reference to knowledge all the Muslim thought appears to hover around this version, and this is the basic view of the Muslim philosophy, and this present there as the basic view point. If this problem is considered from Islamic point of view, this thing is present everywhere that knowledge of the unseen is not possible, and know the things as they in reality exist is beyond our knowledge. Keeping in view this background, the exact meanings of supplication of the Holy Prophet can be understood. He says "O Allah inform me of the reality of things with the real knowledge of things". If it were impossible completely, the Holy Prophet would not have offered this prayer. The fact is concealed in this prayer is that knowledge of reality of things is not impossible. Muslim philosophers diverted their attention only to this side.

The other thing which I want to express is that the methodology of Mulla Sadra is also reconciling and he had tried to reconcile inductive philosophy with philosophy of spiritual experiences. He had tried his level best to connect both philosophies and then reconcile them with the principal of *Irfan* (wisdom of the reality of spiritual knowledge). Which was to bring into notice through Ibn-al-Arabi and his diciple Mulla Sadruddin Qunavi. After that he had linked it with *Wahi*. He also then interpreted revelation in the light of Shia tenets. In this way Mulla Sadra had reconciled Shia faith with philosophy and completed it with connection with the traditional philosophy of Islam. All the methodology of Mulla Sadra is based on reconciliation of philosophy with faith of Shi'ite spiritual interpretation in the light of traditional Muslim philosophy of Sunnah.

This reconciliation method was first adopted by a Jewish philosopher of Alexandria named Philo for congruity of Plato's philosophy and Judaism. Following him, another Christian philosopher of Alexandria named Plotinus adopted the same method, and the foremost Muslim Arab philosopher al-Kindi, al-Farabi and Sheikh Ibn-i-Sina introduced it among the Muslim which is the basis of their knowledge of belief whose have major representations. This tradition was followed in sub-continent by Sir Syed Ahmed Khan and Iqbal in the educational and philosophical world. Following Sir Syed Ahmed Khan, movements of naturalism surged up in religion, philosophy and poetry. Sir Syed and his followers were called naturalists. Hali, Azad etc. wrote poems with reference to nature and subsequently all our literary, poetic attitude fell a prey to romanticism, naturalism, narcissism, modernism, existentialism, logical positivism, pragmatism and utilitarianism. We gave up our ways of writing in literature and poetry we were chained in colonialism and neo-colonialism. Thinking and practicing in this way now we even do not feel aversion. On the contrary we take them to the signs of progress, triumph, success, and on thinking this we are surrounded by these civilizational tumults, on which were relaying our forefathers and now all the Europe is mourning it. In his book entitled *Reconstruction of Religious Thought in Islam* with the gists of Western science, naturalism, physics, psychology and sociology etc. they have deterred these branches to be the extension of Islamic culture and civilization. These old as well as new Muslim thinkers

Muslim Theory of Knowledge In The Philosophical Perspective of Mulla Sadra And Iqbal

appeared to have the same congruing and reconcilianal attitude. With reference to this attitude of philosophizing the ultimate of Iqbal and Mulla Sadra to be congruous, I feel that a great misfortune of Muslim philosophy and Islamic *Ilm-al-Kalam* (knowledge of belief) that instead of discovering new attitude of another field of knowledge they have destroyed all of their mental energies whereas it was not necessary that they should copy their ugly examples of Jewish and Christian attitudes and their religion, philosophy and science. The thing which has been termed as wisdom by the Holy Qur'an, has not come into being among the Muslims. In its place, the Muslims have heard awkward Jewish and Christian beliefs due to which the real spirit of the Holy Qur'an has been crushed, and Qur'an's own beliefs and subjects fell a prey to doubts. Instead of building their own culture and civilization in this wisdom of Islam, Muslims applied labels on the results obtained by the others, Muslims tries to Islamize them. Right from al-Kindi, al-Farabi, Ibn-i-Sina, upto Mulla Sadra and Iqbal are suffering from the same tragedy because all these people gave preference to philosophic and scientific beliefs, over the Holy Qur'an's contents. All these philosophers have tried to apply Islamic parchment over the results obtained by others. By stretching they have invented the method to apply it over the results obtained by Greek philosophers and Western learning and science but thus was a futile effort. With reference to congruity also the attitude of Mulla Sadra and Iqbal in concordant to the thoughts of Shia sect, and Iqbal had with him the result of modern European learning and Sunni beliefs Mulla Sadra had with him Greek philosophers and their Muslim commentators. My question is as to why Mulla Sadra, Iqbal and other Muslim intelligent scholars have turned new philosophy and science as "basic" and they have interpreted the Holy Qur'an in congruity with these branches of knowledge. This is such an obvious tragedy that it does not need to be explained with regard to its injurious effects. If they have admitted the Holy Qur'an to be basic and they have interested and explained Greek philosophy and European learning and science, then this is advancement in the right direction, but alas! the reply of the second part of this query is in the negative.

What is knowledge? If I offer argument according to the sacred *Hadith* (saying) of the Holy Prophet in which he says "O Allah! Inform me of the reality of things", then knowledge will be defined as "to know the reality of things". Then the Holy Qur'an says: "Allah, the sublime has appraised Adam of the names of things and informed him of reality of things". The Holy Qur'an also says: "Allah, the sublime acquainted Adam

Understanding Iqbal's Philosophy

reality of things by which Adam came to know about reality of things." Now the research as to "what is knowing". The answer to this question is that knowing and acquaintance are not always used in the same content. Sometime knowing is used in its simple sense. For example: do I know Aslam? This means in what sense? 1) Only familiarity and acquaintance. Other sense applies to practical and technical knowledge. 2) The second sense of "know" refers to knowledge and technical and practical knowledge. For example, how he rides the horse? How he drives the car? 3) However, the right method of knowing is real fact. For example, I am aware of the fact, that Mulla Sadra was the resident of Shiraz. Also that after this some thing happens. I know that you are sitting in front of me. I know that Pakistan is a friendly country for Iran or a neighbouring country. In such cases, one cannot be well informed about this without knowing the real facts about the happening. To know a certain case means to take it to be true. However, knowing about his beliefs, weak and strong points of his knowledge and his being hopeful and wondering are quite separate and different things. To know all those facts about him means to know him in the real sense. There are also strong and weak standards of knowledge and understanding. Nevertheless for a philosopher, the high standard only is preferable. He is always in search of such facts which we can save even the slightest extent of doubts and they will never prove to be true. The process of knowing can never be complete without comprehensive testimony because every witness and experiences provides more testimony to a case but has now power to make true. We can only claim for truth, by overlooking long discussion over the understanding. Now we come towards sources of knowledge, which I also call stages of knowledge, which surges to stage by stage and at least reaches the stage of conviction. The only drawback had been that one group of philosophers not only awared it but considered it to be final and ultimate, and ignored others, whereas every one of them completes his mission of knowledge after certainly fulfilling their part. For example teaching experience is very clear among all the stated means of knowledge because in teaching experience we trust in any of our sense and decide over anything as the basis of its performance. The knowledge of existence of natural things and there is obtained attributes by us by smelling and testing by which we get the knowledge of existence. The five senses make the natural world explicit to us. Although mistakes of understanding, cheating and doubt are there but all depend on the right or wrong understanding of teaching sense. These teaching experiences, after passing through the process of confirmation of knowledge. Our mental actions and physical actions confirm our internal elements and external actions confirm external

Muslim Theory of Knowledge In The Philosophical Perspective of Mulla Sadra And Iqbal

elements. Intelligence is one stage higher basis their sense perception. This depends on extracting and stabilizing reasoning. We draw results from different prefaces. During extracting procedure we proceed from the whole to the parts. This method of arrival at the parts from the whole is more dependable and certain where as we arrive at the whole from the experience and individual witnesses, and exercise reasoning. For example, from cases of black crows are drawn the conclusion that since the crow, in our examples appears us not to be white, and as such all the crows are black. Only one single crow can falsify our this reasoning but we are able to understand our surrounding world with the help of our experience of individual examples because after observation of our individual examples when we jump to a certain conclusion, it remains valid and does not turn to be false, so long as no convincing and comprehensive argument is not available to mollify it. However, asked of intelligence, there also exists capability of thinking, and by stages of intelligence we mean ability of practicing in thinking, which achieves results broader than the principles of initial reasoning. Evidence is also essential as the source of knowledge. We accept a news or thing to be true in the authority of an expert or a prophet or a messenger. We have confidence over it being true. We trust in its truth. For example we trust in the authority of television, newspaper, radio, research scholars, astrologers, expert journalists and expert doctors, and accept their results, and trust them more than ourselves. Institution is also considered to be fourth stage and source of knowledge. Whenever conviction is gaining during intuition, we consider it to be reliable. Iqbal and Bergson admit the existence of an organic connection between thought and intuition. Sometime intuition of an expert artist gains such results which had not been possible for study centuries. This is revelation of abrupt results of a certain conviction, this is a flash of dazzling light, just as a quickly returnable high tide in the sea. No one can deny working of intuition. Every one experiences this at any stage, although its attributes and volume can be different. It can be according to the capability of the person experiencing intuition. This can be beyond his capability. Among means and stages of knowledge revelation is also important, although revelation is not the cause supporting any one's argument, just as Mujaddid Alf-i-Sani has stated in his letters because this individual, subject, wise and untransferable but it is strong convincing knowledge for a person who experiences it. Revelation is experienced during dream or same slumber or during existing condition. During revelation man has directed contact with the supreme reality. In this subject matter is more clear than words. Better condition of revelation is *Wahi* which is stronger than all the sources of knowledge. This creates drowsiness in the person to whom any thing is revealed. Its special attributes are quite clear. *Wahi* is related only to Prophets and Allah's messengers. Whatever *Wahi* is having revealed to a honey-bee, it is also a kind of revelation. It has special attributes. It is totally free from distraction and confusion. Thirdly, Allah the sublime has reserved the angel Gibrail. It is he who conveys Allah's words. The fourth attribute is that this connection has been discontinued forever since the death of the Holy Prophet. As regards to meanings and words now only Holy Qur'an is that *Wahi* or guidance and argument which is protected upto the Day of Judgment, and this is the guidance for every kind of faith. This is the critera on which every thing to be tested, and the pack of every kind of knowledge, faith, thought and result of educational research have to be congrued to it, and not that the religion should be stretched and applied to the result of other branches of learning. The mistake committed was that in order to make religion a disputable point, it was congrued to the results of natural world after considering them to be facts which was a basic fact awarding to Greek logic, but there were not congrued to religious thought on considering to be a reality. If discending of Quranic revelation is a real fact, then the result of all wanders of learning cannot be said to be true so long as they after congruing to the Quranic thought and considering it to be true. In the seventh chapter of the book *Mubahis-e-Mashriqiyya*. (The Eastern Discussions), Imam Razi does not consider definition of knowledge to be possible. He says that reality of knowledge is indifferent of acquisition and diffinition. According to him partial knowledge cannot be completed unless the known is not established in mind. Therefore knowledge is not which is gained from the nature of the known. Knowledge is the impression which is drawn on the mind of the scholar. Acquaintance of existence and confirmation is also knowledge which may be present with both existence and exhibition. I would also like to narrate another thing that is among all the means of knowledge elestial revelation is better because this is based on witness whereas all the other means of knowledge or stages are based on intelligence instead of testimony.

Mulla Sadra, like Imam Razi, says that knowledge is also related with the facts which have their individuality and reality depend on the same condition; and definition of such facts is not possible. The reason of which is that things are mostly defined with reference to their individuality which they call to be limited which is formed by qualities and parts. It is evident that all these things are complete affairs. A thing whose existence is its attributes; since existence appears itself as physique; therefore, its definition is not possible. Neverthless, Mulla Sadra considers knowledge

Muslim Theory of Knowledge In The Philosophical Perspective of Mulla Sadra And Iqbal

to be an intuitive situation of the self which every living being which he finds in himself from the very beginning in a way that it contains some vagueness and innate idea which he has not learnt from any experience, nor has it imagination formed it. It is clear due to its being distinguished and explicit. Exactly similar to this Descartes with the help of this consideration has arrived at the thought of Allah, the sublime. They think it to be the basis of reason and be little a thing which is reasoned. My personal view-point is that whenever a philosopher is involved in his complication of thoughts, he has either to breath his last in his net woven by himself like the silky cloth or he invents such a thought for which he does not have any argument. He accepts it without any reason or argument, and then after decorating it with principles of mathematics, intellect and argument; the same is the position of Plato's world of ideas. Aristotle's "initial sense" and innate idea of initial Descartes and Hegel. Despite roaring over educational institutions, with their intellect remains folded. It is same philosophy which is nearest place of the inner world which is not filled through the entire life. When before Kant, Ansalm and Augustine had talked about "perfect absolute", there was no scope of inherent thought. The reasoning of all the philosophy of Descartes and Hegel all philosophical reasoning is based on "axioms" which they call "logical necessity", with accepting innate idea as a basis of knowledge, his philosophy is just a work of a technician which he has used in formulating his thought, which had been cleverly used and completed this philosophy by Descartes and Hegel etc. The philosophy of our friend Leibniz also based on this initial concept, which right from the very beginning in his view, from the beginning of "creation" he had inherited it in his intellect. They do not accept human mind as a clean slate like the empirisists as Locke and Hume which is overcrowded at the time pressing touching senses because its monads and domes of particles are doorless. They have no windows, passage or ventilator through which the external stimulus may enter. Due to doorless monads all the knowledge will be considered to be within intellect. Expcricncc only cxplains clearly in upon whatever is already present within mind. This mollifies the thesis of John Locke that our mind is a plain slate which means that it learns from clean experience. (*Tabala Rasa*) Our mind has not a prior experience of senses. For this there is no plausible decisive argument with Locke nor with windowless monad for Leibniz any basis although John Locke also cannot escape from accepting pure thought which is different from some impressions. Locke this theory is nothing beyond the echo of Socrates conception of ideas which Plato already had formed as idea and Aristotle identified them as a "forums" which are existed in philosophy openly in the history of philosophy.

Perhaps Locke was also compelled not to say anything beyond slate of mind because clean slate could not provide clear basis of knowledge. Berkley tried to solve this problem with partial pure notions and partial notions. Pure thoughts are these notions which are not concerned with certain person or event these are such complete notions which Plato had named. Absolute idea which is comprehensive, and secondly, that partial conception which covers a particular person or happening pure conception are for communication and exchange of understanding which according to them is language. Completion is invented only for nomenclature. These pure impressions are themselves present, whereas partial notions are our mental thoughts which are impressed on our mind and become mental thoughts. Thus by getting our pure perceptions impressed on our mind and become mental perceptions whereas in the mental perceptions are formed initial and secondary which according to new theory of Locke which is a new theory of vision, our senses feel length, width, depth, opposition, firmness, movement. Lord David Hume congrued to thoughts of Locke, Berkeley and those who lived prior to them because all the understanding, marks, designs and conceptions of human mind.

Designs and impressions impress human mind. They become basis of memory, thinking and they thus maintain connection among them and through teaching become the basis of learning. Then these singular conceptions become basis of mutual relations. Association of conceptions happens with relation and cause and what is casual this theory of Hume is more scientific than all the other philosophers. However, Hume also thinks of his these thoughts, heavily cold and ironical because apart from offering Locke's experimental reasoning in naturally healthy and correct language, did not do anything which did not result but in scholastic learning and doubt.

Wale's philosopher Richard Price emphasized understanding of intellect and sensibility of heart. He said that to have sense does not mean that we are aware of their connections and extensions and through them we get knowledge of their causes, essentials and possibility. Experience is unable to give us knowledge of intellectual facts, virtues and evil standards is also beyond its reach, although he does not say anything regarding operation of understood. Experience plays an important role in knowledge but Hume does not have to say any thing about the knowledge over and above senses.

Muslim Theory of Knowledge In The Philosophical Perspective of Mulla Sadra And Iqbal

Kant said that we cannot know things as they really are, and they are beyond the limits of our knowledge. Kant said that transcendent reality is unaccessible. Thus Kant said that nature is subject to our principles of thought and artificially created and intellectual inventive sayings which depend on ourselves and individual. They do not at all represent complete reality. Thus he presented a new aspect in the old scholarly tradition that things have their own apparent special shape and form. Contrary to this scholarly theory that external things assume the shape and form according to mental figures, we cannot see things as they are, we apply attention our mental. Instead of changing itself to their form and shape moulds them to its own shape and form. Since the process of marks and sketching is similar in all the human beings and is unchanging; therefore, certain meanings are assigned to the external world. Thus although Kant extricated religious principles from reasoning process but the basis of moral faith which he offered was a dream of another submission during which he slept, and he shooks the solid grounds of religious principles because intellect does not provide solids ground for practical religion and morality due to which we are certain declared religions of psychology and things beyond nature as against intellect, and a psychological, and mental disease, and announced by discussion and movement which resulted from verbal analysis of these perceptions declared to be packed in a bottled of language, entangled together, but Hegel declared theories of Kant as unconnected with each other and also as a whole, and drawing result from one theory to another. He painted and to same difficulties of thinking system of Kant and its structure is not progressive. He said that the structure of Kant's theories about unseen world is not active and progressive, and visible world and the real world which is different from the subjects of the world comes to an end. However, if it is not possible for us conceive things as they are, we cannot term them as "they appear", and by a magic we cannot create a reason or the intricacy of practical wisdom of religion, morality and law. Thus theory of Kant is locked dome which is more doorless than Monad, which even his efforts could not and make active and progressive. This is not the occasion for more discussion on the misunderstandings of Kant. We shall criticise it at same suitable place because even Kant's conception of wisdom is also faulty from which he deleted the most supreme quality of revelation which is *Wahi*.

Iqbal has also discussed theories of Kant in his *Lectures*. He also feels that morality had to fall a pray to beneficiality due to the fact that faith cannot concede to intellect, due to which irreligrousness progressed but when Iqbal says about Kant to be gift of Allah to Germany his statement cannot be understood because he had demolished the intellectual basis of religion. Similarly Ghazali's doubt provided basis of deterioration of Islam because when disappointed by dissolution process when he diverted himself towards septic revelations, then after having been despaired by wisdom, philosophy and reasoning basis of knowledge was up-rooted in the Islamic world. Therefore according to Ghazali intellect was to end and not accessable. This he created a fence between thought and intuition.

According to Mulla Sadra, unavailable things, who are forbidden and whose acquisition impossible have the capability to be present in mind heaven we declare them to be actually available. We also declare that association of Allah is forbidden and two defects cannot gather there. The forbidding attitude of a thing or impossibility attitude of a thing improved in the knowledge of a thing. Every thing has knowledge evidence and intuitive evidence which means that this has also intellectual existence. Mulla Sadra says, with reference to Ibn-i-Sina:

"If a thing or its example is present in the world and the one who perceives its, is also its perception."

Sometimes they declare intellect as an addition or association. Kant has also referred to extension of intellect that knowledge is actually self-created because we cannot perceive things as they actually are but we mould things prior to experience in that shape. We do not prepare our mind according to the nature and variety. Without additions knowledge and relative, self-created nature of things, and therefore knowledge has to be changed with the change in information. Thus knowledge is a thing wherein addition and reference is found, which means that it should be added or referred to anything. This is such a situation which on one side is reference, and on the other side it has reference. Mulla Sadra has also pointed to disparity in theories of knowledge of Ibn-e-Sina.

According to Sheikh Maqul, the *Hikmat-al-Ishraq* is the name of evident knowledge outwards appearance in itself is the kind of illumination. Then there are different situations of illumination. Sometimes illumination is illumination for itself, which means that it becomes visible over itself. It is called self-illumination. Sometimes it is illumination for other which means that it comes out in open. During the first place, the illumination has its own knowledge and its own

Muslim Theory of Knowledge In The Philosophical Perspective of Mulla Sadra And Iqbal

understanding just as illumination on illumination (Allah). Enhancing illumination is illumination of self. The gist of statement of Sheikh-al-Ishraq is that a thing having its own knowledge is it has light and illumination both for itself, and that both these shining things should have luminous connection between them. This is knowing other things beyond itself. This is knowledge of others, which means that knowledge is the name of knowing things free from material impurities; which may be the knowledge of its own self as of any other thing. If an identity exists in itself, then it is in itself knowledge or intellect. If not so, and it is associated with any other thing, then this knowledge is also for that things. John Locke has also named the pure knowledge of a thing as the name of that thing or knowledge of the whole like Mulla Sadra he calls it to be the knowledge of the whole. He does not consider it to be the knowledge of a particular thing because thus additional description of the attitudes accepted of the thing will be essential. According to Mulla Sadra knowledge is the name of existence. Knowledge of conception is divided into comprehensive and partial confirmation etc.

Iqbal, in his thesis entitled *Development of Metaphysics in Persia* has written that Mulla Sadra considers the theory of decision about knowledge and the known as the basis of knowledge. In the chapter entitled "Iranian's subsequent thought" has mentioned Mulla Sadra, and said that "According to Mulla Sadra reality is all the thing. Even that it is nothing out of there. Real knowledge depends on decision about subject matter and decision about the thing. He says that Vee Gobenian thinks that philosophy of Mulla Sadra is the renewal of the philosophy of Ibn-i-Sina. However, he overlooks the fact that Mulla Sadra theory that subject - matter and the thing must have connection is the last step which the Iranian intellect advanced towards complete unity. Apart from this, the philosophy of Mulla Sadra is derived from the beyond - nature of initial Babi religion. Iqbal, referring to Asha'irah writes that according to him knowledge is the name of mutual connection between the knowing person and the known thing which has external position. Ibn-i-Maskawaih says knowledge is the name of acquiring resemblance or similarity of external things."

In his thesis *Development of Metaphysics in Persia* Iqbal has thrown light on the theory of Ibn-i-Maskawaih. Iqbal writes, "All the human knowledge commences with senses, and continues changing in perceptions step by step. Reality determines initial stages but evolution of knowledge means that we may be able to think quite independent from the matter. Thinking starts with matter but its purpose is fore thought so that we may free ourselves from initial conditions. Therefore any capability which the mind has to presence or repeat a thing, and in which external fact is overlooked, we reach a higher step of thought. Even higher than this is the where thought shapes perception, and gets itself separated from the matter to the extent that is the result of arrangement and comparison of perception and understanding".

It cannot be said about this that it has freed itself from the apparent external cause of senses but on the fact that imagination is based on perception we cannot ignore the mutual difference in the nature of imagination and perception. The continuous change through which parts (perception) are passing also influence the nature of this knowledge which is based only on perception. Therefore, there is absence of the continuity and stability of knowledge of parts. Contrary to this whole (conception) are not influenced by the law of change. Parts are made change but the whose remains unchanged.

According to the theory of knowledge of Mulla Sadra the knowing man reaches the known with the help of senses but whatever is known is not precisely the same thing about which is known, which means that external existence and mental existence are not harmonious. Above and separate of our five senses, thing and intellect - also have their sources of knowledge.

The second attitude of philosophy of Mulla Sadra is its reconciling and connective attitude. In the history of philosophy it so happened that different philosophers offered different theories, and those who come afterwards, created connection among them and reconciled them, passed them through a single string. Mulla Sadra created connection between theories of Ibn-i-Sina, Ibn-i-Maskawaih, Ibn-al-Arabi, Ishraqi and Imam Razi, he also created connection between the theories of Imam Jafer Sadiq and Imam Baqir relative to Shia tradition, he provided basis for beyond nature thoughts on the back of which Islamic thought and belief appear to stand which took birth during current time in the form of Mulla Tabatabai, the commentary which is published from Qum by Muhammad Kawakbi, doubted the importance of Mulla Sadra. Regarding philosophical tradition exegesis, closely connection of Mulla Sadra is with Quranic commentary written by Ibn-i-Sina, *Mishkat-Anwar* and *al-Ishraq* of Suhrawardi. Mulla Sidra emphasizes external as well as internal attitudes of commentary. He also confuses that the meanings of the Holy Qur'an are known only to Allah, but so far as apprising of these who "have correct knowledge" is done. According to Mulla Sadra, the faith and knowledge inside a human being should essentially be disclosed to him. However, it can be said that regard to explaining knowledge Mulla Sadra, remaining in the middle of Mu'tizilah, and other scholastic philosophers, he used them for his benefit but he did not totally depend on any of them but he used all their positive arguments and subjected them to his own thoughts. There is complete harmony of the results of congruous attitude of thoughts of Mulla Sadra and Iqbal. The only difference is that Mulla Sadra's direction is towards Shia belief and Iqbal's direction is towards Sunni belief. Iqbal appears to explain purely even Shia thought according to Sunni conception. Just Sadra derives Shia thoughts from Sunni thoughts.

In his religious experience, Iqbal also does not ignore its pausing side in his religious experience completely and he insists or organizes relation between thought and intuition, but there is wider scope in the inner experience of Mulla Sadra because he thinks inner experience to be a pausing experience, and insists on the use of wisdom reality truth in daily life; and believes that this should not be confined to intellectual problems because after coming into practice, it is deprived of its attributes. Religious experience and inner experience of Mulla Sadra, not denying inner experience of pause of intuition and intellect are nearer to each other in their real nature. It is also a common view of Mulla Sadra and Iqbal. Newer if Iqbal's religious experience cannot be transmitted, then Mulla Sadra regards to be constructive and better more than intellect and general reasoning. Since Mulla Sadra has tried it to make it harmonous with consciousness prophethood, he does not create any sort of major confusion but with Iqbal its position is that with the confusion resulting from consciousness of prophethood and consciousness of mysticism confusion is created which results from the situation that both of these have the same kind because by declaring all the experiences of reality as "partial", causes consciousness of prophethood to be superior to all these.

Some partnership of views between Iqbal and Mulla Sadra is also commonly shared. Both Iqbal and Mulla Sadra do not admit nature to be static. Islam declares nature to be moving. According to Islam, the spiritual basis perpetual existence which we observe in difference and change. If society is based on the perception of truth of reality, then it is

Understanding Iqbal's Philosophy

necessary that in his life he should think of both the static and changing situation. According to Iqbal change is that reality which the Holy Qur'an has declared it to be Allah's major sign. According to Iqbal change is the essence of nature and existence. Every thing is continuously in motion. Moon, stars trees and stones. All the life is the name of motion. To Iqbal motionlessness appears to be a illusion. Every particle of nature is restless. Continuous movement is the basis of existence. Iqbal does not agree to the theory of Aristotle and other Greek philosophers that nature is static. This existence is capable of being revealed. Similarly Mulla Sadra says in his theory of existence has surrounded every thing, which he says to be in motion. He says it to be solid and connected. It is this existence which is capable of revealing. During descent the existence moves downward but during its basic nature it means moves upwards. Ibn-i-Sina was firm on gradual movement which means from one point to another point which is only an intellectual process, during which we observe a body by placing it at different points and perception because a complete wholes but there is no lack of intimacy or awareness, among the bodies which have come with the external atmosphere and are in motion. Mulla Sadra is not convinced of beginning and end of movement, because you will have to accept peace before movement and after the end of movement. Therefore like Iqbal without considering beginning or end is convinced of continuous movement. Motionlessness is also meaningless for Mulla Sadra. For Mulla Sadra stress of gist of conception in movement is on love. According to Iqbal also the cause of starting movement. Just as the basic movement theory of Mulla Sadra apprises of the shapes of existing things, and the nature of external movement continuous to change and brings in varieties of betterness in nature. According to Iqbal also in the conception of love and warmth are the basic causes of life and change. According to Iqbal, one single jump of love covers all the stages which is not possible by another means. According to the conception of mystics, nature continues to obliterate, afterwards continuous to suppress in a new shape, and new form, but according to Mulla Sadra a thing does not obliterate but shows existence of things in a new form. According to Mulla Sadra also in the light of his theory of evolution, like Ibn-i-Maskawaih, Rumi and Iqbal, life continues to move from stationary position to botany, animals and humanity. Presently, in his essay published in July, 1999 of *Iqbaliat*, criticizing conception movement theory of Iqbal, with reference to the deceased Salim Ahmed, has said that theory of the East about tranquility above nature is correct, and movement theory of the West is wrong, and that Iqbal was wrong in his theory of movement. Secondly, even on the traditional basis static view point has a

Muslim Theory of Knowledge In The Philosophical Perspective of Mulla Sadra And Iqbal

preference over movement. First thing according to Islam is that nature is in motion. It does not hence any thing like being motionless, and Iqbal had expressed his reaction against the stationary theory of the East. However, here discussion on this point is not possible, we shall discuss at any other place that movement is the law of nature and peace above nature is not a reality. Some people, including the deseased Dr. Fazl-ar-Rehman think that Iqbal did not study writings of Mulla Sadra, otherwise he would not remain contented with a brief statement about him in his thesis entitled *The Development of Metaphysics in Persia*, and in his *Lectures* he has not at all mentioned Mulla Sadra, whereas it is Iqbal's habit that he refers the philosophers and commentators from whom he gets benefitted. It is possible that he might not have studied him directly but he is not unaware of basic discussions of Mulla Sadra, because there is so much harmony in basic thoughts of Iqbal and Mulla Sadra that which shows that Iqbal was not only intensily aware of the thought of Mulla Sadra but he also accepted influence from his thoughts. For example, with reference to conception of *Khudi*, movement love, theory of knowledge, theory of evolution and time and place, Sadra influenced Iqbal.

Chapter 4

IQBAL AND THE PRINCIPLE OF DYNAMISM IN ISLAM

The paper analyses and elucidates Iqbal's message that the renaissance and advancement of the Muslim world can be achieved only by using the spirit of Islamic culture, with dymanism as its most important component. Iqbal has pointed out in *The Reconstruction of Religious Thought in Islam* that the greatest achievement of Muslims is the derivation of the inductive and experimental methodology from the Holy Qur'an and its establishment in place of the Greeks' abstract and deductive methodology, which had engulfed the human race of that period. In this way the Muslims laid the foundations of modern science rind technology. Modern Europe's intelligentsia has also admitted this fact, which has been illustrated by extensive quotations in the taken from them through the Iqbal's above cited book.

Iqbal, in his above-cited book, has stressed the role of Intellect in the solution of the basic problems confronting the present day Muslim world. He considers *wajdan* or Intuition synonymous with *Iman* and *Ishq* as only an advance form of *Khirad* or *Intellect* (synonymous with knowledge)

The gist of Iqbal's reasoning is that as religious experiences and visions are endowed with the essentials of science and the experimental spirit, religion, and specifically Islam can perform a basic role in the solution of fundamental human problems by virtue of being a living, dynamic and creative time.

The need for a critical review of all our traditions and other intellectual heritage is emphasized with the advice to reject, as myths, those not supported by intellect.

A strong plea is made for accepting the Unity of God and the Unity of Mankind, which are the basic foundations of Islamic thought as well as that of Iqbal's philosophy. This belief is capable of establishing a human society on the foundations of universal peace as the starting point of a "New World Order", which Islam came to establish on earth. This World Order is synonymous with the "Kingdom of God" or the "Islamic State".

Iqbal and the Principle of Dynamism in Islam

It is here pointed out that the Eastern, and particularly the Muslim world, is devoid of amplitude and advancement because, in spite of being the custodian of eternal principles, it has not understood and adopted the principle of dynamism which may deep abreast of the constantly changing conditions of human civilization and society and may protect Islam from being reduced to ideology and idealism rendered immobile by traditionalism.

That essential principle of Islamic dynamism is *Ijtihad*. The events leading to the loss of spirit of *Ijtihad* by Muslims, in the course of their history, are related and the need is stressed for adopting it again as a pre-requisite for the renaissance of the Muslim world to that becomes to the Islamic world. The mechanics of *Ijtihad* and its operation are discussed in detail.

Shedding light on the spirit of Islamic culture Iqbal in the fifth lecture of his book, *The Reconstruction of Religious Thought in Islam*, has said:-

"The first important point to note about the spirit of Muslim culture then is that for purposes of knowledge, it fixes its gaze on the concrete, the finite".

According to Iqbal the real achievement of Muslims is that in their search for Truth and in the comprehension of science and technology they rejected the deductive methodology of the Greeks after testing it and substituted it with their own inductive methodology. In the formation and understanding of their ideology and goal, in the compilation of history and the philosophy of history and in the creation and formulation of physical and psychological sciences they arrived at such far reaching conclusions through their inductive thinking as led to revolutionary advancement of thought in the history of human thinking. Analysing Greek philosophical ideology, with reference to Robert Briffault's book, *The Making of Humanity*, Iqbal says:

"In fact the influence of the Greeks who, as Briffault says, were interested chiefly in theory, not in fact, tended rather to obscure the Muslims' vision of the Qur'an and, for at least two centuries, kept the practical Arab temperament from asserting itself and coming to its own. I want, therefore, definitely to eradicate the misunderstanding that Greek thought, in any way, determined the character of Muslims culture".

So, in Iqbal's view Muslims remained strangers to the comprehension of the real spirit of the Holy Qur'an for about two hundred years. In his view these thoughts of the Greeks played the role of suppressing the intellectual, potential and creative expression of the power of the thought of the Arabs instead of providing guidance to them. But Muslims were, after all, the custodians of the Holy Qur'an therefore their original thinking ultimately defeated the Greek thought. Consequently, the encounter and interaction of Islamic philosophy with Greek thought resulted in the Muslims' abandonment of the Greek way of thinking and adoption of the Holy Qur'an's own inductive methodology. After freeing themselves from the abstract Greek thought the Muslims formulated experimental thought or methodology for shaping their science and technology. Robert Briffault, the author of *The Making of Humanity*, who has been cited by Iqbal also writes about the encounter of the Greeks' deductive and the Arabs' or Muslims' inductive methodology and the resulting science and culture produced thereby:

> "It is strongly believed that the modern European civilization would not have even appeared if the Arabs had not existed, and it is conclusively believed that the European civilization could not have assumed the special character which has enabled it to surpass all the previous evolutionary stages. For although there is not a single aspect of European growth in which the decisive influence of Islamic culture is not traceable, nowhere it is so clear and momentous as in the genesis of that power which constitutes the permanent distinctive force of the modern world, and the supreme source of its victory - natural science and scientific spirit".

According to Robert Briffault, Europe has not been somewhat influenced by Islamic culture and by Muslims' rational approach and scientific methodology or inductive thinking, but owes its entire renaissance to the inductive methodology of Muslims. This inductive thinking reached Europe through Spain. He says:

> "Europe's real renaissance was not created in the fifteenth century but earlier under the influence of the cultural revival initiated by Arabs and Moors. The cradle for Europe's rebirth was Spain not Italy. This continent, falling into the abyss of barbarism, had reached

the darkest depths of ignorance and degeneration, though the cities of the Arab world, like Baghdad, Cairo, Cordoba and Toledo had become strong and important centres of civilization and intellectual pursuits by that time. It was there that the way of life appeared which later had to assume the form of a new stage of human evolution in the future. A new life started appearing as soon as the influences of this new culture were felt".

Briffault considers inductive methodology to be the most prominent facet of Islamic culture, which resulted in the shaping of modern science. This advancement of Islamic science alone is responsible for the growth and development of modern science. He says:

"The benevolence of the Arabs to our science does not consist of startling discoveries or revolutionary theories, science owes a great deal more to the Arab culture, it owes its very existence to it. The ancient world was pre-scientific, as we have roved above. The astronomy and mathematics of the Greeks were foreign importations, which the Greek culture could never thoroughly absorb. No doubt the Greeks systematized, generalized and theorized, but the patient ways of investigation, the accumulation of positive knowledge, the minute methods of science, detailed and prolonged observation and experimental inquiry were altogether alien to the Greek temperament. Only in Hellenistic Alexandria was there any approach to scientific work in the ancient classical world. What we call science arose in Europe as a result of a new spirit of inquiry, of new methods of investigation, methods of experimentation, observation, measurement, of the development of mathematics in a form unknown to the Greeks. That spirit and those methods were introduced into the European world by the Arabs".

Similarly, he says about experimental methodology:

"The Arabs did not create only those branches of mathematics which were to become indispensable tools for scientific analysis and assimilation, but also laid the foundation of the methods of experimental research which together with mathematical analysis gave birth to modern chemistry".

Chapter five of Briffault's book, *The Making of Humanity*, is "On Science" and comprised the influence of Islamic culture, of its science and technology and the inductive methodology on modern Europe. This chapter clearly shows that the Islamic inductive methodology provided the basis of modern scientific thought as well as that of scientific and psychological subjects. This admission is not restricted to Briffault alone. Other European scholars also had to admit this fact in spite of their severe prejudice. Friedrich Engles writes in the introduction to his book, *The Struggle for Existence.*

"The seed of invigorating free thought struck root among Latin nations after being received from Arabs and being nurtured by the neo-Hellenic philosophy. It prepared the ground for the conquest of matter in the eighteenth century. This was the big revolutionary progress which the human race had never witnessed before".

According to Iqbal the spirit of Islamic culture or, in other words, the principle of dynamism in the structure of Islam, is this inductive methodology which freed the Muslims from the abstract thought of Greek science. Through their inductive methodology Muslims concentrated their attention on the tangible and the finite, spent their energies on research, inquiry and creativity which made them instrumental in the advancement of modern science. According to Iqbal this inductive methodology was not the result of Greek or any other culture, but was obtained by Muslims directly from the Holy Qur'an. In this connection he has described the magnificent efforts made in the direction of shaping the inductive methodology and criticizing and rejecting the abstract thought of the Greeks by Ibn-i-Taymiyyah, Ibn-i-Maskawaih, Iraqi, Khwaja Muhammad Parsa, Naseer-ud-Deen Tusi, Imam Ghazali, Ibn Hisham, Ibn Haitham, Ibn Khaldun etc. Simultaneously, citing Roger Bacon, Spengler, Einstein and other Western scholars, as well as the cultural centres of the Muslim world and by comparison of the Islamic and Greek learning Iqbal has authoritatively established the factors which created the modern scientific, inductive methodology. In this way Iqbal is teaching Muslims that the Qur'anic methodology is inductive and experimental, or scientific, in common parlance. Hence, using the scientific methodology, Muslims should revive their classical sciences in the present age, on the one hand, and on the other hand should also reshape their beliefs in accordance with the scientific and experimental principles. The spirit of Iqbal's *The Reconstruction of Religious Thought in Islam* is the great possibility of religious revival in the present-day scientific era on account of the presence of the element of thinking in religion and religious experience.

Iqbal and the Principle of Dynamism in Islam

Also, because of the existence of the element of thinking in religion the religious experience can be considered similar to that or other sciences. The gist of entire reasoning is simply that religious experiences and beliefs are endowed with the essentials of science on account of having experimental spirit. Consequently, religion or Islam can perform that basic role in the solution of important problems of the human race in its capacity of being a living, dynamic and creative cultural and social power. In addition, the creation of the Islamic world is not only possible but the dangers besetting the present-day man can also be brought home to him in the proper way through Islamic education on account of the latter's being shaped on towards the new experimental and scientific subjects he has adjudged these as the Muslims' heritage.

Consequently, he does not give the inductive intellect a basic status only for subduing nature and shaping and compilation of the physical sciences, but adjudging religious experiences, he insists on utilizing inductive intellect and experimental methodology in religious experiences and beliefs also. This is especially pronounced when Iqbal accepts the element of thought in introspection or religious experiences. Consequently, Iqbal himself insists that:

"Yet it cannot be denied that Faith is more than mere feeling. It has something like a cognitive content, and the existence of rival parties - scholastics and mystics - in the history of religion shows that idea is a vital element in religion".

Besides this Iqbal considers *wajdan* also an advanced form of intellect. Consequently, he says.

"In fact, intuition, as Bergson rightly says is also a higher kind of intellect".

After this Iqbal himself admits:

"The search for rational foundations in Islam may be regarded to have begun with Holy Prophet himself. His constant prayer was: "God! Grant me knowledge of the ultimate nature of things".

Understanding Iqbal's Philosophy

In the same way Iqbal brings *Wahi* close to the rational intellect when he extends its orbit beyond the limits of the Divine *Wahi* restricted to the prophets and apostles. He says:

"Indeed the way in which the word *Wahi* is used in the (Holy) Qur'an shows that the (Holy) Qur'an regards it as a universal property of life, though its nature and character are different at different stages of evolution of life. The plant growing freely in space, the animal developing a new organ to suit a new environment, and a human being receiving light from the inner depths of life, are all cases of inspiration varying in character according to the needs of the recipient or the needs of the species to which the recipient belongs".

Study of the above mentioned extract of Iqbal brings out the reality that he includes Intellect among the indispensable components of religious experience and on this basis considers experimental science and inductive methodology indispensable to religion. He considers even *wajdan*, the basis of religion, to be advanced form of intellect. When he considers an animal developing a new organ to suit a new environment and a human being receiving light from the inner depths of life he sees *Wahi* in a separate and distinct from the "Prophetic Wahi" which is close to inductive intellect. Iqbal argument on the finality of prophethood also supports the fact that he considered the appearance of inductive intellect as a key to the glory of human intellect and the solution of all human problems in the present age. Accordingly, he writes:

"The birth of Islam is the birth of inductive intellect. In Islam prophecy reaches its perfection in discovering the need of its own abolition. This involves the key perception that life cannot for ever be kept in leading strings, that in order to achieve full self-consciousness man must finally be thrown back on his own resources".

This is the reason why he looks upon the Holy Prophet as a preceptor of humanity who stands at the junction of the old and the new world and has the status of a liaison between both. Hence, about the Holy Prophet, he says:-

"Looking at the matter from this point of view, then, the Prophet of Islam seems to stand between the ancient and the modern world. In so far as the source of his revelation is concerned he belongs to the ancient world, in so far as the spirit of his revelation is concerned he belongs to the modern world. In him life discovers other sources of knowledge suitable to its new direction".

So, he admits an organic relationship between *Wahi* and intellect and the organic relationship or spirit is the manifestation of or rational intellect, with the support of which alone the present-day man, in his own words, "will be thrown back on his own resources" and plan the solution of the economic, political, ethical, social and technical problems of the present day's complex society. There is no hesitation in admitting that Iqbal assigns only limited significance to intellect in religious experience and, conferring superiority upon religion over philosophy considers religion to be the manifestation of the entire essence of man and regards philosophy to be compelled to accept man's central position with reference to the value of religion.

However, it is not possible to completely deny that what Iqbal considers to be the stepping stones for reaching the Truths of *Anfus*, and *Afaq* and approaching the outer limits for reconstruction of religious beliefs is none other than inductive intellect, whose appearance, according to Iqbal himself, is connected with the manifestation of Islam, and which has great similarity with *wajdan* in the light of his own extracts mentioned above. Hence, in Iqbal's words *wajdan* is only a higher kind of intellect".

In this way Iqbal considers one form of *Wahi* also to be close to inductive Intellect and considers the manifestation of the Holy Prophet of Islam and the finalization of the prophethood to be an important relationship between *Wahi* and inductive Intellect of the present age. He recognizes the extreme necessity of trusting man's inductive Intellect for the solution of the problems of the present age. In the alternative the continuation of prophethood will have to be admitted so that continuous guidance in life's affairs may be available eternally. However, in view of the termination of the process of *Wahi* resulting from the termination of prophethood and the availability of basic fundamental guidance in the Holy Qur'an for the doctrinaire guidance of mankind the dependence of man on inductive Intellect for the solution of the problems of the present and the coming ages is a natural necessity.

So far there is no appearance of any kind of misunderstanding or ambiguity in Iqbal's thought. On the other hand, when Iqbal says that "Human intellect is nature's effort at self-criticism" it becomes even more clear that Iqbal considers Intellect to be basic in the solution of the problems of the present age. Also, as for the spirit of *The Reconstruction of Religious Thought in Islam* explanation and reconciliation of Islamic beliefs in the light of the modern physical and psychological sciences, as Iqbal himself writes in the preface of his book.

"Your creation and resurrection", says the Holy Qur'an "are the creation and resurrection of a single soul". A living experience of the kind of biological unity, embodied in this verse, requires today a method of physiologically less violent and psychologically more suitable to a concrete type of mind. In the absence of such a method the demand for a scientific form of religious knowledge is only natural. In these Lectures, which were undertaken at the request of the Madras Muslim Association and delivered at Madras, Hyderabad Deccan and Aligarh, I have tried to meet even though partially, this urgent demand by attempting to reconstruct Muslim religious philosophy with due regard to the philosophical tradition of Islam and the more recent developments in the various domains of knowledge".

He writes further; "The day is not far off when Religion and Science may discover the hitherto unsuspected mutual harmonies".

However, contradiction appears to exist in Iqbal's thought when, departing from the thesis of his book in prose (*The Reconstruction of Religious Thought in Islam*), and adopting fault-finding with intellect as his thesis, he questions the achievements of the present age in his poetry. When Iqbal himself adopted the line of Intellectualism and, looking upon the present-day problems confronting the Muslims, from scientific, applied and realistic points of view, he supported Intellectualism and experimental methodology, invited Muslim towards dynamism in Islamic culture in the light of the scientific knowledge of the new era and presented inductive thought as a new dynamic principle for Islam a contradiction became a little more apparent. He went a step further by affirming the component of Intellect in the inner experiences of religion and adjudged *wajdan* as "only a higher form of intellect", confirmed an organic relationship between Intellect, and soul, tried to establish, in his *Lectures* the harmony between religion and science, which is the spirit of the present age. However, in a more important and actually more effective part of his teachings, he found fault with this inductive Intellect, rational logic and experimental methodology and adjudging them contrary to each other established a dividing line between them, Iqbal in his *Lectures* had never talked about considering Love (*Ishq*) the leader in preference to the

Iqbal and the Principle of Dynamism in Islam

Intellect. The *Lectures* were in prose. Prose can be used for rationalization and so he preached the rationalization of the Intellect and individual thought as a leader. However, in verse in which belief plays a very prominent role and intellect a low keyed role he found fault with Intellect and advised having recourse to Love for guidance. These conflicts between Love and Intellect do not exist in Iqbal's prose but are very prominent in verse. The Iqbal's point of view about Love is unclear and ambiguous and it is hardly possible to understand the meaning of Love or its interpretation and elucidation. Thus, the Iqbal's term Love needs clarity and is not communicable, because Love has no meaning other than a vague and inexplicable mystery in the conflict between Intellect and Love. As opposed to this Intellect has a clear meaning and methodology, which is capable of providing guidance. The question then arises as to how did Iqbal establish a case against Intellect. In *Ruzgar-i-Faqeer* Iqbal has distinguished between Intellect and Love thus:

"Intellectual reasoning cannot affirm the existence of the *Wajib-al-Wujud*. The method of His affirmation is inner vision or religious experience. The way of God's cognizance is not Intellect but Love, which is called *wajdan* in philosophical terminology"

Citing Iqbal, Yusuf Saleem Chishti thus describes the struggle between Intellect and Love within himself:

"I had started the study of philosophy in 1914 and Plato was my first preceptor, the impressions of whose books had been prominently imprinted upon my head and heart. After this I studied Aristotle whose "Metaphysics" overwhelmed my studied thoughts for years and this book prepared the way for speculative dogmatism, i.e. considering Intellect to be adequate for being the criterion between right and wrong, between good and evil, superior to religious beliefs and revelation of the Truth. After a few visits Iqbal advised me to study Bergson so that the incapacity and poverty of vision of Intellect may become evident. His world famous book, *The Two Sources of Morality and Religion* shattered the spell of materialism and creative evolutionism and ethics; the' two sources of religion' ultimately prepared the way for my taking refuge under the shelter of *Tasawwuf* (Islamic mysticism)".

This statement of Yusuf Saleem Chishti facilitates the understanding of Iqbal's point of view, which moved him from Intellect to Love. The struggle between Intellect and Love is riot new to Iqbal but has been

Understanding Iqbal's Philosophy

viewed as a very important question by all the scholars from the olden to the modern times. However, Iqbal's contradiction to the gallows in his verse, which in his prose he adjudges as inductive Intellectualism and thus the very object and goal of Islam and religion.

We have strong objection to the statement of Dr. Khalifah Abdul Hakim that:

"As lqbal's point of view about life became progressively stable and mature he became increasingly critical of rational intellectualism".

This is so because Iqbal's *Lectures* is a masterpiece of his intellectual, ideological and mental maturity in comparison with his poetry. Thought and intellect is more pronounced in his prose than in poetry. Poetry reflects the emotional condition of the person, whereas his rational condition is expressed more explicitly in prose. The *wajdan* and emotional aspects are evident in Iqbal's verse because it is an attribute of verse to exhibit such expressions. Poetry cannot bear logical and philosophical rationality the same way prose itself becomes poetry if it is filled with expression of emotion and *wajdan*, and loses the component of intellect, reasoning and thought. In prose as well as in poetry expression has produced an artificial combination of Love and intellect in Iqbal. This combination or encounter does not produce any meaning except an absurd and meaningless conflict and it cannot be understood as anything other than as a mere intricacy of technicalities. Consequently, intellect has a close organic relationship between *wajdan Wahi*. Intellect, *wajdan* and *Wahi* are the branches of thought which have different 'stages of preferences in their search for and Reality, which Iqbal has staged one against the other on account of terminological vagueness, in spite of accepting them at least partially, in his *Lectures*. Love, which has been called *wajdan* in philosophical terminology really acquires full communications of the Truth and intellect gets only its partial communication. Iqbal also understands the truth that:

"Thus, in the evaluation of religion, philosophy must recognize the central position of religion and has no other alternative but to admit it as something focal in the process of reflective synthesis. Nor is there tiny reason to suppose that thought and intuition are essentially opposed to each other. They spring up from the same root and complement each other. The fast grasps Reality piecemeal, the other grasps it in its wholeness. The first fixes it gaze on the eternal, the other on the temporal aspect of the Reality. The one is the present enjoyment of the whole Reality, the other aims at traversing the whole by slowly specifying and closing up the various regions of the whole for exclusive observation. Both are in need of each other for mutual rejuvenation".

To Iqbal thought and *wajdan* or intellect and *wajdan* have the same goal and have the same field of inquiry. In logic's terminology the intellect with partial communication of Reality is deductive and that which communicates the whole Reality is inductive. So deductive and inductive Intellect alone are the means of reaching the Absolute reality. *Wahi* is a mixture of these deductive and inductive intellects. When intellect, in its most sublime form, reaches and unites with Absolute Reality it does not only establish its own communication with the Absolute Reality, but also gains control over the disclosure of this communication. The Holy Qur'an which exists safe and preserved for the insight and guidance of mankind is the most dignified form for the communication of the Absolute Reality by the Absolute Spirit. It is within the capability of the average human intellect to he close to the Absolute Reality itself trough contact with the Holy Qur'an. Love, if translated into religious language, can be called *Iman*. Love, *wajdan* and *Iman* are similar technical terms in their meaning. If they were merely they could have never been able to guide human intellect, not to say the intellect of the present day man. They would create confusion and stalemate in human intellect instead of progress. Dogmatic love would produce jealousy in their lives instead of obtaining solution, and the nation possessing such thinking would fall a prey to decline instead of making progress.

In our view *Iman* is a much better word than Love. *Iman* is not devoid of the component of thought. The concept of *Iman* as belief in a being whose existence is rationally impossible is a popular though incorrect thought. *Iman* can require you to believe in a Being or Essence which is apparently invisible or cannot be known in a tangible way, but cannot compel you to have faith and belief in a Being or Essence or concept which is intellectually or logically absurd. *Iman* has an aspect of Intellectualism and is the name of the intellectual relationship with a Being, Essence or Concept. Prophet Ibrahim's *Iman* can be an example of this who reached the intellectual conclusion of accepting the stars, the moon and the sun as God on account of their gigantic sizes. Similarly, drinking of poison by Socrates and rejecting all his desires for escape was based on the intellectual attachment with and conscious comprehension of his ideology, principle and belief. This intellectual attachment is *Iman*.

However, this intellectual attachment varies according to the shrewdness and intellectual depth of the believer. The stability of the *Iman* as an ideology or principle depends upon the depth of intellectual attachment with it, as also depends the exhibition of this intellectual attachment in the form of action—Blind belief in any principle results in shaky and unhealthy *Iman* which can also be called deficient *Iman*. This *Iman* may create the urge for some action but cannot have the perseverance and firmness which can or should be exhibited by the believer with intellectual comprehension. In short, if Iqbal has used the world of Love in the sense of *Iman* and intellectual attachment with an ideology or in principle it can have a practical and real meaning, otherwise this technical term of Iqbal would be dogmatic and ambiguous which would serve no purpose except creating confused thinking.

The influence of Bergson on *Tasawwuf* is prominent in Iqbal's criticism of intellect. Romanticism pervades in Iqbal's thought on account of his being a poet. The same romanticism has constantly guided Iqbal towards intellect's opposition. Consequently, as Ali Abbas Jalalpuri says:

"Iqbal's Love is the echo of Bergson's ardour, i.e. the creative power of life which has sustained the system of life".

Really Iqbal adopted this term of "Love" from Maulana Rumi and used it in the same sense as Bergson used the term "ardour of life". In this way Iqbal presented the term Love in a new but unique sense. Consequently, unless and until *Iman*, Love, *wajdan* or *Wahi* is based on intellect it will not be able to produce creative activity.

This admixture of intellect and *wajdan* has confused Iqbal in another place. If Iqbal considers the components or intellect and thought included in religious experiences and regards the inner experience stable, consequential and worthy of attention like other scientific experiences, the religious experience should also be stable, consequential and repeatable like other experiences, otherwise this experience would not attain the status of other experiences, and all the efforts which Iqbal has made in *The Reconstruction of Religious Thought in Islam* for harmonizing religion and religious experiences with science, philosophy and the demands of the present age would be nullified. If the nature of some inner experience is not capable of solution, impossible to relate and transfer, how can it form the basis of knowledge and be the foundation stone of some system whose establishment can be useful and purposeful for the human race?

Iqbal and the Principle of Dynamism in Islam

The claim of Iqbal obtains verification from observation of religious experiences, because the religious observation or visions of prophets are available in a communicable form in the Holy Qur'an and other revealed books. Innumerable Muslim and non-Muslim Sufis (Islamic mystics) have detailed the inner visions of their souls in their writings. The Sufis exchange these inner feelings with one another and have also coined special technical terms for communicating their experiences. These terms are well known and their purport is authentic and agreed upon among the Sufis. Often these experiences are also liable to tautology in the process of communication, narration and comprehension. Hence, it is absolutely wrong to assert that the inner experiences of Sufis are non-communicable. On the other hand they are communicable in every way, and it is also possible to deduce inferences from them. Like other experiences religious experience also uses a special type of symbolical and technical language. However, as the inner experience deals with an intangible Reality it would be difficult to communicate the latter with the methodology of the communication of the experiences of the tangible Reality. Nevertheless, the inner religious experiences would become increasingly more communicable with the development of science and maturity of human intellect. The following stand of Iqbal deserves attention:

"It is neither possible to establish an incontestable intellectual argument in favour of the existence of God, nor can intellect provide an adequate answer to the objections that intellect itself raises against the Existence of the Creator of the Universe -----. So, if a belief in the Existence of God can be created it can be done only ugh inner vision".

This is so because if the inner vision is devoid of the component of thought, it would be without the Universal Spirit, or the guidance of *Wahi* and would be nothing short of apostasy. If Iqbal considers *wajdan* itself to be a form of intellect and *Wahi* its the higher form of intellect and admits the element of intellect or thought in the religious vision how can he say that intellectual reasoning cannot be incontestable for the Existence of God? Any argument based on the existence of religious vision and *Wahi* would also be an intellectual argument, but the religious vision not based on intellect would not arrive at any inference except apostasy and spiritual disorder. Hence, it must be understood that intellect alone is the incontestable argument on the Existence of God. Intellect is inescapable, though it may emanate from the Universal Spirit or it may be *wajdani* intellect, or may be based on the principles of inductive or deductive logic. Deviation from intellect would not lead man to anything except destruction. Perhaps that is why Plato had said: "What would be more unfortunate for a man than being against intellect?"

We consider intellect a superior attribute. We can accept or reject the products of *Wahi* and *wajdan* also after testing them on the basis of intellect. Actually, a little deep insight would show that *Wahi* and *wajdan* are not in conflict with intellect, but that *Wahi* and *wajdan* are included within the realm of intellect. If *Wahi* and *wajdan*, which are shadows of the Universal Spirit, emanate from the Holy Prophet, or from our own inner consciousness, are not anti-intellect how can they be considered contradictory to intellect.

Wahy and *wajdan* also have a system of argument in spite of which sometimes we do not readily understand the syllogisms of *Wahy* and *wajdan*. This is so because *Wahi* transcends the limits of time and space and many of its syllogisms and concepts exhibit themselves only gradually with time. The syllogisms and concepts of argumentational intellect, not being based on *Muhkamat* are capable of and liable to changes and these ranges are possible any time. The *Muhkamat* and *Mutashabihat* of intellect are mutually interchangeable. However, though changes are possible in the interpretation of the *Muhkamat* of *Wahi,* the *Muhakamat* themselves do not change. Also, the *Mutashabihat* of *Wahi* and *wajdan* continue changing to *Muhkamat* with time.

The single reason for the existence of mythological traditions among Muslims is their acceptance of these traditions on faith without testing them on the basis of intellect. In the present age if the Muslims desire socio-economic, ideological, ethical, scientific and intellectual advancement abreast with other nations of the world they will have to review their entire literary and scientific heritage critically in the light of intellectual insight instead of accepting it on faith and will have to destroy all those legends and myths which are nauseating to intellect. On the contrary, they will have to accept the traditions which produce creative feelings an concordant with the demands of the present age, and help in the shaping of an advanced ideological and democratic society. Human feelings can be expressed correctly on the basis of intellect alone. If intellect is ignored and only sentiments are promoted it would not be possible to keep the expression of these sentiments in balance, and the growth of human life on mere sentiment would make it desolate and sickening.

Iqbal and the Principle of Dynamism in Islam

Islamic teachings have the attributes suitable for shaping the best society and have the ability to organize such an advanced society in the modern age as would be concordant with the essentials of modern technology. If blind faith has its play and intellect is ignored they would create desolation and establish a static and oppressive society which is frightening even to imagine. Unfortunately, if such a society is created the human race would witness the opening of a new dreadful floodgate in the wake of blind religious fanaticism, which would result in engulfing the human race in severe anguish. So, if the Muslim intelligentsia desirous of building a human civilization based on the immaculate teachings of Islam they will have to test and compile Islamic teachings on intellectual basis and, in Iqbal's words, will have to activate the Islamic principles of inductive intellect and explain the eternal and universal nature of Islamic teachings.

For the purpose of recasting Islam in accordance with the present day's needs Iqbal views Islam as an ideology of life which bases its growth on the dynamic concept of the universe. Establishing the foundations of his collective system of life on the individual's own value system he considers all concepts of nationalism, race and colour as false. For that reason, looking for the psychological basis of the human race, he adjudges the human race and the sources of its life to be spiritual. Iqbal claims that Islam alone has provided mankind with real psychological foundations. Constantine's efforts to shape a collective system based on Christian teachings could be attractive only because Christianity itself potential for providing such a basis. Hence, he had no choice but to turn to the ancient Greek gods and then he tried to mould it into a system with philosophical explanations. Iqbal cites a contemporary historian of civilization who, after detailing the cultural poverty of the pre-Islamic world, had expressed amazement at the rise of Islam with new social principles from the Arab world, and which eventually exhibited itself as the bright destiny of the human race. Regarding the author's surprise as meaningless Iqbal says:

> "There is, however, nothing amazing in the phenomenon. The world-life intuitively sees its own needs and, at critical moments, defines its own direction. This is what, in the language of religion we call prophetic revelation (*Wahi*)".

Understanding Iqbal's Philosophy

The question is as to the nature of the principle which presented Islam as a new cultural system, on the basis of which Islam, declaring all relationships based on nationalism, blood, race and colour as false, provided a new psychological basis to humanity, which is established on dynamic concept of the universe. Stating this principle, Iqbal says:

> "The new culture finds the foundation of world-unity in the principle of *Tauheed* Islam, only practical means of making this principle a living factor to the intellectual and emotional life of the mankind. It demands loyalty to God, not to thrones"

Shah Waliullah writes about the basic importance of *Tauheed* for human life"

> "Therefore, the belief in *Tauheed* is the fountainhead of all virtues and the root of all kinds of good and reform, because the sincere obedience to the Lord of the Universe alone is really the most important source for the acquisition of human felicity. Hence, the most effective scientific method for perfecting humanity and acquisition of human felicity is none other than *Tauheed*".

"Shah Waliullah himself explains its reasons also:

> "This (belief in *Tauheed*) directs man's attention completely towards the Transcendent Heavenly Kingdom in its most immaculate form. Its status and importance is obvious from the fact that *Tauheed* is the heart of all forms and shapes of virtue, just like the heart in the human body, whose illness makes the whole body ill and whose improvement improves the whole body".

In short, *Tauheed* is to be interpreted in accordance with the demands of the present age in order to shape it on inductive principles in the intellectual and *wajdani* life and to keep it alive as a living Reality for human civilization: This is necessary to shape a society which, freeing the human race from the prejudices of colour, race and class distinctions, endows it with economic prosperity and sound cultural values. It would also he able to shape the human society on the basis of human unity and equality, free from extortion, would provide new leadership for the creation of the *New World Order* and the foundations for the *Tauheed* or unity of mankind and the unity of human rights.

Iqbal and the Principle of Dynamism in Islam

Iqbal himself admits in his *Lectures* that:

"The inner experience is only one source of human knowledge. According to the (Holy) Qur'an there are two other sources of knowledge - Nature and History, and it is in tapping these sources of knowledge that the spirit of Islam is seen at its best".

Obviously, intellectual methodology is needed more than the *wajdan* one for either of these sources of intellect. Therefore, intellectual methodology or, in logic's language, inductive methodology is the only criterion or methodology which the Muslim world can accept as a tool in the present age for the elucidation of Islamic beliefs. Iqbal himself has presented several examples of accepting intellect as the methodology even in the first century of Islam. Iqbal had said about intellect:

"People who have dedicated their lives for developing their intellectual powers are God's selected best and most useful servants." Please find out and

Bergson himself had very high opinion about intellect and philosophers:

"Philosophers teach us respect for the individual and the rights of all persons through intellect alone both cases we transcend the limits of the family and the nation and arrive at the concept of humanity".

The authority of intellect is obvious from Iqbal's all works in prose. He has attempted reshaping of a new Muslim theology in his *Lectures* only by utilizing the inductive methodology. Iqbal, harmonizing the Islam's concept of *Tauheed* and, fixing its limits in Islam, he critically examines the efforts Muslims in this direction.

In Iqbal's view there are two kinds of principles in Islam. One kind are the eternal principles which never change or alter. The limitations of time and space have absolutely no control over them. They remain eternally established at every place in every age and in every environment. These are the principles through which an ideology can establish itself in collective life. They have element of change in their nature. Iqbal understands that the basic reason for the failure of Europe's cultural movement is its being devoid of the ideals of such eternal principles. Similarly, Iqbal says that the Eastern particularly the Islamic movement, is devoid of amplitude and progress, because in spite of possessing eternal principles it has lost the principles of dynamism which could have kept it informed of the consistently changing conditions of human culture and society and would have protected Islam from becoming an ideology and idealism which has been spoiled by the mildew of immobility.

According to Iqbal, *Ijtihad* is that principle of dynamism in the structure of Islam which guides it towards harmonizing it with creative and consistently changing cultural and social conditions of humanity. In other words the *Ijtihad* is the new elucidation and interpretation of Islam's concept of *Tauheed* in the light of inductive intellect in concordance with the demands of the present age, whose foundation is the scientific and intellectual research and inquiry as opposed to apologetic and conformative tendencies.

"The word (*Ijtihad*) literally means to exert. In the terminology of Islamic law it means to exert with a view to form an independent judgement on a legal question. The idea, I believe, has its origin in a well-known verse of the (Holy) Qur'an -'And to those who exert We show Our Path!" We find it more definitely adumbrated in a tradition of the Holy Prophet.

Here Iqbal relates the incident of Ma'az bin Jabal, a famous companion of the Holy Prophet, which he experienced in the presence of Holy Prophet's at the time of his appointment as the governor of Yemen, in which he had talked about trusting his own judgement in the event of his failure to get clear guidance from the Holy Qur'an and the Traditions of the Holy Prophet about a particular problem. According to Iqbal *Ijtihad* is the sincere effort of a Muslim to find the will of God about a matter on which a clear order does not exist in the Holy Qur'an and the Holy Prophet's Traditions. The Omayyad Caliphs presented *Jabriat* in support of their tyrannies and brought in the all-pervasive nature of God's will as a licence for major sins like the murders instigated by them. They argued that whatever they did was in accordance with God's Will and Pleasure, in the absence of which they would not have been able to do that.

The science and technology of the present day world has influenced the infrastructure of old civilization and culture everywhere and has confronted the human race with ever new problems. These include the mutual alliances between world nations, the growing world population, hunger, poverty, unemployment, illiteracy, the economic, political and cultural domination of large nations over small ones and the monopoly of large nations on science and technology through which they have divided the small nations dishonestly and inequitably into regions of their respective influences and have also entangled the nations under their influence in different problems.

The people of the Muslim world want to change their economic condition and reorganize their economic and social structure in accordance with their beliefs and ideology. They want to replace the existing world society and economic structure with a new world order and economic system. However, there are four major obstructions in their way which need removal of. It is necessary to keep them in view while elucidating and interpreting Islamic beliefs today.

The first one is the mentality inherited by us from the colonial system, which is controlling us. This mentality reigns supreme over our offices, high government positions, our policy making institutions and in the shaping of our education system. This mentality is devoid of that creative thinking through the help of which a nation can plan its own and its society's reconstruction in the light of its ideology and principles, making use of the experience and progress of other nations.

The second obstruction in the prosperity and progress of the Muslim world is the oppressive attitude of world powers. The Muslim world has been divided into the regions of the communist and Western influences under their diplomacy. These two regions are mutually at war for the benefit of their respective supporting world powers. Secondly, these world powers have divided the world between themselves extremely inequitably. Thirdly they have converted the Muslim world into a market place for their (usually obsolete) armaments on the one hand and have kept their economic progress in check by creating and keeping unresolved the problems of Cyprus, , Palestine, Kashmir and other similar conflicts.

The third and the biggest obstruction in the path of the Muslim world, including Pakistan, is their political instability. No doubt the people of the Muslim world want to shape their political system on the basis of Islamic ideology. However, the Muslim world has been kept strangulated from the Omayyad period to the present times by dictatorships and quasi-dictatorships and is breathing its last.

The fourth basic reason is the completely static character of the reactionary elements of the Muslim world. But the class which understands Islam, is still attached to the revolutionary values of Islam and considers it as the manifesto of its welfare in this world as well as in the hereafter is presenting itself in a very strange a role nevertheless, this class can be capable of right leadership of the Muslim world in the present age if it shapes its Islamic character with the creative thinking which would be in accordance with the demands of the present age. This class can become a means of the economic welfare, national individuality, Islamic ideological democracy of the Muslim world as well as become a bulwark for its protection from the domination of other world powers and, becoming the fore-runner of Islamic revolution on the basis of its revolutionary character, can really acquaint the world with the new world order. However, the fact is that the reactionary character of this class has reached the proportions of desperation. It is devoid of the comprehension of Islamic character of universal revolution. It has made Islam a puzzle of ritualistic worship and social taboos and to resemble a dark room which has no door, no window, ventilator, or even a hole through which somebody may enter it, or through which it may receive even a wave of fresh air.

In the same lecture Iqbal describes Islam in the light of juristic *Mazhabs* (Any of the five recognized schools of Islamic jurisprudence). According to him *Ijtihad* has three degrees:

1. Complete authority in legislation which is practically confined to the founders of Schools.

2. Relative authority which is to be exercised within the limits of a particular Scool. This means that if a Hanafi would elucidate and interpret any principle he would necessarily have to follow the principles compiled and organized by the founders of the Hanafi School. This would restrict his orbit of freedom to the limits set down by the founders of this system, whereas the founders themselves had unlimited freedom.

3. Special authority which relates to the determining of the law applicable to a particular case left undetermined by the founders. This degree deals with the application of the law. There are many principles of jurisprudence which are deeply related to practical aspects of life to which no preconceived

conditions can be effectively applied. The founders of the system have considered suitable only those interpretations and explanations which conform with the possibilities of time and place and have left the decision for the manner of their application to the judgement of the people applying them. They have freedom to use their judgement and fully utilize the freedom given to them by the founders."

As Iqbal has concentrated his attention on the first degree only we will also discuss the same and shall defer discussion of the other two degrees to some other occasion. This is so because the latter two conditions have created very little controversy.

Iqbal rejects the accusation of objectors. that the jurists of the Sunnat-wal-Jama'at sect have imposed restrictions on *Ijtihad,* he also admits that though in principle they did not reject the option of permission for *Ijtihad,* in practice these jurist schools subjected *Ijtihad* to conditions which made it impossible to operate. In our view the jurists had themselves closed the door of *Ijtihad* by making it conditional in that way. They realized that if it was not possible to deny full freedom for elucidation or codification through *Ijtihad* it would be better to impose conditions which would make it utterly impossible for the later jurists to do *Ijtihad* in practic Therefore, Iqbal's view is not acceptable that the founders of Sunnat-wal-Jama'at sect never denied the need for *Ijtihad* and that its door was closed later. Really the harsh conditions imposed by the founders themselves had closed this door. As nobody fulfilled the conditions for *Ijtihad* nobody could practice it, and he who neglected these conditions was considered an outcast. Iqbal has stated the following reasons for closing the door of *Ijtihad:*

1. I. The controversy about the Holy Qur'an being *makhlooq* (created) or *qadeem* (eternal)

2. Ascetic Sufism

3. Destruction of the intellectual centre, Baghdad.

In our view two more basic reasons have been overlooked. The first reason has been stated above, i.e. the unintelligible attitude of the founders about *Ijtihad* and the obstructions placed in its way. The second basic reason was monarchy and the entry of non-Arab people into Islam together with their science and technology and their presentation of such interpretations of Islam as were suspected of encouraging democratic thinking in contrast with monarchy and *qadr* in contrast with *jabr*. Anybody who has understood the affairs of the early years of the Islamic era can very easily understand the admixture of monarchy and *Khilafah*.

Thus, the spirit of the concept of *Ijtihad* had been crushed during the Omayyad period. Now, we would be disappointed if we want to shape our Islamic ideology of dynamism in such a way that it can perform the function of guiding Muslims in the solution of economic and social problems confronting them in every age, which may shape an economic and social system that would be the cradle of creative character without detriment to the eternal character of Islam and, instead of strangulating Muslims, would give them feelings of freedom and rejuvenation of human intellect, which in its turn would be the source of delight and satisfaction though creative feelings and tendencies and which would encourage people to rise for struggle to master the expanses of *Anfus-o-Afaq* after raising new desires and longings in them. The state of affairs at present is that though the eminent jurists of the early days had elucidated the features of an extremely organized social order in accordance with the requirements of their times the later jurists gave up this method clue to the limitations on *Ijtihad*. The situation now is that the juridical system organized by the eminent founders of jurisprudence had been done after full consideration of the social, cultural and scientific conditions of their age. The social, cultural and intellectual level of the juridical system and the social standards created by the products of science and technology of that age pertained to that age. It was necessary for the jurists of each age to reconstruct the Islamic jurisprudence of their age with the scientific, technological, social and intellectual advancements of their age in view so as to maintain the potential for freshness and advancement in it. In actual fact our jurisprudence became static due to the closure of the door of *Ijtihad* and the human society advanced much in science and technology. Consequently, at present the cart is before the horse. The jurisprudence, which guides a society is itself in need of ordinance. Iqbal had understood this state of affairs and stated in his *Lectures*:

"What the religious scholars of the present day do not understand is that the existence and the destiny of nations does not depend upon the degree of their being organized but on the personal virtues, capabilities and potentials of their people. Even otherwise the individual's existence completely disappears in an over-organized society. Though the society becomes enriched by the wealth of the collective thinking of its environment it loses its own real spirit. In these circumstances the decline and fall of the nation cannot be stopped by viewing our past history with unjustified reverence or start rejuvenating it by our own efforts".

This lecture shows that even in the periods of decline the Muslim intellectuals have been deeply conscious of the deterioration in the framework of their antiquated system of jurisprudence of the system based on it, the absence of the potential for advancement in it and the need for the reconstruction of Islamic jurisprudence according to the demands of every age. He makes special mention of Ibn-i-Taymiyya who reacted strongly against this deterioration and suffocation in jurisprudence. After this, Iqbal has talked about Ibn-i-Hazm and the Sanusi and Wahhabi movements who had felt the needs for this change, took part in the organization of the new system of Islamic jurisprudence and again set the Islamic principles in motion which had become unnaturally static".

Iqbal has paid attention to the efforts at reorganization of the Islamic jurisprudence in the present age only in other regions of the Islamic world. In the course of the discussion of *Ijtihad* and compilation of Islamic jurisprudence he has made special mention of the efforts made by Turkey in changing its political and social structure according to its needs, created by the changes brought about in Turkey after the Ottoman Caliphate. However, it is strange that he has overlooked the efforts of Sir Syed Ahmad Khan, Syed Ameer Ali and others in the Indian sub-continent in reorganization of Islamic jurisprudence.

Iqbal has invited the sub-continent Muslims towards Haleem Sa'id Pasha and other Turkish thinkers. Though we admit that Sir Syed Ahmad Khan and other reformers of the Indian sub-continent have taken some faults in the interpretation of Islamic beliefs, Shah Waliullah, Mawlana Hamiduddin Farahi some other Muslim reformers have certainly shown leadership in this direction which should benefit Turkey and other Muslim countries. Their good point should be adopted and defects should be overlooked. Iqbal's indifference to the controversial opinions prevailing in the sub-continent may have been prompted by his desire to avoid entanglement in regional controversies its a participant. Iqbal has described two aspects of Turkish thought. They are the members of the Nationalist Party and it was the movement of secular nationalism under Western influence rather than an Islamic movement. Criticizing their thoughts, Iqbal neither accepted their nationalism himself nor considered it worthy of attention. On the contrary he said:

Understanding Iqbal's Philosophy

"Personally I think it is a mistake to suppose that the idea of State is more dominant and rules all other ideas embodied in the system of Islam. In Islam the spiritual and the temporal are not two distinct domains, and the nature of an act, however, secular in its import, is determined by the attitude of mind with the agent does it. It is the invisible mental background of the act which ultimately determines its character. An act is temporal or profane if it is done in a spirit of detachment from tile infinity of life behind it, it is spiritual if it is inspired by that complexity. In Islam it is the same reality which appears as the Church looked at from one point of view and the State from another. It is not true to say that the Church and the State are two sides or facets of the same thing. Islam is the single unanalysable reality which is one or the other as your point of view varies".

Together with this Iqbal says that the soul, when viewed in relation to time and space, appears in material form and when matter is viewed with its end object and goal it is called soul. Thus, Iqbal changes matter and soul from antonyms to synonyms and looks upon the soul as the single element which is based on *Tauheed*. Iqbal considers this concept as justification for the concept of the unity of man, equality, freedom and the individual as well as the collective welfare of the human race. He considers all concepts and ideologies obstructing the progress of the above as false and absurd. Iqbal bestows a basic and key status on the Islamic system of collective State and considers the reform and improvement of the State to be the duty of religion because the State has the status of a human institution which unites human beings into collective whole, organizes their individual and collective efforts and, activating the collective power of human beings, results in the collective exhibition of the individual and collective efforts of the human race.

In modern times Iqbal wanted the reconstruction of religious thought in Islam for the improvement of the State and for making it a creative power, for casting the Islamic State into an ideological mould, for including it in the people's ambitions and freedoms and for making the people self-supporting in meeting their present day economic needs. He was strong supporter of the concept that:

"The only alternative open to us, then, is to tear off from Islam the hard crust which has immobilized an essentially dynamic outlook on

Iqbal and the Principle of Dynamism in Islam

life, and to rediscover the original verities of freedom, equality and solidarity with a view to rebuild our moral, social and political ideals out of their original simplicity and universality".

Though Iqbal stated the above as the views of the Grand Vizier of Turkey to him:

"He (the Grand Vizier) reaches practically the same conclusion as the Nationalist Party, that is to say, the freedom of *Ijtihad* with a view to rebuild the law of *Shariah* in the light of modern thought and experience".

Rashid Ahmad Siddiqui has stressed the need for *Ijtihad* in his own distinctive style and he has said that the thoughts devoid of dynamism decay and fade out. Hence, *Ijtihad* is really presenting old thoughts in new ways. He says:

"There is nothing new in the world. Old thoughts only adopt new forms after revolving in new moulds in various ways. The forms are innumerable, in the absence of which the world would decay and disappear".

This means that *Ijtihad* is not a new discovery, but is only an old matter or principle recast in new moulds, which would disappear or become decayed and meaningless if not so recast in new moulds. Confusions also said the same thing in his own way that the work philosophers is to present old wine in new bottles, i.e. to present old thoughts in a new style. This is so because unless the old concepts are presented in new forms, in accordance with the demands of the time and circumstances, it is very difficult to obtain guidance from them. Therefore, philosophers state these thoughts in new language and form so that the thoughts never lose their freshness. Mian Bashir Ahmad, the former ambassador of Pakistan to Turkey, has said the same thing in one of his articles titled "Zindah Falsafah" in the following words:

"A better way of making belief's firm and immaculate is to shed the light of new thinking on them periodically. The better which is strong and based on intellect and experience would emerge from every test in a better and stronger shape. The decayed thought would be destroyed by encounter with new knowledge."

Understanding Iqbal's Philosophy

In view of the demands of the ever-changing conditions of the present day it is essential that Islam, which is not the product of any race, country, colour or language, but is an ideology which transcends all these be pesented in a universally acceptable form for obtaining guidance in the problems created by the closeness and intermixing of nations, and for fulfilling the social, economic, cultural and legal demands of the technical and complex life of today. But such guidance is not possible unless Islam is viewed in its real dimensions and its real shape, is highlighted after washing away the local colours of the Arab and the non-Arab. The real question is whether the Holy Qur'an is to be used as a decoration for the shelf or as a mandate for the solution of the complexities of the life's problems of practical. If it is a decoration piece for the shelf the Muslims have conferred this honour on it with great effort. For years Muslims do not touch it nor see what this Holy Book contains. However, if it is not meant for his and, on the contrary, it is a mandate for providing guidance in the battlefield of life it will have to assess the complex economic and ethical conditions of today and command action accordingly.

Only the work of seeking guidance from the Holy Qur'an in accordance with the current conditions is *Ijithad*. This very requirement has highlighted the need for elucidation and interpretation of this mandate in the new language and form.

As for the delegation of the right of *Ijtihad,* Iqbal supports the views of the Turks that:

> "Turkey's *Ijtihad* is that according to the spirit of Islam the *Khilafah* or *Imamah* can be vested in a body of persons, or an elected assembly."

This is so because Turkey's *Ijtihad* is that the *Khilafah* should also be vested in a committee or elected assembly instead of being concentrated in a single individual. According to them the same assembly would be empowered for *Ijtihad*. Giving argument in support of this Iqbal says:

> "The republican form of government is not only thoroughly consistent with the spirit of Islam, but has also become a necessity in view of the new forces that are set free in the world of Islam."

Iqbal and the Principle of Dynamism in Islam

Though we do not disagree with the transfer of *Khilafah* to an elected democratic assembly we consider it inappropriate to restrict the right of *Ijtihad* to such an assembly. This would also be contrary to the spirit of democracy and "It" be close to the nature of communism in which the presidium presides over the destinies of the country and the people have no right to raise their voice against those decisions. The most serious danger in this would be that the president of the elected democratic assembly would be able to keep the *Ijtihad* on the Holy Our'an and the Holy Prophet's Traditions subservient to his will and interests by virtue of his authority, and nobody would be able to utter a word against it due to the restriction of the power of *Ijtihad* to the elected democratic assembly. Therefore, confining of the power of *Ijtihad* to an individual or an institution would be a serious mistake. Perhaps Iqbal did not realize the possible defects of restricting the power of *Ijtihad* to the elected assembly. We also disagree with the point of view Turks, which was accepted by Iqbal, that the concept of worldwide *Khilafah* could never succeed in fact. The concept of Islamic *Khilafah* was never unsuccessful in its essence and spirit. It was always liked by Muslims as an ideology and it has no logical contradictions. As for its expression in fact it is obvious that the Omayyad and Abbaside monarchs also derived the power for their authority from the same concept. Though they certainly crushed its spirit they did not dare to change its status. If the institution of *Khilafah* had continued to exist in its spirit in the same way as it did in its apparent form the concept of worldwide *Khilafah* would not have been confronted with the present state of affairs. It was only through the worldwide favours and blessings of the *Khilafah* that the Muslims could establish that grand civilization whose banners flew with full powers and glory over the greatest part of the known world of their period. Syed Nazir Niazi has described the meaning of *Khilafah* in a wider sense than the Turks and Iqbal, which is perhaps the newest and most effective elucidation of the *Khilafah*.

Chapter 5

IQBAL'S PHILOSOPHY OF REVOLUTION

Before talking about Iqbal's philosophy, I consider it necessary to explain that the term of revolution is usually applied to political revolution, which means a sudden and complete rejuvenation and immediate change. In addition, this change also includes the concept of subversion or destruction for reconstruction. In the third world revolution also means the overthrow of the established government by martial law or in some other way and capture of the political power by some dictator or a new ruler. The murder of hundreds of thousands of people in the Russian and French revolutions etc. and establishment of new governments was also called a revolution. In the modern world revolution is considered nothing more than a phobia, because the change expected by the people from political revolutions does not follow it. The revolution is restricted to mere change of personalities and the appearance of some new faces in the wake of the revolution. In the third world, and particularly in Pakistan, as the word revolution has become attached to martial laws the average person along with the intellectuals become wary of this word. However, as I have applied revolution to such an intellectual and notional change which would herald a new cultural and social change, only this concept of revolution should be kept in mind which aims at such changes in the intellect and thought which would gradually bring about a new order. I have not used the word evolution because the evolution of a concept or order of things is based on its own foundation, for example, the evolution of the Western mode of thought. However, Iqbal does not want the evolution of any existing order in his thought. He does not want evolution of the existing order based on the foundations of materialistic metaphysics. On the contrary, he created a new spiritual metaphysics in his order of things in the light of modern physics and away from materialistic thought and metaphysics, which is not composed of evolution but revolution and whose attribute is dynamism and not quietism. Hence when I talk about Iqbal's philosophy of revolution I use revolution in a very broad sense. As Iqbal considered Islam to be a social and cultural movement I am presenting revolution in the meaning of that social and cultural revolution which Iqbal wanted to bring about at the intellectual, social, and cultural levels. He was not in favor of establishing any order by overthrowing the government overnight by means of destructive measures. On the other hand he was really the herald of a metaphysical order whose foundation was spiritual instead of the existing metaphysical order based on materialism. Instead of justifying this point of view of his by the traditional concepts of matter, he used the researches of modern physics in the light of which matter came to be considered mutable rather than immutable and imperceptible instead of perceptible. He based the foundation of his metaphysics on the concept of destructibility of matter from fission of the atom and conversion of electrons and protons into energy or power, leading to its destruction. On this basis he adjudged the basis of the universe to be spiritual rather than material. With this revolution in the metaphysical thought Iqbal explained religion and provided a new inductive foundation to religion. In addition, he also established a new route for knowledge by establishing an organic relationship between intuition and thought and considering the religious experience as a scientific experience, like other experiences of material nature. In this way, by presenting new social, cultural and rational explanations for Islam and its principle of *Tauheed* in his *Lectures*, he pointed out new principles of *Fiqh* by entrusting the new *Ijtihad* for society, state and economy to parliament, which could be used to prepare a new social and cultural framework. In this way, it was the graft of this very revolution in Iqbal's thought which endowed his homeland with the concept of Pakistan and procured the excellent leadership of Quaid-i-Azam. It is the purpose of this paper to plead for focusing attention on Iqbal for bringing about this scientific, intellectual, and cultural revolution, for laying the foundations of the Islamic revolution in Pakistan in the light of Iqbal's thought, so that Pakistan may be moulded into a new Islamic Welfare State in the light of his philosophy, and the Islamic world may reach its goal of renaissance on the basis of unity and dynamism.

Iqbal's dynamic metaphysics is based on "Absolute Existence" or the dynamic concept of God. Iqbal does not accept Aristotle's concept of God being "The Unmoved Mover". Aristotle thought that God can be adjudged as the source of all movement only by being considered "The Unmoved Mover". According to him if God be considered as dynamic some other center for movement will have to be formulated. Hence, he hypothesized that God is the first cause of the long series of movements and changes, but is stationary Himself. He also argued that if God also is moving we will have to accept the impossibility of the explanation of God's movement. So he says that God is that primal cause which is the cause of the Universe' movement but is Himself beyond movement and change. However, when Aristotle, adjudging God's status as intellectual, says that God is a 'thought' he accepts God as an action and a movement on account of being a thought as well as its object. Neither can 'thought' be considered to exist by itself nor can 'thought' be without movement and action. Movement is a property of 'thought'. Now, when Aristotle himself says that God is "the Thinking Thought" he really wants to say that the 'thought' of God exists inside Himself and His movement and 'thought' are within His own Essence, without being dependent on any other thing or object.

He Himself is the mover of His movement, is not dependent on anything else for His movement or 'thought' and His movement and 'thought' are in Himself. He Himself has the power and authority over His 'thought' and movement. As the problem is not solved even by accepting God as Unmoving the very concept of God is movement. In spite of all this His movement is within His own Essence whose real character is known to Him alone. Unlike Aristotle's thinking He is not the primal cause of movement but is Himself wholly and completely movement. He has within His Essence the subject as well as the object of His movement. Therefore, His thought also relates to His eternal Perfection in His own time and space. In reality the bounds of eternity and time and space are also meaningless with reference to Him because these terms have been created by Man which lose their meaning in reference to Him.

Ali Abbas Jalalpuri has presented a detailed discussion of Iqbal's concept of the Deity or the Essence of God, With respect to the transcendental and Assyrian concepts of God, i.e. the discussion whether God is beyond or in the universe Ali Abbas Jalalpuri considers Iqbal to be a believer in the Assyrian concept. Notwithstanding that I consider it inappropriate to bracket Iqbal with any one concept of Deity, whether transcendental or Assyrian. This is so because in Iqbal's concepts themselves we see signs of negation of Assyrian concepts. Iqbal accepted the Islamic concept of God in contradiction of the Assyrian or transcendental (Semitic) concepts. In the Islamic concept God is the Omnipotent, the Perfect, the Eternal in His own Essence, who is also our personal God. He is beyond this universe as well as this universe is one of His unlimited potentials. Hence, the assertion of Ali Abbas that Iqbal, like Bergson and Alexander, did not construct the Islamic Divinity on the basis of presenting the Assyrian theory of *Wahdat al-Wujud*, but gave scientific form to the Assyrian theory, shows lack of comprehension of Iqbal's concept of God. This is so because, really, Iqbal fought against this concept all his life. Iqbal did not fully accept either Assyrianism or transcendentalism, but emphasized the Qur'anic Concept of the Deity, which fuses in itself the basic component of both the transcendental and Assyrian concepts. According to the Islamic concept God is the Complete, Most Perfect, Absolutely Omnipotent, Essentially Eternal, Independent Essence which transcends the universe, Who created the universe from Absolute non-existence with His extraordinary attributes. The creation is based on evolution for its growth and completion. Hence, the explanation of the universe of Nature such a creative act of the Self, which is offered at the present stage from the human point of view, whose bounds cannot be defined, in which Nature is a live and consistently expanding celebrated Unity, whose growth cannot be restricted from outside, whose limits are internal, if any, is Iqbal's concept which has been formed from the concordance of the transcendental and Assyrian concepts. Iqbal had more interest in the Qur'anic concept of God than the Assyrian or transcendental concepts. According to Iqbal God is a live and effective Power in the creation of the universe, Who is not isolated from mankind but has deep relationship with them. Iqbal did not accept the concepts of *Wahdat al-Wujud*, because in this concept existences do not rise above entities of equal ranks, while in *Wahdat al-Shuhud* the Essence has a higher rank than Existence. S.M. Raschid has made Iqbal's concept of God so much borrowed from Hegel's concept of the Absolute in the same way as Ali Abbas Jalalpuri has entangled it in Assyrian and transcendental concepts. Really there is no concordance of thought in the Hegel's concept of the Absolute and Iqbal's concept of the Living, the Self-subsisting, the Eternal God. Dr. Muhammad Ma'ruf has rightly pointed out in his book *Iqbal and His Contemporary Western Religious Thought* that S.M. Raschid could not adequately comprehend the concepts and thoughts of Iqbal and Hegel. This is so because there is no similarity at all between the Hegel's concept of the Absolute and Iqbal's concept of God.

Iqbal's concept of God is the one of a Being Absolutely Omnipotent, Absolutely Perfect and Eternal in His own Essence Who transcends the universe, which is one of His unlimited potentialities. This universe is the expression of His extraordinary power of creation. He is completely dynamic, which dynamism depends entirely on His own Being which does not admit any lack, but is the symbol of His being Live Self-subsisting, the Eternal. He transcends the boundaries of time and space as well as those of the Beginning and the End. These time and space are His own creation, and do not apply to His Essence. He is the Essence of Elegant Attributes. His Existence is also Potential. When some potential makes its appearance

Understanding Iqbal's Philosophy

His attribute becomes evident. His Attributes like His Essence are All-pervasive and Countless. Iqbal's dynamic concept of the universe has emerged from this very dynamic concept of God.

The universe which is a constant movement has come into existence from absolute non-existence into existence by the extraordinary attributes of God. The Holy Qur'an has said, "God is the Light of the Heavens and the Earth". In other words if God has personified Himself with anything it is Light. Light is that unique form in which God has expressed Himself. Light is not the name of any solid article, but appears in movement, energy and light. Now, viewing with reference to the universe and matter, the atom or the smallest indivisible part of matter when split changes into energy. Within it are found electrons, protons and an unknown number of other centers of energy which are in constant motion. This means that matter by splitting of its smallest indivisible particle changes from perceptible matter into non-perceptible power and energy. This energy, which modern physics accepts as convertible into light, shows the reality that the existence of the universe itself is a particle of light, a wave or current of light, which means that the reality of the universe is light. Now consider the concordance between the Light of God and the Light of the universe, i.e. the universe is only a wave of the Light of God. This very Light appeared as an effulgence to Hadhrat Musa on the Tur. The heart of Light is being moulded from God into the universe. Many universes are being or will be benefitted from this Light and many universes will be annihilated by the ceasing of some specific wave of God's Light. If the moulding of this wave of Light on emanating from God into a universe demonstrates a movement which is specifically assignable to God its comprehension is not difficult, though there is no precedence for it. This very wave of Light is the creator of different objects in the form of the universe. The combination of time and space is the creator of objects, The same wave of Light, which is completely a motion, by coming into existence through explosion, condensation, ascent and descent appears in different ever-changing forms by radiation and spreading and changing from motion into quiescent and stationary states. If everything is moving one moving object will see the other object stationary, because both are in motion with the same energy and velocity. Motion will be felt only when there is some change in its velocity, style and form. Life collects energy in a material form and evolves. Motion can be witnessed by your body being in constant motion, by changing of your cells and tissues, by the movement of the earth and the growth of the mountains. Non-living objects show their movement by their fragmentation and re-assembly.

Still, the act of motion is related to every object by its quality and quantity. But motion is certainly the property of all objects.

Life also is a property of the same Light. Motion itself is a portion derived from life. Life itself is motion. If the mountains are growing and if they increase the objects on or in them it obviously means that they also have life. If the electrons and protons are moving within atoms they are expressions of life in the atoms. The cells and tissues of the human body have life and move. Life has different forms and expressions at its different levels. Life appears in constantly changing forms in minerals, plants, animals and mankind. The heap of dust which becomes a cup acquires its life by becoming the cup. We do not perceive some subtle levels and stages of life, but life rages through and appears in every thing and produces the act of change. In the same way sensitivity, which is a property of life is also present in minerals, plants and animals. It has different levels. The change appearing in some stones by touch, and wilting or changing color of some plants reflects their sensitivity. Sensitivity also appears in its different forms by its density and its subtlety Man has such a level of sensitivity as has the perceptive capacity to distinguish, feel and decide whether to do or not to do some act. When Man evolved, or was created by God in the form of Adam, as a result of the continuation, succession and effect of centuries, arrived at the level of perception he descended from his first level. The fruit which he ate was the same ability to distinguish at the level of perception and he distinguished between himself and his sexual opposite, and by the realization of her presence he gave birth to an action which resulted in his transfer from paradise to the earth's orbit. By adopting this motion of Man's or Adam's sensitivity he grew on the earth. By the distinction between himself and his opposite sex he acquired the perception which enabled him to remain in possession of the potentiality of changing his life into a new form. Consequently, through Adam and Eve life started moulding itself into different forms.

Life is one of the innumerable possibilities which can appear from life and sensitivity. Hence the possibility which appears becomes a fact. Destiny is the appearance of any possibility. When some object is faced with the appearance of one of the occurrences selected from the innumerable possibilities that occurrence is called the destiny or fate of that object. This destiny is not pre-determined, but every object makes its own destiny by selecting one incident out of the innumerable possibilities. This means that destiny is the name of the occurrence of one possibility out of the innumerable open possibilities. Hence, history which presents itself in the shape of the arrangement of innumerable incidents is also the name of the appearance of one incident out of the innumerable possible incidents. History is the function of the conversion of possibility into incident. As the appearance of an incident out of possibilities is the destiny of history, which it selects out of its innumerable possibilities, history is the destiny of any object which moves from possibility into fact. This, the metaphysics of motion, is the characteristic of Iqbal's thought, which in turn is based on his dynamic concept of God, universe and history. Iqbal's concept of the individual and society is formed on the basis of this dynamic philosophy of God, the universe and history.

In this dynamic metaphysics of Iqbal the individual, *Khudi* and society are involuntarily in motion. In Iqbal's view *Khudi* is the intuition of Man's own individuality and uniqueness. by which it distinguishes itself and creates as well as goes around the orbit of its action. In Iqbal's view the appreciation of one's individuality and uniqueness has three stages which he has stated in *Javid Namah* and at the end of his last lecture "Is Religion Possible?"

زندہ ءِ یا مردہ ءِ یا جاں بلب
از سہ شاہد کن شہادت را طلب
شاہدِ اوّل شعورِ خویشتن
خویش را دیدن بنورِ خویشتن
شاہدِ ثانی شعورِ دیگرے
خویش را دیدن بنورِ دیگرے
شاہدِ ثالث شعورِ ذاتِ حق
خویش را دیدن بہ نورِ ذاتِ حق
پیشِ ایں نور ار بمانی استوار
حیّ و قائم چوں خدا خود را شمار

Iqbal's Philosophy of Revolution

بر مقامِ خود رسیدن زندگی است
ذات را بے پردہ دیدن زندگی است

"Whether alive or dead or on the verge of death you be
Obtaining testimony from three witnesses you should be

First witness, a sense of existence of the Self
Seeing one's Self with help of light of the Self

Second witness, a perception of existence of others
To see one's Self with help of the light of others

Third witness, perception of Existence of God
And seeing one's Self with the Light of God

Before this establish the Aiman's Light of God
Consider your Self Live and Eternal like God

Realizing your own status is life
Seeing the Essence Unveiled is life".

These verses contain the explanation of Iqbal's philosophy of *Khudi*. *Khudi* or the individual's self-identification consists of three levels or stages. At the first level he views his own Self, analyses himself in the light of his qualities, deeds, longings and ambitions. He acquires the knowledge of his own Self, and finds out what he is. Is he a mere lump of flesh or has some other quality also which establishes his identity or personality? The individual or *Khudi* is also the realization of one of the innumerable possibilities, which God creates and establishes with his extraordinary attributes. *Khudi* appears in the form of the center of our actions and efforts. This same center is the inner entity or the essence of our personality. This should be called "Ego". The same "ego" is active behind our likes and dislikes, our decisions and intentions. The "ego" appears directly as our existing and real Self. The knowledge of "ego" is not inferential in any sense, but is the direct comprehension of *Khudi* itself. It is an Intuition and Intuition alone provides the believable foundation of its being real. Ghazali considers *Khudi* as a separate entity, higher than intellectual experiences and conditions. According to him it is a virtue which is single, indivisible and immutable. Many kinds of experiences come and go but the spiritual virtue remains unchanged.

Understanding Iqbal's Philosophy

However, this definition does not provide us with any clue as to the nature of *Khudi*. Firstly, it is a metaphysical existence, and it has been supposed to exist so as to explain our experiences. However, do our experiences enter into it in the same way as color in a body? Do they have the same relationship with *Khudi* as conditions or properties with material particles? This is certainly not so. Secondly, as Kant points out the indivisibility and immutability of the spiritual virtues depends upon the uniqueness of experience. But this uniqueness neither proves its indivisibility nor its immutability. Thirdly, this theory is unable to explain the expressions of the schizophrenic personality. Now psychology considers *Khudi* as a mere heap of human experiences. But Iqbal not only denies its being a mere mixture of human experiences, he considers *Khudi* as different from Intellect and Experience, and considers its acquisition as dependent upon concentrating on the depths of the inner consciousness and using Intuition. Nevertheless the expression of *Khudi* after being exposed in Intuition like this is very difficult. According to Iqbal *Khudi* is a continuous current of life, feelings and influences which is a discontinuous change within ourselves. It is a mere motion which is present as a unit behind the multifarious feelings, which strings them together, and produces the phenomenon of multiplicity in unity and unity in multiplicity.

According to our above-mentioned statement *Khudi* also is purely a motion which is part of our continuous feelings and reflections and which is present in our experiences and feelings like a unit which links them together on a string. Thus, it constitutes a dynamic unit in the experiences and reflections of our perceptions, which are part of the continuous process of ever-changing experiences and their unlimited possibilities. In other words human *Khudi* is also a name for a creative current of perception which is continuously progressing with production of its unlimited possibilities and which is propelled by the desire for expression. In this human ego we witness the effulgence of God in the same way as we see the manifestation and warmth of the sun in innumerable water-filled cups, or witness the presence of the river's flow and flood in the river's current. Like our above-mentioned explanation about life and its gradual ascent from minerals, through plants and animals to Man, perception also progresses through rise and fall in different stages and conditions. Its revolving circle starts with the primal source of life and perception, i.e. God. A very subtle and pure ray of Light emerges from God which, becoming gradually materialized, appears in extremely subtle particles of Light. These particles of Light, evolving from the particles of air through the particles of water appear in such particles of soil which are indivisible any further and are invisible. These particles are converted into such particles of soil through multiplying and assuming material form, as produce different elements in different objects. All these elements by their mutual combination and interaction create life and its perceptions. Life and perception are not two different things. On the contrary as life becomes gradually more and more pure it acquires maturity of perception and the perceptions become more dynamic, mobile and reliable. As life gradually becomes more and more impure the senses become gradually less and less lasting and less and less mobile. This revolving circle of life reverts to its original condition from God, particles, or in the material universe from minerals, insects, plants, animals, to elegant and chosen persons and Man. It keeps on moving between union and separation and the perception continues traveling through its stages in the company of life. Consequently, when the human *Khudi* attains self cognizance it progresses from *Khudi* to *Bekhudi*, from individualism to collectivism, from Man to society, and finds its place through the visions of history. Perception moves from individual to collective perception and for its cognizance creates cultural and social norms in the same way as God, transforming Himself from a concealed treasure to congregational elegance, created a system for being known. In this state of affairs the new needs, desires, ambitions and longings of Man created in him a restlessness, a warmth, a feeling of disappointment, and gave him a new strength which created in him the power of dynamism and activism. Iqbal calls this "Love". The human life started with the longing for absorption, and the ardent desire for reaching and meeting the Beloved. The desire for everlasting continuation of the human race was the strongest force in its creation. The very foundation of human society is based on Man's desire to establish and continue the human race. The foundation of all economic struggle, all institutions, the formation and evolution of all civilizations, cultures and societies as well as the sum and substance of "Self" is this continuation and betterment of the human race. Every religion, every belief, existence and institution lasts only as long as it regards the continuance and betterment of the human race as its ideal. In this way the creation of the collective personality of a society, its personality and identification is associated with the betterment and continuance of the human race. Hence any society which is based on the collective existence of people cannot be useful unless it is dynamic itself. The human society is not an artificial entity, but is a natural collection which ensures the satisfaction of their needs. This is so because Man is a social animal which not only likes to live in society but is compelled to do so for his own continuance. He creates different institutions according to his innate and natural needs.

Understanding Iqbal's Philosophy

We have stated above that history is the destiny of some object which moves from possibility into reality and history is the act of moving from possibility into reality. In addition we also state that history is also the record of the society's ups and downs. When the different components and actions of society, changing from possibility to reality, leave some records, and when these records are eventually saved, we create our own trails for the preservation and continuance of our race and for balancihg and prolonging our dynamism. In this way, in the words of Byling Brook history teaches us philosophy through the examples of the rise and fall of human civilization, and shows us the ways of shaping the institutions for our environments on proper lines. In this way history changes from a science to an art. Iqbal called history a gramophone record. But Iqbal also calls history a molder of man and his destinies because we ourselves move forward fixing our own speed with history's help. In the same context, with reference to the Holy Qur'an, Iqbal adjudges history as a fountainhead of mutually associated events of knowledge, which is a necessary means of establishment and stability of *Khudi* in nature. Thus, history becomes such a fountainhead of the Signs of God which becomes a means of acquiring knowledge from the Self and the universe. In Iqbal's view history is an inductive science, because it derives its inferences from individual examples through logical reasoning. It was this inductive study of history which created in Muslims the habit of inductive methodology. Iqbal does not consider the science of history restricted to historical generalities. On the contrary he says that the Holy Qur'an has established a basic principle of historical criticism. The same science of historical criticism introduced the science of humanities, testing of traditions and use of intelligence. In any case in Iqbal's philosophy of history it is not a mere collection of facts, but in its capacity of being the signs of God is in itself a reliable source of knowledge. This is so because history is a reliable record of human activities as a member of society which moves us towards organizing a series of inferences about the past, present and future through induction, and warns us about the transfer of objects from the realm of possibility to that of fact. Here the question arises whether the knowledge of God is restricted to the universal principles with reference to possibility, or extends to all the details. In the view of Iqbal as well as in our view, as possibility includes the universal principles and there are all possibilities of the universal principles being within the knowledge of God, the knowledge of God about generalities is proven to include that of details. He knows the whole universe of possibilities and that of fact, including all their details. Now the selection of any specific possibility turning into fact is the function of possibility itself. So the knower of this knowledge completely covers possibility and occurrence, but the responsibility for the results of this occurrence will rest squarely on the shoulders of the person selecting it. Its responsibility will not extend to its knower. This is an important problem which demanded reference in view of its importance. Now, as the bestower of this power of the occurrence of possibility is also God the question arises as to why God bestows the power of doing evil. The reply is that God has fully demonstrated the virtue and evil to Man, the source of evil is present within himself and the one persuading towards evil is present in the outside. However, Man's nature has been provided with the criterion for distinguishing between virtue and evil. Man certainly feels restraint and abhorrence at the time of committing evil as well as after it but he paralyzes his capacity to select properly on account of being overcome by greed, anger and jealousy. Hence, the disposition for selection of virtue and feeling pleasure after doing a virtuous act has been endowed in Man by Nature or God Himself. In the same way the disposition for restraint on sin, and feelings of pain and shame after committing it is also found in Man. Even if goaded by being human he does commit a sin God has kept the door for forgiveness open, even though society may or may not forgive him. In spite of this if somebody misuses this right of selection he alone is accountable for it. If the mistake history becomes such a fountainhead of the Signs of God which becomes a means of acquiring knowledge from the Self and the universe. In Iqbal's view history is an inductive science, because it derives its inferences from individual examples through logical reasoning. It was this inductive study of history which created in Muslims the habit of inductive methodology. Iqbal does not consider the science of history restricted to historical generalities. On the contrary he says that the Holy Qur'an has established a basic principle of historical criticism. The same science of historical criticism introduced the science of humanities, testing of traditions and use of intelligence. In any case in Iqbal's philosophy of history it is not a mere collection of facts, but in its capacity of being the signs of God is in itself a reliable source of knowledge. This is so because history is a reliable record of human activities as a member of society which moves us towards organizing a series of inferences about the past, present and future through induction, and warns us about the transfer of objects from the realm of possibility to that of fact. Here the question arises whether the knowledge of God is restricted to the universal principles with reference to possibility, or extends to all the details. In the view of Iqbal as well as in our view, as possibility includes the universal principles and there are all possibilities of the universal principles being within the knowledge of God, the knowledge of God about generalities is proven to include that of details. He knows the whole universe of possibilities and that of fact, including all their details. Now the selection of any specific possibility turning into fact is the function of possibility itself. So the knower of this knowledge completely covers possibility and occurrence, but the responsibility for the results of this occurrence will rest squarely on the shoulders of the person selecting it. Its responsibility will not extend to its knower. This is an important problem which demanded reference in view of its importance. Now, as the bestower of this power of the occurrence of possibility is also God the question arises as to why God bestows the power of doing evil. The reply is that God has fully demonstrated the virtue and evil to Man, the source of evil is present within himself and the one persuading towards evil is present in the outside. However, Man's nature has been provided with the criterion for distinguishing between virtue and evil. Man certainly feels restraint and abhorrence at the time of committing evil as well as after it but he paralyzes his capacity to select properly on account of being overcome by greed, anger and jealousy. Hence, the disposition for selection of virtue and feeling pleasure after doing a virtuous act has been endowed in Man by Nature or God Himself. In the same way the disposition for restraint on sin, and feelings of pain and shame after committing it is also found in Man. Even if goaded by being human he does commit a sin God has kept the door for forgiveness open, even though society may or may not forgive him. In spite of this if somebody misuses this right of selection he alone is accountable for it. If the mistake in the right of election is punishable its correct selection is also worthy of rewards. It is the Divine Will that He preferred a specific selection for a particular person's destiny and nobody has the power to object.

As we have explained above society is essential for the *Khudi* and the very continuance of Man, because being a social animal Man cannot live his life in isolation. This very nature of sociability has led Man to create different institutions for his inter-relationships, out of which State is the most important and in fact the real institution. All other institutions are affiliated to it and their function is only to ensure the continuity of the State, to keep moderation and balance within it and to devise plans for its evolution and progress. The most primary form of this institution is the family, with its progressively higher forms of brotherhood, tribe and finally nation and State. Iqbal has devised very fundamental principles to keep this institution based upon justice and fair play. Iqbal considers the human society or State a basic training institution for evolution and progress of human *Khudi*, which is an evolutionary, live and dynamic organ. But, because Iqbal places on religion the foundation of the metaphysics of his thought we cannot comprehend his attitude towards State and its different institutions. So let us briefly review Iqbal's concept of religion.

Defining religion in the words of Professor Whitehead, Iqbal writes, "Religion is the system of well known truths which, if followed sincerely and understood as they should be, will change morals and character"

By acceptance Iqbal means having faith in the system of the truths of religion. In the words of Fariduddin Attar, Faith, without the aid of Intellect, finds its unmarked way like a bird. In Iqbal's view religion is not mere feelings but includes the component of Intellect also, for which reason the existence of thinking is inescapable for religion. Hence, in Iqbal's view some intellectual basis is needed for religion's principles and beliefs even more than for science. For the same reason Whitehead regards every period of religion to have a component of Intellect. That is why Sufis and debaters came into existence very early in Islam. In Iqbal's view the prayer of the Holy Prophet "O God apprise me with the reality of all things" was the starting point of the basis of Intellect which, together with the Greek philosophy, appeared as a strong cultural power. Still this cultural potential of the Greek philosophy was conceived to exist in the Holy Qur'an to a limited extent among the people of insight. The passage from the deductive trend of the Greek philosophy to the inductive trend is the acquisition of Islamic culture itself, which, moving the Muslims from abstract theories and concepts, led them towards comprehension with senses and, together with Intellect and mind, gave the concept of the reality of hearing and sight. After two hundred years the Muslims started feeling that the holy Qur'an's own spirit was contrary to the Greek philosophy. The substance of this revolt appeared in the logical discourses of Ghazali and Ibn-i-Taimiyya. In Iqbal's view Intuition and natural thought are not mutually contradictory but, being derived from the same fountainhead are mutually complementary. One attains the grasp of the Absolute Reality in stages and the other in its entirety. One sees the eternal aspect of Reality and the other temporal. In other words while Intuition seeks the pleasure of enjoying the Reality in its entirety, thought treads the path with cautious steps and fixes the peculiarities and limits of its different components so as to view them individually one by one. Both need each other for their freshness and strength. So Intuition and Thought are not different from each other, but Intuition is only an advanced stage of Thought, and both have an organic relationship with each other. In Iqbal's view, unlike Kant and Ghazali, thought is not incapable of reaching the destination but is able to reach the Boundless Reality with the deepest dynamism concealed in itself. Thought in its intrinsic value is dynamic, not static. Thought appears in its entirety within the limits of time, which we comprehend with reference to one another, while beyond time its entirety is preserved *The Lauh-i-Mahfuz* in the words of the Holy Qur'an. All the undefined possibilities of knowledge are present in it from the very beginning, which make their appearance in the form of defined concepts in the continuity of time. In this way the unlimited and undefined possibilities, becoming limited in the continuity of time appear in the form of limited concepts of knowledge, and in this way in every action of knowledge also thought, transcending its limits, enters into limitlessness, and so thought is freed from its limitations. In the breaking of its limits and in the achieving of its limitlessness alone thought gets that dynamism which keeps it oscillating between limitlessness and limit Hence, religious thought also, like the flame of longing, is busy in restlessness for acquiring its limited accessibility from its inaccessibility.

The religious experience, which forms the foundation of this Intuition, instead of exhibiting the comprehended, can only explain the controversies of logic. This is so because of the difficulties in the faithful expression of its attributes of concentration, and the uniqueness and individuality of the Sufi's moment of ecstasy. This increasing expression of his condition exhibits and promotes the development and expression of the component of feelings. But feeling itself is a great source of knowledge, which fully preserves the grandeur of knowledge in his religious experience, and makes it possible to acquire the knowledge of the comprehended due to the presence of the component of Intellect. Thus thought oscillates between the temporal and non-temporal limits of the Truth. Hence, by the merging of the Sufi with the Eternal Essence the continuity of time is not negated because in spite of its uniqueness the momentary and ephemeral Sufistic - observations are not separate from daily feelings and perceptions. Very soon the Sufi returns from his Sufistic or prophetic condition to the world of physical occurrences. In Iqbal's view it is clear that Sufistic observations are also as real and as reliable in the acquisition of knowledge as some other universe of our observations. In this way in Iqbal's view the revealed books, and particularly, the Holy Qur'an are a reliable source of knowledge, which is the universe of the spiritual observations of the Holy Prophet which was divinely revealed to his heart. In Iqbal's view the echo of the spiritual experience of a prophet is the vehicle of far-reaching results for mankind. This echo is creative. The prophet, returning from his spiritual incidents, enters the current of time, so as to create a new world of goals with the superiority and the powers of the whole world. The pleasure of Union is the last stage for a Sufi as is clear from the statement of Shaikh Abd al-Quddus Gangohi that the Holy Prophet would have never returned from the celestial world because the spiritual experiences of a prophet produce such powers which, changing the man's universe, bring a new universe into existence. The appear in the form of a social and cultural power. Defining prophethood Iqbal says, "This is that form of the perception of saint-hood in which the occurrences of union exceed their limits and search for the means of discovering or re-shaping those powers which are the creator of collective life. In other words in the personality of prophets the limited center of life is absorbed in its unbounded depths, so that it may re-emerge with a new power and strength. It annihilates the past and opens up new paths of life to it." By this concept Iqbal elevates religion much above a system of mere beliefs and rituals to a social and cultural movement which shapes the collective form of Man on the basis of *Tauheed* and binds this cultural power of religion with the science of *Tauheed*.

Iqbal, by moving away from the traditional concept of religion and presenting it as a scientific and cultural movement, makes religion itself a social, cultural and scientific current which is moving, evolutionary and constantly acquiring ever new dimensions, instead of leaving it as a puzzle of inert, immobile theories and beliefs. This means that in Iqbal's view this principle of *Tauheed* is continuously moving towards evolution in its social environment. The seed of *Tauheed* also produces social and cultural fruits around itself and appears in its ever new forms in every human historical as well as existing environment. In Islam *Ijtihad* is really another name for scientific reasoning for is-lam's principle of *Tauheed,* which we do for our guidance in our special historical as well as existing, individual and collective environments, so that we may live our lives in life's fast moving evolution. By accepting three sources of knowledge, i.e. the worlds of Nature, Self, and History Islam has accepted the principle that in the explanation of the principles of *Tauheed* these worlds cannot be overlooked. Therefore, it is very necessary to keep in view the worlds of Nature, (the physical world), Self, (psychological and observations' world) and History (the social and cultural world) in the explanation and clarification of *Ijtihad*. In Iqbal's view, as the universe is not a static and immobile entity but a moving reality, life also is a mobile reality. When life is the name of an incessant movement, and all social, cultural and civic institutions surrounding it are part of a motion, how long can the rules and regulations of life remain immobile and static? Therefore, even the principles which Islam has called eternal and absolute also contain within them the components of motion, evolution and progress, and together with the needs and conditions of the evolving life they also continue evolving. This is that revolution which Iqbal presented in the form of a constantly evolving system of life and concepts in contradistinction of the concept of religion as an immobile and static religion with fixed beliefs and rituals. Iqbal has reasoned in favor of the principle of *Ijtihad* on the conversation of Ma'az Ibn Jabal, Governor of Yemen, with the Holy Prophet in which the former expressed the desire to use his own religious insight to express and apply Islamic principles after the Book of God and the Holy Prophet. The history of Islamic *Fiqh* also shows that the leaders of *Fiqh*, have used this principle freely in Islamic legislation and, with their religious insight, have leaned heavily on *Ijtihad* in accordance with their existing environment. Hence, in Islam the need and importance of *Ijtihad* for legislation and religious matter was never abandoned in any period and environment. On the other hand, with the increasing depth and complexity in the evolution of life, its need and importance is increasing. It is the principle of *Ijtihad* alone which has maintained Islam as a living reality in its competition with other religions. Hence, if Islam claims to be the religion for all humanity and all ages it is incumbent on it to be capable of fulfilling the needs of Man universally and in all ages. In addition, in my view Islam insists on its acceptance and practice from all its believers. The practical aspects of religious doctrine which tailor to the temporary, and temporal needs of different cultures and civilizations should not be emphasized to the extent of turning them contrary to Islamic principles. Distinction should also be made between the requirements of Islam and Arab society of the time of the Holy Prophet. Islam should insist on its adherents to obey its commandments, but the Arab society of the Holy Prophet's days and its social norms should not be considered Islam and it should not be confined to them. The traditions of the Holy Prophet should not be confused with conformity with the Arab society. On the other hand the essence of the Holy Prophet's traditions, i.e. the highlights of character should be emphasized. This is so because the cultural, social and civic norms of the days of the Holy Prophet have changed much due to the passage of long time. Applying the social norms of those days to the present age is tantamount to turning the wheels of history backwards. This is obviously un-Islamic because Islam is the name of organizing history on its own principles rather than dragging it back. The main principle is that, keeping Islamic principles and their spirit in view we should shape our civic, cultural, civic and social institutions in such a way that they should clearly reflect the spirit of Islam together with modernism.

After explaining this basic principle we want to explain that the State which Islam wants to create is such an ideological State as is based on the concept of *Tauheed*. In Iqbal's view the ideology of *Tauheed* is the basic principle of our individual as well as collective lives. The ideal Islamic State will not be shaped on the principle of race, language, geography or collective gain. On the other hand the Islamic concept of *Tauheed* is the basic principle of shaping it. According to this the State and its government is a trust of God, where the ultimate authority rests in God and the pillars of the State are obliged to establish the ultimate authority of God in, the State and, being the vicegerent of God on earth create such a collective theology where the law of God may reign supreme, and should select their advisors by mutual consultation and opinion, who would establish Islamic justice, clean economic ways and virtuous society. Iqbal calls this State and the machinery as well as the system for its administration "Spiritual Democracy", which should be governed through such a parliament the members of which would possess Islamic character and would legislate on the principle of *Ijtihad* and with due regard to the requirements of the times. In Iqbal s view the legislation of such an elected parliament, enforced by the powers of the Islamic State, would create a *Fiqh* which would satisfy our timely needs on the one hand and, eliminating sectarianism, would reflect our collective perceptions and would be able to create unity among us. Iqbal has two expectations from such an ideological Islamic state. One is the establishment of a precedence which would start the work of change in the other States of the Islamic world, and will result in the establishment of this ideal spiritual democracy in them, which will ultimately lead to the molding of all the democracies born out of this concept of Islamic State into a federation. In this way the Muslim world will witness the dream of Islamic renaissance come true. The second expectation of Iqbal from this Islamic State, which would be the embodiment of spiritual democracy, will be solving the economic problems of its poor population on the principle of *Qul al-Afv*. The land and all resources belong to God which concept makes it incumbent on the Islamic State to disallow the continued concentration of these resources in a few hands, and must take periodic initiatives for the just and fair distribution of these resources. In Iqbal's view the just and fair distribution of resources and their produce and the elimination of all kinds of feudalism and capitalism is the act of reverting to the real spirit and principles of Islam. For this Islam has undertaken to establish of *Ushr*, *Qul*

Understanding Iqbal's Philosophy

al-Afv, and benevolence in addition to *Zakat*. When Islam introduces the economy of charity and benevolence in place of the economy of usury it uproots economic distinctions completely. The State to be established on the principles of Iqbal's "Spiritual Democracy" must be considered bound to provide education, medical treatment, home, and justice and fair play to all people. In this State the society is strengthened collectively in addition to conferring dignity on the individual's individuality, and such institutions, associations and pressure groups are formed as continuously draw the society, the State and its pillars to progress and evolution. Its goal would be to keep the society and its life dynamic and to keep the society constantly flourishing through *Ijtihad* according to the requirements of every age and environment and with due regard to the ideology of Islam. This alone is the essence of Iqbal's philosophy.

On the basis of this very philosophy of revolution Iqbal presented the concept of Muslim nationalism in contrast with the nationalism nurtured by the geographical, racial and linguistic movements of Europe. He adjudged this philosophy of revolution as the charter of the Nation of Islam and created the concept of this Islamic nationalism throughout the Islamic world. This philosophy was also a reaction against the movements of migration, Arab nationalism and the concept of a single nation propounded in the Indian sub-continent. This Islamic nationalism was not related to homeland, province, race, collective interests or economic ends. On the contrary it was based entirely on the creed of *Tauheed*. It contained the lesson of Islamic unity from the banks of Nile to the city of Kashghar for the defense of the Haram. Iqbal conferred this new enthusiasm on the nation of Islam from Lahore to the lands of Bukhara and Samarqand and talked about making Tehran as the center of the Islamic world.

ایک ہوں مسلم حرم کی پاسبانی کے لئے

نیل کے ساحل سے لے کر تابخاکِ کاشغر

اک ولولہ تازہ دیا میں نے دلوں کو

لاہور سے تا خاکِ بخارا و سمرقند

طہران ہو گر عالم مشرق کا جنیوا

شاید کرۂ ارض کی تقدیر بدل جائے

Iqbal's Philosophy of Revolution

"The Muslims should unite into one body for Haram's defense
From banks of the Nile to where the city of Kashghar is

I have given a new enthusiasm to the hearts
From Lahore to the lands of Bukhara and Samarqand

If Tehran becomes the Geneva of the Eastern lands
Perhaps the destiny of the whole world may change."

This same Islamic nationalism was the most powerful weapon of the Indian Muslims against the Hindu imperialism, which brought about the defeat of the British, Hindus and their camp followers, as well as the establishment of Pakistan under the leadership of Quaid-i-Azam. Thus, Pakistan was an ideological State based on the principles of Islamic nationalism, which should have been established on that ideology from the very outset. Unfortunately the absence of Iqbal's ideology and the dearth of leadership of Quaid-i-Azam's character made the country the victim of the plunder by feudal lords, landlords, capitalists, *Mullahs* and *Peers*. Consequently, Pakistan was deprived of the State based on the ideology of Islam and Islamic nationalism. This made Pakistan the helpless prey to sectarian, racial, linguistic, provincial and group prejudices. Pointing out an old malady of the Muslims Iqbal had said that Muslims lacked spiritual enlightenment, which he had attributed to the Islamic Nation's attachment to monarchy, and the institutions of *Mullahs* and Sufis. This means that though the malady of the Muslims is due to external causes, the above three are very important among the internal ones. These maladies are slowly consuming their body corporate. Iqbal gave the solution of monarchy in the form of "Spiritual Democracy", annihilated *Mullaism* and the resulting sectarian mentality by assigning the right of *Ijtihad* to parliament. He discarded the institutions of *Tasawwuf* and *Peers* on the basis of their being born in the *Ayyam* and are based on the "Philosophy of Goats". Distancing himself from the philosophy of *Wahdat al-Wujud* of Ibn al-Arabi, Hafiz and Plato he adopted that of *Wahdat al-Shuhud* of Mujaddid Alf-i-Thani. Thus, rejecting these three institutions responsible for the Muslims' downfall he established new ways, because in Iqbal's view these institutions were symptoms of the static and stalemate life, and were devoid of the spirit of Iqbal's philosophy of dynamism. Hence if Iqbal's spiritual democracy, Islamic nationalism and spirit of *Ijtihad*, which is based on the inductive method and is associated with an elected parliament, is accepted and, instead of the *Ajami* philosophy of *Tasawwu*f Iqbal's ideology of *Khudi* is adopted the Islamic world can benefit from both the spiritual as well as the material revolution. The same was the subject matter and the *raison d'étre* of Iqbal's *Lectures* and poetic works, through which he satisfied the demand of the youth of Islamic Asia and Africa that the time was rife for the assessment of the basic principles of Islam so that Islam might be understood as a system which concerns the whole of the human race. In addition to this Iqbal also considered the changes in Central Asia in addition to the new current of awakening among Muslims as the prime movers of this movement. On this basis he undertook to review Islamic theology and in this way, by the comprehension of new concordance between religion and science, established a new theology which, in the words of Maulana Saeed Ahmad Akbarabadi, laid the foundation of a new theology. It also created, in our thinking, a new philosophy of revolution, which is a blessing for the whole human race in addition to Muslims. Still, as Iqbal stood for dynamism and revolution he, not only made himself dynamic and vocal, but also made it clear that in philosophical thinking there is no such thing as absolute and final. As and where we advance forward new ways for thought open up. Many more ideologies, and perhaps more important than those presented in his *Lectures* will present themselves to us. In any case it is our duty to keep a careful watch on the growth and development of human thought and carry out independent criticism in this field. It is this point of view of Iqbal alone which is the spirit of his philosophy of revolution and tells us that we should continue critical examination of our religious, political, cultural, and social concepts along with the evolutionary progress in human thought, and should always remain in search of a new world for ourselves because the spirit of the lives of nations is the struggle of revolution.

Chapter 6

THE SOCIAL PHILOSOPHY OF IQBAL

In the present-day world Iqbal has nurtured an intellectual, moral and social vision on the Islamic world much needed by the Muslim nation, dazzled by the glamour of Western civilization and culture. During his educational period in Europe Iqbal had perceived its intercultural, moral and social decline and had likened the apparently shining European civilization and culture to a frail nest on a flimsy branch. He had declared this civilization and culture to be a deadly poison for Muslims, and was never prepared to call it a blessing for them: He aroused the Muslims from slumber from the shores of the Nile to the land of Kashghar, and guided them away from the path adopted by European societies which are leading them to their death. There were three groups of people in the Muslim world who were under the influence o European science and technology, civilization and culture. One had made the *Asharite*[1] and Ghazali's[2] interpretations their refuge and they were not prepared to abandon their adopted path at any cost. They considered the light of the new knowledge and scientific developments as dubiousness and heresy. The second group wanted to break off from the Islamic path. It had either embraced the West completely or was prepared to accept communism as their *deen*[3]. The third one interpreted Islam and organized Islamic learning and thought in the light of the new science and knowledge. Though some of them, looking upon Islam in the Western framwork, reduced it to a puzzle, there was no dearth of the thinkers who did not allow Islamic thinking to be hurt at any cost. Iqbal was among such people who were never impressed by Westernism or communism. On the other hand Iqbal opposed and criticized them severely and established the Islamic social concepts in detail.

To Iqbal history is a continuous process. To him history is not a mere collection of facts but is a continuous creative process, which operates by interaction of the opposing forces of vice and virtue. The individuals and nations rise by treading the path of virtue and become leaders of mankind. On the other hand the nations which elect the path of vice and make it their wont are removed from their high position and destroyed by God. The Holy Qur'an has placed the stories of the rise and fall of nations on the scale of their virtue and vice. The only reason for the destruction of the nations of 'Ad,[4] Thamud[5] and Bani Israil[6] virtue was their turning away from virtuous values and adoption of vice as their permanent way of life. The source of these theories of Iqbal about history was his concept of time, which he has repeatedly explained in his philosophy and works. According to this, time is a creative activity. It is a process which is constantly creative, gives birth to ever new conditions and events. To Iqbal this creative activity is not purposeless, as the famous philosopher Henri Bergson[7] thinks, but has a clear and fixed purpose:

"The alternation of the day and the night is the creator of all events
The alternation of the day and the night is the Essence of life and death.

The alternation of the day and the night is the warp of the coloured silken thread
With which the *Zat*[8] makes its gown of Attributes
What is the reality of thy life

Except that it is a current of time without the day and the night."

Life is a continuous, flowing, ever changing and evolutionary process to which the concepts of resting and quietitude are foreign and which does not think in terms of stopping.

"Quietitude and stability are but a mirage
Restless is every particle of the universe

Stops not the caravan of existence
Because every second of the Majesty and Glory of God is manifesting anew
Thou considereth life a secret
Life is only the taste for flight
Ever running is the river of life
Everything exhibits the notion of life."

Iqbal's philosophy of history has no concept of repeating itself but exhibits the flow of the river of life. It is neither a recollection of some past events from which, according to Bernard Shaw[9] we do not derive any experience, nor does it repeat itself in quick succession According to Iqbal history is constantly moving forward because otherwise it reduces historical facts to a mere machinistic movement, which does not have evolution; motion and progressivity. In Iqbal's view, by informing us about the stories and tales of previous nations, history helps us in arriving at a suitable course for deriving positive and better results from our own social and revolutionary systems, keeps the individual and society informed of its past and helps them in handling, the problems of the present and for planning the future. In this way history is a very useful field of knowledge about which Iqbal expresses his opinion thus:

> "What is history O thou ignorant of thyself
> A tale, a story, a fable!
>
> It informs thee about thyself
> It makes thee useful and a man of action
>
> To the soul it is illuminant wealth
> For the nation's body it is like the nervous system
>
> The decreasing flame brightens up by its warmth
> Tomorrow appears in the lap of its today
>
> Its lamp is the star of the fate of nations
> It is the source of perpetual enlightenment
>
> Its decanter has a century old wine
> Its wine has lasting ecstacy
>
> Adhere to history and become perpetual
> Get life from the disillusioned breaths".

The concept of history of Iqbal is closely related to his social philosophy, because it is only a person's concept of history which determines his point of view about individuals and society. After adjudging life to be a creative action Iqbal considers the individual's status. To him an individual is God's most elegant masterpiece, and he considers God's slavery in no way inferior to the Divine Dignity. He has the vision of an individual who would reflect Divine Beauty in his attributes, would manifest Divine Attributes in his human body. Iqbal's individual is the center piece of the universe and the vicegerent of God. Iqbal's concept of the individual is indebted to his Quranic thought, in which be assigns the place of pride to Man which is higher than the assigns the place of ride to Man which is higher than that of angels and which is only next to God's place.

Iqbal's theory of Man is also closely related to his theory of time and the universe. He has called time to be ever-changing and progressive and has likewise given the concept of dynamic universe. He considers the concept of the eternity of matter wrong and an ignorance. To him the real source of the universe is light. According to (God is the Light of the heavens and the earth)"[10] Holy Qur'an. He regards the entire universe to be God's Light. Explaining this theory Iqbal says:

"In this way physics, feeling the need for a critique of its fundamental theories, ultimately shattered its own idol, and the experimental technique which had been created to support materialism is now rebelling against it. Einstein[11] has dealt a deadly blow to materialism".

According to Iqbal matter is not a permanent entity *per se* but is a series of interlinked occurrences and creations. However, science itself cannot be considered to be the only method of unfolding the secrets of the universe and leading to the Truth cannot be considered to be the function of science alone. On the contrary, science can only encompass the truths which can be seen and experimented with and which are material and external. To him the whole universe is a mere reflection of a Reality and is unfinished:

"This universe is perhaps unfinished still
Because the ethos of 'Kun fa yakoon' are resounding constantly"

In the view of Iqbal the universe is dynamic, a purposeful dymanism, and a creation with an end. This universe is not static but constantly susceptible to change. The universe is the masterpiece of God. which is not indebted to matter for its existence. However, the material macrocosm has a real existence and its knowledge also deserves reliance. To him the essence and origin of the universe is spiritual and that the universe is not the ultimate truth and the real objective, but is a field whose crop we have to harvest later. It is a place of action, the rewards and punishments of which we shall experience later. Man occupies a very dignified place in Iqbal's above stated concept of the universe, because this universe is an examination hall and the real importance belongs to Man and not to the examination hall. This universe is no more than an examination hall which God has created for Man. The universe has been created for Man and not Man for the universe. So Man is not the slave and dependent on the universe but the universe is the subservient servant of Man. Man is its master and controller:

"Thou art neither for the earth nor for the sky
The universe is for thee not thou for the universe."

Fixing Man's position is not difficult after understanding this relationship of Man and the universe because Man and not the universe is the desired entity. All the modulations of nature are for the purification of Man's character and beauty and form the enhancement of his greatness, by which Man benefits from God's Essence and feels His reflection within himself. When Man understands his own status he understands God also.

Iqbal likes to see the individual in the shape of *Mard-i-Kamil*[12] or *Mard-i-Mumin*[13] who may have creative qualities like the universe, who may be morally and socially so much liked as to arouse angels envy. Iqbal' *Mard-i-Mumin* is neither Nietzche's[14] superman nor the fountainnead of blind nationalism and the master of limitless power and resources, who may be dreaming of being master of the whole universe and of subjugating all mankind with the power of his material resources, and who commits genocide. On the contrary, Iqbal's *Mard-i-Mumin* is the fountain of mercy for mankind and a source of benignness and munificence. He is consistently creative, whose creativity is the source of peace and tranquility for mankind: he is a portrait of compassion and kindness for humanity, all his actions are positive and productive he enjoins what is right and forbids what is wrong.[15] He leads people to the right path and by his word and deed proves himself to be an embodiment of service of God: he does not cause the slightest hurt to anybody by his actions. His personality is at once extremely tough and mild.

"He is the dew drops which provide coolness to the tulip's heart
He is the storm which strikes fear in the oceans depths."

Huzur Sarwar-i-Kainat[16] Muhammad was the *Mard-i-Kamil* and the *Mard-i-Mumin* par excellence. Iqbal places other prophets also in the same rank. The companions of the Holy Prophet were also *Mard-i-Mumin*. He considered the period of the Guided Caliphs as the golden age of human history. *Khudi* (Self) individual ego or "Self-cognizance" is the most fundamental quality of the *Mard-i-Kamil* to Iqbal. He considered it most important for the *Mard-i-Kamil* to be true to the saying of the Holy Prophet:

"He who has understood himself has understood his Lord."

In this way he can understand his status in the universe and in this world. Unless a person is conscious of his Self, individual Self or his consciousness he is not above the rank of the lowliest of the low[17] Iqbal considered individual Self or consciousness of the Self to be the most valuable asset of the individual. According to him unless and individual become conscious of his Self he cannot be conscious of his status and station in creation, and without this consciousness he cannot engage himself in any dynamic and creative activity, which is the purpose of his existence. He remains unsuccessful as long as he remains away from his purpose. He is the losing person who incurs God's wrath. The *Mard-i-Kamil is* the one who is fully conscious of the purpose of his being created, his status of being a servant of God and his ideal of life. Attainment of these qualities brings the happiness of kingship even in poverty, about which Iqbal says: "If the consciousness of the Self is kept kingship is attained, if not disgrace is the lot".

Iqbal has given a high place to community also. He regards the security of the individual to be based on the community just as a wave is a wave inside the ocean only and ceases to be such outside it. Hazrat-i-Ali[18] has stated that individuals outside the community are like the goat which falls prey to the wolf[19] i.e. the status of the individual outside his community or group is reduced to one of no avail. Some people have distinguished between the individual Self and the collective Self. Immanuel Kant[20], Henri Bergson and Nietzsche consider the individual as but naught outside the society's life. Consciousness of Self has a wide scope but the individual Self exists even without the Self of the society and the country, which is the source of virtue and character. It is the source of all values. This individual's Self is meaningful. Our feelings and our very existence depend upon it. This is a secret unravelling of which is impossible, and it maintains its existence even after abandoning the community and the society. It enlightens our life. This is so because the society or the community is restricted by space, whereas the essence and ardour of life are temporal and are not different from ourselves. Is Bergson justified in saying that the society's life is an artificial mantle round our real existence, which has only a temporary and periodic relationship with our life, because we are associated with it only to fulfil a social need, and

The Social Philosophy of Iqbal

like the realists nobody except us is aware of our desires, happiness, longings, hopes and disappointments. In one of his lectures he said:

"The individual *per se* is a nominal existence, or it may be considered to be in the class of intellectual abstracts, reference to which makes it easy to understand discussions about society. In other words an individual, in the life of the community to which he is related, is like a temporay and ephemeral moment. His longings, his way of life, his entire physical and mental capacities, and in fact, even the days of his life are moulded into the needs of the community of the collective life of which he is only a partial expression. The reality of the individual's actions is not more than the helplessness and evoluntary performance of the task which the community administration has entrusted to him. The nation has a separate existence and it is basically wrong to consider it a mere sum of its individuals. For this very reason all the social and political plans based on this premise are in need of very careful review. The nation is not only a sum of its present individuals but is much larger than that. Consideration of its nature will show it to be boundless and limitless, because its constitutent parts include the very many future generations, which though constantly beyond the immediate vision of the society, are capable of being considered the most important constituents of alive community".

Thus, though Iqbal considers the individual important and essential he does not place him above the ethical concepts and values of the society's life. In spite of Iqbal's belief in the individuality and Self-consciousness of the individual, he wants to keep him dependent on the community for the survival and glory of the nation. This is so because the individual derives his status from the nation and has no standing by himself. Civilization and the individual are interdependent. Self-consciousness, individual ego and the Self depend upon social life for their evolution and culmination. In *Zarb-i-Kaleem* Iqbal has also talked about the ulcers which are sufficient to destroy a nation. Immorality, dissentions, political decline and grouping together for slefish ends are the biggest enemies of any society in his view. They are caused only by a nation's detachment from its concept of life's ideals and ethos.

Iqbal's period had two characteristics. One was that materialism and science were at there climax. Scientific concepts had eclipsed all old beliefs and theories. Objectivity suffered by the hands of the realists and subjectivity prospered and his followers criticized Hegel's[21] objectivity. Scientific thought and standards declared everything spurious and absurd if it could not be tested on the touchstone of scientific principles of verification and experimentation. This shocked religion, ethos and metaphysical thinking very badly. However, it was also a bitter truth that science itself did not always conform to its own principles or verification. This was a different, though an important question. The logical positivists had denial everything which was not established by experiment and could not be tested with the principles of verification. This influenced people's faith in religion, metaphysics and ethics. Along with this the destruction caused by the First World War, engulfing the whole world and resulting in extensive genocide pushed all people into fear, terror and death. The people of the whole world had been plunged into a sea of pain and misery. Realism was a reaction to the loss suffered by the human subjectivity at the hands of Hegel's objectivity. English philologists in America brought to light seismological problems. There was demand for knowing the explicit and correct meaning of the words and phrases we use, because unless we know the implication of a word, its correct application and its scope and meanings, it cannot give its correct acceptation. Similarly, unless we know the purport of a word or sentence, we can neither establish the meaning of somebody else's sentences nor can we transmit out thought to him. Realism, logical positivism and philology weakened gregarious, ethical and metaphysical concepts. People's belief and faith in them was shaken and even the concepts given by them about life's problems and the relationship of the individual with society ceased to remain accepted. Secondly, the static conditions of religious, ethical and metaphysical disciplines themselves produced in them a special non-evolutionary attitude. They failed to provide the guidance needed by the people of the new social order regarding the rise of the new sciences and learning, industrial revolution and the new social problems, created by these changes. Though capitalism vanquished the European feudalism, it was itself instrumental in creating innumerable problems. The concentration of wealth in a few hands and the unspeakable lot of the laboured made capitalism a vexacious disaster and the proletariat of this society staged a strong reaction against the bourgiosie. In Iqbal's view the communist society was nothing more than a negative reaction to the whole capitalist system. He writes in a letter:

"No doubt the power of capitalism is a curse if it exceeds the limits of the happy mean. But its complete elimination is not the right way as the Bolshevists propose. To keep its power within reasonable limits the Holy

The Social Philosophy of Iqbal

Qur'an has prescribed the law of inheritance, prohibition or usuary and the system of *zakat*[22], etc., and considering human nature, this is the only practical system. Russian Bolshevism is a strong reaction against the selfish and short-sighted capitalism of Europe. But in fact that European capitalism and the Russian Bolshevism are two extremes."

The results appearing form the promulgating of communism and socialism in Russia are not encouraging enough to deserve being exemplary. On the contrary, this experience has proved that Marx's dream of the celestial paradise descending down to the earth did not come true, because in practice Russian socialism has assumed the character of imperialism and it also contains two classes: one the Proletariate which has been deprived of all the comforts and facilities of life and is at the mercy of the ruling junta, and the other is the ruling class which anjoys the unshared control of the whole country's resources. The solution of the problems of the proletariate planned by Karl Marx[23] proved worse than the captalist system, not to say of its being considered as equivalent to capitalism. The capitalist system has departed but the socialistic imperialism must also disappear soon. Iqbal had the premonition of the failure of socialism in Russia. He wrote:

"The Russian nation itself, experiencing the shortcomings of its own present system will be obliged to incline towards a system whose basic principles will be either purely or approximately Islamic. At present, however laudable the economic ideals of Russians may be their practical program cannot win any Muslims sympathy."

We have reached the stage when Muslim should perceive socialism's failure in Russia and turn to Iqbal and become aware of the weakness of the principles of the socialist impeialism which, having been born from the evil bosom of capitalism, itself, exists as a perverse system.

Iqbal, after getting rid of the capitalism of the West disliked Russian socialism also and considered Bolshevist beliefs to be contrary to Islam. The question now arises whether he has the social philosophy which would form the infra-structure of his own society. Iqbal equally disliked dictatorship and the form of the present day Western style democracy. According to him "The Western pharmacopaea has sweetend medicines, but their effect is merely soporophic". He does not consider the anarchic Western Democracy as exemplary. He is convinced of the Islamic consultative system, which is sometimes called Islamic democracy in the new terminology. The present day democracy has the same defect which had been pointed out by Socrates[24] several centuries ago, that in this system persons are counted and not weighed. He used to say that:

"What could be more ridiculous than the democracy which has been hamstrung by the mob, where emotions reigned supreme, government was merely a debating society; where the military commanders were selected, dismissed and killed without rhyme or reason, where the simple minded farmers and merchants were selected in alphabetical order to work as the members of the supreme court. How could a new and natural moral code develop in Athens under these conditions and save the country from destruction?"

"The demon of despotism is parading in the mantle of democracy

Thou considereth it a beautiful ferry."

This applies mutatis mutandis to the present day democracy also. Iqbal also has said:

"Democracy is a form of government in which persons are counted and not weighed."

The question then arises as to which is a better system than this. Bertrand Russell[25] has adjudged communist democracy as necessary for the present age. But this also has demonstrated the same basic defect, namely that there are no restrictions on the election of members of assemblies in democracy and on the *modus operandi* of their members, so as to stop them from framing a law, albeit by majority vote, which would be contrary to the accepted values and recognized principles. For example, the British Parliament, overlooking the accepted values, has given legal protection to homosexuality and paederasty. In the absence of any restrictions on democracy it adopts the path stated above in the example of the British Parliament. So the best procedure is to make democracy subservient to some eternal principles. What are those principles? In Iqbal's view they are the principles established by the code of life of Islam, i.e. the Holy Qur'an. It is essential to place the basic foundation of Islamic democracy on the creed of its faith in prophethood, the firm belief in life after death and accountability for deeds, and this is that three-sided restriction which can protect democracy from going astray, and simultaneously fulfilling the needs of the present age, can stop it from

The Social Philosophy of Iqbal

apostacy. In the same way Iqbal wants to keep the state in close relationship with *deen,* because in his view, without this the State becomes a fountain of perversity instead of being a source of virtue.

"What is the difference if the reigns of government are in the hands of the bourgiosie?

The system of the bourgiosie is the same as that of the imperialists.

"It may be the majesty of kingship or the mockery of democracy

If religion is separated from politics the latter becomes mere tyranny."

Here the concept of *deen* itself needs some explanation. In our society the concept of *deen* has been restricted to the priest calling the *azan*[26] into the new born baby's ears, performing of the wedding ceremony at puberty and conducting the funerals prayers after death. However, the social of *mazhab* and *deen is* much wider than this. 1f we look at the social life and the *mazhab* and *deen* during the Holy Prophet's time the fact cannot be denied that the *deen* during the Holy Prophet's time on the citizens of Medina was really a way of life, the acceptance of which revolutionized their social, intellectual, ethical and political affairs. Islam during the Holy Prophet's time addressed the problems of that civilization and society, presented its point of view and guided the individual as well as the society in finding their solution. During that period Islam did not comprise only some beliefs and methods of worship, but was a code which used to affect their very lives in every way and, entering their affairs strived to straighten them. Every aspect of Holy Prophet's life at Mecca as well as at Medina shows an enlightening way of thinking about the social, ethical and political problems of the times, and was a constant guide. The Holy Prophet had included the righteous *deen* of Islam in every problem of the individual and the State. The study of Islamic and specially the Qur'anic education will show its pervasiveness over the entire life. Iqbal had a concept of *deen* vibrating with life and acting as a lodestar. The *deen* preached today is not that of the Holy Prophet. He had instructed people to style their lives completely in the Islamic fashion.

"Enter the Islam completely" (Qur'an)

Understanding Iqbal's Philosophy

Unlike Christianity and Hinduism Islam is not a *mazhab,* but, like communism, is a system of life, which fixes the positions of the individual and the society as well as presents a viewpoint on their mutual relationship. Consequently, a person cannot be called a Muslim unless he enters the Islamic precincts completely.

Now, by considering the relationship between the individual and society the truth will dawn on you that in the view of Iqbal both the individual and the society are important, both have high positions and are inseparable from cacti other. Aristotle[27] has called Man a social animal.

This means that one cannot live his life in isolation. He needs mutual cooperation for fulfilling the needs of his life and for keeping it progressive. The individual and society are essential and under obligation to each other and society are essential and under obligation to each other for their existence and development. Some social philosophers emphasize the protection of the person's individual ego and that of his wishes, ambitions and longings. According to them the individual's individuality should not be sacrificed at the altar of society and should be safe and secure at all costs. For this reason they do not favour the present day society and individualism, because the individual has been effaced in the overtones of the society, although the individual himself is the society on which society self depends. He has been fettered by society and community everywhere. How rightly has Rousseau[28] said "Man is born free but is fettered everywhere."

These chains are those of customs and rites and the present day man is groaning under the bondage of society and civilization. The realists had protested against these very chains on mankind and had tried to exhibit and protect the individual's individuality. They called everything absurd and defective which had throttled the subjectivity of the individual. But complete freedom of the individual from all manner of social restrictions will also not be conducive to the survival of society. The tragedy of the present age is the desire of every individual to enjoy his rights but still be free of responsibilities. A society cannot survive unless its members adopt a responsible attitude in sharing their rights and obligations, which may promote the society. The society also, falling a prey to stalemate, dies a slow death when it is deprived of the upbringing of both and ceases to perform the duty of strengthening the individual's worth, capabilities and potentials. Consequently, Iqbal wants to create a society where the individuals work for society's stability and the where the individuals work

The Social Philosophy of Iqbal

for society's stability and the society may engage itself in the training and education of the individual and in promoting happiness and bliss for them. Iqbal presents something unique about society and its organizational institutions, i.e. the State. In his view it is essential for the State to be endowed with high ideals, i.e. the State is the reflection of on Unity of God. So the objective of the State is the creation of a system which we can call the reflection of the Unity of God. Just as Iqbal emphasizes the individual's relationship with God and adjudges the individual to be the picture of God's elegance, he wants to see his society and State to be the reflection of Divine Attributes. To him only such a society and such a State can be considered exemplary, which would have the beauty of the Divine countenance and Attributes both from the viewpoint of the individual as well as that of society.

Iqbal has talked about different social institutions also in his social philosophy. he regarded woman as a colour in the picture of the universe, and equal to man in rights. He was desirous of seeing woman as an active member of the present day society. He considered current system of isolation of women unnecessary. Nevertheles he wanted protection of the woman's virtues at any cost, so that the Muslim society leave her active in here special fields of activity, instead of dragging her in every walk of life in their apish pursuit of a ways of the West. This was so, because society would not be able to remain secure if the woman abandoned her special fields. Similarly, lqbal's views about education was that education has two basic goals. One is the upbringing of the individual, promoting his creative potentials and enabling him to comprehend the inner secrets of his life and existence as well as those of the universe. The other goal is to endow him with the understanding of community's needs and demands, so as to enable it to make adequate contribution to the vast cultural heritage of mankind and be a message of happiness to the human society.

Iqbal considered a living society to be the reflection of the social, cultural, economic, ethical and scientific tendencies of its own time. It builds its foundation on the benefits resulting from the technology, social changes, cultural concepts, intellectual reasoning, psychological movement.-. and special religious beliefs of its time. Iqbal wanted the Muslim society also to benefit from the twentieth century's scientific, economic and social acquisitions, to avoid the dark aspects of the new civilization and adopt its bright aspects. However, Iqbal did not accept that an exemplary society could he formed only by totally aping the present day European civilization and its beliefs. He considered faith in the concept of the unity of God, and the resurrection preached by the Holy Qur'an and Islam as unavoidable for this purpose. In his view only the realization of accountability and a Divine power can keep a society pious. Iqbal considered the Qur'anic concept of economic justice and social equality to be the only solution for the concept of internationalism, fromation of the World State, liberation from the horrors of wars, economic depression, unemployment and the universal psychological unrest of the present day world.

Foot Notes

(1). The *Asharites* are a branch of early Muslim thinkers and are followers of Abul Hasan Ali Ibn Ismail al-Ashari (873-935)

(2). Abu Hamid Muhammad Ghazali (1030-1111 C.E.)
The Asharites as well as Imam Ghazali's thinking is based on what is now termed 'fundamentalism'. i.e. a belief in the absolute correctness of the Holy Qur'an and the authentic sayings of the Holy Prophet. They strived to cleanse the crystal of Islamic thought of the taint of Greek philosophy. For more details see the following references:

Muslehuddin, Muhammad (1984) - *Islam, Its Theology and Greek Philosophy* (Second Edition). Published by The Islamic Publications Ltd., Lahore, Pakistan: Appendices A and B respectively, and

Nadvi, Muhammyad Hanif (1956) - *Afkar-i-Ghazali*. Published by the Idara-i-Thaqafat-i-lslamia, Lahore, Pakistan.

(3). *Deen* and *Mazhab* are often interchangeable used and variously translated into English, which gives the false impression of their synonymity. However, in Islamic literature they are used as technical terms and are not synonymous. *Deen* means a way of life, covering all human activity in which sense Islam is a *deen* or a way of life based on the Holy Qur'an and the traditions of they Holy Prophet. *Mazhab* is one of the five recognized *fiqh* systems or systems of Islamic jurisprudence.

(4). The 'Ad people are famous in Arab tradition, according to which their eponymous ancestor ('Ad) was fourth in generation from the prophet Nuh. They lived over a vast tract of land in Southern Arabia extending from Oman to Hadhramaut.

(5). The Thamud people are also a part of Arab tradition, according to which their eponymous ancestor was the third in generation from the prophet Nuh. They were cousins of the Ad people and occupied the north west corner of the Arabian peninsula.

Both these people are referred to in the Holy Qur'an as those who incurred God's wrath on account of their materialism and deviation from the path of God.

(6). The name of Jews used in the Holy Qur'an.

(7). Henri Bergson (1859-1941). French philosopher and Nobel Prize winner in literature in 1927. He was one of the most influential but controversial thinkers of the 20th century in spite of being a lucid writer with suggestive powers. The root belief of his philosophy is that the ultimate reality is a vital impulse, whose nature can be grasped only by a mind capable of transcending the limits of intellect. Though science can provide useful generalizations concerning the nature of the universe, only philosophy, based on the "immediate data of consciousness" can give absolute knowledge of the nature of real time, change, creation and human freedom.

(8). *Zat is* the Essence or the Nature of God as distinct from His *Wujud* or Being, and *Sifat* or Attributes.

(9). George Bernard Shaw (1856-1950) British playwright, litterateur, socialist pamphleteer and lecturer. He was one of the most influential figures in contemporary literature and won the Nobel Prize in 1926. He is most famous as a playwright and produced 50 plays, many of which are among the classics of Western theatre. He was very unconventional. His plays combine wit and satire on contemporary society.

(10). The Holy Qur'an 24:35.

(11). Albert Einstein (1879-1955) - He is considered one of the greatest physicists of the 20th century. He taught at several German universities and technological institutions, and in 1933 he accepted a position at the Princeton Institute of Advanced Studies, which he occupied till his death. He is most famous for laying the foundations of the Theory of Relativity (1915), though his work covers Brownian movement (1905), and photo-electric effect of quantum mechanics (c.a. 1910). He won the Nobel Prize in 1921.

(12). *Mard-i-Kamil* The perfect man. One who has realized his full potential as a servant of God *(Khudi)*. The highest iealised model of *Mard-i-Kamil* is the Holy Prophet

(13). *Mard-i-Mimin* - The true believer in and follower of the Holy Qur'an and the traditions of the Holy Prophet.

(14). Friedrich Wilhelm Nietzsche (1844-1900). Though he is famous as a German philosopher he was a very multi-dimensional personality - university professor, civil servant, medical orderly and even became insane at the end of his life. He is the author of many books, of which the most celebrated is *Also Sprach Zarathustra* (Thus Spoke Zarathustra), published in 1892. He was against the other-worldliness of Christianity. He held that what men want most is power over self and creative mastery. He preached that the "other world" is an illusion, and instead of worshipping God who lives in an which he called *Uebermensch* or Superman for which philosophy he is famous. The Nazis made use of this thought to develop their philosophy of life and politics which produced Adolf Hitler and his followers.

(15). The Holy Qur'an 3:14.

(16). His Eminence, The Chief of the Universe. This is a respectful title of the Holy Prophet.

(17). The Holy Qur'an 95:1-8.

(18). *Karamallahu Wajhohu* (May God look at his face with His Mercy). This is an expression of respect used for Hazrat-i-Ali.

(19). "Beware of dissensions because a stray person is the portion of the Satan, just as the stray goat is the portion of the wolf."

(20). Immanuel Kant (1724-1804) - Famous German philosopher. In spite of financial difficulties and interruptions in his education and writing work he became prominent and held several academic and administrative positions, and became the Rector of the University of Koenigsberg. Though he was a prolific writer on philosophy his two most celebrated and

The Social Philosophy of Iqbal

quoted books are *Critique of Pure Reason* (1791) and *Critique of Practical Reason* (1788).

(21). George William Frederich Hegel (1770-1831) - He is a famous German philosopher and the last in a succession of four (Kant, Fichte, and Schelling) who, in the latter part of the 18th century and the first quarter of the 19th century, developed the idealistic philosophy of Germany. He was an idealist, i.e. he believed that we must ultimately explain the universe as the manifestation of a rational principle. He maintained that the universe of objects (material universe) is not only related to an Intelligence, but that it can be nothing but the manifestation of that Intelligence. He believed in evolution on the basis of the concept of the survival of the fittest, i.e. the concept of a continuous struggle, confrontation, wrangle and combat.

(22) *Zakat* - A system in Islamic economics in which a tax is levied on the property of a person in excess of the prescribed limits. The proceeds of this tax are used exclusively for the financial support of the indigent.

(23). Karl Marx (1818-1883) - He is the famous German economist, originator of communism and the author of *Das Kapital*, in which he has argued against private property and has explained communism.

(24). Socrates (Fifth century B.C.) - He is a famous ancient Greek philosopher. He believed that to know one's self is a more pressing task than to know about nature. He claimed hearing a "divine voice", frequently, which gave him guidance to act or not to act. This is very controversial and several conjectures have been presented to explain it. His religious beliefs differed from these of the State religion of Athens, for which he had to drink the famous cup of hemlock rather than compromise his beliefs. The Socratic method, named after him dialectic, consists of question and answer.

(25). Lord Bertrand Arthur William Russell (1872-1970) British philosopher and mathematician. In his own words "Three passions, simple but overwhelmingly strong, have governed my life: the longing for love, the search for knowledge and unbearable pity for the suffering of mankind". He was most actively interested in social and political problems. Though in his youth he was a socialist and member of the Fabian Society but he was as much disappointed with Russian communism as he was with Western capitalism and imperialism.

(26) *Azan* - The Muslim's call to prayer, which publicly testifies to the Unity of God and the prophethood of Muhammad.

(27). Aristotle (384-322 B.C.) - A Greek philosopher and a pupil of Plato. Most of Aristotle's literary productions have perished, making it difficult to compass his philosophy. Aristotle differed from Plato in that he based his philosophy on observations of the physical universe, while Plato hated it on account of its ephemeral character. He also differeed from Plato in regarding the physical universe as complete and

(28). J. J Rousseau (1712-78) - A French political philosopher and author. He was perhaps the most influential person in French literature and philosophy. He wrote many books, of which *Social Contract* and *Confessions* and *What I Believe* are famous.

Chapter 7

RECONSTRUCTION OF ISLAMIC THOUGHT

In spite of the widely accepted importance of Iqbal's *Lectures* titled *The Reconstruction of Religious Thought in Islam*, in the field of Iqbal Studies, the works published on it are very limited. Only a few books have been written with reference to the *Lectures*. This is due firstly to the fact that the *Lectures* are in English language and, secondly, they address profound literary and philosophical problems. The language of literary and philosophical problems is usually more difficult and delicate than the common language, which renders their comprehension difficult for the average reader. Consequently, the average researchers shy away from this serious responsibility. In addition, *The Reconstruction of Religious Thought in Islam* is a book which is one of the greatest importance among those written after the period of our downfall. It leads us to comprehension of the spirit of our cultural and civilizational progress and the basic causes of our decademe as well as points out to us the ways of understanding the requirements of the new age and the reconstruction of our present and future and shows us the principles on which our renaissance is possible. After studying the Western civilization and phenomenon of our downfall with deep insight Iqbal has raised questions in this book, on the answer to which depends the shaping of our present and future collective well being. It is obvious that these basic questions and their answers are such delicate subjects that attempting their solution is very difficult. The new book of Professor Muhammad Uthman, *Fikr-i-Islami kee Tashkil-i-Nau* (The Reorganization of Islamic Thought) is a bold and thought-provoking book on the *Lectures* of Iqbal whose review is the subject of this paper.

Several other books are also available in Urdu about *The Reconstruction of Religious Thought in Islam*. Included among these are: *Khutbat-i-Iqbal per Eik Nazar* (A Glance at Iqbal's *Lectures*) by Muhammad Sharif Baqa, a book of the same name by the distinguished theologian Maulana Saeed Ahmad Akbarabadi and the *Muta'alliqat Khutbat-i-Iqbal per Eik Nazar* (A Glance at the Matters Concerning Iqbal's *Lectures*) by Dr. Syed Muhammad Abdullah. In addition to these Dr. Khalifah Abd al-Hakim, has given an abstract of these *Lectures* at the end of his book *Fikr-i-Iqbal* (Iqbal's Thought).

Understanding Iqbal's Philosophy

All these works, though admirable and conducive to a good comprehension of Iqbal, do not amount to much with reference to a book of the calibre of the *Lectures*. The truth is that the work on Iqbal's *Lectures* does not at all equal in authenticity the work on his verse. Consequently, till now, despite its defects and shortcomings, the translation of the late Syed Nazir Niazi *Tashkil-i Jadid Ilahiyat - i - Islamiyah* (The Reconstruction of Religious Thought in Islam) is the only available source for study of the *Lectures* to some extent for the Urdu readership. Mir Hasan al-Din had translated one or two *Lectures* but that also could not be completed which restricts its utility. The abstracts of the *Lectures* prepared by Dr. Khalifah Abu al-Hakim is not very useful.' It does not create anything except misunderstanding and confusion in the comprehension of Iqbal. It can only create a superficial understanding about the *Lectures* in students. It does not even create an interest for study of the *Lectures*.

The book of Muhammad Sharif Baqa, *Khutbat-i-Iqbal per Eik Nazar* (A Glance at the *Lectures* of Iqbal) is a good introduction to the titles and subjects of the *Lectures*. However, it has neither reached the depth of the *Lectures* nor has done justice to its subjects initiated by the Iqbal. At best it can be regarded as a student's effort. In reality it must be admitted that even the utility of the *Lectures* has not been understood. These *Lectures* are spread over the vast canvas of the religious, intellectual, theological, political and practical problems created for the Muslims in the evolution of the new life in the Indian subcontinent and the Muslim world, and by the continuous struggle between them and the West. In the whole Islamic world the basic challenges faced by religion itself and by the Muslim *Ummah* for its existence and continuity have been addressed in the background of Islam and its relationship with the West by Iqbal in an unprecedented manner. This was due to the fact that in the Indian subcontinent the *'Ulema* understood Islam only with the perception of a special traditional system. Most of the eminent *'Ulema* were only good teachers in religious seminaries, but totally lacked the perception of the current thought and the political, social and economic problems confronting Muslims. In fact the conduct of some of them proved detrimental to the Muslim independence movements by knowingly or unknowingly continuing to play in the hands of the powers operating against the Muslim interests. These *'Ulema* were ignorant of the advancements of the Western philosophy, Western theology, new psychology and new technology. In contrast to them the new educated mind was adopting the Western ways completely. The changes continuously created by the slow and insidious hold of the Western

Reconstruction of Islamic Thought

civilization on the cultural, political and ethical life of Muslims under the guise of new technology, seriously affected the collective life of Muslims. The greater number of our *'Ulema* could not comprehend this state of affairs, and failed to understand the special nature of the problems facing the Muslims in the present day world. Consequently, the demands of life have continued to pull Muslims towards Western culture and have been consistently creating uncertainty and doubt against religion itself and particularly Islam even in the face of the preaching and edicts of the *'Ulema*. The modern-minded class of Egypt, Turkey and the Indian subcontinent itself was offering such explanations of Islamic teachings as reflected the lack of ambition and indicated submission to the Western culture as well as ignorance of both Islam and Western culture. In these circumstances Iqbal formulated some basic questions with the background of Western philosophy and Islamic theology. In this way, with reference to the spirit of their times, the Muslim *Ummah*, particularly those of the Indian subcontinent became aware of these basic questions, the answers to which were essential for the organization of the Muslims' new social, cultural, political and economic life. Iqbal was the first to raise these questions in the Muslim society. In the history of philosophy the answers often have not been considered as important as the questions. This is so because the formulation of a question gives birth to new intellectual discussions which lead the human mind to new fields of knowledge and opens new dimensions of vision. It is these questions which lead to the rise and evolution of knowledge. Iqbal understood the spirit of his time and raised new intellectual questions with the background of the basic customs of his time. Even if Iqbal had not offered answers to these questions he would have enjoyed unique eminence. But the greatness of Iqbal lies in his not leaving these questions hanging in the air and tried to provide their answers with serious thought and deep insight. These *Lectures* of Iqbal area mirror of our national perceptions. Again, as Iqbal himself has said in the "Preface" to the *Lectures* that:

"It must, however, be remembered that there is no such thing as finality in philosophical thinkings. As knowledge advances and fresh avenues of thought are opened, other views, and probably sounder views than those set forth in these lectures are possible".

We neither do nor should insist on the finality of the thoughts presented in the *Lectures*. On the other hand, as said by Iqbal in the above reference:

Understanding Iqbal's Philosophy

"Our duty is carefully to watch the progress of human thought, and to maintain an independent critical attitude towards it".

This means that just as Iqbal viewed the Islamic and Western knowledge with due regard to the growth and development of human thought in his own age we should also keep a careful eye one the growth and development of human thought of our own times, and should organize the perceptions of today in the light of Iqbal's scientific and intellectual conclusions. The conclusions of the nineteenth century physics brought about the destruction of religion and old theories by attacking them in such a manner as created an intellectual stampede in the realm of old theories and religion. As religion was attacked and criticized by Freud through psychology, by Marx through economics, by the Vienna Circle through linguistics, by Darwin through biology and by Kant, Hume, Locke and Berkeley through experimentalism and was equated with mythology and evolution of Voodooism by George Fraser the whole world witnessed the insult of religion. This led to the concept that religion was nothing more than some blind beliefs, and an unintellectual and illogical labyrinth of some rituals, which might have been somewhat useful for man in the medieval times, but was only an obstacle on the road to progress and an instrument of oppression in the hands of the strong against the week. The critics of religion used this self-made testimony of physics against religion. However, in the twentieth century, as physics itself started contradicting its own basic theories and affirmation of some fundamental axioms of religion Iqbal, arguing from the fallacies of the claims of classical physics and support of the claims of religion through modern physics for the confirmation of the beliefs of religion, established the rationality and acceptability of the truths of religion on the basis of the existence of concordance between religion, physics and other sciences. thus, he took the stand that "by carefully watching the progress of human thought" we can create new angles of vision for the truth of religion.

By far and large our scholars have studied the *Lectures* without taking the trouble of understanding the basic problems by pondering over this basic stand and way of thought of Iqbal, and without identifying the basics of Iqbal's thought, the various subjects and problems of the *Lectures* have been viewed only in a cursory way.

A well-known book of the late Mawlana Saeed Ahmad Akbarabadi known as *Khutbat-i-Iqbal per Eik Nazar* (A Glance at the *Lectures* of Iqbal) has been published by the Iqbal Institute, Srinagar, Kashmir. the

Reconstruction of Islamic Thought

erudition of the author is widely accepted but the conclusion is imperative that the method adopted by him in the explanation and appreciation of the *Lectures* of Iqbal stands on very weak ground. According to him Iqbal's *Lectures* amount to be the theology of the modern age and this theology is far superior, firmer and better promoter of faith and insight than the classical theology. Careful examination will show Iqbal's theology to be only an extension and continuation of the classical theology. Actually it must be said that it was the theology of Plotinus and his predecessor the Jewish philosopher Philo, whose theology provided the rational foundation for finding concordance between Islam and Greek philosophy to al-Kindi, al-Farabi, Ibn-i-Rushd and other Muslim theologians. Earlier Muslim theologians continued to establish concordance between Islam and Greek philosophy. Sir Syed found concordance between Islam and naturalism which was the prominent thought of his time the same concordance appears to us as a way of thought in the *Lectures* also the requirements of every age call for the rationalization of old theories and thought. Confucius used to call this 'presenting old wine in new bottles'. By establishing concordance between the physics, science, technology, modern psychology, biology and sociology of his age with Islamic beliefs Iqbal established the rationale for religion. Iqbal's theology is not different form that of his predecessors in spirit. The Mawlana has presented three arguments for distinguishing Iqbal's theology from that of his predecessors, however, he does not support his hypothesis, but attests that this hypothesis has been advanced in poetic high sounding language in a hurry without rationality. Iqbal himself nither claimed this nor this eminence needed such irrational claims. In addition, the discussions on the various subjects of the *Lectures* is so short, ambiguous and incomprehensive that it could not do justice to Iqbal. These important and serious discussions could not be conducted in such a cursory manner. In fact, on reading this book mind becomes confused about Iqbal's *Lectures*. The attitude of Mawlana Saeed Ahmad Akbarabadi is unnecessary praise of the at some places and is apologetic at others. Would that he had viewed the Iqbal's discussions within the vast expanse of Islamic theology and had pointed out these discussions in the history of Islamic theology, which would have facilitated the understanding of Iqbal's discussions with reference to the traditions of Muslims theology. Like Dr. Muhammad Alba'hi of Egypt. Mawlana has also shown some differences with Iqbal. Though a detailed discussion of these is not possible here the objections of Muhammad Alba'hi betray lack of comprehension of Iqbal. The support which the Iqbal provided to every movement created in the Islamic world was a demand of the times, because the start and growth of any movement

Understanding Iqbal's Philosophy

anywhere in the down-trodden and suppressed Muslim world was in itself a great matter. Every action which could motivate Muslims was laudable to Iqbal. Its being appropriate or otherwise was of less importance at that time. Later, if this movement started drifting form its path Iqbal would point out that also. The objection of Muhammad Alba'hi had resulted from a lack of understanding of the state of affairs created by colonialism. Instead of clarifying the correct position of Iqbal, Mawlana has thrown his weight also in favor of Muhammad Alba'hi. Thus, this book is the result of an incomplete effort.

With reference to the *Lectures* of Iqbal the book compiled by Dr. Syed Abdullah, titled *Muta'allaqat-i-Khutbat-i-Iqbal* (About Iqbal) is also a very well-known book. Included in this book are "*Iqbal awr Dini tajrubah*" (Iqbal and Religious Experience) by 'Abd al-Hafiz Kardar, "*Allamah Iqbal ka Junubi Hind ka Safar*" (The Trip of Iqbal to South India) by Dr. 'Abd Allah Chaghatai, "A'alam-i-Khutubat-i-Iqbal" By Dr. Ghulam Husain Zulfiqar, "Allamah Iqbal ka Tasawwar-i-Taqdir" (Allamah Iqbal's Concept of Destiny) by Muhammad Munawwar, *(Iqbal ka Tasawwar-i-Baqa-i-Dwam"* (Iqbal's Concept of Eternity) by Muzaffar Husain, "*Khutbat Main Ulamah-i-Islam kay Havalay*" (References to the Philosophers of Islam in the *Lectures*), "Iqbal our Fakhr al-Din Razi" (*Iqbal and Razi*) by Dr. Amin Allah Wasir, the "*New Gulshan-i-Raz jadid Khutubat kay Aienay Main*" (The New Secret Rose-garden in the Mirror of the *Lectures*), and "*Iqbal awr Shabistari*" (Iqbal and Shabistari) by Dr. Saiyyid 'Abd Allah. The papers of Professor Muhammad Munawwar. Muzaffar Husain Chaudhry and Abd al-Hafiz Kardar are important with reference to the subject matter of Iqbal's *Lectures*, while those of Syed Abdullah, Abd Allah Qureshi, Amin Allah Wasir and Dr. Ghulam Husain Zulfiqar cover the introductions to and histories of the personalities of the *Lectures*. Some discussions in this book are admirable. Though the purpose of the *Lectures* that can be discerned in this book its effect is blurred and unclear on account of the book having been written and compiled without any solid theme. It does not provide satisfactory guidance for the comprehension of the *Lectures*.

In the background of all this work we want to review Muhammad Uthman's book. *Fikr-i-Islami kee Tashkil-i-Naw* (The Restatement of Islamic Thought) and study its special features.

Muhammad Uthman was a well - known specialist of Iqbal Studies. The *Hayat-i-Iqbal ka Jazbati Dawr* (The Emotional Phase of Iqbal's Life)

Reconstruction of Islamic Thought

and *Asrar-u-Rumuz per eik Nazar* (A Glance at the *Asrar-u-Rumuz*) or Iqbal's philosophy of *Khudi* are admirable works. His point of view in the study of Iqbal is not abstract but practical and applied. He has always seen and shown Iqbal as a man down to earth, living, having feelings and a real life. He is shown as man of life and blood who becomes a victim of disappointments in adversity and is happy in prosperity. The Iqbal of Muhammad Uthman is an Iqbal full of life and away from the limitations of creeds.

Two characteristics of *Fikr-i-Islami* are very prominent. Though it is not lacking in errors of proof-reading and existence of unfilled blank spaces left for the English equivalents at some places this book is an example of its good calligraphy and beautiful printing on high quality paper. The efforts of both the author and the publisher in this direction are admirable. The second quality of this book is its simple and easy language. Muhammad Uthman by presenting elegant subjects and discussions in extremely easy and simple language has brought the lovers of Iqbal studies so close to these *Lectures* that even a person of average education can read and understand very easily the subjects and discussions of the *Lectures*. Now these *Lectures* of Iqbal are no longer the 'prohibited tree' for the average person. This work is so basic that Muhammad Uthman deserves all praise. The title of each lecture is on the lines of the titles established by Iqbal. He has offered elucidation of each lecture separately. In this way the Professor Uthman has adopted the style of interpretation instead of translation. It can be said with confidence that Muhammad Uthman has first pondered over each lecture, has fixed its contents and has then briefly described the contents of each lecture. In such works the author usually interjects his own opinions freely, but Muhammad Uthman has explained and interpreted the *Lectures* objectively rather than subjectively, in which he has been successful. Thus, this book deserves the best attention out of those written for understanding the *Lectures*. At several places Muhammad Uthman has also made an effort to describe the purport of Iqbal in detail and in conformity with the modern style and methods. Here also the style of the author is one of understanding and explaining Iqbal. Muhammad Uthman has also written a comprehensive preface himself before writing the interpretation, which is very important is itself. It shows the depth of vision of the Professor on these *Lectures*.

Simultaneously with these qualities one cannot help noting shortcomings at some places and feeling that in each lecture there is need for some more discussion of some subjects. Though such feeling is possible for any book but it is felt this book for more than one reason and in more than one way. This is so because if rendering of the *Lectures* in easy language was aimed at that aim has been achieved but if the understanding of the *Lectures* was the object it leaves scope for more explanation on many subjects which appear during the study of these *Lectures* and no work on them has appeared so far. It will also be appropriate to mention here parenthetically that in the beginning of the first lecture the occult incident related by him about his early life does not find a solid reference. This is so because it neither resembles a prophet's spiritual experience nor has any relationship with a saint's inner events. The basic question raised by Iqbal in this first lecture itself needs attention and explanation. Merely saying that "Yet it cannot be denied that faith is more than mere feeling. It has something like a cognitive content" is an incomplete assertion till, by establishing the nature of intellect in religion, we bring into human understanding an entity which would make spiritual experience verifiable like other experiences of science and social learning. How can an experience which cannot be verified and tested objectively be moulded into the form of a science? In any case, the reason for this ambiguity appears to be that the true nature of spiritual experience could not be defined as to the sense in which it is objective. It was necessary to explain the concept of the component of intellect in religion. In the same way Iqbal has adjudged Islam as the expression of the inductive reason but nothing is known about the state of inductive reason in Islam. Also, the question arises as to why Islam is against deductive intellect when the source of knowledge is not entirely induction but is composed of both the ways, i.e. deductive and inductive knowledge.

Again, calling only deduction to be the cause of Islam's decline and basing all hopes on induction for the renaissance of Islam betrays undue criticism of deduction and unnecessary dependence on induction which is a dilemma which can give birth to many new confusions.

How deduction has weakened Islam and the reason for its being not in concordance with the disposition of Islam are important question. The majority of Muslim theologians were not independent in their intellectual conclusions form the Greek deduction. Is it not an intellectual fallacy to base the foundation of knowledge on induction? The Holy Qur'an stresses the need for the study of the universe on the basis of both induction and deduction. Many examples of this can be presented form the Holy Qur'an. To adjudge pure induction as the source of knowledge is itself only half truth. The other half truth is that ignoring deduction amounts to repetition

Reconstruction of Islamic Thought

of the same delusion as that of the supporters of deduction about induction. It is also not permissible to adjudge pure induction as the foundation of modern knowledge and science. Both modern knowledge and science use deduction as well as induction in arriving at intellectual inferences. However, this subject will be discussed in detail at some other place as to the results of this logical delusion in the *Lectures*. The same kind of logical delusion has been created by the supposition that if the Islamic education had evolved and developed on the path of induction it would have taken the place of the new European civilization. The first point has been explained above that the Islamic civilization would not have reached its climax merely by induction. Secondly, it has also been supposed that the modern European civilization has reached some climax. If mere acquisition of technology is considered as civilization muslims can reach the stage of the Western civilization with mere technology. But is not technology only a part of civilization? Also, is acquiring technology the climax of civilization even in spite of the havoc created by it? technology has imprisoned man in conditions of fear, terror, starvation, disease and war to a much greater extent than the services it has rendered to him. This is due to the fact that technology, which we are adopting, considering it the climax of European civilization, being deprived of balance is under the influence of blind mechanization, and man is standing on the pyramid of these destructive armaments. Would the Islamic civilization have reached the same climax with induction? To adjudge the Western civilization as an evolved form of Islamic civilization is also a notional delusion and a very dangerous one, because it has given birth to the thinking in the Islamic world that adoption of the European civilization, together with faith in God and the Holy Prophet will attain the objectives of the Islamic civilization. This notional delusion has made the Muslim intellect a victim of Western civilization. The intellect based on induction will arrive at the same conclusion when passing through more stages of evolution. This onesidedness of thought will lead to similar inferences. Muhammad Uthman has missed this and several similar problems and questions. He has not brought his intellect into play to express any opinion on several such subjects emanating frogs the background and foreground of the *Lectures*. These controversies have been presented as a sample, otherwise Iqbal's *Lectures is* a ocean concerning which such questions have arisen and can be raised with reference to the identification of our cultural and civilizational identity which can create a new insight.

Similarly, the standard of attaining results for prophets set by Iqbal may be somewhat comprehensible if considered with the interpretation that Iqbal has set this standard only for the prophets with a book. If the standard of results be applied as roof for every prophet's prophethood it will be impossible for every prop to measure up to such a standard. This is so because innumerable prophets were killed immediately on claiming prophethood without the results of their prophethood making appearance. Their prophethood has been attested by some prophet succeeding them. Here the question rises whether prophethood itself has been attested by some prophet succeeding them. Here the question rises whether prophethood itself has ever proposed this standard for its attestation. It is difficult to answer this question in the affirmative. In the same way in the matter of the "Termination of Prophethood" the question remains unanswered whether the human intellect has reached the stage at which it can fix its own path and whether this argument is sufficient for "Termination of Prophethood"? The other question is about the nature of the principle established by Iqbal about spiritual democracy and spiritual purification of the individual. What is the form of this spiritual democracy?

In the same way the question of conferring the right, of *Ijtihad* on parliament following the example of Turkey deserves consideration. This is so because extinguishing the individual's right of *Ijtihad* and conferring it on parliament raises the question about the parliament's capability. The question also rises whether parliament can bridle the selfish motives of the ruling classes. In view of all this what is the assurance for the correct use of the right of *Ijtihad* by the parliament it is appropriate not to extinguish the individual's right of *Ijtihad*. This is so because often such eminent personalities can have the compelling power of keeping the ruling classes on the right track. Also making parliament the law-giver will create a form of theocracy whose eradication has always remained the distinctive feature of Islam. Similarly, Muhammad Uthman could bring under discussion such and several other questions in the interpretation of the *Lectures*. However, as the impossibility of discussing all subjects in one book is well known some very important questions have been left undiscussed in his book also. Muhammad Uthman could be expected to bring under discussion numerous questions of this nature. It is quite possible that he will include these matters in some other forthcoming book of his. Still, notwithstanding the serious feeling of incompleteness the present book can be regarded a good effort and a helpful guide in the comprehension of Iqbal.

Chapter 8

IQBAL AND DEMOCRACY

Introduction

Even apart from Iqbal's concepts democracy is a controversial subject which needs viewing with deep insight. Evidence exists in Iqbal's verse as well as prose which gives the impression of his strong opposition to the concept of democracy. Iqbal was a particularly strong critic of the present day commonly held concepts of Western democracy. As Iqbal has pointed out several basic defects of the Western concept of democracy it would be appropriate to clarify that he was against the well known and widely understood Western concept of democracy only. This also was with special reference to the conditions prevailing in the Indian sub-continent, where the Muslims were a minority and the Hindus a majority. In opposing the Western concept of democracy Iqbal also had the fact in view that the promulgation of the Western democratic system In undivided India, with Muslim minority and Hindu majority, would result In perpetual political power for the Hindu majority and slavery for the Muslim minority. This fact should not be ignored in connection with Iqbal's opposition to democracy. Still, the question arises whether the unaltered Western democratic system was acceptable in a new, Islamic society outside the mixed Muslim and non-Muslim society. Iqbal's reply to this also is almost in the negative. However, the system of government which Iqbal considers indispensable for the spiritual freedom of Muslims, according to the concept of *Ijtihad* and "spiritual democracy" has the Islamic democratic consultation as its foundation and spirit. Sovereignty belongs to the people in Western democracy and they are answerable to none except themselves. As opposed to this, sovereignty in Iqbal's "spiritual democracy" befits God alone. The Muslims are its guardians by virtue of being God's Vicegerents. They are empowered to establish an Institution, by mutual consultation, some form of election, or by vote, In the present day parlance, for the administration of their affairs, in conformity with the dictates of God and Holy Prophet. In this way, based on the Islamic concept of consultation, Iqbal strongly supports the establishment of a parliament or consultative assembly for the Muslim society, elected by the majority of Muslims. This assembly would produce new interpretations or *Ijtihad* in conformity with the demands of the present age, so as to bring justice and prosperity to the Muslim society and harmonize them with the demands of the present age. This is the basic point of the "spiritual democracy' of Iqbal. We explain below the basic concepts with reference to Muhammad Iqbal.

What is Democracy?

In the commonly known Western sense democracy is a system of government in which sovereignty belongs to the people and the legislature is created by their majority opinion, which is obtained through votes. This legislature is the highest legislative organization of the country. Mawlana Muhammad Hanif Nadvi explains democracy thus:

"Democracy is composed of two Greek components; one means the people and the other means government and law. Technically, It is applied to a system of government in which the greatest number of people participate".[1]

The Encyclopedia of Philosophy explains the concept of democracy thus:-

"The correct meaning of democracy is that this is a form of government in which citizens have the direct collective right of political decisions, and the principle of the rule of the majority is accepted as the law. This is called direct democracy. Secondly, It is the system of government In which people do not exercise political rights Individually but through elected representatives and the latter are responsible to them. This is called representative democracy. Thirdly, this is a form of government which is generally representative democracy but the powers and activities of the majority operate within a special Institutional framework, which is constitutionally so framed as to allow people to enjoy their collective and individual rights. These rights relate to freedom of expression and religion. This is called balanced or constitutional democracy. Fourthly, the word democracy is also used for the political and social characteristics of a system which are not covered by the above mentioned three definitions of democracy, but which do aim at eliminating economic and social distinctions, especially the distinctions resulting from the right of individual ownership and distribution of wealth. This is called social and economic democracy".[2]

Dr. Khalifah Abdul Hakim in his book titled, *Fikr-i-Iqbal* (The Thought of Iqbal) considers democracy to be an ambiguous concept like many other social concepts. He says:

"Democracy is also like those ambiguous concepts which have no meaning. In the present day world every nation desires for and 'strives to establish democracy, or claims to be the custodian of the correct democracy, and considers the claims to other forms of democracy baseless and imposturous".[3]

However, notwithstanding the various ambiguities about democracy it has the basic attribute that "The most common meaning of democracy, which appears to be acceptable to all, is that no Individual or class rules over the people against their will".[4] Further explaining this Hakim says:

"Democracy is a system in which sovereignty should not belong to the king or the rich, the reins of government should be controlled neither by the feudal lords nor the capitalists and industrialists. The people's representatives in the legislatures should be persons of sound judgment freely elected by the people".[5]

A brief definition of democracy would be, in Abraham Lincoln's words, "The government of the people, for the people, by the people". In other words democracy is a form of government in which people participate by expressing their opinion through votes. They have the feeling of participation in their affairs in a government established only for the common weal by the common consent of the people. This feeling of people's participation prompted Abraham Lincoln to call it "the last best hope of this world", and Jefferson had called it "a respect for the people's opinion".[6]

In short, democracy is a system of government in which:

1. Sovereignty belongs to the people.

2. The people establish the parliament or the country's highest legislature by their common votes, and the legislature is answerable to them.

3. The government is established for the common weal and prosperity.

4. It is also elected by the common vote.

In other words democracy *per se* is not the purpose or goal but is only an instrument of government of a country in which the country's people participate directly.

The Common Arguments against Democracy

As stated earlier, the concept of democracy is of Greek origin. Consequently, the first proceedings against democracy were also initiated In Greece by Socrates, who was regarded as one of the seven wisest persons of his time. The criticism levelled by Socrates against democracy at that time has always been repeated by its critics *mutatis mutandis*. In fact democracy's critics neither have a stronger argument than those of Socrates nor any convincing argument in favour of any other system, except sub-consciously taking shelter behind fascism or dictatorship under some excuse. Socrates had said that:

"What would be more ridiculous than democracy which had been hamstrung by the mob, where emotions ran supreme, government was merely a debating society, where the military commanders were selected, dismissed and killed without rhyme or reason, where the simple minded farmers and merchants were selected in alphabetical order to work as members of the Supreme Court".[7]

Later, criticising the system again he says:

"Is it not naively superstitious to imagine that wisdom would be attained by mere majority? On the contrary, is it not universally experienced that the people participating in gatherings are very much more foolish, violent and cruel than those who prefer seclusion? How shameful is it that those orators should rule humanity who indulge in high sounding rhetoric which can be linkened to empty brass vessels which keep sounding on being hit till somebody stops them by putting his hand over them".[8]

Iqbal and Democracy

Socrates suggests the solution of this problem to be to "entrust government's leadership to the wisest person.[9]

After condemning democracy to the gallows the solution presented by Socrates in the form of "the wisest person" will be examined at the proper place. We should first identify Socrates' criticism, which is:

1. This system of government is hamstrung by the mob, i.e. decisions are made by majority opinion, which means that the decision made by the majority opinion is considered sound.

2. This system of government is dominated by emotions.

3. Such a government is a debating society, i.e. every matter is decided after debate in the parliament.

4. Simple minded farmers and businessmen are elected, or in otherwise power is captured by feudal lords and capitalists.

5. Rhetoricians gain power.

6. Those living in public are more violent and cruel than the ones who prefer seclusion.

These are the basic objections raised more or less by all. It would be better to point out the criticism of other critics of democracy before analysing Socrates' criticism, so that the objections against this system and the analysis of other systems in comparison may be explained in detail. Wil Durant writes in his book, *The Story of Philosophy* on the tragedy of Western democracy:

"Democracy, which was intended to free mankind, itself became a mechanism of giving voting rights to the witless crowd. The protest of the individual against this mechanism was Ineffective like the individual's voice against the crowd in the East, so much so that even leaders became a part and parcel of these lifeless machines. They became Insensitive like their deluded followers, who were only counted in elections".[10]

So, Wil Durant has the same objections as Socrates, that the power of decision rests with the majority. Even Rousseau who was among the founders of the new democratic system, also objected to the decision making by the majority. Consequently, he says:

"If we take the term In Its strictest sense there never has existed, nor will ever exist, a true democracy. It is contrary to the nature of things that the many govern and the few be governed".[11]

Tahseen Firaqi in his book, *Maghribi Jamhuriat Ahl-i-Maghrib Kee Nazar Main* ("Western Democracy in the View of the Westerners") has assiduously assimilated the objections of very important Western thinkers and writers against democracy. They include Rousseau, Nietzsche, Carlyle, Belak, Donnelly, Agneish, Bernard Shaw, Laiky, Spengler, Lawrence, Eric Fromm, Harold Laski, Rene Guenon, Joseph Schimpter and Bertrand Russell. In addition, there must be many more who have raised objections against democracy. However, it must be admitted that of all their objections against democracy none is worth mentioning are more than those of the first critic, i.e. Socrates. For example Carlyle also considers a wise man more important than many idiots. He is also in search of a wise man, and considers democracy to be the rule of the idiots. Belak, Donnelly and Bernard Shaw prefer a wise man over the majority and consider democracy to be synonymous with the appointment of some unscrupulous people through elections organized by several incompetent persons. When Laski says that the creation of a conflict between the majority and the minority is the work of the election agent he also supports the stand of Socrates. He has another objection, that is voters do not have mature judgement needed for voting. That only a rich person can contest a democratic election is an important objection against democracy which has been levelled by Laiky, Spengler, Russell, Eric Fromm and Schimpter. They have said that poverty and democracy do not go together. As it were, election is an arena In which only the rich can enter, The American intellectual, Joseph A. Schimpter calls democracy a government established with the people's approval, and says that we cannot call it the people's government but the one established by their approval. In the same way the famous French intellectual, Rene Guenon, who later accepted Islam with the name of Abdul Wahid Yahya, raised the objection against democracy. In his book, *Crisis of the Modern World* that the lower and backward classes of the populace form the majority and they are devoid of judgement and ability, while the classes with ability constitue a minority. Hence, the superior cannot emanate from the inferior, which is approximately what Socrates had said, namely that thick-headed farmers and businessmen acquire power in democracy and the dream of the government of the people becomes ridiculous".[12] Tahseen Firaqi has cited the whole of this objection of Rene Guenon in his above mentioned book. Consequently, this discussion of the critics of democracy is largely based on this book, where it has been put together to some extent. Gai Eaton (Islamic name Hasan Abdul Hakeem), who was a native of Switzerland, criticising the materialism of democracy and the misleading concept of majority, says:

"As for the problem of the common people, the poor simpletons mark the ballot papers as voters in favour of the person who has promised them better houses and cheaper food".[13]

Professor Muhammad Munawwar also levelled some important and basic objections in one of his papers titled, "Iqbal's Idea of Democracy" on the complete absence of ethical values and destruction of the higher ethical principles in democracy. These objections point out misdemeanors of the candidates in obtaining votes and of voters in giving them, which influence the entire ethical structure of society. The objections of the professor are obviously very important and correct. The Western democracy has bequeathed all these evils of the countries of its origin in their colonies, and has destroyed the ethical, social and political structures of the latter. However, the countries gaining independence from this colonial system did not organize this Western concept of democracy under their own cultural and social principles, and instead of accepting the experiences the West in a constructive spirit have blindly followed them. Consequently, the virtues of the West could not be established in our countries but we did adopt their vices. Perhaps virtue, on account of its durability is slow, and vice, being apparently bright is fast in its influence. Consequently, the scarceness of morality in democracy exposed by Muhammad Munawwar cannot be denied, because ethical values are really alien to Western democracy. He writes:

"But the glaring drawback that transpires is the non-visibility of any moral fibre in the system. Rights are mentioned whereas the question of right and wrong is ignored. What sort of people as human beings are to be elected? Certainly they must be suitable individuals, but are they suitable morally as well? What sort of people as human beings are those who elect their representatives? Are they upholders of human values and hence they elect those who have respect for what is good for humanity? Are they elected because they can spend lavishly on election campaigns, can brow-beat others into voting for them on account of their muscles or just due to their positive capabilities? Does in the Western democracy, even legal equality prevail? Are there no racial or territorial prejudices at work? Does Western democracy stand for teaching man's respect for man and try to make human beings genuinely human? Does it create feelings of sympathy and sacrifice for others? It is quite obvious that Western democracy is not essentially for forming government of good people, elected by good people and making people good".[14]

In fact these objections can be raised against any system devoid of prophetic consciousness. However, In contrast with democracy-fascism, imperialism and dictatorship are completely devoid of the very concept of ethics. People are at least counted in democracy, while they are driven like despicable wild beasts in systems other than democracy. Scrutiny of the methods of formation of the governmental structure of the systems other than democracy would show them to be much more cruel, vindictive, narrow minded and destructive ethical values than democracy. The crimes committed by all the democrats of the world are much less than the cruelties and crimes of one dictator. Examples are available even in Islamic history of the way in which the neglect of the mechanism for the transfer of political power created moral evils. The non-observance of this mechanism for the transfer of political power created the dispute between Hadhrat Ali and Amir Muawiyya and brought Yazeed, Ameer Muawiyya's son to political power after his death. During his reign several prominent companions of the Holy Prophet and his grandson, while his whole family was scarified at the altar of dictatorship by substitution of the voluntary *baiat* (*baiat bil raza*) with the *baiat* by force (*baiat bil jabr*). If the system of the *baiat* of Hadhrat Abu Bakr Siddique and Hadhrat Umar Farooq had been continued as an effective system for the transfer of political power, the pathetic tragedy of the martyrdom of the oppressed Imam would have been avoided and the *Khilafah* would not have been changed to monarchy. The fundamental essence of democracy is the transfer of political power and establishment of the governmental structure by majority opinion. It is unrealistic to expect anything more than this from democracy. It can resist the devastation of ethical values only with the help of other ethical ideals and cultural limitations. We will have to seek guidance from our deen for his and will have to fix the objectives and the mutatis operandi of democracy in the light of prophetic consciousness. After achieving this democracy will be a means of accomplishing ethical values instead of breaking them down, as in the present conditions when all systems are devoid of ethical values, work on the principle of "might is right" and are not even remotely concerned with the eminent status of humanity and dignity of man. In fact the very object of Islam is the reorganization of democracy in the light of Islamic principles and its application to Islamic society, through which alone it can gradually evolve into a government elected by 'pious people, for pious people', which would be instrumental in promoting virtue and endeavoring In the pursuit of the common weal. Expecting this from any other system is self deception. If a good king or dictator in power per chance takes interest in the common weal it should be considered only fortuitous. The dictatorial, fascist and monarchical systems cannot be expected to do that.

In the same way the gist of the objections of Laski, Repaird, Eric Fromm and Russell on democracy is also that it is a trick of the capitalist class, which brings incompetent people to political power through press, specious language and wealth. Lord Russell says the same thing in various ways. So, an analysis of all the objections against democracy compels us to admit that the critics of democracy have not gone beyond its first critic, Socrates, while this democratic system has laboured its way to a mighy system in spite of all these criticisms. Democracy's being a controversial system is a criticism levelled by various classes. Directly or indirectly it has been entangled in various confusing concepts such as social democracy, economic democracy, constitutional democracy, noble democracy and people's democracy. It has no clear and identifiable form. The different forms of democracy, appearing in different circumstances prevailing in different societies and resulting from centuries of experimenting are in themselves in need of definition, so that a society may be able to adopt any of the forms it prefers to suite its circumstances. It would be better to review Iqbal's criticism also before discussing these criticisms.

Iqbal's Criticism of Democracy

The basic objections raised by Iqbal against democracy in his works are not different from those raised by Socrates. Iqbal expressed the following thoughts about democracy:

ہے وہی سازِ کہن مغرب کا جمہوری نظام
جس کے پردوں میں نہیں غیر از نوائے قیصری
دیوِ استبداد جمہوری قبا میں پائے کوب
تُو سمجھتا ہے یہ آزادی کی ہے نیلم پری

Understanding Iqbal's Philosophy

مجلسِ آئین و اصلاح و رعایات و حقوق
طبِ مغرب میں مزے میٹھے، اثر خواب آوری
گرمیِ گفتار اعضائے مجالس الاماں!
یہ بھی اک سرمایہ داروں کی ہے جنگِ زرگری
اس سرابِ رنگ و بو کو گلستاں سمجھا ہے تُو
آہ اے ناداں! قفس کو آشیاں سمجھا ہے تُو

A. "The Western democratic system is the same old orchestra
Whose notes have nothing but the melodies of Caesar,

The demon of despotism is treading of democracy the path
Thou considereth it to be the fairy of freedom

The constituent assembly, reforms, grants, concessions, and rights
In the Western medical system tastes are sweet but the effects are soporific

The heat of the debates of assemblies may God protect us
This too is a sham quarrel to deceive others

Thou considereth this mirage of attractions to be a garden
Ah O simpleton / thou considereth the cage to be the nest".[15]

متاعِ معنیٔ بیگانہ از دوں فطرتاں جوئی؟
زموراں شوخیِ طبعِ سلیمانے نمی آید
گریز از طرزِ جمہوری، غلامِ پختہ کارے شو
کہ از مغزِ دو صد خر فکرِ انسانے نمی آید

B. "Thou seekest the treasures of unfathomed wisdom from people of mean nature

Surely, Ants cannot attain the wisdom of a Sulaiman

160

Iqbal and Democracy

Flee from the mechanisations of democracy, follow an experienced sage

For the brains of two hundred donkeys cannot produce the wisdom of one man".[16]

فرنگ آئینِ جمہوری نہاد است
رسن از گردنِ دیوے کشاد است
گروہے را گروہے در کمین است
خدایش یار اگر کاوش چنیں است
زمن دہ اہل مغرب را پیامے
کہ جمہور است تیغِ بے نیامے

C. "The West has founded the democratic system
It has loosened the rope from the demon's neck
A host of people are running like robbers
While many hungry mouths are running for a loaf of bread

One group lies in ambush for another one
May God help it if these are its ways

Convey the message from me to the West
That the populace is an unsheathed sword".[17]

اس راز کو اِک مرد فرنگی نے کیا فاش
ہر چند کہ دانا اسے کھولا نہیں کرتے
جمہوریت اک طرزِ حکومت ہے کہ جس میں
بندوں کو گنا کرتے ہیں، تولا نہیں کرتے

D. "Some European sage has unveiled this secret
Though wise men keep these secrets concealed

Democracy is a form of government in which
People are counted but their worth is not assessed".[18]

تو نے کیا دیکھا نہیں مغرب کا جمہوری نظام

چہرہ روشن اندروں چنگیز سے تاریک تر

E. "Hast thou not seen the Western democratic system
Whose face is bright but the inside is dark (darker than Changiz?"[19]

ہم نے خود شاہی کو پہنایا ہے جمہوری لباس

جب ذرا آدم ہوا ہے خود شناس و خود نگر

F. "We have ourselves bestowed democratic role on monarchy
Then has man become somewhat self conscious and self-cognizant".[20]

اٹھا کر پھینک دو باہر گلی میں

نئی تہذیب کے انڈے ہیں گندے

الکشن، ممبری، کونسل، صدارت

بنائے خوب آزادی نے پھندے

میاں نجار بھی چھیلے گئے ساتھ

نہایت تیز ہیں یورپ کے رندے

G. "Cash them away, into the street
The eggs of the yew civilization are rotten

Elections, membership, council, presidency
Sham freedom has invented strange noozes

The carpenter has also been scraped
Very sharp are the Europe's planes".[21]

یہاں مرض کا سبب ہے غلامی و تقلید

وہاں مرض کا سبب ہے نظامِ جمہوری

H. "In the East bondage and mimicry has caused the malady
In the West the democratic rule causes the disease".[22]

Iqbal and Democracy

We have assembled some verses from Iqbal's Persian and Urdu works containing some criticism of democracy so that a consolidated comprehension may be acquired of Iqbal's criticism of democracy, freed from emotional and humourous diction. Consequently, the following objections arise from the background of the verses:

1. The Western democratic system is the same old European Ceasarism or imperialism, and the old capitalistic despotism of Europe is operative behind the smoke screen of democracy. Hence, the system bears only a deceptive resemblance to freedom.

2. Parliament or legislative assembly is only a debating society and an institution established by capitalists for the protection of their own interests.

3. Just as the assembling of two hundred donkeys' brains cannot produce a human brain the majority of the common people cannot produce a wise man, or in the Iqbal's words 'a man of attested Intelligence'. We should avoid a democratic system which makes decisions by simple majority and does not seek a wise man or a man of Faith. Democracy is a system in which the simple majority of persons makes decisions without considering the ability of these persons, whereas one wise man is better and more effective than thousands of simpletons

4. Though the Western democracy has a bright face, its Interior is darker than that of Chingiz. Due to the general awakening of the common people brought about by the influence of the awakening created by the Muslims in Spain and Baghdad Europe has presented imperialism in the wrappers of democracy. The democratic institutions such a selection, membership, council and presidency etc. are the rotten eggs of the new civilization. Europe has invented these in the name of democracy.

5. Iqbal says that the bane of the Eastern people is their enchantment with blind following of the ways of their ancestors and the root of all ills of the West is this democracy in which the numbers of persons are considered instead of their intellectual worth.

Reflection on Iqbal's criticism of democracy would give the feeling that his criticism of democracy is the same as that levelled by Socrates or other critics of democracy. We want to present a fundamental matter about Iqbal's criticism of democracy before analysing it. This fundamental matter is the Iqbal's farsight which discerned the psychological problem constituting the background of his criticism of democracy and this was interconnected with the special political atmosphere of that time.

The Background of Iqbal's Criticism of Democracy

During Iqbal's time the concepts of democracy and democratic thinking, like one person one vote, right of representation, joint and separate electorates were moving fast from the West to the East and were increasingly becoming popular. Under the conditions prevailing in the Indian sub-continent, resulting from the British terminology, all big and small nations there had been designated Hindus. Thus the Hindus were elevated to the status of majority by herding together all the different nations of the sub-continent, although the real Hindus were a minority. This catapulted the Hindus into a majority and relegated all other nations to the status of a minority. The latter included the nation which had formerly ruled the sub-continent, i.e. Muslims. The relegation of Muslims to minority status meant that in the event of the sub-continent gaining independence under the concept of one person one vote, the political power In India would have been transferred to the Hindu majority, and the Muslims being a minority would have become subservient. Consequently, Iqbal supported the right of *Ijtihad* for the consultative assembly or parliament of an Islamic State, but did not support this right for the parliament composed of the non-Muslim majority which would have been established in united India, and he plainly said:

"In my opinion this (*Ijtihad* by parliament) is the only way by which we can stir into activity the spirit of life in our legal system; and give it an evolutionary outlook. In India, however, (with Hindu majority and Muslim minority) difficulties are likely to arise, for it is doubtful whether a non-Muslim legislative assembly can exercise the power of *Ijtihad*".[23]

This extract reflects Iqbal's thinking that he did not like any system or state of affairs in united India which would enable the Hindu majority to influence the interests of the Muslim minority. This is the reason for which democracy was not acceptable to Iqbal in any form in the united India. Not only to Iqbal, this state of affairs could not be acceptable to any Muslim. This was so because the Hindus' dream of their renaissance included the annihilation of Muslims from the sub-continent on the pattern of Spain. In these circumstances Iqbal's support of democracy in united India would have amounted to his recommendation of slavery for

Iqbal and Democracy

Muslims. This is the social psyche which made Iqbal a critic of democracy in united India. But was Iqbal an opponent of democracy even in an Islamic State and was he not prepared to accept any form of democracy? Judgement should be passed on this only with much caution. To prove Iqbal to be an all out rejector of democracy, on the basis of a few of his verses, would be against the truth, because Iqbal was a supporter and friend of democracy in an Islamic State where political power would be in the hands of Muslims.

An Analysis of the Criticism of Democracy

The objections resulting from the above - mentioned verses of Iqbal have been levelled even by democracy's supporters. These are the defects of democracy and it is desirable to remove them, but the outright rejection of the system is not at all right. This is so because comparison of these defects with other non-democratic systems leaves no choice but to adopt democracy. The systems presented in contrast with democracy are the worst examples of despotic dictatorship in which the individual is not even counted, leave alone assessing his worth. The individuals in the democratic society are at least consulted, whereas in other systems every dictator, acquiring power by force cosiders himself to be the Angel Gabriel, the man of Faith and the Perfect Man. Consequently, the gleaners of power convince such a dictator that the world has never produced a wiser and more intelligent person than him. Searching for a wiser person is even more difficult than obtaining the moon. Nobody has an instrument which can search for such a person. Moreover, having found such a person it is neither always possible to obtain people's consensus in his support, nor is it necessary that he would be able to comprehend the affairs of the State. In these circumstances the power for enforcing his decisions would not be the common consent but the power of the bullet, and he would appear in the form of an absolute dictator on the strength of this power. The question is as to who beside his own claim, would decide that he is a man of Faith and proven truthful. In social environment finding such a person in every election may be possible for a village council, but is impossible in the present day State comprising millions of people. Insistence on or support of such concepts is equivalent to establishing and maintaining a State on perpetually shaky foundations. This is an abstraction with which the present day State cannot be bracketed. How many such wise men has any State been lucky enough to acquire since the time of Socrates? Surety those acquiring political power by force have compelled people to call them wise men a and men of steel. In the present day and age talking of such concepts cannot be considered short of knowingly or unknowingly gaining favours from dictators. Lastly, it cannot be ensured that such a wise and righteous man also has the ability of operating the political system of a country.

The second objection levelled against democracy is even more meaningless than this, i.e. only capitalists and rich people can acquire political power through democracy. The question is whether the poor people and labourers acquire political power in monarchy and dictatorship? Such a thought is no less than folly. Surely some slaves became kings and some poor and middle class people became dictators. But poverty was not instrumental in their becoming kings and dictators, in that, somebody conferred political power on them on the basis of their poverty and excellent ability. In actual fact the internal wire pulling and intrigue provided such military power to these kings and dictators which enabled them, not only to ascend the pedestal of political power but also to join the ranks of capitalists. Also, a labourer does not remain a labourer after ascending the pedestal of political power. His mental and political approach acquire the character of those of the capitalists. Hence, it is a pure fallacy that only capitalists acquire political power in democracy. On the contrary these people acquire political power under every system. The people of the labouring and poor classes also who acquired political power through democracy outnumber those who did so by force. Hence this objection is a mere jugglary of words.

The third objection also deserves little attention, because the opinion of two hundred persons should be considered more reliable than that of one as one person is more liable to err than two hundred persons. A solitary person dispensing political power, surrounded by flatterers and overloaded with problems cannot make a better decision than two hundred people elected by a social unit. These people have the common will as well as the power of validation, whereas the dictator has no power of decision except his own egoism. The people of Pakistan, who have a twenty to twenty-five year experience of dictators climbing the pedestal of political power through the bullet instead of the ballot, know well the game played by these "men of Faith" "men of God", and "men of iron will". They know that these men have used every cunningness to frustrate the democratic ambitions of the people. Certainly, one human brain cannot evolve out of the brains of two hundred donkeys. However, are the two hundred persons always idiots? Besides, how can it be ensured that the one individual preferred over two hundred persons would measure up to the desired standards required by these critics of democracy? Infact every dictator regards himself as the Universal Spirit and others as donkeys. This is the psyche which also exists in the sub-conscience of the opponents of democracy. Considering the common people to be donkeys and the dictator as the Universal Spirit is nothing short of insulting the populace and flattering the dictators. These attitudes result only in strengthening the hands of the dictators. The establishment of Pakistan, which has resulted from the common vote, testifies to the appropriateness of the collective decision of the Muslim *Ummah*. They are worthy of trust, whereas the decisions of the Jamiat-i-Ulema-i-Hind, Jama'at-i-Islami, Majlis-i-Ahrar-i-Islam, Khaksar Organization and many other "righteous" people were in conflict with Muslim interests, indifferent to the future of Islam in the sub-continent, fostered by false personal egoism and completely against the interests of Islam. If the right of final vote had been in the hands of these "righteous" people Pakistan would not have come into existence. The establishment of Pakistan is a masterpiece of the sound judgment of the common people of Pakistan.

The majority of democracy's opponents in Pakistan, by depriving the people of Pakistan of their voting rights, wants to chastise them for their decision in favour of the establishment of Pakistan, and in the name of religion wants to thrust on them their own self-made "theocracy of the righteous". This will be an oligarchy in which the power of decision would be in the hands of these "righteous" persons. Consequently, It is only proper for Muslims to beware of the advocates of dictatorship in preference to democracy. Dr. Khalifah Abdul Hakim writes:

"There appears to be no course open to Muslims except to abstain from looking up dictatorship in opposition to democracy, and to use their inelligence and practical sagacity combined with sacrifice, for slowly reforming the democractic system so as to make its virtues more prominent than its defects".[24]

The correct approach is that in matters of decision making on concepts and articles of faith nobody except God, His ordained Holy Prophet or His Book has the right to make even the most infinitesimal alteration. In these matters it is more useful and effective to assess the worth of people than merely counting them, so much so that even in the interpretation of the *deen* people would be assessed. At the time of *Ijtihad* in *deen* both the opinion and the worth of the *Mujtahid* would be kept in view. Still the worth of the *Mujtahid* would be assessed more rigorously than his opinion. In other words the worth of people would have to be assessed in matters pertaining to *deen* and doctrine, but in matters of State, administration, participation of the greatest number of people in this decision making is more appropriate than their personality. Precedents for this are available from the immaculate life of the Holy Prophet himself. He was bound by God and the Holy Book in matters of *deen* and at the time of the Battle of the Trench and on several other occasions concerning State administration. He asked for and accepted counsel in spite of having full authority. We cannot adjudge the Holy Prophet to be bound by consultations but other sovereigns certainly do not enjoy the same status. Prophet is appointed by God whereas other sovereigns do not have the same status. Hence, it is only proper to compel them to consultation and abiding by it, so that they do not become autocractic. Mawlana Muhammad Hanif Nadvi has explained this matter to some extent in his book, *Isasiyat-i-Islam* (The Basics of Islam):

"The distinction between right and wrong in matters of deep and doctrine is doubtlessly not bound by majority opinion. The Truth is the Truth even if it may be accepted only by one person and opposed by the whole society. However, when considering matters of State administration the criterion for decision would be the suitability of the course of action instead of the strength of argument".[25]

"This is so because application and not experience is important in democracy".[26] Here, considering the majority opinion alone as decisive is proper. Maximum participation of the people makes it more acceptable by the people, and if some decision enjoys common acceptance it is conducive to the increased stability of society.

The fourth objection to democracy becomes meaningless when we compare democracy with other systems and see that the heart of dictators is much darker than that of Chingiz., compared pared with that of democratic rulers. Every ruler from Oliver Cromwell to those of the present day are the worst examples of oppression and fascism. They do not want to hear anybody's opinion, leave alone accepting it. All their powers are wasted in suppressing their opponents, and psychologically they suffer from the complex of non-acceptance of the people. They are permanently paranoid, which makes them psychologically suffocated, leading them to hard - heartedness and cruelty. They become bent on suppressing every opposing thought and its expression. If the silence of the graveyard can be called peace it abounds in dictatorships. If the expression of the differences of opinions and views, listening to others and

Iqbal and Democracy

the acceptance or rejection of each other's views after their consideration is regarded instability then it certainly exists in democracies. A little reflection would show that this right of decision making is also a product of democratic disposition. Dictatorships force decisions by power, force and fear. There cannot be two opinions about considering dictators darker than Chingiz.

In the fifth objection Iqbal says that the charm of ritualism is the bane of the Easterners, and being ensnared by democracy, that of the Westerners. Iqbal has very rightly diagnosed the malady of the East. He wants the East to abandon blind ritualism and be the architect of its own destiny, making use of the experience of the West but with due regard to the environments and the problems of the East when applying those experiences. He goes to the extent of advising against blind by them following the West even in the matter of democracy. On the contrary, the East should reorganize democracy according to its own conditions and goals. When Iqbal adjudges democracy to be the bane of the West he has in view the unbridled democracy adopted by the West, which is harmful even to its own civilization. By adjudging the Western civilization as being devoid of prophetic consciousness and being enamoured by the visible, i.e. materialism, Iqbal means that If it were to reorganize itself in the light of prophetic consciousness it can avoid the problems which are leading it. O decline. The absence of prophetic consciousness alone has brought the decline of ethical values in the Western style democracy. If we organize democracy in the light of our concept of sovereignty and Islamic, ethical values democracy can help in the enlightenment and glory of ethical values also. It has the potential for being cast into a system in which good people may be elected for parliament in order to enlighten and glorify the higher ethical values, and participate in the progress of virtue. This also can be expected only from democracy because in other systems even a good hearted-person cannot protect himself on account of being caught in the struggle for political power.

Two Basic Attributes of Democracy

All definitions of democracy have two basic points. One is making some arrangements for participation of public opinion in the framing of a country's or nation's councils of executive and legal administrations. At the time of shaping the country's administration, conducting political affairs and enforcing administrative decisions it is necessary to keep in view the opinions of the people on whom these decisions would be enforced, so that their acceptance of these decisions may be obtained through their own free will rather than under any force of authority. Now, compare this attribute of democracy with other systems. In theocracy decision making on country's affairs and administrative matters was the prerogative of the select ecclesiastical group. They played with the people's destinies as they pleased, and claimed this right under religion, i.e. the power of the Church. Following in their footsteps kings started designating themselves as the 'Shadow of God', implying that their power was bestowed upon them by God. Consequently, they presented themselves as protectors of God's people and co-sharers in the Will and Intentions of God. The clergy derived their power and authority from the institution of the Church, but the powers of kings resided in their inheritance, their own military strength and the Divine right to rule. The same applies to the dictators of the old as well as the present age, who acquire their right to rule over their people by the sword or the bullet. Decide for yourself whether these dictatorships and monarchies are not the products of the law of the jungle in which "might is right". What can be a bigger insult to human conscience and dignity than these monarchies and dictatorships which are born of the power of the sword or the gun. Supporting them is 'tantamount to crime against human dignity, and all those who support these dictatorships and monarchies are criminals against humanity, because support to them resembles the support the law of the jungle. When offered the choice between the ballot and the bullet the present day conscientious man would select the ballot in preference to the bullet. The ballot is the expression of respect for man's rights and opinion in the affairs of the State and the bullet is the emblem of the use of power and force for subduing him.

Peaceful transfer of political power is the other attribute of democracy. It is a means of transfer of political power from one hand to the other, a better formula than that which has not been established by the human race. There are only three ways for the transfer of political power. One is the method of inheritance by the son on the death of the ruler. The second method is the snatching of political power by force. The third one is this democratic way in which those to be ruled elect their own ruler by their own vote. The first or the second method is current in monarchies. After the death of a king either his son ascends the throne or some other person usurps political power by his military might. In dictatorships military power is the only way for transfer of political authority. Now consider both these methods of transfer of political power and also view the method of the transfer by common vote and decide which one is safer, easier and more peaceful that has human dignity, honour and magnificence. It is a fact that there is less than one percent possibility of a man of Faith acquiring political power by the first method of inheritance. In the Muslim history of the Indian sub-continent a good ruler has seldom acquired political power in this way except Awrangzeb, Tipu Sultan and a few others. Among these also, the former had to use the sword to ascend to political power and even a pious person like Aurangzeb could not escape the ignominy of having to shed the blood of his brothers and father. If such a pious ruler could not avoid being implicated on account of adopting this wrong way to political power the less said the better about other rulers. The whole human history is a tale of woes resulting from the atrocities of kings and dictators. In these circumstances change in government or transfer of political power by common vote, alone is proper for human dignity and humane perceptions. In human history the number of people killed in connection with transfer of power in the democratic way bears no comparison to those killed at the time of transfer in monarchies and dictatorships. Hence, there is no alternative to adopting the method designed by democracy for transfer of political power. All monarchies and dictatorships fail in comparison to it.

Democracy comprises of only these two basic concepts, i.e. participation of the people in the affairs of the State and transfer of political power through the ballot instead of the bullet. All other aspects and definitions of democracy are only explanations and clarifications of these two basic concepts, and these explanations and clarifications can be modified by every country and nation according to its own ideologies and conceptions.

Iqbal's Concept of Democracy

Iqbal's criticism of democracy was firstly because of the creation of special circumstances and secondly was the pointer of some basic defects of democracy. If corrective measures for these defects are adopted these objections not only cease to exist but democracy becomes even acceptable to him. This criticism of democracy by Iqbal cannot be taken to imply his support for monarchy or dictatorship, as our dictators have done in attempting to justify their dictatorial behaviour by quoting some verses of Iqbal against democracy. However, such attempts have always been rejected by the people. The dictators' attempts are equivalent to dishonesty with Iqbal's thought. Iqbal has always rejected monarchy and dictatorship and has considered them as un-Islamic systems.

In his *Lectures* Iqbal has designated "spiritual democracy" as the goal of Islam and has adjudged its establishment as a fountainhead of hope for the human race. He says in his lecture on *Ijtihad* in Islam:

"The growth of republican spirit, and the gradual formation of legislative assemblies in Muslim land constitutes a great step in advance. The transfer of power of *Ijtihad* from individual representatives of schools to a Muslim legislative assembly, which in view of the growth of opposing sects, is the only possible form *Ijma'* can take in modern times, will secure contributions to legal discussions from laymen who happen to possess a keen insight into affairs."[27]

Iqbal, not only liked the democratic experiment in the Islamic State of Turkey, consisting of a Muslim majority, but also accepted their *Ijtihad* that the elected parliament of an Islamic country should have the power of elucidation, interpretation and explanation of Islamic laws. In Iqbal's view, the interests of the Islamic *Fiqh* whose reconstruction and consolidation in the new ages in conformity with its demands, was his ardent desire, would be best served, If this duty would be assumed by the elected parliaments of Muslim countries. This was the reason for Iqbal considering the growth and development of the democratic spirit and the gradual establishment of legislative assemblies in the Islamic world as a "great progressive" system. This also shows that Iqbal was critical of democracy in the sub-continent on account of its special circumstances, but welcomed it in the Islamic world where Muslim constitute the majority. Iqbal was even convinced that if the system of the Divinely guided *Khilafah* had continued. It would have been reshaped into democratic institutions and legislative assemblies, and the legislature, instead of individuals, would have legislated by collective decisions. According to him individuals got the right of *Ijtihad* on account of the absolute monarchy of the Umayyads and Abbasides who wanted to make themselves powerful instead of making any legislature to be its fountainhead. The ardent desire of Iqbal for an Independent legislature can be gauged from the analysis of the tragedy of the journey from the *Khilafah* to monarchy during the period from the Divinely-guided *Khilafah* to the Omayyad and Abbaside *Khalifahs*. He says:

"Possibly its (*Ijma's*) transformation into a permanent representative institution was contrary to the political interests of the kind of absolute monarchy that grew up in Islam. Immediately after the fourth *Khalifah*, it was, I think, favourable to the interests of the Omayyad and Abbaside *Khalifahs* to leave the power of *Ijtihad* to individual *Mujtahids* rather than encourage the formation of a permanent assembly which might become too powerful for them".[28]

This means that in Iqbal's view, frustrating the efforts to establish a permanent legislative assembly or *Ijtihad* assembly was the achievement of Muslim monarchies. In view of this are not the people who want to prove opposition to the establishment of legislative assembly or parliament from Iqbal's works blowing the trumpets of the Rings dictators? Iqbal considers the following to be the only solution of the problems of Muslims:

"For the present every Muslim nation must sink into its own deeper self, temporarily focus her vision on herself alone, until all are strong and powerful to form a living family of republics."[29]

Iqbal even believes that:

"The teaching of the Holy Qur'an that life is a process of progressive creation necessitates that each generation guided, but unhampered, by the work of its predecessors, should be permitted to solve its own problem".[30]

These two extracts clarify Iqbal's desire that *Fiqh* should not be an obstruction in the way of Muslims in living their lives at present, but should be explained and interpreted according to the demands of the present day world where necessary. They should obtain and use maximum guidance from their predecessors. This means that it is desirable to keep in view the experiences of predecessors while new path in reshaping of *Fiqh*. Still there is no harm in differing them. Secondly, Iqbal desired that all Muslim countries should establish legislative assemblies in their respective areas, should interpret *Fiqh* according to their circumstances and should benefit from each other's experiences and then all should unite to form a federation or administration of Islamic republics, and thus should pave the way for the unity of the Islamic world. According to him this was a practical and exemplary state of affairs which the Muslims could adopt and can still do so. This, according to Iqbal, is the demand of the renaissance of Islam in the present day world.

"It seems to me that God is slowly bringing home to us the truth that Islam is neither nationalism nor imperialism but a League of Nations which recognizes artificial boundaries and racial distinctions for facility of reference only, and not for restricting the social horizon of its members".[31]

With reference to the *Ijtihad* of the Turks, Iqbal considers democracy indispensable for Islamic State. He says:

"Let us now see how the Grand National Assembly has exercised the power of *Ijtihad* in regard to the institution of *Khilafah*. According to the Sunni Law the appointment of an Imam or *Khilafah* is absolutely indispensable. The first question that arises in this connection is this: Should the *Khilafah* be vested in a single person? Turkey's *Ijtihad* is that according to the spirit of Islam the *Khilafah* or *Imamah* can be vested in a body of persons, or an elected assembly. The religious doctors of Islam in Egypt or India, have not yet expressed themselves on this point. Personally, I believe the Turkish view is perfectly sound. It is hardly necessary to argue this point. The republican form of government is not only throughly consistent with the spirit of Islam, but has also become a necessity in view of the new forces that are set free in the world of Islam."[32]

After understanding Iqbal's detailed stand underlined above what further resoning is necessary to bring his democratic perception into evidence. Here, Iqbal, adjudging the democratic system of government to be exactly in accordance with the spirit of Islam, considers it indispensable in the present age. In fact, going a step further he considers the courageous reinterpretation of the Islamic *Fiqh* as essential, and states clearly:

"Equipped with penetrative thought and fresh experience the world of Islam should courageously proceeds the work of reconstruction before them. This work of reconstruction, however, has a far more serious aspect than mere adjustment in modern conditions of life."[33]

Iqbal did not want only remodelling of Islam according to the dictates of the present age, but he wanted to see an insight among Muslims which could interpret the Islamic principles so as to provide them guidance in the present day and age. He has advised to keep the Russian Revolution also in view in this connection so that arrangements can be made for the State to provide economic assistance also to the people. Consequently, He says that on the one hand the experience of the Western world and 'the new economic experiments tried in the neighbourhood of

Muslim Asia must open our eyes to the inner meanings and destiny of Islam."[34]

According to Iqbal, while reinterpreting Islam we should keep in view the new *Ijtihad* of Turkey, the denial of prophetic consciousness of the European civilization and its unbridled inclination towards materialism leading to ethical decline, and the Russian experience in which the maximum emphasis has been placed on the economic aspect. 'In the opinion of Iqbal' Europe today is the greatest hinderance in the way of man's ethical advancement"[35], and 'The Idealism of Europe never became a living factor in her life and the result is perverted ego seeking itself through mutually intolerant democracies whose sole function is to exploit the poor in the interests of the rich"[36]. Consequently, humanity is passing through a period of extreme commotion. According to Iqbal the present day spiritual or even material needs of the present day human race can neither be satisfied by the Western capitalist system nor by the Russian communism but only by Islam. He has provided very good analysis of the situation and a reasoned cure when he says:

"Humanity needs three things today - a spiritual interpretation of the universe, spiritual emancipation of mankind and basic principles of a universal import directing the evolution of human society on a spiritual basis."[37]

"Let the Muslim of today appreciate his position, reconstruct his social life in the light of ultimate principles, and evolve, out of the hitherto partially revealed purpose of Islam, that spiritual democracy which is the ultimate aim of Islam".[38]

According to Iqbal the spiritual interpretation of the universe should be made under the principle of *Tauheed* whose spirit leads from the visible to the invisible. Islam is the only way for the spiritual freedom of mankind and establishment of 'spiritual democracy' is the basic universal principle which will lead to the evolution of human civilization on spiritual basis. Now let us see what this spiritual democracy is:

Iqbal's Concept of Spiritual Democracy

After understanding the fact that Iqbal considered the establishment of 'spiritual democracy' indispensable for Muslims and comprehending his views that this democracy should be established through "an elected assembly"³⁹, and that "the republican form of government is thoroughly consistent with the spirit of Islam"⁴⁰ it becomes easy to understand the concept of spiritual democracy. Iqbal, warning the West about the epemerality of its civilization said:

دیار مغرب کے رہنے والو! خدا کی بستی دکاں نہیں ہے

کھرا جسے تم سمجھ رہے ہو، وہ اب زر کم عیار ہوگا!

تمہاری تہذیب اپنے خنجر سے آپ ہی خودکشی کرے گی

جو شاخِ نازک پہ آشیانہ بنے گا' ناپائیدار ہو گا

"O people of the West the God's world is not for exploitation
What you consider to be economically genuine will turn out to be worthless

Your civilization will commit suicide with its own dagger
The nest built on a frail branch will be unstable."⁴¹

This was due to the fact that the Western civilization was enamoured of the visible, had distanced itself from prophetic consciousness, had ignored the real purpose of the creation of the universe and life, and had accepted matter as its goal instead of keeping it at its proper place of being only a means for understanding the reality. In the same way, in the social sphere, the West separated politics from *deen* and an unbridled democracy held sway everywhere which, while endowing man with unrestricted freedom estranged him from the real purpose of his existence. According to Iqbal the real reason for this was the separation of politics from *deen*. Consequently, he clearly warned that:

جلالِ پادشاہی ہو کہ جمہوری تماشا ہو

جدا ہو دیں سیاست سے تو رہ جاتی ہے چنگیزی

"It may be the majesty of the royalty or the funfare of democracy.
"If *deen* is separated from politics the latter becomes mere tyranny."⁴²

Considering *deen* essential for encompassing the entire life, Iqbal believed in keeping politics also subservient to it and wanted the shaping of political systems only under the guidance of *deen*. Iqbal's spiritual democracy is synonymous with harmony between *deen* and politics. Sovereignty is the sixth pillar of *deen* and *deen* cannot be established without sovereignty and the State.

Man as God's Vicegerent on Earth

According to Islam man is the spiritual leader, is God's vicegerent on earth, and the establishment and enforcement of God's Will on earth is a duty and Divine Command for the entire human race. Not any one person but the entire human race inhabiting the earth constitutes spiritual leadership and has been commissioned for the enforcement of God's Will on earth. God's Guidance, the Holy Qur'an is His last Command, and the Muslims, being its acceptors are specially obligated to enforce it, not severally but collectively. This responsibility devolves on all Muslims and not only on any one class of society. All Muslims are answerable for that before God. Every Muslim will be examined for the part he had played in establishing the Islamic system and enforcing God's Will. If somebody falls short of his responsibility in this respect he will be answerable for his shortcoming. In other words establishment of God's Kingdom on earth is incumbent not only on one group but is the Divine Commission for all Muslims. Hence, all Muslims must initiate action for enforcing God's Will. According to Iqbal the sovereignty of the universe belongs to God. Sovereignty, authority and power befits Him alone and if somebody considers the exercise of these attributes to be his prerogative he is guilty of idolatry:

سروری زیبا فقط اس ذاتِ بے ہمتا کو ہے

حکمراں ہے اک وہی باقی بتانِ آزری

"Sovereignty befits only he Unique Being
He is the only Sovereign, all the rest are false idols."[43]

Sovereignty of the State

Sovereignty of a State in the political sense befits God alone, and the Divine Command for the Vicegerent of God, i.e. man is to use this authority transferred to him for the enforcement of God's Will. In the Western democracy this sovereignty belongs completely to the people. A country's people can declare intoxicants lawful or unlawful as they wish and are fully empowered to deal with lewdness in the same way. This is so because sovereignty of the State is considered to be their statutory right.

Understanding Iqbal's Philosophy

Sovereignty in 'spiritual democracy' is not the right of any individual or nation but that of God. Mankind, being Vicegerents of God is obligated to enforce His Will and nobody is empower to alter it, exercise their own will. There can be various interpretations of the Will of God in an Islamic "spiritual democracy" but any change in even a word or its purport in the real source of the Law, i.e. the Holy Qur'an, is not possible. This leads to the shaping of a responsible democracy having a positive and permanent value system for controlling society, which can create social and cultural stability instead of producing social anarchy, promotion of lewdness and unbridled freedom. The eminent Iqbalist, the late Bashir Ahmad Dar, casting light on the political philosophy of Iqbal, changing Abraham Lincoln's famous saying about democracy being 'the rule of the people, for the people, by the people', under Islamic concepts writes about sovereignty:

"If we could change the famous saying of Abraham Lincoln on defining democracy in the light of the Islamic democracy it would read 'Rule of God, for the people, by the people'. The government established by the people is in the interests of humanity, but such a government must be operated under the laws framed by God. Man can never be the sovereign. Sovereignty befits God alone. People govern through their representatives under the laws framed by God."[44]

Moreover, as stated above, this sovereignty is the joint heritage of all Muslims, and so no single class can claim the interpretation of the Holy Qur'an, Hadith and the Sunnah as its exclusive right. It is the joint right of all Muslims and jointly they evolve a system which can help them in establishing the Will of God in any state. Now, it is obvious that the joint will of Muslims cannot be included in a monarchy or dictatorship, and all Muslims cannot discharge their responsibility of establishing the Will of God through either of these systems. Hence, this leaves the single alternative in which decisions can be made on the basis of the joint opinion of the Muslims. In the early days that alternative was the *baiat* through which people used to renunciate their right of opinion in favour of the *Khalifah* by surrendering their hands into his, which also demonstrated their confidence in him. In the present age the vote is the instrument for expressing opinion and for showing confidence in the ruler. This vote is the emblem of a Muslim's opinion and will and his confidence in the ruler, through which every person, i.e. every Muslim considers himself to be a partner in the conduct of government and regards himself an equal partner in the responsibility of his ruler's actions and conduct. He can evaluate the ruler throw vote of no confidence and can call to account the ruler of the state who fails to enforce God's will. it is not possible the present day complex and mechanized states to assemble in the mosque or an open space for a common *baiat*, or expression of opinion. To adopt the current method of vote in preference to the old time *baiat* is like reliquishing travel by camel in favour of car, rail or ship. In these circumstances if somebody insists on travelling by camel we can only pray for the one with such an unsound mind.

Sovereignty and Theocracy

It is necessary to remove a common misunderstanding here. In Islam sovereignty does not belong to the people, but is only a trust from God and they are only custodians of the sovereignty of God. Remember that in Islam sovereignty is the joint trust with all Muslims and not with any particular race, society or class. Hence, no aspect of theocracy applies to Islam. In theocracy sovereignty lies in some group, which considers itself to have been commissioned by God and presents itself to be the interpreter and propagater of the Will of God. In our society some conservative religious scholars have endeavoured to acquire this portion of theocracy, but it has never been accepted. Hence, in Islam the responsibility for enforcing God's Will falls on all Muslims. No group or class has the sanctity and the authority to present itself as ordained for the interpretation and enforcement of God's Will. By adjudging the Islamic State a form of theocracy, Mawlana Abul A'ala Mawdudi has presented an incorrect image of the ideal Islamic State. The Mawlana says:

"The Islamic State, the establishment and promotion of which alone is our goal, is neither a theocracy nor a democracy as understood in Western terminology. It is a unique political and cultural system intermediate between them. The intellectual confusion preying on the minds of the present day Western educated people about 'Islamic State' is really the product of Western terminology, which necessarily carries with it Western concepts and rallies the whole plethora of Western history before the mind. Theocracy in the Western terminology is a combination of two basic concepts, viz., (i) Divine rule in the sense of legal sovereignty and (ii) the ecclesiastical class which, presenting itself as God's representative and interpreter, would practically enforce this Divine rule in a legal and political form."[45]

Understanding Iqbal's Philosophy

According to Mawlana "Islam contains only one component of this theocracy and that is the belief in God's sovereignty. The second component certainly does not exist in Islam. As for the third component we have the Holy Qur'an, with its comprehensive and detailed commandments, for the interpretation of which we have such instructions in the sayings and actions of the Holy Prophet for sifting the Truth, through which we have access to authentic procedures for distinguishing the right from the wrong."[46]

In disagreeing with this opinion of the Mawlana one feels that his point of view was not clear about the Islamic State as well as theocracy. This is so because the Islamic State is an ideological State based on the concept of *Tauheed*. It is in no way connected with any concept of theocracy because the basic substance of theocracy is not Divine rule but the concept of the superiority of a special class in the name of God, which considers itself a group of the self-righteous people who are interpreters of God's Will. Probably, Mawlana's this very concept of theocracy produced the inclination in among the members of his party to consider themselves righteous and led them to claim their right on the State and its government as a consequence of if. In reality Islam is not connected with any group of the righteous people, but imposes the responsibility of God's Vicegerency on all Muslims. Adjudging this very concept of theocracy to be contrary to the spirit of Islamic governmental system Muhammad Mazharuddin Siddiqui says:

"The basic reason for theocracy being excluded from Islam is the absence of any special class in Islamic society specifically entrusted with the preaching and service of Islam. All Muslims are expected to mould their lives according to Islam wherever and whatever they are, to adopt Islamic concepts and introduce new methods of their presentation. Islam has vigorously opposed monpolistic tendencies in religion and has bestowed the high rank on every Muslim by making him personally responsible before God. Islam has not distinguished between "a religious person" (the clergy in Christianity and the *mawlvies* in Islam) and "a common person" and has prohibited monasticism in all its forms."[47]

Mawlana Muhammad Hanif Nadvi says that Islam does not have theocracy in any form because 'in the fourteen hundred year history of Islam there is not a single incidence in which the 'Ulema (religious scholars), *faqihs* and *muhaddithéen* as an institution or class have ever acquired political power or have even expressed their longing or even a desire to do so[48]. Therefore, saying that the Islamic State also is a theocracy of a kind or in a sense is tantamount to impressing on the minds a wrong concept about the Islamic State. In Islam every Muslim's opinion is equally respected because every Muslim has been accepted to be God's Vicegerent and a custodian of his trust and answerable to him.

Some Arguments in Support of Democracy

A survey of Islamic history would lead to the conclusion that the Holy Prophet neither appointed any of his relations as his *Khalifah* nor hinted towards any of his close friends for the *Khalifah* and leadership after himself. He only signalled to Hadhrat Abu Bakr Siddique for the leading prayer, which also does not establish his right for the Khilafah after the holy Prophet. After the death of the Holy Prophet all the claimants for the *Khilafah* based their claims to that high office only on the basis of their services to Islam. None of them presented any credentials from the Holy Prophet entitling him to the *Khilafah* or the *Imamah*. This clearly means that the Holy Prophet delegated to all Muslims the right of electing the *Khalifah* or their ruler after his death, so that they could entrust this authority to whomever they considered most suitable. Then at the time of the appearance of differences between the *Ansars*. the *Muhajireen* and the supporters of Hadhrat Ali the action which played the decicive role was the *baiat* of Hadhrat Omar at the hands of Hadhrat Abu Bakr Siddique. This means that Hadhrat Omar used his right in favour of Hadhrat Abu Bakr Siddique and then, following his example, the remaining companions of the Holy Prophet also cast their vote in favour of Hadhrat Abu Bakr Siddique. This was the first method of *baiat* or voting adopted by the Muslims. After this, Hadhrat Omar did not appoint anybody as his successor but, suggesting some people, advised the companions to elect any one of them for the *Khilafah* and obtain *baiat* i.e. obtain the general consensus of the Muslim's to this election. The allegation that Hadhrat Omar had not been elected but nominated by Hadhrat Abu Bakr Siddique is an oversight of facts. It is worth noting that though Hadhrat Abu Bakr Siddique had nominated Hadhrat Omar the *baiat* was obtained for him also, which alone gave credence to his *Khilafah*. Hadhrat Omar was not exempted from the procedure of the *baiat* by virtue of his nomination by Hadhrat Abu Bakr Siddique. The nomination was only suggestion. The same applied to Hadhrat Ali. That is why the deviation of Hadhrat Ameer Muawiyya from this principle led to his opposition by several companions of the Holy Prophet. And when the attempt was made to extort the *baiat* from Hadhrat Imam Hussain in favour of Yazeed the Imam preferred the sacrifice of his entire household to supporting Yazeed:

$$سر داد نہ داد دست در دستِ یزید$$
$$حقا کہ بنائے لا الہ اللہ ہست حسینؓ$$

"He gave his head but not his hand in Yazeed's hand (as *baiat*) By God Hussain is the very foundation of Lailaha."[49]

No other human civilization has any precedence of so much respect and reverence for *baiat*, or vote as used in the present day political parlance. Can there be any stronger argument in support of democracy? Again, does not the division of Muslims into the three groups of Ansars, *Muhajireen* and Hadhrat Ali's supporters on the basis of political stand, after the death of the Holy Prophet, prove that the people in an Islamic State can belong to different opinion groups on the basis of differences on an issue. Also, if different schools of thought can emerge from the juristic explanation and interpretation of religion, why can the people not be polarized into different associations on the basis of the elucidation, clarification and enforcement of the political system of the Holy Qur'an, and why can they not struggle for the establishment of the political framework in the light of their respective stands? It must be remembered that the initial Islamic society, had limited resources and needs which led to its being characterized by its simplicity. As the society grew and expanded the Muslims managed their affairs by planning their courses of action by *Ijtihad* in the light of the Quranic knowledge adapted to changing conditions. If the original straightforward society had continued in its efforts at evolving its own course in the same manner the Islamic system would have traversed the evolutionary path and would have reached the conclusions reached by the present day human race. The Divinely guided *Khalifah* can provide only doctrinaire guidance in our effort to meet the demands of the present day's complex and mechanized world. We can make decisions by the analysis of our cicumstances in the light of the present day conditions. Gloating over past glories, any attempt to bracket the present age with the old times is a vain effort, because the current of history moves forward and not backwards. Hence the same method of *baiat* had progressed, it would have assumed a shape which would not have been different from the present day vote or ballot. Also, instead of viewing the *baiat* superficially we must understand its real spirit, which is getting or giving opinion. Voting is also the same obtaining or giving opinion and the act of changing government or transferring political power by the same seeking or giving opinion is the real spirit of democracy.

Arguments from the Holy Qur'an and the Hadith

Though deductions about any particular form of government are not possible from the Holy Qur'an and the Hadith literature, the basic fact emerging from these sources is the requirement of deciding our affairs, that is the business of the society and the State, by mutual consultation, and that the Muslim populace is the ruler as well as the ruled simultaneously, and all of them are answerable to God for their deeds. Therefore, Muslims must shape a system of government in the operation of which they can all participate. Muslims must shape the government and conduct its business by mutual consultation: In the days of yore the *baiat* was the form of opinion or vote, and was the vehicle of expression of opinion. The same *baiat* or opinion at present is expressed through vote under the new technique. The Holy Prophet commands:

"Beware, each of you is like a shepherd and is accountable for those he rules, and the highest chieftain of Muslims who rules over all is also a shephered and is accountable for those he rules over."[50,51]

This means that every Muslim is accountable to God and the people for his actions to God on the day of judgement and to the people in this world. Similarly, the ruler of Muslims is also accountable to God and the people. All rulers, i.e. all Muslims are empowered to elect and appoint their ruler and to hold is by an individual. Obviously, this ruler is neither ordained by God, nor is by an individual or group but has to be appointed by Muslim masses. There can be no way of doing this except by election. Anybody who claims to be the ruler or tries to become one by means of force is a usurper. If he tries to obtain *baiat* or vote by treachery, temptation or force, the Muslims have no alternative but to obtain resist from him. In the present age both forms of obtaining resistence can be used, i.e. education of public opinion against him and expression of lack of confidence, and, in the event of failure of the democratic methods for peaceful removal of such a ruler from power, the combined power of the people can be used.

There cannot be a stronger argument than the Holy Qur'an, Surah al-Nisa: 58 in which God commands:

Understanding Iqbal's Philosophy

"God doth command you to render back your trusts (i.e. authority and confidence to those to whom they are due, i.e. trustworthy people); and when ye judge between man and man, that ye judge with justice."[52]

How can this verse be practised by Muslims? Obviously, political power and authority is the most valuable trust and the only way to consign it to the care of the trustworthy people is that of *baiat* or vote. God commands in The Holy Qur'an, Surah al-Nisa :59,

"O ye who believe, obey God and obey the Apostle, and those charged with authority among you."[53]

Now, the meaning of obedience to God and His Apostle is clear, i.e. all authority belongs to them alone and that their command is the real Law. Obedience to the people in authority is also clearly commanded and it is required that they should be from among you. The requirement that the people with authority should be from among Muslims clearly shows that they should be elected from amongst Muslims. This is so because a person acquiring political power by force can neither be one from among the people nor does he consider himself to be so. He does not consider himself in any way less than supernatural and the shadow of God on earth. If he is from among the Muslims he would be accountable to them. Still obedience to the people in authority is enjoined in good deeds but not in wrong or bad ones. On the other hand it is an act of virtue to remove from authority in such circumstances. There is a Hadith in *Sahih Bukhari* as well as *Sahih Muslim* narrated by Ibada Bin Sammit, which says:

"We will not dispute with our rulers till we see open incredulity which may be a Divine argument with us against them."[54]

This means that differing from, disputing with and deposing, a ruler who openly defies the Commandments of God and His Holy Prophet is incumbent on all Muslims, because 'obedience is only in virtue and not in vice[55] Besides this there are several verses in the Holy Qur'an and in *Hadith* literature in which Muslims have been commanded to conduct their affairs with mutual consultation[56]. This consultation covers the entire field of shaping the government, removal of the usurper government and mutual human relations. A Muslim who contents himself with mere advice disobeys the spirit of this command. Advice includes the method of its enforcement and accountability for refusal to enforce it. Therefore, if Muslims establish a consultative assembly its status would not be merely that of a consultative board but would include the authority to fix the limits of the ruler's authority, establishing the internal structure for the enforcement of God's commandments and accountability in the event of the ruler's failure to do so. Also, this consultative assembly would be elected because they cannot be deemed to be from among us till we elect them with our consensus.

Essentials of Democracy

As stated above Iqbal's objections to democracy highlight the defects pointed out by other intellectuals as well. Therefore, democracy can be considered only as a technique for shaping governmental system. This is a method by which people elect their own representatives for the legislature. These representatives are bound to enforce the commandments of God, and the Holy Prophet. In case of neglect or shortcoming Muslims can hold them accountable and remove them with the same vote and even no-confidence motion can result in extreme cases. These representatives are accountable to God, the Holy Prophet as well as God's Vicegerent on earth, i.e. to the Muslim populace. Accordingly, there are certain prerequisites for the formation of a successful, ideological Islamic government which should be introduced gradually into the society. They are essential for making this system of government exemplary, successful and stable. These are:

1. To make the system of Islamic government succeed every Muslim individual, including men and women, should be equipped with religious as well as secular education. It is incumbent on the Islamic State to give the highest prority to the improvement of the status of Muslim education immediately on acquiring political power, because without education the people can neither understand society's problems nor distinguish between good and bad and cannot even fully benefit from the enforcement of the *deen* and its blessings. Therefore, progress in education, both religious and secular, is an essential demand of democracy.

2. Every Muslim should pay attention to economic betterment because democracy itself cannot take root in any society without economic prosperity. It is incumbent on every Islamic State to improve the people's economic, medical and residential conditions, i.e. arrange for food, clothing and home. This can be achieved only by increasing lawful occupations for people, to guide and help them in this respect and put in place the economic planning which would result in equitable distribution

of society's wealth among Muslims to free them from the fear of poverty. Every Muslim can appeal to the Islamic State for seeking an occupation and satisfaction of his economic needs, and can obtain economic protection for himself by recourse to legal means. Economic prosperity of the people is essential for the success of democracy.

3. The rule and superiority of law is very essential for the success of democracy. A. system of justice should be established which would enable a common man to hold the ruler accountable, and should be able to question the ruler for any excesses of his. It should be easy to obtain justice. The oppressed should not have to beg for justice, but the State should punish the aggressor and should meet out justice unrequested. The highest placed aggressor should not be above the law, and the meanest oppressed should not be left deprived of justice. To provide justice is the legal obligation of the State.

4. Satisfaction of the above three requirements for democracy would lead to the automatic satisfaction of the fourth one. However, it is necessary to give full attention to that as well. This is the ethical and political training of the masses. The more attention the Islamic State would bestow on this the more the people would acquire political and ethical awakening and power, which would enable them to be useful to their country's political system. This can also lead to the control of the defects of democracy and its being moulded into an exemplary system whose benefits and blessings would emanate from it and reach even the common people.

Iqbal and Application of Democracy to Pakistani Society

All discussion of democracy, *Khilafah* or Islamic system in our country during the past sixty years have been the masterpieces of idealistic abstrast thought. Only Mawlana Mawdudi, Dr. Khalifah Abdul Hakim, Mawlana Muhammad Hanif Nadvi and a few other scholars, though rejecting the basic concepts of Western democracy, have considered its basic spirit to be somewhat concordant with Islam. In the same way Iqbal, notwithstanding his declaring the Western civilization to be the greatest hinderance in the way of man's ethical advancement, has adjudged the approach towards the tangibility of Western civilization and its religious experimentation in the spirit of inquiry as thoughtfulness. Nevertheless many people, under the cover of Western civilization, have rejected Islam's consultative system, which is only an early form of Western democracy, in a manner which has provided stability to the country's dictatorship and has frustrated the people's democratic and Islamic aspirations. This has given the impression that Islam supports dictatorship. Every dictator raised the slogan of Islam's rejection of Western democracy in order to stabilize his dictatorship. With this alleged rejection of democracy by Islam they provided a licence for their dictatorship. This period has also produced a generation of people who provided arguments from Islamic history in support of dictatorship. This went so far that a well known religious scholar declared that 'the first martial law was enforced by Hadhrat Abu Bakr Siddique."[57] Thus, martial law was defended in this country. The Consultative Assembly was said to have the function of advice only and it was up to the ruler or the dictator to accept or reject the same. The Consultative Assembly was nominated and, reducing it to the status of a mere consultative board, the 'Islamic system' was enforced under the dictator's own authority. However, under the people's strong pressure some progress since has been made, though unwillingly, and ultimately a limited democracy has been restored somehow. In spite of passing through all the crises may God keep Pakistan as the first real democracy of the Islamic world whose leading role may be followed by other Muslim countries. We are confident of the restoration of a completely Islamic or, in Iqbal's words, a "spiritual democracy" if the country proceeds in the right direction, albeit with limited democracy. Still it is very necessary to introduce and watch the above-mentioned prerequisites for democracy, which are also its goals.

I want to emphasize here that the complete Islamic democracy cannot be established with a stroke of pen. The enactment of the above-stated prerequisites are essential for establishing an ideal democracy. Democracy will gain stability, progress and stature as education spreads among the people, improving their economic condition and imparting political and ethical training to them. All this will lead to general social welfare. According to Ewing "The success of democracy depends mainly on the creation among its citizens of a consciousness of good and evil without any confusion."[58] Consequently, getting rid of the limitations of adages and idealism the country's resources and problems should be viewed in a practical and feasible way, and efforts should be made towards the Islam's idealistic system of government, or Iqbal's "spiritual democracy". The work of establishing assemblies in the country on the basis of adult franchise should continue. The opportunities for the fulfilment of the ambitions of dictators and political fortune hunters should be removed and national disputes should be referred to the Supreme Court.

Understanding Iqbal's Philosophy

The judicature should be strong enough to issue judgements in the interests of the national weal and without fear or favour of the rulers, instead of entrusting the destiny of the people to them. The count president should be empowered to order a referendum on specific problems in times of need. Consequently, we present the following suggestions with reference to the Pakistan's special conditions and problems so that Iqbal's "spiritual democracy" may strike roots in the country:

1. As has been clarified in the Objectives Resolution it should be a part and parcel of the constitution that the establishment of Islam's "spiritual democracy" in the country is the object of our lives. If somebody establishes dictatorship or martial law by force he would be a traitor to the constitution, country, God and the Holy Prophet. The country's sovereignty resides in God, and the Holy Prophet and the Holy Qur'an and the Sunnah are the basic ingredients and sources of the country's constitution. By virtue of being the Vicegerents of God on earth all Muslims are the custodians of the Supreme Sovereignty of God and the Holy Prophet.

2. By virtue of being God's Vicegerents on earth all Muslims are jointly responsible for enforcing Islam's "spiritual democracy". Consequently, fixation of the destiny of Islamic society will rest with the consensus of the *Ummah* and the *Ummah* will create the Consultative Assembly, through its elected representatives. Members of this Consultative Assembly can be elected from all walks of life. The government, i.e. the Executive will be created by the Consultative Assembly and will be answerable to it. This a assembly will have full legislative powers; it will be authorized to *Ijtihad* in the interpretation of the Holy Qur'an and the Sunnah and will be answerable to the people for its decisions. The people will be empowered to reject or alter the *Ijtihad* of the Consultative Assembly through a referendum. Still, the shaping of the government, legislation, and dismissal of government will be enacted by the common Muslims of the country instead of a single institution, person or authority. The people will be allowed to form political parties to achieve these objectives. If the different schools of juristic thoughts are acceptable for the interpretation and explanation of *deen* they should also be similarly acceptable for the attainment of political objectives of the country and the shaping of the Islamic political system. They have the right to state their stand and to obtain its acceptance by the people as long as the effort is in conformity with the democratic principles. At the time of the election of the first Divinely guided *Khalifah* the Muslims had been

divided into three political schools of thought, i.e. *Muhajireen, Ansars* and Supporters of Hadhrat Ali. If these schools had thrived they would have progressed in the form of political parties with different opinions instead of being divided into shortsighted religious groups. They would have been capable of managing the country's affairs with tolerance, endurance and patience instead of being shortsightedly violent in their own stands. But autocratic monarchy stopped the natural political evolution of Muslims and laid the foundation of their downfall.

3. It will be the basic duty of the Islamic State to help and guide every citizen in his effort to be an exemplary Muslim, and will furnish free education to every citizen, provide free justice and above all provide occupation for every citizen or, in the alternative, to assume complete responsibility for his economic needs. Every citizen will have constitutional assurance for the above four rights and will be entitled to obtain these rights through legal procedures. This is necessary also because as Whitehead says: "Democratic society is not established till people acquire a philosophic outlook by general education."[59]

4. Initiatives will be taken for the gradual elimination of the privileged classes on social, religious, political and economic levels and efforts will be made for the equitable distribution of country's resources among all the citizens.

5. The State will guard the interests of Muslims throughout the world, whenever they are ruled as an under - privileged class and will help them in gaining independence and establishing the Islamic way of life.

6. The State will invite all mankind towards the Islamic system, will provide all possible help to all the oppressed and down-trodden people, will cooperate with peace loving nations to prevent oppression, and will do every thing possible for establishment of world peace and will protect all mankind from adventurers and enemies of humanity.

These are the standards and ideals of the Islamic State or "Islamic spiritual democracy", which we should always in view and which have been repeatedly explained by Iqbal in his thoughts and works, and for the attainment of which he has repeatedly urged Muslims. If we start moving towards the attainment of these ideals gradually through democracy we can fulfill Iqbal's dream in which he has said:

ایک ہوں مسلم حرم کی پاسبانی کے لئے
نیل کے ساحل سے لے کر تابخاکِ کاشغر

"Muslims should unite into a single body for *Haram's* defence
From the shores of the Nile to the land of Kashghar."⁶⁰

This was the new fervour produced by Iqbal from Lahore to the land of Bukhara and Samarqand, i.e. he created the longing in Muslims to mould themselves in the frame of independent "Islamic spiritual democracy" shape new societies on the basis of equality and freedom and revive Islamic civilization and culture; i.e. to become the messengers of Teed of God and *wahdat* of humanity, and strive for peace and 'prosperity for all mankind:

اک ولولہء تازہ دیا میں نے دلوں کو
لاہور سے تا بہ خاکِ بخارا و سمر قند

"I infused a new fervour in ail hearts
From Lahore to the Lands of Bukhara and Samarqand."⁶¹

References

(1). Nadvi, Muhammad Hanif - *Isasiyat-i-Islam*. Published by the Idara-i-Saqafat-i-Islamia, Lahore: p. 205, 1973

(2). *The Encyclopedia of Philosophy*. 2: 77-78

(3-5). Hakim, Dr. Khalifah Abdul: *Fikr-i-Iqbal*. Published by Bazm-i-Iqbal, Lahore, Fourth Edition, p. 281, 1968

(6). Firaqui, Tahseen: *Maghribi Jamhooriat, Ahl-i-Maghrib kee Nazar Men*. Markaz-i-Tahqiq, Dayal Singh Trust, Lahore: p.3, 1983

(7-9). Durant, Wil (1885) - *History of Philosophy*. Urdu Translation (*Dastan-i-Falsafah*) By Syed Abid Ali. Published by Maktaba-i-Franklin, Lahore: P. 44

(10). Durant, Wil (1885) - *The Pleasure to Philosophy*. Urdu Translation (*Nishat-i-Falsafah*) by Dr. Muhammad Ajmal. Published by Maktaba-i-Khawar, Lahore. p. 101, 1966.

(11). Rousseau, Jean Jaques - *Le Contract Sociale*. Vol. III, Chapter IV, p. 762

(12). Guenon, Rene, *The Crisis of the Modern World*. Urdu Translation (*Nai Dunia ka Bohran*). Published by Suhail Academy, Lahore. pp. 69-78 (cited Tahseen Firaqui in *Maghribi Jamhooriat, Ahl-i-Maghrib Kee Nazar Main*, p. 45

(13). Eaton, Gai: *The King of The Castle*: Chapters 3, 4

(14). Munawwar, Professor Muhammad "Iqbal's Idea of Democracy". (*Iqbal Review*, Vol. 27, No.1; p. 104, 1986)

(15). Iqbal, Dr. Sir Muhammad: *Bang-i-Dara*. Published by Shaikh Mubarik Ali, Lahore, Pakistan, Third Edition 1930, p.26

(16). Iqbal, Dr. Sir Muhammad: *Payam-i-Mashriq*. Published by Dr. Javid Iqbal at Shaikh Ghulam Ali & Sons, Lahore, Pakistan, Thirteenth Edition. 1971. p. 158

(17). Iqbal, Dr. Sir Muhammad: *Zabur-i-Ajam (Gulshan-i-Raz Jadeed)*. Published by Dr. Javid Iqbal at the Pakisatan Times Press, Lahore, Pakistan. Ninth Edition 1970, p.233

(18). Iqbal, Dr. Sir Muhammad: *Zarb-i-Kalim*. Published by Maktaba-i-Jamia, Dehli, India. First Edition 1941: p. 150

(19). Iqbal, Dr. Sir Muhammad: *Armaghan-i-Hijaz*. Published by Kapoor Arts Printing Works, Lahore, Pakistan. First Edition pp. 218, 1938

(20). Ibid., p. 217

(21). *Bang-i-Dara*, p.335

(22). *Zarb-i-Kalim*, p.164

(23). Iqbal, Dr. Sir Muhammad (1930): – *The Reconstruction of Religious Thought in Islam*. Published by Shaikh Muhammad Ashraf, Lahore, Pakistan (1982) : p. 174

(24). *Firk-i-Iqbal*: p. 298

(25-26). *Isasiyat-i-Islam,*: p. 212

(27). Reconstruction: pp. 173-74

(28). Ibid., p. 173

(29). Ibid., p. 159

(30). Ibid., p. 168

(31). Ibid., p. 159

(32). Ibid., p. 157

(33). Ibid., p.179

(34). Ibid., p. 179

(35). Ibid., p. 179

(36). Ibid., p. 179

(37). Ibid., p. 179

(38). Ibid., p. 180

(39). Ibid., p. 157

(40). Ibid., p. 157

(41). Ibid., p. 150

(42). *Bal-i-Jibril*, p.62

(43). *Bang-i-Dara*, p. 296

(44). Dar, B.A. - *A Study of Iqbal's Philosophy*. Published by Shaikh Ghulam Ali & Sons, Lahore, Pakistan. pp. 276-7.

(45). Mawdudi, Mawlana Syed Abul A'ala: *Islami Riasat*. Published by the Islamic Publications, Lahore, Pakistan: pp. 479-80

(46). Ibid., p.480

(47). Siddiqui, Muhammad, Mazharuddin - *Islam and Theocracy*. Published by the Institute of Islamic Culture: pp. 42-43,

(48). Isasiyat-i-Islam,: p. 181

(49). Khawaja Mu'eenuddin Chishti

(50). *Sahih Bukhari* – "Kitab-ul-Ahkam": Bab

(51). Ibid.

(52). The Holy Qur'an. Surah al-Nisa: Verse 58

(53). Ibid: Verse 59

(54). *Sahih Bukhari*

(55). *Sahih Bukhari*

(56). The Holy Qur'an. Surah al-Shoorah: Verse 38

(57). Mawlana Muhammad Malik Kandhalavi, Member Consultative Assembly of Pakistan made this *Ijtihad* in support of Martial Law. The *Ijtihad* was published in all newspapers countrywide and was the target of criticism.

(58). Ewing, A.S. *The Basic Problems of Philosophy*. Urdu Translation (*Flasafe ke Bunyadi Masail*). Published by the National Book Trust India, New Delhi, India: p. 14

(59). Whitehead, A.N. – in: Ibid., p.14

(60). *Bang-i-Dara*, p. 301

(61). *Zarb-i-Kalim*, p. 15

Iqbal and Democracy

Explanatory Notes

Ijtihad - The efforts of jurists to determine the right course of action in new situations the light of the sources of the *Shariah*. A *Mujtahid* is the person who makes an independent *Ijtihad*.

Mawlana Muhammad Hanif Nadavi (1908-1987) - He was a research fellow in Institute of Islamic culture, Lahore, Pakistan. He has written many books on Islam, Islamic Philosophy, Qur'an and Islamic Fiqa.

Dr. Khalifah Abdul Hakim (1901-1959) – Professor of Philosophy in Hyderabad University Deccan, Principal Amir Singh College, Srinagar, Kashmir, Director Institute of Islamic Culture, Lahore. *Islamic Iqbal*, *Prophet and his Message*, *Fikr-i-Iqbal* and *Meta Physics of Rumi* his well-known books.

Abraham Lincoln (1809-65) - The sixteenth president of the United States of America. He was a lawyer by profession, and rose rapidly in politics from a member of the House of Representatives of the State of Illinois (1834) to the office of the President of the United States (1860-65). His presidency is famous for the successful conduct of the Civil War which had been fought on the issue of abolition of slavery. With all his responsibilites, which were increased manyfolds by the Civil War, he could find time for reflection and meditation. The favourite subject for his meditation was the inscrutable Will of God. He is also famous for his definition of democracy cited in the text.

Thomas Jefferson (1743-1825) - The third president of the United States of America. He was a planter, architect, scientist, educator, and an ardent speaker on human liberty. He is the author of the famous Declaration of Independence. He was elected to the presidency in 1800. The American nation was divided at that time and the federal administration was very repressive against those who were advocating a weak federal and strong state political structure. He was against this policy. During his presidency he successfully gathered round him a group of very loyal subordinates. He did not try to achieve his goals by coercive measures as his predecessors had done, but by strong faith, hard work, high priority for public interest, systematic habits of thought and effort, encouraging science and free inquiry, and by his strong zeal for the 'holy cause of freedom'.

Understanding Iqbal's Philosophy

David Herbert Lawrence (1885-1930) - English novelist, poet and essayist who was one of the most gifted literary figures of the twentieth century. He was a radical and warned his country men of the coming dangers resulting from the West's abuses of power, and the dangerous power vacuum created by World War I.

Harold Laski (1893-1950) - He was a British socialist, a member of the Fabian Society and the British Labour Party. Professionally, he was a professor of History, first at the McGill University at Montreal, Canada (1914-16), then at Harvard University, U.S.A (1916-20) and lastly the London School of Economics. In Canada and U.S.A his views were looked upon with disfavour. He also wrote editorials for the *Daily Herald* (1914-16), and while at the London School of Economics he concentrated on writing books on politics and political philosophy. During the course of his life his views changed from socialism, (in which he defended the rights of special groups, such as labour and religious classes against the State) through individualism (under the influence of John Stuart Mill) to strict Marxism.

Hadhrat Ali (600-661) - He was the Holy Prophet's cousin and son-in-law by marriage with his daughter Hadhrat Fatima. He was the first among the youth of Mecca to accept Islam and was on of the most trusted and closest companions of the Holy Prophet. At the time of the Holy Prophet's immigration from Mecca to Medina in 622 he stayed behind in Mecca to settle outstanding affairs. He also slept in the Holy Prophet's bed to overstall suspicions among the Quraish and in doing so risked his own life. Hadhrat Ali was always in the forefront of the struggle for the establishment of Islam at all levels. He is very famous for his prowess during *Jihad* for which he has become proverbial in Muslim society as well as in Islamic history and literature. Iqbal has frequently alluded to his qualities of bravery and leadership. In addition to all this he was an eminent scholar and lecturer of Arabic. He has a place of honour in these fields due to his poetry and his famous book, *Nahj-al-Balaghah* (Ways of Eloquence), which is a collection of his sayings, lectures, sermons and letters. During the rule of the first three divinely-guided *Khalifahs* he fully cooperated with them. However, when he was elected to the *Khilafah* after the martyrdom of Hadhrat Usman in 656 Hadhrat Amir Muawiyya did not take *baiat* at his hands. A period of controversy and struggle between him and Hadhrat Muawiyya ensued which lasted till his martyrdom in 661 by a man seeking personal vengeance. Views differ on the apportioning of blame for this fighting. However, the motivating force behind this fighting is agreed upon to be the clannish rivalry between the Bani Hashim (Hadhrat Ali's clan) and Bani Umayya (Hadhrat Ameer Muawiyya's clan). It also appears to have been caused by the latter's ambition for monarchy, which is supported by the fact that Hadhrat Amir Muawiyya was not duly elected, but declared himself to be the *Khalifah,* and enthroned his son Yazid at the time of his death. However, this unfortunate affair resulted in the first schism in Islamic history and the end of the Divinely-guided *Khilafah,* as well as its usurpation by monarchy. The Islamic world has suffered for about fourteen centuries from its effects.

Hadhrat Amir Muawiyya (602-680) - He was the son of Abu Sufyan who was a rich merchant of Meeca. Abu Sufyan was One of the strongest enemies of Islam and was the leader of the Quraishi in all the military combats between Muslims and the pagan Quraish. He accepted Islam only after the conquest of Mecca and was forgiven by the Holy Prophet for all his anti-Islamic activities. The unfortunate role played by Hadhrat Amir Muawiyya in Islaimc history has been broaded to in the previous note. However, in spite of these shortcomings he did some good work. He reorganized the army, created a navy, and attempted to take Asia Minor from the Byzantines, in which he did not succeed. His armies moved east as far as Central Asia and west as far as Algeria.

Yazid (642-683) - He was the son of Hadhrat Amir Muawiyya and was nominated by the latter to the *Khilafah*. This action confirmed the conversion of the *Khilafah* into monarchy, which has continued since then in the Islaimc world. Hadhrat Imam Hasan and Hadhrat Imam Husain the two sons of Hadhrat Ali - did not take *baiat* at the hands of Yazid on account of the latter's illegal appointment to that position by his father, as stated above. The controversy between Yazid and the two brothers culminated in the martyrdom of both the brothers, that of the former by poisoning and the latter's in the Battle of Karbala, in which many other Muslims were also martyred. This battle is one of the most painful chapters of Islamic history and sealed the future, of the divinely-guided *Khalifah* forever, till now at least.

Baiat - Oath of allegiance to the *Khalifah*

Khalifah - *Khalifah* is the person responsible for keeping order and enforcing the laws. This term as used in the Holy Qur'an denotes a deputy who takes care of and manages the affairs of the original. The original, accordingly, is the group of the ruled people who authorizes the deputy to keep order and enforce he law of the *Shariah*. *Khilafah* is the political system or institution in which the *Khalifah* works. (Kurdi, Abdulrahman Abdul Kadir (1984) - *The Islamic State - A Study based on the Islamic Holy Constitution*. Published by the Mansell Publishing Ltd., New York, pp. 23-24).

Deen - *Deen* and *Mazhab* are often interchangeably used and iously translated into English, which gives the false impression of their synonymity. However, in Islamic literature they are used as technical terms and are not synonymous. *Deen* means a way of life, covering all human activity, in which sense Islam is a d*een* or a way of life based on the Holy Qur'an and the traditions of the Holy Prophet. *Mazhab* is one of the five recognized *Fiqh* systems or systems of Islamic jurisprudence.

Ummah - A nation constituted on the basis of ideology and not geographical boundaries, e.g. the Muslims.

Oliver Cromwell (1599-1658) - Parliamentarion, General in the English Civil War, and Lord Protector of England, Scotland and Ireland after the Civil War. Although he fought the Civil War to a successful conclusion, terminated the cruel rule of Charles I and improved the governments Lord Protector, he did not free it from military control to elevate it to a rule by national consent as is required in democracy.

Awrangzeb (1618-1707) - He was the sixth and the last effective Mughal Emperor of India. He ascended the throne at a time when the cause of Islam in the Indian sub-continent had been badly damaged by the lax and permissive rule of his predecessors. He had to seize the throne by fighting against his father and brothers. After acquiring authority he tried his best to expand his rule and enforce Islam. However, he met very severe opposition from the Marathas, Jats, Rajputs and Sikhs. He spent the greater part of his reign in fighting against them. He could not succeed in his aims as all his efforts amounted to being too late. Though his treatment of his father and brothers leaves much to be desired it is also true that he has been much maligned by the combined efforts of the, British and Hindu intelligentsia. All their accounts of Aurangzeb and his reign should be read with much caution.

Fath Ali Tipu Sultan (1749-1799) - He was the Sultan of Mysore and is famous in the history of the Indian sub-continent of the late eighteenth century. At the initiative of his father, Haider Ali, he was trained in military tactics by French officers. He fought several wars with the Marathas and the British. The last one with the British was fought on May 4, 1799 in which Tipu Sultan was martyred and the State of Mysore fell to the British. This defeat was due to treachery, mainly that of Mir Sadiq, who was Tipu Sultan's prime minister. Tipu Sultan was an able general and administrator and was a man of letters in addition. He has the place of a *Mujahid* and a martyr in the history of the sub-continent, especially in Muslim literature, particularly in Iqbal's works, such as *Javid Namah*. He was also eulogised in the marching songs of the Indian National Army organized in Burma by Mr. Subhas Chandra Bose during World War II with the intention of invading India and seizing it from the British. Thus, he was the symbol of India's independence, and anti-imperialism for Muslims and Hindus alike.

Ijma - Consensus among jurists.

Fiqh - Islamic jurisprudence

Imam and Imamah - Literally 'leader'. The term is used in common tolerance for the person who leads prayer. However, in Islamic literature the term is used for an overall leader and is almost synonymous with *Khalifah*. *Imamah* is the institution in which the Imam functions as the *Khalifah* functions in the *Khilafah*.

Tauheed - To believe and testify that God is one and to fulfil the demands of that belief by struggling in and making sacrifices for his cause.

Professor Muhammad Mazharuddin Siddiqui - He has written a many books on Islamic Philosophy on Iqbal and Muslim's Philosophy and Islamic Culture.

Ansars and Muhajireen - The *Ansars* were the residents of Medina who welcomed the Holy Prophet and the Muslims who migrated with him from Mecca to Medina and were called *Muhajireen*.

A.S. Ewing (1875-1961) - He was renowned modern English philosopher. He was a teacher of philosophy. He has written a many books on philosophy, social problems etc.

Chapter 9

IQBAL AND THE IDEOLOGY OF PAKISTAN

The most prominent of the many characteristics of a philosophy bearing creative wisdom is that it not only penetrates deep into the masses, but itself provides the leadership endowed with the creative wisdom and potential for bringing about large scale changes in society. Such leadership is a portrait of the elegance and majesty of the above philosophy and with its limitless capabilities and powers, establishes and organizes a body of men, out of the whole society, which brings about a universal social revolution, based on the foundations of this philosophy. This philosophy thus penetrating a society, reorganizes it and assembling the society's creative potentials infuses revolutionary sprite into it. It is this revolution which, freeing mankind from oppression and coercion gives a new meaning to their character, by which individuals unite among themselves on the one hand and individuals encourage the creative activities of the society on the other. It, thus, exhbits its own creative character by stirring up the dormant potentials of the society:

The basic purpose of the Pakistan movement or the ideology of Pakistan was the affiliation of an ideology with a land. After the deep study of Europe's materialism, Iqbal realized that the European civilization was nurtured by the materialistic concept of struggle for existence, which means that everything is struggling to maintain its existence and is annihilating everything else in its pursuit of self-preservation; combat and mutual enmity is universal.

Sartre's[1] philosophy is based on the concept of "the existence of the other person being hell". Combat, strife, struggle, wrangling and hostility are the basic principles civilization of materialism on which the materialistic European is founded.

Hegel's thesis, anti-thesis and synthesis also base the evolution of its absolute idea on the same feelings.

Fichte[2], Comte[3] and other European thinkers also base their concept of "the individual being society's adversary and society being individuals adversary" on the same ideology. The ideology of historical dialectical materialism in Marx's works is also shaped on the same feelings of hostility, combat and enmity based on the concept of struggle for existence. However, Marx changed the struggle between individuals and between society and the individual into inter-class struggle, but did not change the basic concept of struggle being the motive for human action. This was due to the constraint that he had based his theory on the same materialism on which the capitalist civilization had been established. Therefore, both capitalism and communism are founded on the bases of materialism and both consider progress and evolution to be the product of wrangle, combat and struggle. The anarchy of thought and intellectual, confusion created by this in Europe has worn out the intellect and nerves of European thinkers. Their attitude has become so peevish that they have started considering life to be purposeless. Behind this concept of purposelessness and absurdity of life is the European mind, born out of Europe's materialist civilization which, having traversed the maddening stages of wrangle and combat, and having considered the existence of the other person fiendish, considers the attainment of purpose in life absurd. This concept of purposelessness has not only pushed the Western civilization towards the first stage of decline but has also exposed its hollowness.

The Intellectual Foundations of Western Civilization

Iqbal has clearly explained this aspect of Western civilization, He has aware of the juiced weakness of this 'nest built on a frail branch'. The apparent brightness of the current European civilization was to him no more than the elegance of non-precious stones. According to Iqbal the present day advancements of the European civilization are the remains of the civilization established by Islam. Iqbal has clearly explained this in *Javid Namah*. Communism itself was born out of materialism's perverse bosom. However, communism demolished one pillar of European civilization, which was nationalism, based on racial pride. Communism not only abolished the concept of geographical nationalism, but also annihilated racial pride with it, and for the first time presented to the European or Western civilization the concept of social equality in human society in a practical way. In addition to this communism played an important role in creating momentous changes in the society's concept of economic motives and on the basis of this realization created an ideology in their system. In this way communism gave the concept of an ideological society to Western civilization for the first time. But in spite of good and praiseworthy successes of communism its basic defect was its being shaped on the foundations of materialism. In their system also life depended upon evolution, hostility and combat. Consequently, it also halted after a short progress and the Western civilization remained deprived on its righteous leader.

On getting a clear understanding of the inherent weakness of Western civilization Iqbal also passed through a strange period of distraction, helplessness, intellectual conflict and being split between hope and fear. This is the period referred to by Iqbal himself in his letters to Atiya,[4] Professor Muhammad Uthman has talked about the same emotional period in Iqbal's life, when he would be lost in thinking. He was foreseeing the death of one civilization in the ear future re and had seen the ruins of another one form Sicily and Spain to Samarqand and Bukhara.[5] The custodians of the latter civilization were then enthralled into slavery everywhere. They wane suffering from a deep feeling of defeatism. Their spirit of *Jihad*[6] and *Ijtihad* had died and they were in a stalemate everywhere. All their dragoman and intellectual potentials, fretting away in non-creative activities, where leading to the annihilation of their own existence. Sectarianism, seditions and false prophets were appearing among them. Edicts of heresy were being issued on petty matters, *bida'ts* were common, and indeed the correct teachings of Islam were being amalgamate ed with *bid'ats*.[7] *Bid'ats* were so prevalent that Muslims ignored the essential commandments of the Holy Qur'an, like prayers, but celebrated *bid'ats* with great efforts and are still doing so. Interpretations and exegeses of the Holy Qur'an were being used for wrong ends. *Ijtihad* was the forbidden tree for scholars. Defeatism, confusion and anarchy had engulfed Muslim society like a flood. In addition to this were the activities of the wars of the Crusades, for annihilating the Muslims all over the world. They were using their efforts with the full force of politics, learning, prudence and tactics. The Hindus in the Indian sub-continent were hand in glove with the British to destroy Muslims. Communism had banished us from Samarqand Bukhara and Tashkent. We had long been thrown out of Spain. After annihilating us from Romania, Bulgaria etc. our removal was complete from Europe at least and we were being constantly attacked in Asia also. It appeared that though the Western civilization was dying it would not stop short of strangulating us also. The Hindus in the Indian sub-continent and the Judeo-Christian clique in the Middle East lent a helping hand in this.

Iqbal and the Ideology of Pakistan

Iqbal was faced with two problems. One was the strategy to safeguard the existence of Muslims in India after Spain. This was a political and cultural question. The second problem was an intellectual and philosophical one, and this was whether a human society could be established on any basis other than materialism. Was the materialism's interpretation of the inter-relationship between the individuals themselves, and between them, the universe and society final? What was Man's destiny if the above was correct? Was it the existing purposelessness, abuse reality of life and destruction and decimation of mankind? Alternatively, was it possible to elucidate and interpretation of the relationship between the universe and Man, the individual and society, and the individual and God on any principle other than materialism and was it possible to establish a philosophy on its foundations?

The Ideological Foundations of Islamic Civilization

The thorough grasp of the Holy Qur'an, wide mastery of the Islamic learning and deep study of the European philosophy and science convinced Iqbal that the civilization of which Islam is the standard bearer, in contrast to the European civilization, can in no way be founded on materialism. On the contrary it is established on spiritualism. In the Islamic philosophy life's development is not based on hostility, combat, enmity, hatred and strife. On the other hand the evolution of human life according to Islam depends on love. In Islam one person is not an enemy of the other but one individual is a companion, intimate friend, comforter and a partner of the other in affliction and suffering. Neither is the individual an enemy of the community nor is the community an adversary of the individual. One individuals essential for the fulfillment of the personality and the exhibition of the socially creative potentials of the other. If only one person had inhabited the earth, or if people had become disinterested in each other, or were constantly hostile to and combatting each other, this excellent edifice, which humanity has established on the earth after the toil of centuries, would not have been built.

Only Man consoles Man. The positive side of human character consists of love, cooperation, compassion, friendship and companionship. People enduring difficulties and hardships in their efforts for manifestation of the virtues of human civilization, in the creation and shaping of human societies, in the establishment of the family and likewise for the very existence of Man, and training and education of the young ones, is the product of the feelings of love alone. However, exaggerated love starts exhibiting its negative tendencies and love turns into hatred, and this hatred, created by exaggerated love, produces anarchy in human society. Love is the positive aspect and hatred the negative aspect of human character. Sartre's thinking that one individual is hell for the other is the vehicle of negative thinking. On the other hand serious thinking will show one individual's existence as a blessing for the other. Without going into details serious observation of the evolution of life in the Universe will show the truth that life grows and flourishes with love and closeness. Love and closeness are basic principles of love's growth. Whenever a human society will shape its community's relationships on the principle of love and unity it will attain its spiritual eminence. The materialistic philosophy of life, based on combat, force, hostility and struggle for existence tends to bring the outside evils into the human soul and the philosophy based on love and unity tends to bring out human virtues form inside out. The former binds a person to *Jabr*[8], while the latter is based on *Qadr*.[9]

The entire European philosophy, being inclined to go inside from outside is based on *Jabr*, while the Islamic philosophy, being inclined to the outside from inside insists on *Qadr*. Capitalism and communism are born of the same mother, i.e. materialism and so are similar in nature and in application. Their philosophy are inclined to be from outside towards inside. That is why they could not solve human problems.[10]

In Iqbal's view, by restricting human culture to materialism, the Western civilization provided it with a very weak foundling and that is why there are ever-growing possibilities of its committing suicide. Consequently, he planned to build human civilization on the sound and real spiritual foundation, Religion, provided him with the most solid foundation for it. This is so because throughout human history religion along has been the standard bearer of spiritualism and religion alone provides the foundation which enables Man to direct his activities from inside out. The study of religion rewarded him with the realization that the foundation of a revealed religion is based on Faith, which is the highest form of intellect. Materialism on the higher form of intellect, i.e. *Ilham*[11] to or the still higher form, called *Wahi*.[12] *Wahi* is the power been the foundation of religion, which has been the guiding force for Man since the time in human history when Man had not even been awakened at the intellectual level. It has accompanied mankind continuously during his entire evolution throughout human history. The foundations of the teachings of *Wahi* are based on three things, i.e.

Iqbal and the Ideology of Pakistan

    (i)   Unity of God *(Tauheed)*
    (ii)   Prophethood *(Risalat)*
    (iii)   The concept of resurrection and accountability for deeds *(Ma'ad)*

In the concept of God's Unity the universe and everything in it has been adjudged to be God's creation, the Overlordship of God has been emphasized, His Unity and Uniqueness has been insisted upon, and, having admitted Him as the Creator, the Lord and the Master, obedience to Him has been set to be the human destiny.

In the concept of brotherhood the presence of a connecting link between God and human beings has been emphasized and the relationship between God and Man has been confirmed. Adjudging the correctness of the messages and instructions so communicated between these two and considering them to be emanating from God, subservience to them has been emphasized. The perception of accountability for human beings has been created with the concept of resurrection, in that on your return to God you will have to explain the extent to which you had been obeying God's commandments. It has been explained that those obeying God's commandments would be honored and those disobeying them would be adjudged to be in error. Those held in honour would be rewarded and those in error would be punished. The teachings of all prophets and religious persons have been based on these very three foundations. Any differences between them are trivial. In this manner religion continued to be propagated among mankind along with the progress of human history till the advent of Hazrat Muhammad, the Last Prophet of God. He confirmed the teachings of the earlier prophets and presented the teachings of all of them in the most perfect and complete form in all respects, in the shape of the divine *Wahi,* or the Holy Qur'an. This was the first stage, when God guaranteed the safety of His *Wahi* and announced the closure of the series of *Wahi* through the same prophet. After obtaining the complete knowledge of the civilization established by Hazrat Muhammad and that of the European civilization, which followed on its heels one can comprehend God's decision of discontinuing the chain of *Wahi*. Progress and evolution of human society had created the ability in human understanding and civilization to the extent to make it difficult for anybody to change the Divine *Wahi,* and the human intellect obtained enough insight with the help of different kinds of knowledge to be able to shape and build human civilization itself in the light of the Divine *Wahi*. Iqbal accepted this highest state of religion and adjudged it as the principle on which human civilization can be shaped on the world-wide basis in the new world order.

The Basic Pillars of the Ideology of Pakistan

In this context Iqbal had two important problems before him. One was the creation and understanding of the correct sense of Islamic eduction, so that the Muslims could know the features of Islamic ideology in detail. His book titled *The Reconstruction of Religious Thought in Islam* was an effort to test religion on the standards of modern knowledge and present it to the present day Man. Along with this book he wanted to reconstruct Islamic *Fiqh*[13] and to write an exegesis of the Holy Qur'an in the light of the new thinking and knowledge. But, unfortunately, death did not spare him. The sole purpose of all these efforts was to remove Islamic teachings from other spurious directions and present them in the contexts of the matters which could help in the solution of the present day's human problems and which could provide the basis for the revival of Islamic civilization. His intention was also to open the door for *Ijtihad,* which had remained closed for centuries.

India's taverns have remained closed for three hundred years
It is only timely that thy avours be general O dispenser of wine *(saqi)*

However, far more important than all this was the solution of humanity's burning problems on the basis of religion. Iqbal prepared the plan for the establishment of an Islamic Institute at Pathankot, in the Punjab, India, and for this purpose he wanted to invite Syed Abul A'ala Mawdudi from Heyderabad, Deccan to the Punjab to participate in his efforts. However, unfortunately that project could not start under Iqbal's supervision. An important problem for Iqbal was the explanation and interpretation of Islam in conformity with the demands of the spirit of the times, which could shape human civilization on the basis of spiritualism and religion and which would establish universal brotherhood among men.

The other important problem before Iqbal was the protection of Islamic ideology from isolationism and abstruseness. Bare ideology and abstract theory has no value and is no more than a pleasant concept. The importance of communism also was recognized only when Lenin[14] enforced it in Russia. Iqbal did not want to view Islam as a mere theory or an abstract way of life. He desired to see it promulgated in a practical form. He was deeply conscious of the fact that the beauty and the miracle of Islam can appear only when an Islamic society is organized' under Islam's teachings and when the Islamic ideology pervades through the actions of the populace. Iqbal tried to strengthen the grasp of Islamic belief and ideology among the common people with the help of his poetry. However, he was confronted with the problem of creating a leadership, which would be the vehicle of an unshakeable faith in the Islamic ideology, and at the same time be endowed with the intellectual and cultural understanding of the present times; which would be conversant with the European languages; and which would be strong enough to face the internal pressures of the so-called Muslims and the external pressures of Hindus, British and communists against the enforcement of Islamic ideology; which should have a crystal clear character and should be like a rock in its purpose and will. It was, the good fortune of Iqbal's thought that the true believer who had reached the zenith of *Khudi*[15] and whom Iqbal had made the center of his thought actually existed in the solid world of real life. He was the one whose 'soft character would cool the delicate tulip' and the 'storm of whose political sagacity and intelligence would frighten the oceans hearts'; whose insight could not be dazzled by the false effulgence of European cunnilingus; who had committed to heart all the lessons of truthfulness, nobility and justice, whose heart was teeming with the deep love for Muslims and who was also endowed with the potential of converting the dram of Islamic renaissance into reality Iqbal had to assume the practical leadership of Muslim for a short period of time. However, he was the thought, and the Quaid-i-Azam Muhammad Ali Jinnah was the action, the incessant action, which was overflowing with the faith in Islamic ideology. Organization was all that was needed. Consequently, when after a long and important communication with Iqbal, the Quaid-i-Azam undertook the responsibility of organizing the sub-continent's Muslims under the Muslim League, his very first step was his affiliation with a movement for a land based on Islamic ideology. Iqbal provided the right personality of Islamic ideology, gave us its knowledge and provided us with an eminent leader in the person of the Quaid-i-Azam. In the Presidential address of the Muslim League Convention of 1930 at Allahabad he also gave us a manifesto which contained the practical proposals for affiliation with a land based on Islamic ideology. The sub-continent's Muslims took the oath of allegiance at the hands of the Quaid-i-Azam on March 23, 1940 and resolved to centralize their efforts for the establishment of a sovereign state on the basis of Islamic ideology by combining the Muslim majority provinces of the north-west and the Province of Bengal on the east of the sub-continent.

Understanding Iqbal's Philosophy

Thus started the plan for translating Iqbal's thought into action under the leadership of the Quaid-i-Azam. If Iqbal had not existed the sub-continent's Muslims would have had an undetermined destiny. Similarly, in the absence of the Quaid-i-Azam, if Iqbal had not existed the sub-continent's Muslim would have had an undetermined destiny. Similarly, in the absence of the Quaid-i-Azam Iqbal's ideology would have been the victim of isolationism and abstruseness. The destiny of the sub-continent's Muslims would have remained at the mercy of the Hindus and the naive Muslim leaders. The controversy about the comparative greatness of the Quaid-i-Azam and Iqbal is naivete and childish. Iqbal was the lighthouse of eminent thought and Quaid-i-Azam was the incessant action. Iqbal and the Quaid-i-Azam are respectively the intellectual and the practical architects of Pakistan. Their thinking and active mutual cooperation, sincerity, mutual understanding and feelings of loyalty and sacrifice for each other, converted into reality the possibility of affiliation with a land based on the ideology of Islam on the one hand and on the other succeeded in preserving the cultural entity of the sub-continent's Muslims.

"Fortunately, the solution for this problem has been found in the promulgation of Islamic law and in expanding it further in the light of the new concepts. After long and deep study of Islamic law I have reached the conclusion that at least every individual's economic rights can be protected by enacting this legal system after its proper understanding. However, its application is not possible without one or more independent Muslim States."

Consequently, for the promulgation of the Islamic economic system in a practical form the sub-continent's Muslims needed a country which would be completely under their control. In the present age no nation can establish its entity without making itself economically stable and without establishing a strong economic system. Hence, the subcontinent's Muslims needed Pakistan to enable them to establish their unique economic system, distinct from communism and capitalism.

The question arose as to why Muslims could not attain economic strength while living alongside with Hindus in the sub-continent. Iqbal has answered this clearly:

"At least the new constitution has provided the Indian Muslims with the unique opportunity of organizing themselves in line with the progress in India and the Muslim Asia."

Iqbal and the Ideology of Pakistan

In addition, Iqbal bad the deep perception that:

"The future of Islam in the form of an ethical and political power in Asia was mainly based on the complete organization of Indian Muslims."

The organization of the Muslim nation is the salvation for the East,
The Asian nations are still unaware of this secret

The purpose of the future political progress in India and Muslim Asia was the emergence of movements of political awakening among Muslims and the destruction of the network of the colonial system on the basis of the nations' right of self determination and transfer of political power to the people. As far as the other Muslim countries were concerned Muslims were in majority there. Hence, in view of the nations' right of self determination and their democratic rights, supreme authority had to be transferred to them at all costs. However, in the Indian sub-continent, thought Muslims existed as a separate nation transfer of political power to them was not possible. This was so because Hindus lived in India as a majority nation. Most Muslim movements were founded on the notion that because power had been taken away from Muslim it must be restored to them alone. These movements were organizing, the Muslims on the basis of return of power to them over the whole of India. However, this military organization had the weakness that their leaders lacked the feeling based on the emergence of the concept of self determination. Even if Muslims had acquired poor over the entire sub-continent by military strength it would not have been possible for them to retain it for a long time, and the sub-continent would have been engulfed in civil war. It had the added danger that an organizationally stronger majority would danger that an organizationally stronger majority would have completely annihilated a disorganized minority. Consequently, the best peaceful solution of the sub-continent's problem was to transfer power separately to both the large nations of the sub-continent in the respective areas of their majority not he basis of the right of self determination. This is what actually happened and solved the cultural problem which was referred to by Iqbal in his letter dated March 30, 1937 to Quaid-i-Azam Muhammad Ali Jinnah. Its basic concept was based on affiliation with a land of Islamic ideology.

The Strong Advocate of Pakistan's Ideology

Though Quaid-i-Azam Muhammad Ali Jinnah took part in practical politics with and in apprenticeship of Dadabhai Naoroji[16] and Mr. Gopal

Understanding Iqbal's Philosophy

Krishna Gokhale[17], the centre of his early activities was restricted to free Indians from the domination of the colonial system. Consequently, when he joined the Congress he did not have the concept of the Hindu or the Muslim nation, but that of the Indians. Outwardly the Congress was claiming to be the representative organization of all the citizens of the sub-continent and not that of the Hindus or the Muslims, and that, broadly speaking, it aimed at ending the colonial system and attaining freedom for India. On joining the Congress the Quaid-i-Azam also worked for Hindu-Muslim unity, as a result of which the Jinnah Hall was constructed in Bombay, and Hindus gave him the title of the "Messenger of Peace". The Quaid-i-Azam was at first personally in favour of joint elections thought, respecting the Muslim sentiment, he later stressed separate electorates. The difference between the Quaid-i-Azam and Congress surfaced openly after the publication of the Nehru Report[18], commenting on the Nehru Report, had said:

"In my youth I was very fond of keeping hounds, but I have never seen
any hound treating a rabbit as the Nehru Report has treated Muslims".

The famous English newspaper, the "Times of India" said:

"The unanimity of Muslim feelings in the Assembly was unexpected and worrisome to those shaping up the Nehru Report as the Joint demand of India, Hence, such a claim appears ridiculous".

Dr. K. K. Aziz[19] considered the Nehru Report as the point of termination of the efforts at Hindu-Muslim unity and said that by presenting the Nehru Report and rejecting the amendments proposed to it, the Hindus had severed relations with Muslims permanently. His words are:

"Right at the termination of the Khilafat Movement the short Hindu-Muslim honeymoon ended and opposition and enmity surfaced once again. However, this time its intensity had increased and no possibility remained for their unity. The Nehru Report sealed this tension and peace disappeared from India for ever".

Quaid-i-Azam, Muhammad Ali Jinnah who was once considered to be the ambassador of Hindu-Muslim unity made the comment "This is the

Iqbal and the Ideology of Pakistan

parting of the ways", on the acceptance of the Nehru Report and rejection of his amendments to it.

The Quaid-i-Azam, then, abandoned efforts at Hindu-Muslim unity after the Nehru Report and presented his famous fourteen points at the Muslim League Convention at Delhi at the end of March 1929. These were:

"(i) The form of the future constitution should be federal with residuary powers vested in the provinces.

"(ii) A uniform measure of autonomy should be granted to all provinces.

"(iii) All legislatures of the country. and other elected bodies shall be constituted on the definite principle of adequate and effective representation of minorities without reducing the majority in any province to a minority or even equality.

"(iv) In the Central Legislature, Musalman representation shall not be less than onethird.

"(v) Representation of communal groups shall continue to be by means of separate electorates as at present; provided it shall be open to any community, at any time, to abandon its separate electorate in favour of joint electorate.

"(vi) Any territorial re-distribution that might at any time be necessary shall not, in any way affect the Muslim majority in the Punjab, Bengal and North-Western Frontier Province.

"(vii) Full religious liberty, i.e. liberty of belief, worship and observance, propagation, association and education, shall be guaranteed to all communities.

"(viii) No bill or resolution or any part thereof shall be passed in any legislature or any other elected body if three-fourths of the members of any community in that particular body oppose such a bill, resolution or part thereof on the ground that it would be injurious to the interests of that community, or in the alternative, such other method is devised as may be found feasible and practicable to deal with such cases.

"(ix) Sind should.be saparated~from the Bombay Presidency.

"(x) Reforms should be introduced in the North-West Frotier Province and
Baluchistan on the same footing as in other provinces.

"(xi) Provision should be made in the constituent giving Muslims an adequate share along with the other Indians; in all the services of the State and local self-governing bodies having due regard to the requirements of efficiency.

"(xii) The constitution should embody adequate safeguards for the protection of Muslim culture and for the protection and promotion of Muslim education, language, religion, personal laws and Muslim charitable institutions and for their due share in the grants-in-aid given by the state and by the self-governing bodies.

"(xiii) No cabinet, either central or provincial, should be formed without there being a proportion of at least one-third Muslim ministers.

"(xiv) No change will be made in the constitution by the Central Legislature except with the concurrence of the States constituting the Indian Federation."

These demands were rightfully founded and did not hurt any nation's rights. The purpose of presenting these demands was the safeguarding of the Muslims' rights in the sub-continent, so that the Muslim existence could be accepted as a separate and distinct nation, and their cultural, religious, economic and political welfare could be safeguarded. These points neither discriminated against any nation nor were intended to insult any one. This was a positive initiative, so that as two nations existed in the sub-continent, Muslims as a nation had the right to protect their economic, cultural, social and religious individuality. Though the hope for Hindu-Muslim unity had been frustrated by the rejection of the Quaid-i-Azam's these fourteen points, he kept the door open for preserving at least a working relationship between the tow nations. He always tried to obtain cooperation from Hindus. However, when the

Iqbal and the Ideology of Pakistan

Hindus adopted the trend of non-cooperation and lack of amity in every affair the question of safeguarding the national pride stared the Muslim in the face, as to how they could protect their political future in the sub-continent. The nation's sage, Sir Muhammad Iqbal provided leadership at this juncture. He examined in detail the problems of the sub-continent's Muslims in his presidential address at the All-India Muslim League Convention at Allahabad in December 1930 and advised them that:

> "It is my desire that the Punjab, North-West Frontier Province, Sind and Baluchistan be consolidate into a self-governing State, either within or outside the British Empire. It appears to me essential for the an organized Islamic State"

He gave the following reasons for it:

> "If we want to keep Islam alive as a cultural power it is necessary to establish its centre in a specific area"

Conflict between Secular-Geographic and Islamic Nationalism

Earlier, Iqbal, under the title of "Islam and Nationalism", in the he above address, had already rejected the Congressite and National Muslims' concept under which they were propagating the ideology of Indian nationalism the sub-continent and were presenting the fallacy of the Hindus and the Muslims being one nation.[20]

Iqbal had explained the concept of Islamic nation at many places in his prose and poetry. Throwing light on Islam's concepts of nation he said in the above mentioned address:

> "In India also, like other countries, the structure of the Muslim society is indebted to the spirit of Islam alone, because a special spirit pervades throughout Islamic culture. By this I mean that the internal unity and the external similarity of the Muslims is derived from the laws and the institutions which are associated with Islamic civilization".

Iqbal presented the same thoughts to Quaid-i-Azam in a letter, saying that "I am confident that you appreciate the fact that the constitution has at least provided the unique opportunity to Indian

Muslims to organize themselves in conformity with the political advancements in India and Muslim Asia. As we agree to cooperate with other progressive organizations of the country we should not forget the fact that the future of Islam in the form of an ethical and political power largely depends upon the complete organization of Indian Muslim".

Iqbal emphasized in the same letter to Quaid-i-Azam that:

"I propose that the All-India Muslim Convention give an effective reply. You should hold a session of the All-India Muslim Convention in Delhi immediately and invite the Muslim members of the new provincial legislative assemblies and other prominent Muslim leaders to it. The political ideal of the organization of Muslim Indians as a distinct political unit should be reiterated in this convention with all possible force. It is essential to clarify to the internal Indian and the external world that the economic problem is not the only problem of the country. From the Islamic point of view India is the bearer of important consequences in the shape of cultural problems for almost all Muslims. In any case it is not less important than the economic problem."

The thoughts expressed by Iqbal in his Allahabad address contained deep reelections on the problem of Muslims in India. Muslims never felt their national identity endangered during the period of their power in India. After the 1857 War of Independence the Hindus entered into an understanding with the British and busied themselves in the he-efforts for their renaissance in cooperation with the British power: They considered their former rulers (Muslims) as adversaries and planned to destroy them gravelly. This was so because they were conscious of the fact that a tiny little country like Britain, which has occupied India by force for economic benefits, rather than for the advancement of any ideology, would not be able to retain its poor for a long period of time. As Britain would have to leave India some-day it would be futile to entertain hostility towards it. As their former rulers would be their adversaries after the departure of the British it was considered necessary to obtain British help to annihilate the Muslims. Consequently, they started to suppress Muslims in political, social, economic, educational and ethical fields. At the very beginning of 1900 the Hindus felt the beginning of the retreat of the British colonialism on the world level. So they started uniting the Indians in the name of Indian nationalism under the so-called Indian National Congress. They were then faced with the problems of winning over the Muslims. They could not accomplish the plan for Ram Raj by ignoring Muslims

Iqbal and the Ideology of Pakistan

completely because the Muslims then had their identity as a united and powerful nation. Despite this, the Hindus acted fast and started their efforts of crushing the Islamic and cultural identity of the Muslims. These efforts were an eye opener to the Muslims and, set them thinking about the protection of their cultural existence. Constantly Shah Waliullah[21], (earlier) Sir Syed Ahmad Khan[22] played an important role in raising the individual identity of the Muslims and in laying the foundations of the two-nation theory.

Iqbal, giving a perceptible and consistent form to this two-nation theory in his Allahabad address declared that the only way for the protection of the Muslims' future and for the solution of their cultural problem was the establishment of an independent State in north-western India. After the termination of the First World War when Britain announced its intention to quite India the problem arose once again that, in view of nations right of self-determination and the new concepts of democracy, the cultural existence of the Muslims in India would be at the tender mercy of the Hindus. This was so because the Muslims could not conquer India militarily, and democratically, the power would be transferred to the larger nation or the Hindu majority community of India. Allamah Iqbal proposed the solution for this cultural problem that for the purpose of shaping the Islamic ideology on the lines of individual identity and for making it a cultural power and for giving it a it was necessary perceptible form to affiliate it in the Muslim majority areas of the north-western India. This provided a positive foundation to the concept of Pakistan. Quaid-i-Azam Muhammad Ali Jinnah also studied deeply the special cultural and political condition of India and, experiencing the failure of all efforts for unity with Hindus, reached the conclusion that the Hindu-Muslim unity in India was like the union of two opposites, hat was the biggest obstruction to the practical promulgation of the Islamic ideology in India. The Muslim would be able to absorb the Islamic ideology in their lives only when they would be able to promulgate it after holding power. Hindus would not be gracious enough to allow the Muslims' concept of life to bear fruit. The Quaid-i-Azam accepted the conclusions arrived at by Iqbal and said, after a study of the conditions later, that he agreed completely with the views of Iqbal about the protection of the cultural heritage of Muslims and that there was complete harmony in their views. He says:

"There is complete harmony between mine and the deceased's (Iqbal's) opinions. After a deep study of India's constitutional problems I also had to draw the same conclusions and ultimately these opinions resulted in the birth of a united Muslim India, which was shaped yesterday, March 23, 1940 in the Lahore Session of the All-India Muslim League, which is commonly called the Pakistan Resolution."

The arrival of Iqbal at the ideology of Pakistan was due to his inspired study of the practical, intellectual, intuitional and political conditions, while Quaid-i-Azam arrived at this conclusion through practical politics. But the sincerity and the correspondence between those leaders provided them with good opportunities of understanding the problems, and both reached the same conclusion. This conclusion was that if Islam had to establish a separate identity as an authentic and inherent power in the he subcontinent it would have to avoid isolation and abstruseness, and would have to affiliate itself in a practical way with a land where its followers would be in the majority. When Iqbal and Quaid-i-Azam scrutinized the geographical conditions of India they discovered a belt of Muslim majority areas comprising the Punjab, North-Western Frontier Province, Sind, Baluchistan and Kashmir, which was contiguous, geographically harmonious, militarily acceptable and economically self-supporting. Bengal was included in the he proposed Pakistan when Sir Fazl-ul Haque[23], under the leadership of Quaid-i-Azam presented the Pakistan Resolution in the Muslim League Session on March 23, 1940 in the Minto Park, which has no ben renamed Iqbal Park, and where the Pakistan Minaret now stands in its full glory and majesty. this tract of land was named Pakistan by Chaudhry Rahmat Ali[24], though the thinking behind it was that of Iqbal. The invigorated power of the sub-continent's Muslims supported it and the excellent planning of Quaid-i-Azam performed the historical role of converting it from a mere concept and an ideology into a reality, and of placing it as exhibition of evidence of success. In the words of Quaid-i-Azam the Pakistan movement was neither a British trick, nor did the narrow-mindedness of the Hindus constituted its *raison d'étre*. Its real reason was the feeling of the sub-continent's Muslims that they should make Islam as part of their lives and establish Islam as a power in the present age in order to free mankind from the destructive rolled capitalism and communism and their origin, i.e. materialism, and to revive the Islamic civilization, based on spiritualism,, so-that the present day Man might acquire the right ideology of life and the human race might live in peace, security and freedom from anxiety. Quaid-i-Azam explained the positive aspect of the Pakistan movement as follows:

Iqbal and the Ideology of Pakistan

"Did you reflect on the motive power of the demand for Pakistan, the raison d'etre for a separate country for Muslim? The need for India's partition was neither the Hindus' narrow mindedness nor a British trick. This was the basic demand of Islam."

A study of the movement for the ideology of Pakistan in the light of Quaid-i-Azam's thinking will show that the Pakistan movement started the day when the first non-Muslim accepted Islam in the sub-continent. We held the unshared sovereignty over India for a milleneum, and the same movement, when it matured after contact with the British and the Hindus, it moulded itself into the perceptible form of Pakistan. Quaid-i-Azam's words are:

"Pakistan had been created when the first Hindu accepted Islam in India. This happened even before the establishment of Muslim rule in India. The foundation of nationalism for Muslims is *Kalima-i-Tauheed*[25], neither country nor race. When the first individual accepted Islam in India he ceased to be a member of his earlier nation, but became one of a separate nation. A new nation had been created in India."

So, Pakistan was not a movement for Muslims to escape into a corner of the Sub-continent for fear of the Hindus. On the contrary the positivetaspect of the Pakistan Movement was one of practical association of the Muslim majority provinces with Islam. Its object was the creation of a society in the light of Islam's spiritualism where, Man, after protecting himself from ruination at the hands of the individualistic approach of materialism in the capitalist system or the collectivist approach of the communists system may shape and construct his own Self or Essence, where society may devote its entire attention to the building up of the personality of the individual, and where the individual may become the messenger of glad tidings of peace and security for mankind by utilizing his creative potential in making the society beautiful, compassionate and ever better than before. This was the Pakistan's ideology for which the sub-continent's Muslims had presented the tribute of their innocent lives and blood of their martyrs.

To mould the Pakistan's ideology into a perceptible shape it is necessary to understand it in its correct perspective. We should not use it as a mere slogan and should shape it into plash and institutions such that Pakistan's ideology may transcend a mere gratifying slogan and penetrate into people's inner self. The people should realize that there was surely no other solution for then problem. Similarly, in view of the demands, needs, problems and challenges of the present age we consider Pakistan's ideology basic need for our national identity. Moreover, this ideology cannot assume a perceptible shape unless we establish such institution under it as would give the feeling and knowledge of Pakistan and Islamic identity to the people of Pakistan.

In the present age many movements for ideological, national, political and personal identity have arisen all over the world. A very important problem of the present day youth is as to who they are, what they are, and what they have to do. The colonial system has gifted mankind with depriving the individuals and nations of their ideological, national, rational, cultural and social identity and has tried to pain them artificially in the colour of the Western civilization and culture. It has destroyed their national institutions, has robbed them of their social and cultural characteristics and the unique beauty of their character, Immediately on the breakdown of the colonial system the people and the nations enthralled in the he shackles of that system faced the problem of their identity and that of their culture, society and nationhood. The Pakistan's ideology provides an answer to this same question and determines the ideological basis on which we can lay the foundations of our national and social identity, and under the same national and social Islamic identity we can shape such social, cultural, political and financial institutions as can help us in creating our identity in the correct sense.

The second basic aspect of Pakistan's ideology is the procurement of economic and social justice. As we have fully explained above Iqbal considered the economic problem as a basic problem and advised its acceptance as a challenge.

His letters to Quaid-i-Azam inform us that Iqbal was highly conscious of the need for social and economic justice. Consequently, under the Pakistan's ideology we will have to establish institutions of social and economic justice, which would enable every citizen of Pakistan to obtain civic, economic and social justice from superior persons and those in authority, by force, if necessary, One should be able to take legal and ethical action for social and economic justice. This is so because Pakistan's ideology will remain a mere pleasurable though unless we succeed in providing social and economic justice to every citizen, and nobody has the right of ruling over Pakistan who would be slack in providing social and economic justice to the people.

Iqbal and the Ideology of Pakistan

The third basic aspect of Pakistan's ideology is that we should step down from dreamland to the world of reality and, in conformity with the demands of the present age, should establish institutions, which would equip Pakistan with modern technology. The importance of science and technology in the present age is obvious. We can be in line with the modern advanced world only by acquiring and using modern science and technology. Modern technology is the heritage of the whole human race. It is not the property of any one nation and country but is the result of the joint efforts of the whole humanity. Consequently, in this heritage of the human race we should also play the role of technology, like our ancestors. This is so because technology alone has changed the once un-lettered Western nations into the advanced nations of today. If Muslims acquire technological knowledge and excel the Western and the communist worlds in this field they will acquire a basic position in presiding over the destinies of the human race. Failing this their own destiny will lie at the mercy of the nations, which have reached the zenith of progress through technology. In this paper the effort has been made to high light the lines which would play fundamental roles in making Pakistan an exemplary country, and flourishing as advanced State.

By way of explanation of this concept attention is invited to Iqbal's *Javid Nama*, in which Iqbal hag pointed out the sources of the power and strength of the Western world. He has shown that this power is not based on the many positive and negative aspects of Western culture and society but on science and technology. Though the whole reference is worth reading the climax is contained in the verses in which he says:

> The power of the Europeans is from science and technology
> Its lamps is lighted by the same fire
>
> If thou hath intelligent thinking that is sufficient
> If thou hath perceptive temperament that is sufficient

Understanding Iqbal's Philosophy

Footnotes

(1). Jean-Paul Sartre (1905-1989) French writer who was a supporter of the philosophy of existentialism. He held the view that human life had no purpose beyond the goals set by the individual himself for his material well-being. He considered Man as a "useless passion". His philosophy was the epitome of the materialism of Europe. He propagated his views in his novels, plays, essays and philosophical works, which are numerous. He refused the Nobel Prize for Literature in 1964 on the ground that it was unfair to the reader to add the weight of such extraneous influences to the power of a writer's moves. About 1950 he started taking interest in Marxism and tried to reconcile Marxism and existentialism. However, he did not succeed in this and his main theme continued to be the inevitability of conflict among men for material gain, which is a reflection of the lack of a purpose of life higher than material benefits.

(2). John Gottlieb Fichte (1762 - 1814) he was a German philosopher who expounded ethical idealism. He derived his philosophy from Kant. He gave special attention to socialism and German patriotism his philosophy was characterized by its intense moral earnestness and enthusasm, which was very vividly conveyed his speeches rather than by articles. He was a very good orator.

(3). Augustus Comte (1798 - 1857) He was a French philosopher and founder of the positivistic school of philosophy and originator of the development of sociology as a science.

(4). Atiya Begum Faizi, She was an Indian student in Germany and England and was closely associated with Iqbal during the period 1906-1908. Her writings, especially the short biography titled "Iqbal" (first published in 1947) relates some little-known facts and anecdotes of Iqbal and also contains some not very familiar poetry of his.

(5). See the two poems lilies "Saqlia" (Jazira-i-Sicily) and "Bilad-i-Islamia" (Islamic Cities) in *Bang-i-Dara* (1924) Published by Sheikh Mubarak Ali, Lahore, Pakistan. Third Edition (1910), pp. 1541-142 and 156-157 respectively. The study of the whole of these poems is necessary and is highly recommended for a complete appreciation of Iqbal's feelings of pathos on the decline of the Islamic civilization. However, the sum and substance as well as the climax is contained in the opening verse of the first poem,

Iqbal and the Ideology of Pakistan

Which says:
Cry with an open heart O blood shedding eye
There younder lies the tomb of Hijazi civilization

These two poems also contain details of how the Islamic civilization built up the Europe of today mentioned in the first paragraph of the section "The Intellectual Foundations of Western Civilization".

(6). *Jihad* - It literally means struggle for some good cause. However, its usage in Islamic literature is synonymous which 'Jihad-i-fi sabil Allah', i.e. Struggle in the cause of God. This includes, but is not redirected to, war, if necessary.

(7). Bid'at – Unauthorized innovation in religious matters.

(8). Jabr: - It literally means a compulsion. However, in the terminology of *Tasawwuf* (Islamic mysticism) it means the subservience of human life and actions to the material laws of nature, which also govern inanimate objects. These laws work according to the material laws made by God.

(9). Qadr - It literally means "pre-destination" or "preordination" or "the knowledge of the future", which is known to God alone. However, in the terminology of *Tasawwuf* it means that God has fixed the maximum possibilities of good and evil actions for each individual, which would result in maximum felicity or punishment on the Day of Judgement. God has also given the potential to each person to achieve the higher limits for good through his efforts or to fall to the abysses of suffering by lack of such efforts. So, the destiny of each person is the climax or the anti-climax of his achievements but the actual achievement of these climaxes or anti-climaxes depends upon the extent of the effort of that person, each person has the unlimited autonomy of action in this sense. Modern researches in genetics give us reason to conclude that these limits of human potential are controlled and determined by the genome or the genetic constitution of the person. This determines the individual's physical, intellectual and moral potential and limitations. The effects of this genetic constitution can also be modified to some extent by the person's efforts or lack of them. Also, God, being *Qadir-i-Mutlaq* (absolute Omnipotent) can change these destinies if he so wills. Miracles are one of the manifestations of this attribute of God. These changes can be brought about by the individual's efforts, supplemented by and interaction with prayers and supplications to God. These, again,

Understanding Iqbal's Philosophy

supplemented by God's limitless Divine Mercy and Compassion for His creatures, can change these destinies. God's judgement of the Day of Judgement will be the resultant of the persons original destiny, tempered with God's mercy and human efforts, supplemented by prayers and supplications. It would be clear from this that the Islamic concept of *qadr* or *taqdir* (destiny) is different from fatalism. For more details see "Qur'an aur Tasawwuf by Dr. Mir Waliuddin, Chairman Department of Philosophy, Osmania University, Heyderabad, Deccan, India. Published by Nadwat-ul-Musannifin, Delhi, India, second Edition (1948), Chapter on *Jabr-u-Qadr*", pp. 152-167. (...The author has quoted largely from Iqbal).

(10). The above brief discussion of *Jabr,* and *Qadr* leads us to the comprehension of the contents of the comparison between the materialistic European thought and the spiritual Islamic thought / discussed by the author in the text. This is outwardly difficult to understand and needs some explanation.

In a nutshell, a materialist, a heretic or an infidel *Kafir* is the one who depends upon and is controlled by external influences or *Jabr,* while a man of Faith (*mumin*) is the one who has the ability to shape his own destiny from his own potential on the basis of what has been explained above. Iqbal says:

The infidel is recognized by being lost in his environment
The *Mumin* is recognized by mastering his environment
Destiny changes a hundred times in the twinkling of the eye
Its believer changes from grief to happiness in a short time
Plants and atones are subordinate to pre-destination
The *Mumin* is subordinate only to the of God
The infidel trusts his sword
The *Mumin* fights even without the sword
If the *Mumin* is an infidel he is subordinate to predestination
If he is a real *Mumin* he is himself God's pre-destination.

(11). *Ilham* - Inspiration.

(12. *Wahi* - Direct revelation from God, specifically to prophets.

(13). *Fiqh* -Islamic Jurisprudence.

(14). Vladimir llyrich Lenin (1870-1924) - He was the strongest and most active believer in communism. He brought out Karl Marx' *Das Kapital* from the library shelves and promulgated its philosophy in a

Iqbal and the Ideology of Pakistan

practical form in Russia. He did not live long after the establishment of the communist Russian State. However, he is famous as the 'Father of communism' in the U.S.S.R.

(15). *Khudi* – Self, Self-Cognizance. Realization that Man is the best creation of God and that this high position can be attained only by complete submission to God's Will and untainted Love for Him. This Love should not be restricted to observance of mere rituals but active service and sacrifice in His cause. See Iqbal, Dr. Sir Muhammad Iqbal (1915); *Asrar-i-Khudi* and *Rumuz-i-Bekhadi*. Published by Dr. Javid Jqbal at the Kapoor Arts Printing Works, Lahore, Pakistan (Fifth Impression 1940).

(16). Dadabhai Naoroji (1825-1917) - He was a prominent Indian political and social leader. his efforts were mainly concentrated on drawing the attention of the Indian people and the British Government on India's poverty, which he claimed was due to the drain of India's economic resources by the British. He helped in founding the Congress Party in 1885 and was elected its president thrice, in 1886, 1893 and 1906. He became the first Indian Member of Parliament in 1885. He became the first Indian Member of Parliament in 1892. He stayed in England for a long time since 1855. During that period he exerted great influence on the British public opinion by his writings.

(17). Gopal Krishna Gokhale (1866-1915) - He was an Indian nationalist, educator, social reformer and political leader of moderate views. He was the President of the Congress in 1905. He was a member of the Bombay and the Imperial Legislative Assemblies from 1899 to his death in 1915. He believed in peaceful means for attaining independence, and concentrated his attention on the problem of economic drainages of India's resources.

(18). Motilal Nehru (1816-1931) - A barrister and a proinent Congress leader of India. He was the father of Mr. Jawaharlal Nehru, the first Prime Minister of India. Motilal Nehru entered Indian politics in 1920 and played an important role in it. He was the author of the Nehru Report (1928), which outlined a new constitution of India. This report completely ignored Muslim's rights, became the political controversy of the time, frustrated all hopes of Hindu-Muslim unity, and in a way, was the starting point of the concept for the need for Pakistan. This led to the famous

Understanding Iqbal's Philosophy

presidential address of Iqbal to the All-India Muslim League Convention at Allahabad in 1930.

(19). Dr. Khurshid Kamal Aziz.

(20). Strangely enough the nationalist Muslims and supporters of the Hindus and Muslim being one nation were mostly Islamic religious scholars ('*Ulema*). Stranger still was their argument that an Islamic State was not needed to practise Islam, as the "five pillars of Islam", viz., *Tauheed*, prayers, fasting, *zakat* and *Hajj* could be practised in India. Iqbal commenting on this said:

Because the Mullah is allowed to perform the *siajdah* in India, the simple person thinks that Islam is free Mawlana Hussain Ahmad Madani was a prominent *alim* of India in the twentieth century and was the Principal of the Darul Ulum, Deoband, India. He was a staunch believer and supporter of Indian secular nationalism which was very strange indeed. Iqbal has expressed the following views about him:

Ajam (the non-Arab world) still knows not the secrets Hussain Ahmad from Deoband how grossly strange it is orchestration at the pulpit that the nation (*millat*) is based on the country!

How ignorant is he of the stand of Muhammad of Arabia

To Mustafa convey thyself, as he is the complete *deen* If though dot not reach him it is all infidelity *(Bu Lahabi)*

(Iqbal, Dr. Sir Muhammad (1938) - *Armaghan-i-Hijaz*.

Published by Dr. Javid Iqbal, First Edition 1938, p. 278.)

(21). Shah Waliullah (1703-1762) - He was an Indian Muslim religious scholars and reformer. He emphasized the reconciliation of the trend Islamic creed with the world trend at that time. His most important thought was *tatbiq,* which allowed the re-interpretation and re-application of the basic principles of Islam in accordance with the Qur'an and the traditions of the Holy Prophet. He developed this philosophy in response to the situation in India where large numbers of Muslims came increasingly under non-Muslim rule after the death of the Mughal Emperor, Awrangzeb in 1707. Shah Waliullah was not only a scholar but an activist. When the Marathas developed power in India after the decay and disintegration of the Mughal Empire and their forces reached as far as Aligarh, only about eighty miles from Delhi, he was very much disappointed with the impotence of the Mughal court. He then implored Ahmad Shah Abdali, the then ruler of what is now Afghanistan and Iran to suppress the Marathas. Ahmad Shah Abdali did so very successfully at the third battle of Panipat in 1760. Shah Waliullah, thus, saved Muslim lives and honor at a very delicate period of Muslim history.

(22). Sir Syed Ahmad Khan (1817-1898) - He was a very prominent Muslim leader of India in the nineteenth century. He devoted his life to social reform of the Indian Muslim society and to remove the feelings of defeatism created by their downfall and defeat at the hands of the British up to and including the War of Independence of 1857. He was no mere theorist but an activist. Realizing the backwardness of Indian Muslims in the field of Western education, and especially science and technology, he gave high priority to their education in these fields. He founded the Muhammedan Anglo-Oriental College at Aligarh in 1877, which later progressed into the present day Muslim University. The university was granted its charter in 1920. In the political fields he tried to reconcile the Muslims with the British so that they could avoid direct confrontation with them and use all their energies and resources for rebuilding their economic, social, educational and ethical base with which they could ultimately regain political power.

Syed Amir Ali (1849-1928) - He was a prominent Muslim intellectual of India and was a well-known barrister. He was a Judge of the High Court of Judicature at Calcutta. He is the author of several scholarly books on Islamic law and history, of which the two famous ones are *A History of the Saracens* and *The Spirit of Islam*.

(23). Sir Fazl-ul Haque

(24). See his book *Pakistan: The Fatherland of the Pak Nation*. Cambridge, 1947.

(25). *Kalima-i-Tauheed* - The Islamic creed declaring the Unity of God and the prophethood of Muhammad *La Ilah Il-Allah, Muhammad-ur-Rasool Allah*. There is no god except God and Muhammad is his Prophet.

Chapter 10

THE PAKISTAN PLAN AND THE ROLE OF IQBAL

However, India has been assiduously endeavouring to undo Pakistan in a multi-dimensional effort ever since its establishment in 1947. Vilification of all Muslim heroes has always been an important component of this campaign. This paper brings out the details of such a campaign against Iqbal and gives clear explanations contradicting the allegations of Indian and non-Indian pro-Hindu contemporary writers, the chief of which are Dr. Hassan Ahmad of Muslim University, Aligarh, and Dr. Edward J. Thompson. Both have argued that Iqbal was originally a secular nationalist who was conscious of the harmful effects of the partition of India for Indians in general and for Muslims in particular. The paper documents evidence contradicting these opinions and clearly brings out the fact that Iqbal was an Islamist from the very beginning of his career, and that the need for establishing an Islamic State in the Indian sub-continent was an article of faith with him. The above-mentioned two writers have also tried to confuse the issue by mixing up the Pakistan Plan proposed by Iqbal and accepted by the Muslim League in 1940 with the one proposed by Chaudhry Rahmat Ali, who was a student at the University of Cambridge ire the nineteen thirties. The latter scheme was impractical and this fact as well as Iqbal's distancing himself from it have been detailed in the paper. It is interesting to know from the Iqbal-Nehru converstion at Lahore in early 1938 that the Congress was less serious than the Muslims about complete independence. They were satisfied with the freedom of internal administration and were even prepared to accept the continued presence of the British army in India.

The partition of the Indian sub-continent and the establishment of Pakistan has been a perpetual psychological, intellectual political, social and cultural shock to India's Hindus. They have created a world-wide war front against Pakistan. After suffering political defeat the Hindus embarked on agression in Hyderabad, Mangrol, Junagarh, Kashmir, and lastly in East Pakistan in the hope of attaining military superiority. Consequently, along with jeopardising economic and military aid to Pakistan on the world scale they have striven to prove the establishment of Pakistan unnatural as well as ideologically unnecessary and irrational and

The Pakistan Plan and the Role of Iqbal

its continued existence as detrimental to the ideological, political and economic interests of the Western nations. These efforts have been demonstrated in several ways at the ideological level.

Edward Thompson was Professor of Bengali Language and Literature at the University of Oxford. He was largely under Hindu influence ors account of being in the literary circle of Rabindranath Tagore[1]. In the politics of the sub-continent he was always inclined towards Hindus. For that reason tie had established report with Muslim leaders so that he could keep the upper strata of the Hindu and British leadership acquainted with their thinking. He also published an article in the "Observer" and the "London Times" about the Muslims' future with reference to Iqbal in which he reiterated his old stand that Iqbal wanted only a Muslims province within India.

Before starting any discussion about Pakistan It is necessary to understand the Pakistan plan itself. This is so because, without understanding the truth about Pakistan plan, it is impossible to understand the confusion attempted by Dr. Hassan Ahmad, Professor of Political Science at the Muslim University, Aligarh, India in his English book titled, *Iqbal's Political Philosophy - at the Crossroads*.

The concept of Pakistan was neither an inspired nor an innate one, nor was it created instantaneously. On the contrary, it was an ideology which had developed from the centuries old historical, cultural, social and political experience of the sub-continent's Muslilms and reached the stage of the Lahore resolution after the political upheavals and many changes and alterations during the nineteen thirties and forties, and ultimately got the name of the Pakistan resolution.

The second most important fact is that the realization of the impossibility of the co-existence of the Muslims and Hindus was not first presented by Iqbal. It had been first presented by Hadhrat Mujaddid Alf-i-Thani[2] in his epistles, and later by Sir Syed Ahmad Khan in connection with the Hindi-Urdu controversy in which he pointed out the possibility of separation of the two nations. The invitation of Shah Waliullah to Ahmad Shah Abdali[3] for suppressing the Marathas, the basic role of the Hindus in the failures of the struggles of Sirajuddaulah[4] and the martyr Tipu Sultan, barring some specific exceptions, the Muslims' single handed fight for the expulsion of the British in the 1857 War of Independence, and on its failure, being the sole target of oppression together with the rewarding of the Hindus by the British, are facts which awakened the feelings in the Muslims' hearts that the British and the Hindus were jointly plotting against their survival and identity.

The third important fact is that at that time the Hindus had started dreaming of their renaissance. They argued that they had been subservient to the Muslims earlier and were then subservient to the British. The advent of the British had changed their masters but not their destiny. They concluded from experience that the secret of their survival lay in acquiring Western learning, cooperation with the British, adoption of the philosophy of non-violence and were keeping the Muslims enslaved in the fallacy of Indian nationalism. They also understood that as the powerful and brave races coming into India through the western passes could rot escape being absorbed into Hinduism the British and the Muslims would be no exceptions either. The Hindu *bania*[5] thought that the British who had come to plunder India In the name of trade would leave India sooner or later after plundering it, and that at that time their real adversaries and opponents in claiming authority would again be the Muslims whom the British had deprived of authority.

The Hindus got the truth that in view of the rising trend towards democracy based on self-determination, political power would ultimately devolve on the majority community. It was absolutely clear that In terms of the political reforms of 1935 the Hindus alone constituted the majority in the sub-continent. Ail the non-Hindu tribes and communities had already been considered as part of the Hindu nation. The only exceptions were Christians, Sikhs and Muslims. None others could be co-sharers or adversaries of the Hindus in power. This situation could be cured only with the concept of united secular nationalism, and that is why the united nationalism was stressed.

The Congress, which held the political leadership of the Hindus, was striding the policy of obtaining the cooperation of Muslims. The had adorned the show case of the Congress High Command with *Mawlvis*[6] and pious persons. The Congress also embarked on the task of converting Muslims through the movements of *Sanghatan* and *Shudhi*[7]. This clever Hindu poi icy produced some positive results and several prominent and famous '*Ulema* as well as other wise and sobre Muslims were caught in the Congress' net of "one-nation ideology". They performed the basic role in the destruction of Muslims albeit with sincere Intentions and good deeds In contrast with these tactics of the Hindus, the Muslims had no

The Pakistan Plan and the Role of Iqbal

single stand. One group of Muslims had indulged in the old dream of Muslim rule over the whole sub-continent, and was completely unaware of the changes brought about by the new age. The second group was bent upon Islamic revolution in the sub-continent and preferred to form a body of pious people through preaching in the first phase. They considered the whole of India to be the Muslims' inheritance. They were unaware of the truth of the fast changes in the political arena of the sub-continent, and that the Hindus were bent upon acquiring power from the British and also that the British were quitting India, leaving the Muslims at the tender mercy of the Hindus. In these circumstances, instead of quickly designing an acceptable way out of the Muslims' predicament, they encased themselves in the self-made Islamic revolution, busied themselves with making Pakistan and Its leadership the target of ridicule and derision.

The concept of a separate homeland for the Muslims was developed over a long period of time by a large number of thinkers. Among them the prominent non-Muslims are John Bright Belat[8], Quesson and Lala Lajpat Rai[9] and the Muslims are Abdul Haleem Sharar[10], Jamaluddin Afghani[11], Abdul Qadir Bilgrami[12], Hasrat Mohani[13], Gul Muhammad Khan, Mawlana Muhammad Ali Jawhar[14], the Agha Khan[15], Nawab Zulfiqar Ali, Abdul Qadir Badauni[16], Murtaza Ahmad Maikash[17], Sheikh Deen Muhammad, Khairi Brothers, Chaudhry Rahmat Ali[18], their friends and Iqbal. Their concepts were basically focussed on the utter impossibility of the co-existence of the Muslims and Hindus, and the only solution of their problems was to give the opportunity to both of them to centralize themselves in their majority regions. There were two opinions in this respect also one was for the Muslim regions to be a part of India, which should be made up of a confederation of Hindu and Muslim regions or states. The other opinion was that the Muslims establish their separate regions of influence and Independent states, separate from the Hindus. These ideas were being presented by different groups up to 1930. However, these concepts had not yet appeared from any national platform.

Iqbal was a prominent Muslim leader connected with a Muslim majority province. He presented the concept of the establishment of Muslim centricity in the Muslim majority regions in his presidential address to the All-India Muslim League Session in 1930. The Hindu leaders and press as well as their British counterparts for the first time took an adverse notice of it, because this expression of national identity among Muslims had appeared slowly. At first the concept prevailed for the creation of a Muslim province in the north-west of India, so as to solve the

Understanding Iqbal's Philosophy

Muslim problem simultaneously with preserving the unity of India. But the Nehru Report rejected this. Under the excuse of administrative difficulties the Hindu mentality did not accept even a Muslim majority province within the Indian federation and propagated the false impression that the Muslims wanted to secede from India. The Hindu intransigence and their undignified criticism of the Muslim leadership dragged the Muslims to the cross-roads. They were faced with the dilemma whether they bow to the Hindus and throw their very existence at the tender mercy of the Hindus, or should take some other initiative for safeguarding their national identity. During this fast changing and tumultuous period another plan appeared which was called the Cambridge Plan or the Pakistan Plan.

Iqbal's initial thinking was the establishment of a Muslim centricity in the Muslim majority provinces of the north-western India so that the Muslims could live according to the dictates of their system of life. But when even this proposal was not considered worthy of attention Chaudhry Rahmat Ali and his cooperators at Cambridge presented the plan for the creation of a federation of the independent Muslim States of the Muslim majority regions of India. This plan was called the "Pakistan Scheme". In this "Pakistan Scheme" Mysore, Bengal, Hyderabad Deccan were called *Hyderistan*, *Bang-i-Islam* and *Osmanistan* (after the then Nizam Osman Ali Khan) respectively, and Kashmir, the Punjab, North-Western Frontier Province, Baluchistan and Sind were given the joint name of Pakistan. This Pakistan Scheme was also based on the concept of establishing Muslim centricity in the Muslim majority regions.

At that time it was thought that perhaps this Pakistan Scheme presented from Cambridge had also the support and blessings of Iqbal. This scheme was clearly known as the Cambridge Scheme for Palistan, while the scheme of Iqbal for establishing the Muslim centricity in the Muslim majority regions had no name yet. Still, confusion was created when Iqbal presented the concept of an independent Muslim State in his Allahabad address in 1930 in these words:

"It appears to me that such dangerous conditins may appear in India in the near future as may require the creation of a separate front by the Muslims to face them," (i).

He further stated:

The Pakistan Plan and the Role of Iqbal

"As far as my insight goes peace cannot be established in India till the different nations inhabitting India are provided with opportunities which would enable them to develop their society with a happy and judicious combination of their sacred traditons and the demands of the present age." (ii)

According to him the practical way of achieving this was:

"As for me I want to go a step further in these demands. I would like to see the Punjab, the North-West Frontier Province, Sind and Baluchistan amalgamated into one single State. India may get self rule within the British Empire or outside it, it is obvious to me that the establishment of a united Muslim State in the north-western India is the destiny of the Muslims of that region at least." (iii).

The book cited by me was printed by the Khawajah Electric Press, Delhi, India and published by the Maktaba-i-Abbasia, Urdu Bazar, Delhi, India. The translation belongs to the pre-Pakistan period and was published and distributed by the Idara-i-Tulu-i-Islam. This version clearly states the establishment of an independent Muslim State, either within or outside the British Empire to be the destiny of the Muslims. Further on Iqbal says that that proposal of his should not upset the British or the Hindus. Rejecting the opinion of the Right Hon'ble Mr Srinavas Shastri Iqbal even said that the centricity of the Muslims would solve not only the problems of India but that of the whole Asia.

ربط و ضبطِ ملتِ بیضا ہے مشرق کی نجات
ایشیا والے ہیں اس نکتے سے اب تک بے خبر

"The organization of the Muslim nation is the salvation of the East
The Asian nations are still unaware of this secret." (iv)

Still further on Iqbal presented the justification for this independent Muslim State:

"The future of Islam in Asia in the form of an ethical and political power depends largely on the complete organization of Indian Muslims and promulgation of the Islamic Shariah in this country and its extension, which is impossible without one or more independent Muslim States in the region." (v)

On May 28, 1937 Iqbal presented a scheme for a de *nouveac* re-orientation of India to Quaid-i-Azam Muhammad Ali Jinnah. It was presented ire the interrogative form as follows:

"To enable the Muslim India to solve its problems it is necessary to reorient India *de nouveau* to establish one or more Muslim majority States. Do you not appreciate the timeliness of such a demand". (vi)

Consequently, this concept of Iqbal was considered an extension of the Pakistan Scheme and, for the same reason, Edward Thompson also has considered the Pakistan Scheme to be based on Iqbal's concept.

On being asked about the Cambridge Pakistan Scheme Iqbal clarified, with all honesty, that the Cambridge Pakistan Scheme was different from his scheme of the Muslim State in the Muslim majority regions. The former was not his scheme. How can it be concluded from this that he was against the establishment of Pakistan or of an independent Muslim State outside India. It is a travesty of historical truth to use the Cambridge Pakistan Scheme as a smoke screen to declare Iqbal as opposed to the establishment of Pakistan. The characters of this drama have been appearing in the shape of Edward Thompson, Dr Rajindra Prashad[19], Pandit Jawaharlal Nehru[20] and Dr. Hassan Ahmad, of Aligarh. The concept of the centricity of Muslims in the Muslim majority region:, separate from the Hindus, itslf appeared as a result of historical evolution, intransigence of the Hindus, the instigatioin of the *Shudhi* and *Sanghtan* movements, resulting from the attitude of rejecting Muslims, communal riots, the non-cooperation of the Hindus with Muslims in the Hindus efforts to disgrace Muslims in the joint ministries formed in the wake of the 1935 elections. It appeared in the form of the realization that the Hindus were not prepared to keep the Muslims with them at any cost, and that they would incur any risk in their efforts at annihilation of the Muslims. Consequently, the Quaid-i-Azam had to declare in the 1937 Muslim League Convention at Lucknow: "O Hindus, you have hurried to expose yourself."

Waris Mir[21] probably forgot, in his ardent apologetic defence of Iqbal that in doing so he has shown Iqbal to be afraid of the Hindus and the British, as well as confused and that what he was designating tactics

The Pakistan Plan and the Role of Iqbal

amounted to Iqbal's cowardice. In fact Iqbal, who openly and justly criticised the United Nations (then the League of Nations), Western democratic system and power could not be even imagined to be reluctant to present the concept of an independent Muslim State out of fear of the Hindus and the British. The fact of the matter is that Iqbal had clearly indicated the demand for a Muslim State either Inside or outside India as far back as 1930, and had reiterated that demand in his letter dated May 28, 1937 to the Quaid-i-Azam by insisting on his earlier demand for a *de nouveau* re-orientation of India. In these circumstances how can Iqbal be accused of any expedience or political weakness? In fact he repeatedly pressed the Pakistan Scheme at the time of the Second Round Table Conference in England and went to the extent of naming the Muslim State as Pakistan on reference by Chaudhry Rahmat Ali, In this context an extract from *Iqbal ka Siyasi Karnama* (The Political Achievement of Iqbal) by Muhammad Ahmad Khan is presented below for perusal:

"Iqbal went to London in 1931 to participate in the Second Round Table Conference and stayed there for about two months. At this time he had gone to Cambridge also where he addressed a congregation as well. Chaudhry Rahmat Ali was among those who welcomed him." (vii)

This proves at least, that during the Second Round Table Conference (September 27 - November 20, 1931), Chaudhry Rahmat Ali had met Iqbal. The following reliable narrative is interesting in this connection.

Abdul Waheed Khan was a member of the All-India Muslim League Council and an ardent standard bearer of the Pakistan movement. He was a member of the first Constituent Assembly of Pakistan and the Central Minister of Communications. He is the author of several high standard books. He had an interview with Iqbal at Bhopal in 1935. He writes about this interview.

"The appeared to be very satisfied with the new administrative trends in India. The Muslims had contested the elections f or the Central Assembly under the Muslim Unity Board. The intention of "Infusing blood in the dead veins" of the Muslim League had appeared among Muslim leaders. So, Iqbal was convinced of the Muslim India succeeding in the "creation of a new world from its own ashes". This new world had then become famous by the name of Pakistan. Muslim thinkers had started giving serious thought to the Pakistan Scheme presented by Iqbal. On my questioning he stated, "My object in the establishment of Pakistan is not merely the safeguarding of the Muslim national, social and cultural interests but I want an opportunity for the Muslims to establish the ideological foundations of Pakistan, as professed by them, in a part of India for the creation of free independent State, where they can practise Islamic laws arid constitution." After this I asked him about the etymology of Pakistan. This was being attributed to Chaudhry Rahmat Ali at that time and he was popularising this name in London. Iqbal's reply contradicted this theory for which reason I requested him for further explanation. He stated, "When I was staying In London in 1931 for participation in the Round Table Conference Chaudhry Rahmat Ali came to me one day and asked me to suggest a name for the government which would be formed in pursuance of the scheme presented by me in the presidential address to the Muslim League session at Allahabad. I suggested to him to take the first letters of the north-western provinces of India and the "*tan*" from Baluchistan, which would give a meaningful and good word, i.e. Pakistan, and that would be the name of this State. He said that he remembered very well that Chaudhry Rahmat Ali had taken the first letter of each province, i.e. of the Punjab, of the Azad tribal region, of Kashmir, of Sind, and of Baluchistan. Then Iqbal said that the name might be that or something else. The main object was the Muslims' right of governing themselves in their majority regions."

This story proves three things. The first is that Chaudhry Rahmat All used to be in contact with Iqbal during the latter's stay in London in 1931. This period was only nine or ten months after the presidential address at Allahabad in which Iqbal had first presented the concept of Pakistan. The second is that Chaudhry Rahmat Ali did have conversations with Iqbal on his Pakistan proposal. The third is that Iqbal had also coined the word Pakistan.

In short Iqbal presented his concept of Pakistan in December 1930 while Chaudhry Rahmat Ali presented his scheme with the name Pakistan in January 1933. In addition to this, it is also a fact that Chaudhry Rahmat Ali was a believer in Iqbal and had benefited from his guidance, After presenting the Pakistan proposal in the presidential address when Iqbal went to London in September, 1931, Chaudhry Rahmat All maintained contact with him. He was so impressed by this proposal that he did not only talk with Iqbal about it but inquired about its name also. Then he

The Pakistan Plan and the Role of Iqbal

propagated the concept of the scheme with the same name at the time of the Third Round Table Conference In January 1933. All this evidence clearly shows that the first proposer or originator of the concept of Pakistan was not Chaudhry Rahmat Ali, but that he had borrowed this concept from Allamah Iqbal.

The writer questioned Mr. Abdul Waheed Khan to the effect that though his version might be right it contradicted the accepted version, and requested him to give any argument he had in further confirmation of his narration. Mr. Abdul Waheed Khan replied to this in his letter dated November 11, 1974 the relevant portions of which are given below:

"I had two arguments in addition to my own statement and the testimony of Allamah lqbal. (i) I saw neither any stsement nor any booklet of Chaudhry Rahmat Alt before his interview with Allamah lqbal nor even heard him claim that Iqbal told him any such thing. Had Chaudhry Rahmat Ali been the originator of this name it was impossible for him not to discuss it with Iqbal and not to record the latter's reactions to it. However, Chaudhry Rahmat Ali did complain to me in Lahore in 1947-48 that Iqbal did not present any detailed scheme in the Round Table Conference. (ii) The booklet by Chaudhry Rahmat Ali titled, *Now or Never*, seen by me had been published in 1933 and was in the Punjab University Library. However, when I needed it last year it was not there, i.e. somebody had got it issued and did not return it. The booklet which I read had spelled the word "Pakistan" with the first English and not Urdu letters. In this 'T' stood for "Turkistan", 'I' for "Iran" and so on, i.e. the whole concept was different Chaudhry Rahmat Alt had included even some Muslim countries in his "Pakistan." This demand was based on the concept of an indefensible and impractical Pakistan, comprised of parts like Osmanistan and Hyderistan. In his statement lqbal distanced himself from this Pakistan Scheme consisting of Hyderistan and Osmanistan and, Instead of claiming credit for the scheme of Cambridge University students, made a special statement disclaiming the scheme. This scheme was not even feasible from social, political, military and defense perspectives. Iqbal did not consider it feasible because these Muslim regions, surrounded by overwhelming Hindu majority regions, could not survive for long. Iqbal had comprehended this reality as early as 1934 and so did not feel the necessity of supporting this childish Cambridge Scheme. Historically, later events show that, when in 1940 under the leadership of the Quaid-i-Azam the Muslims decided to establish their independent Islamic State, they took notice of only the concept of Iqbal. Chaudhry Rahmat Ali never accepted the federation of just the Muslim majority areas. He never excused the Quaid-i-Azam and the Muslim League for this. He went to the extent of remaining insolent to the Quaid-i-Azam and continued active opposition to Pakistan. Nevertheless, as for the name of "Pakistan", when the Hindu Press repeatedly called the Lahore resolution of 1940 as "Pakistan" the Muslim League also finally adopted the Lahore resolution as its goal of Pakistan. Now, as the interview of Chaudhry Rahmat Ali with Iqbal in 1931 was in camera it was presumed that Quaid-i-Azam or the Muslim League borrowed the name "Pakistan" from the scheme of Chaudhry Rahmat All. As a result of this, though the name of Pakistan became associated with his name his scheme of creating a federation of the Muslim majority regions could not be accepted in practice. This was so because that scheme was only an emotional ambition of some students, which was illuminated its practical application. Thus the scheme of Chaudhary Rahmat Ali was rejected and that of Iqbal became the Muslim League's goal in 1940. In other words there were two Pakistan schemes: one was the proposal of Iqbal, whose initial concept was given by him in his presidential address of December 29, 1930, which was passed on by him to Chaudhry Rahmat Ali in 1931; the other was the Pakistan scheme by Chaudhry Rahmat Ali, which consisted of a federation of different Muslim majority areas. Iqbal had shown his aloofness from the scheme of Chaudhry Rahmat Ali. He remained firmly with his Pakistan scheme till his death. Actually, he wrote in 1937 to the Quaid-i-Azam advising him that the time was mature for pressing its demand. Consequently, the Quaid-i-Azam Initiated that scheme on March 23, 1940, and testified that if Iqbal had been alive he would have been happy in that ultimately the Muslim League also reached the same conclusion as he had drawn earlier and that that was the day of the beginning of ills dream coming true."

A chronological study of Iqbal's thinking will clearly show that his thinking about the future of the sub-continent's Muslims had passed through several evolutionary stages during the eight year period from 1930 to 1938. During this difficult period the played the role of a cautious leader with great responsibility. From the time of the Quaid-i-Azam joining the muslim League till his becoming established as a Muslim leader Iqbal argued with him with great boldness and responsibility about

The Pakistan Plan and the Role of Iqbal

the Muslims' future. He knew that every word of his would result in far-reaching consequences on the future collective life of the Muslims. During this period he continued assaying the Congress' strategems and explaining the nature of the Muslims' problems to the leaders through correspondence and speeches. During this period, while the Quaid-i-Azam assumed the leadership of the Muslim League, the Congress and Nehru tried to mislead Iqbal. However, Iqbal had well understood that the future of the Muslims would be secure only in the hands of the Quaid-i-Azam Twenty three months after Iqbal's death in 1938, by drawing up the Lahore resolution on March 23, 1940, the Muslim League, under the leadership of the Quaid-i-Azam made the final decision about the Muslims' future by focussing the collective struggle of the Muslims on the establishment of an independent Muslim State comprised of the Muslim majority provinces of the north-western India together with the Muslim majority regions of eastern India.

Thompson's malice is exhibited by his efforts to link up Iqbal's demand for Pakistan with the Cambridge Scheme and making an unsuccessful attempt of concealing the truth by trying to mix up two different things. Thompson knew the Iqbal's opinion about the Pakistan Scheme of the Cambridge students. Thompson's attempt to show Iqbal's denial of the way creation of Pakistan with the camouflage of the Cambridge Scheme is strange logic indeed. The attempts to allege Iqbal to be the opponent of a concept which was nurtured in and evolved by the Iqbal's intellect from 1930 to 1938 is the travesty of historical truth. Iqbal had clearly supported an independent Muslim State in his writings, letters, statements and speeches long before 1928. Till 1934 he was desirous of a Muslim majority region in any form, inside or outside India. Then, after 1935 Iqbal gave his full attention clearly to the demand for an independent Muslim State and made a formal proposal about this to Quaid-i-Azam in 1937.

Dr. Hassan Ahmad, is a well known professor with Congressite outlook. To propagate that thought he leaned on the same support which had been used earlier by Dr. Rajindra Prashad and Pandit Jawahar Lal Nehru (viii). The above cited book has several contradictions and refutation of his own stand about Iqbal.

In his letter of July 26, 1934 to Thompson (which has been cited in this book) Iqbal had said that in his capacity of the President of the Muslim Conference it was his duty to support the separation of Sind and

Understanding Iqbal's Philosophy

that the had always believed In the amalgamation of the three north-western provinces of India to be In the best Interests of Britain, India and Islam.

In the same letter Iqbal says that the Muslims had become somewhat enlightened but their leadership was not. This alluded to the leadership composed of Mawlana Abul Kalam Azad,[22] Mawlana Hussain Ahmad Madani[23] and other Congressite *Ulema*, and the Unionist Party in the Punjab, which was a supporter of the British. The Muslim League was then overwhelmed by feudal landlords. Quaid-i-Azam Muhammad Ali Jinnah had not yet appeared as a prominent and universally accepted leader.

Quoting Thompson, Pandit Nehru writes on page 7 of the book:

"Iqbal told me that he had advocated the cause of Pakistan in his capacity of the President of the Muslim League Session. He still felt that this would be harmful to India in general amd the Muslims in particular. Probably, he had changed his mind or had ignored it later. Consequently, it can be inferred that it was not important to him. Considering his general philosophy of life it can be said that his thinking about Pakistan or the partition of India lacked propriety."(ix)

This statement of Pandit Nehru can be considered only as his personal whim. He himself writes, citing Iqbal, that he supported Pakistan's concept in the capacity of his being the President of the Muslim League. This means that at least he did support the concept of Pakistan, though it might have been in any capacity. As for Pandit Nehru's assertion that Iqbal felt that It would be harmful to India In general and the Muslims in particular, neither Pandit Nehru nor Thompson have given any reference to Iqbal's letter, essay or address in which the latter had expressed such feelings. Also, his assertion that Iqbal had "probably charged his mind" --- is in itself only a presumption of Pandit Nehru and he has qualified this assertion also with "probably". Similarly the statement of Professor Edward J. Thompson cited on page 7 of this book that Iqbal had to admit the harmfulness of the Pakistan plan for the British Government, Hindu society and even the Muslim society car, be adjudged as the mere reflection of Thompson's personal thoughts. The Pakistan plan alluded to by Iqbal here as harmful and injurious to Britain, India and the Muslims was the Pakistan plan prepared by the Muslim students in

The Pakistan Plan and the Role of Iqbal

residence at the Cambridge University, according to which Pakistan would be spread over the entire sub-continent, the transfer of power, administration and defence of which would have created difficulties for everyone. It is wrong to attribute this to the Quaid-i-Azam Pakistan Plan.

The author of this book, Dr. Hassan Ahmad has himself admitted that the conversation between Iqbal and Thompson cited by him in this book has not been referred to anywhere by Thompson himself. The Iqbal - Thompson "conversation" referred to by Nehru Is the same as exists in form of "Iqbal - Thompson Letters". Beside this correspondence no reference exists to any interview which might have been held between Iqbal and Thompson and in which any conversation might have beer, recorded between them or, the political future of India and the concept of Pakistan. Dr. Ashique Hussein Batalavi has adjudged the letter of Thompson as fictitious (x).

Iqbal's letters cited by Thompson and Hassan Ahmad show no evidence that he was against the two-nation theory or the concept of a separate Muslim ration, or that he did not want to protect the Muslims from Hindu aggression, or that he did not want a separate Muslim homeland. Consequently, Pandit Nehru's guess that Iqbal had become disappointed at the end of his life and had changed his stand is incorrect. The interview of Iqbal and Pandit Nehru took place in early 1938. We give below the contents of the conversation of Syed Nazir Niazi with Iqbal after the interview so that the truth of Pandit Nehru's secret be exposed as to whether Iqbal had really reneged from his conceptions. Syed Nazir Niazi writes:

"Finding an opportune time I asked Iqbal, "How did the interview with Pandit Nehru proceed?" He replied, "Dr. Chakravarty I came one day and said that whenever he talked with Pandit Nehru about me the latter had expressed great appreciation and respect for me. He was arriving in Lahore that day and Dr. Chakravarty desired an interview between him anti me and hoped that I would not mind. I said that I had no objection and that Pandit Nehru would be welcome at my house whenever it would be convenient to him. I reminded Dr. Chakravarty of the two interconnected problems, i.e. those of India's freedom and the role of Muslims in the struggle for that freedom. The Pandit should come after due consideration of both of them. Dr. Chakravarty came again that evening and said that the Pandit was free and that they would come at eight o'clock. I showed my complete pleasure. He said that he hoped it would not be inconvenient to me as he thought that It was perhaps the time for me to retire. I laughed and said that I would retire a little late that night and insisted that they should come. Consequently, the Pandit arrived at about eight o' clock. Dr. Chakravarty, a few ladies and Mian and Begum if Iftikharuddin were with him. We talked for a fairly long period of time." (xi).

I asked if any special matter was discussed.

Iqbal said:

"No. The conversation was just a review of the current political affairs, and that too was very hurried and superficial. No special problem was discussed except that, when the political trends in Russia, Britain, Germany and Italy came under discussion, the question arose about the effects of the West's colonialism and greed for world domination on the rest of the world in general and on Asia in particular — freedom or slavery and more slavery. The Pandit casually remarked how good it would be if the Muslims would cooperate with the Congress unconditionally, the British would not be able to resist us long and the goal of freedom would draw nearer.

"This compelled me to ask the Pandit as to how the pace of India's freedom would be hastened if the Muslim would accept his suggestion and join the Congress unconditionally, and how it would be that the British Government would not obstruct us. He replied, (rather unconvincibly) that this would be brought about by our continuing our activities and the Hindus and the Muslims abandoning mutual bargaining.

"I inquired from him the details of the activities to which he replied that they would be the same on-going movements, i.e. civil disobedience and non-payment of land revenue. I expressed my doubts on the practicality of the successful continuation of these movements because they had been ineffective till then. I also said that the British army was still in India and wanted to know the strategy for their expulsion. As for the transfer of power 1t was and would continue to be in progress In spite of these movements. I could not see how the freedom's goal could be achieved.

"The Pandit replied that the main purpose was the transfer of power and that that would be hastened if those movements were maintained. The

The Pakistan Plan and the Role of Iqbal

country had achieved some freedom and that its scope would expand if those movements were continued.

"I questioned him about the British army, to which he replied that the British army and its presence in India was inconsequential; we could continue tolerating them till some day the British would leave India out of frustration.

"So, I asked him that the goal was not to gain independence but only internal freedom. Pandit Nehru has the same logic as Mr. Gandhi. Both are aiming at the transfer of political power, and to both independence means internal administrative freedom. ----.

"In fact the fight between the Congress and the government is the fight between two *banias*. The Congress wants to convince the Government of something, which they understand but do not accept. They can and will accept it but only gradually, because the ruler is after all the ruler and the ruled is the ruled. The Congress wants to acquire the reins of internal administration. They are not much concerned with the British army and their continuation in India. They could be useful in the defence of India.

"The whole quarrel is about bargaining but its settlement is very difficult, because both are *banias*. Both want settlement but each wants to have the upper hand.

"I have expressed my disagreement with the Pandit unequivocally. I have told him that he thought that India was under no threat but I thought that it was under a very serious one. He thinks that the geographic and strategic position of India provides complete security and freedom from attack. On the contrary I think we are very vulnerable and will be attacked. The British will not leave India, and it they do leave it will be after much struggle.

"I also told him that even if we accepted his suggestion and considered all his premises to be correct, the very correctness of his premises would provide further rationale for the acceptance of the Muslim demands and an initiative by the Congress for amity with the Muslims. A movement in India can be launched successfully only after creation of confidence in the minds of the minorities in the majority, and the settlement of their mutual rights. However, I got no response from the Pandit on this."

I said:

"It is strange that the Pandit may come to meet and converse with you on a matter like independence and still abstain from responding to your views."

Iqbal said:

"The Pandit arrogantly thinks that the Government would eventually enter into some agreement with the Congress, and so the Muslims can be ignored."

I said:

"If the Pandit thinks so he is wrong. In any case his attitude is very frustrating. He should have at least said something to support his stand. Perhaps he thinks that this course of indifference would slowly destroy the feelings of separate identity among the Muslims."

Iqbal said:

"It appears so. Whenever I tried to convince the Pandit that whatever point of view is accepted, that of the Congress or the Muslim League, political sagacity demands mutual trust and confidence between the inhabitants of this country. He always side-tracked the issue and insisted on the correctness of the concept of mutual understanding, amity and mutual cooperation without any preconditions.

"I even told the Pandit that I was neither the enemy of the Congress nor was irrationally attached to the Muslim League, that I was not siding with any party, but could not help the situation in which compromise and reconciliation were in-escapeable. This reconcilition and understanding is the demand of the separate nationhood of the Mulims and will have to be made some day.

"I had also explained that what I was saying was not just for the sake of argument. I say only what I consider just. I asked the Pandit to listen to me with attention when I say that Muslims have no love for the British;

The Pakistan Plan and the Role of Iqbal

they complain against the British power more strongly than the Hindus, the reason for which is perhaps known to the Pandit, i.e. anti-impeialism. If he was a connoisseur of human feelings he should gauge the Muslim feelings. He would find Mulims to be more anti-imperialist than the Hindus.

"Support for the Congress would not open the way for the liberation and freedom of the Muslims. This is the path of weakness and degeneration, disunity and confusion and not that of strength, which comes from unity and affinity. If power and strength is acquired it would go to the united nationhood or, in the terminology of the Congress to the Indian nation. They would get the freedom as well as the political power in India. This may be achieved by constitutional or un-constitutional struggle, whatever the final decision might be would be in the favour of the majority. Hence, without deciding the status of the people who are taking part in this struggle, *vis-à-vis* each other it would be a major error, and may even amount to suicide to say that the current problem is only that of freedom, all other problems are secondary. Hindus are not as straight forward as the Muslims of the above thinking consider them to be.

"In reality all this mischief has been created by the erroneous concept of the word "nation." Muslims must understand the meaning of "nation" in political terminology. It means some kind of grouping. In the view of the Congress "nation" means the grouping based on the foundations of the native country, in view of which it considers the residents of this country to be a nation. The truth is that this imaginary and fictitious nation has no existence at all in reality.

The Turks, the Arabs, the Afghans are certainly a nation which has geographic, linguistic, cultural and religious unity".

In the light of these extracts indication can be obtained of the trend of the conversation between Pandit Nehru and Iqbal in that Iqbal maintained only one stand all his life that the Muslims and Hindus of the Indian sub-continent are two different nations, they can never unite and co-exist together, that the Hindus and Muslims are not a single nation and that he could not be ensnared by Pandit Nehru:

And when Mian Iftikharuddin said to Iqbal, "Why do you not tell the truth that the Muslims have been influenced by you and that nobody follows Jinnah", Iqbal said in reply to that also, "At least Jinnah listens to things just and true, the Congress is the one which does not listen to truth and justice. Does the Congress really desire freedom? in the same sense as the Muslims?"

After this Iqbal continued, "Mian lftikharuddin, perhaps you will not deny the fact that the Muslim unity is essential and that Jinnah's leadership has succeeded to some extent in this direction. So, should this be destroyed only because Hindus do not like that the Muslims become united as a nation? Excuse me, I am not prepared for this. This unity cannot be sacrificed at the altar of the approbation of the Congress or the good pleasure of the Hindus. (xii).

After perusal of these clear thoughts and declarations of Iqbal any Impression of any intellectual harmony of Iqbal with the Congress or his desire for the co-existence of the Hindus and Mislims melts away into thin air. Syed Nazir Niazi, citing Ashique Hussein Batalavi, has analysed Pandit Nehru's opinion, which the latter had expressed with refernce to Edward Thompson's book, *Enlist India for Freedom*, 1940 Edition, page 58, that Iqbal disliked the partition of India, i.e. the ideology of Pakistan. Syed Nazir Niazi, citing Mr. Batalavi says, This opinion of Pandit Nehru Is based on the statement of Edward Thompson which has been proven to be utterly wrong and fabricated". (xiii)

The perusal of the letter dated June 30, 1933, included in Hassan Ahmad's book will be very ineresting as it will show how disgusted Iqbal was with the Hindu version of nationalism. (xiv) He had realized that "that nationalism would lead to atheism and materialism, which would harm the higher ideals of Islam. Iqbal said, "in these circumstances It is my duty to present the correct concepts before the Muslim youth and I am glad to know that the British also realize that the Indian Muslims have a separate individuality and that they should get the opportunity to be able to plan their renaissance and progress on their own lines. This is my goal, and for this I have even ruined my legal practice, because I have not paid any attention to it for two years. I realize that in doing so I am unfair to my children but still, as a Muslim, I consider Islam's service as my more sacred duty than my children's welfare. Both Islam and Britain are facing difficult times. It is, however, unfortunate that though Britain has the leadership which can understand the problems Muslims do not have such a leadership. You will notice that my interest in politics will not go beyond certain limits. I shall not be a candidate for any seat in the council or assembly under the new constitution."

The Pakistan Plan and the Role of Iqbal

The following matters are evident from the above extracts:

i. Iqbal was disgusted with Hindu nationalism.

ii. He wanted to protect the Muslims from it,

iii. In his view Indian Muslims had a separate identity.

iv. They should get the opportunity for their renaissance and progress on their own lines.,

v. The welfare of the Muslim nation was dearer to him than his children.

vi. Muslims were devoid of leadership.

vii. His interest in politics was up to a limited extent and he was not desirous of power for himself.

After this what further evidence is needed for the self-less and sincere leadership of Iqbal, which is sincerely desirous for the Muslims getting the opportunity for their renaissance and progress on their own lines. Is this very ideology not the spirit of Pakistan which, obtaining nourishment from Iqbal's thought, manifested itself in the Independent State of Pakistan. Iqbal had clearly stated this in his Allahabad address:

> "The establishment of a strong Islamic State in the north-wedtern region of India appears to me to be destined for the Muslims of this region at least." (xv)

Along with the above the following words of Iqbal to his letter dated June 21, 1937 are worth consideration:

> "I understand that the new constitution, establishing a united federation in Inidia, is disappointing.---- Peace cannot be established in India without the establishment of a separate federation of the Muslim majority provinces.---- Personally I think that in the present circumstances the Muslims of the north-western India and Bengal should ignore the Muslim minority provinces. This will prove to be the best action for the Muslims of both the majority and minority provinces." (xvi)

Understanding Iqbal's Philosophy

In addition to this the attention given by Iqbal to the problem of the sub-continent's Muslims in his letters to Mr. Jinnah between May 23, 1936 and November 10, 1937 clearly indicates the perpetual interest of Iqbal in the separate independent homeland for the Muslims. Consequently, neither did he announce the renunciation of his stand in 1933-34, nor was he disappointed 1n his goals at the end of his life. Or, the contrary, at this important juncture he provided guidance, with extreme care, honesty and sincerity, to the leader of the Muslims, Quaid-i-Azam Muhammad Ali Jinnah in the struggle for the establishment of a separate homeland for the Muslims. He helped the Quaid-i-Azam In changing the Muslims' destiny. The Quaid-i-Azam acknowledged Iqbal's help and guidance on several occasions and testified to his services. He stated on March 23, 1940 in addressing the Lahore Resolution session:

"Iqbal is not with us today. If he were alive he would have been happy to know that we have done exactly what he had expected of us". (xvii).

The interest and attachment of the Quaid-i-Azam with the lqbal Day celebrations of March 26, 1940, March 2, 1941 and December 9, 1942 are perpetual witnesses of Iqbal's status, respect and dignity 1n the eyes of the Quaid-i-Azam. The Quaid-i-Azam states:

"Iqbal was a pratical statesman In addition to being a prominent poet and philosopher,--- He was among the few pioneers who had dreamt of an Islamic State for the first time.---Iqbal was an old friend of mine. You know that the All-India Muslim League was only an academic organization in the beginning. In 1936 some of us expressed the view that we should convert this organization into a proper parliamentary one. On arrival In the Punjab in April 1936 Iqbal was the first person I met. I presented my thoughts to him. He immediately volunteered his services and from that time to his last breath he stood with me like a firm rock.---- Iqbal has rendered invaluable services in creating political awakening among the Muslims.---- Iqbal was the best interpretor of Islam in the present age. In this day and age I have not seen a more faithful companion and lover of Islam than Iqbal. What he considered right surely turned out to be right and he stood by it like a firmrock. --- I am not the owner of a realm, but if I get one and have the choice of selection between the realm and Iqbal I would select Iqbal".

The Pakistan Plan and the Role of Iqbal

The Quaid-i-Azam testimony in connection with the attachment of Iqbal with the ideology of Pakistan and the independent Muslim State ranks as the final argument.

Iqbal, in his letter of March 20, 1937 to the Quaid-i-Azam also said, with reference to Pandit Nehru:

"I hope you have read the address of Pandit Jawaharlal Nehru to the All-India National Convention and must have understood his policy about the Indian Muslims. I am confident that you are fully aware of the fact that the new constitution is an unique opportunity for the future political progress of Indian as well as Asian Muslims, Though we are also prepared to cooperate with all other progressive organizations within the country, we should not overlook the reality that the power of Asia's Muslims depends on their complete organization." (xviii)

Iqbal proposed in this letter that the Muslim League should also hold a session of all prominent Muslim leaders and "In this session clear recognition should be obtained for the distinct position of the Muslims in the country's politics. It is extremely necessary to explain very clearly to the Indians as well as to the world outside that the economic problem is not the only problem of India, but from the Islamic point of view social problem is the most important one. The future of Islamic civilization has a greater Importance than the economic problem of Indian Muslims. It is in no way less important than the economic problem.---- In addition to this it will be clear to the Hindus that the political manouvres, however subtle and sly, cannot destroy the cultural reality of Muslims."

In reply to the letter of the late Mumtaz Hassan Iqbal clearly explained this thought, "I do consider the establishment of an Islamic State to be a historical demand but it is not yet clear to my mind whether this new Islamic State would be within the British Empire or outside it."

This means that though Iqbal considered the establishment of an Islamic State to be a historical demand he was not clear about this "new Islamic State" being inside the British Empire or outside it, and remained silent. This also shows that the establishment of an Islamic State was certainly his goal but his stand was not clear about its being within the British Empire or outside it. It cannot be considered from this that Iqbal wanted or was agreeable to keeping it in a confederation with the Hindus, as is the opinion of Hassan Ahmad, Nehru and others.

As for as the use of the word "province" for the "Muslim majority regions" at some places is concerned a reference to the statement of Waris Mir is relevant. He says:

"In this connection the letter dated May 22, 1932 from Dr. Moonje's representative, S. D. Belat to Dr. Iqbal is extremely important. This letter also explains the reason for using the word "province" in the letters to Thompson and Raghib Ahsan. It was stated in this letter that negotiations could be started 1f Iqbal would agree to the use of the word "province" instead of "State" in the context of amalgamation of the Muslim majority provinces of the north-west, and that later Pandit Madan Mohan Malaviya could be included in any final Hindu-Muslim compromise. In this connection Iqbal wrote a letter to Mawlana Muhammad Irfan on June 8, 1932 saying that some days ago he had written a letter to Mawlana Shaukat Ali[24] that he red received a letter from a Hindu gentleman Mr. Belat to the effect that Dr. S.D. Moonje had accepted the scheme which Iqbal had presented in the presidential address to the Muslim League; he was going to consult Pandit Malaviya and that the latter would also accept it for the sake of Hindu-Muslim compromise, though he did not consider it advisable to accept it openly at that time.

This letter was confidential and it also said that Maulana Shawkat Ali had also been consulted and had agreed for a compromise. It can be understood which scheme had been referred to in the above letter. i.e. amalgamation of the Muslim majority provinces of the north-western India. It is possible that Iqbal might have accepted the proposal.

For the establishment of a Muslim province by the amalgamation of the Muslim majority provinces in north-western India for political amity with the Hindus for the time being. It is Important to remember that Iqbal knew about the grant of provincial autonomy in the new constitution. Consequently, Iqbal wanted the establishment of a Muslim majority province by the amalgamation of the Muslim majority provinces in north-western India in the interim, albeit under the British India, so that the same province could become the foundation for the future independent Islamic State. For this reason he accepted the concept of the formation of an Islamic province in the north-western India within British India.

The Pakistan Plan and the Role of Iqbal

Otherwise, Iqbal's real stand remained the same as he had explained in the Allahabad address, i.e. "I am pressing the demand for the establishment of an Islamic State only for the well being of India and Islam. Peace will prevail in India as a result of the balance of power established by this."(xix)

Iqbal, addressing a session of the National League in London on November 24, 1932, during the Third Round Table Conference reiterated that, "in my personal opinion this is the only possible solution of this problem."

How could Iqbal change in 1933 and 1934 what he had considered as the final solution till 1930 and 1932? Thompson, Hassan Ahmad, Nehru and Rajindra Prashad do not provide any answer to this. Lala Lajpat Rai writes, "I have spent a good deal of my time during the last few months in studying Muslim law and history, which has now led me to the appreciation of the impossibility of Hindu-Muslim unity. Even after accepting that the present day Muslim leaders, who have joined the non-cooperation movement, have very good intentions, I think their religion is a definite obstacle in this unity. I had related to you in Calcutta the conversation which I had with Hakim Ajmal Khan and Dr. Kichloo. There is no nobler Muslim in India than Hakim Ajmal Khan, but can any Muslim deviate from the (Holy) Qur'an? I can only wish that I had misunderstood the meaning of the (Holy) Qur'an".

After these testimonies, when the Hindus themselves had given up all hope of Hindu-Muslim unity and were considering it unfeasible, how can it be accepted that Iqbal would have considered any relationship or cooperation with the Hindus as beneficial for the Muslims?

Epilogue

Review of Iqbal's early works and actions belies the theory propounded by some Hindu politicians and their cooperators that he was initially an Indian nationalist and was only swept away into what the Hindus call "communalism" by the "separatist politics" of the Muslim League. This erroneous view reflects complete ignorance of the works, actions and thoughts of Iqbal as well as the basics of Islam. His stay in Europe during the period 1905-08 confirmed his earlier belief, based on the deep study of Islam, that geographic nationalism, with its concomitant secularism, as apolitical philosophy, was contrary to the spirit of Islam and was only a product of Western imperialism, propagated by them for dividing and subjugating mankind and for perpetuating their r rule over non-European people. As early as 1905-08 he had realized the supra-national Ideal of Islam and had set out to achieve It. Space does not permit elaboration of this topic but the reader is urged to read Hussein, particularly pages 1-49, which deal with Iqbal's early life and works. Suffice it to invite reference here to the following two examples. During the period 1905-08 he had declared:

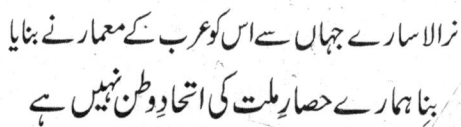

The Arab architect made it distinct from the rest of the world
The foundation of our Millat's citadel is not geographic unity '(xx)

The "Report of the Census of India 1911", XIV, pages 162-164 includes the account of a lecture by Iqbal on Indian Muslims in which he had urged the creation of a separate Muslim homeland In India as the only guarantee for the preservation of Islam in the sub-continent even before 1911. At that time he had declared, "in the interests of a universal unification of mankind the Qur'an ignores their minor differences and says, "Come, let us unite in what is common to us all." "All men and not Muslims alone are meant for the Kingdom of God on earth, provided they say good-bye to their idols of race and nationality, and treat one another as personalities."

Thus, though Iqbal was a patriot he never accepted geographic nationalism as a political philosophy. Far from being swayed by the "separatist politics of the Muslim League" he guided the Muslim Intelligentsia and the Muslim people towards the goal of a Muslim homeland in India. In this homeland an Islamic State was to be established which would be the nucleus for the ultimate creation of a supra-national Islamic State, or at least a "League of Islamic Nations". His aim clearly was Muslim-Hindu amity to speed up India's independence, which would prepare the ground for the real independence of the Muslim world beyond their mere political independence which also is only in name so far.

The Pakistan Plan and the Role of Iqbal

References

(i) Farhat, Razia Bano *Khutbat-i-Iqbal* (Addresses of Iqbal), Published by the Maktaba-i-Abbasia, Delhi, India, p.46

(ii) Ibid., p.40

(iii) Ibid., p.

(iv) Iqbal, Dr. Sir Muhammad (1924): *Bang-i-Dara*, Published by Sheikh Mubarak Ali, Lahore, Pakistan. Third Edition (1930), p. 301

(v) Ibid.

(vi) Khan, Muhammad Ahmad (1977): *Iqbal ke Siyasi Karname* (Iqbal's Political Achievements). Published by the Iqbal Academy Pakistan, Lahore, Pakistan, pp. 898-901

(vii) Ibid., p.903 The author of the book states that Chaudhry Rahmat Ali had coined the word "Pakistan" as follows: "P" from Pujab, "A" from Afghania, "K" from Kashmir, "I" from Iran, "S" from Sind, "T" from Turkistan, "A" from Afghanistan and "Tan" from Baluchistan."

(viii) Ahmad, Hassan: *Iqbal's Political Thought - At the Crossroads*, published by p.7

(ix) Batalavi, Ashique Hussein : *Iqbal ke Akhri Do Sal* (The Last Two Years of Iqbal), pp.561-563

(x) Niazi, Syed Nazir: *Iqbal ke Huzoor* (In Audience with Iqbal), pp. 95-101

(xi) Ibid., pp.334-335

(xii) Ibid., p. 102

(xiii) Batalvi, op.cit. pp. 555-565

(xiv) Ahmad Hassan, op.cit. pp. 2-3

(xv) Cf. Farhat, op.cit.

(xvi) Quraishi, Waheed (Compiler): *Muntakhab Maqalat-i-Iqbal* (Selected Papers of Iqbal). Published by the Iqbal Academy Pakistan, Lahore, Pakistan, p. 309

(xvii) Hashmi, Hameedullah (1976) (Translator): *Iqbal ke Khutut Banam-i-Jinnah* (Iqbal's Letters to Jinnah). Published by Mahboob Book Depot, Faisalabad, Pakistan. Quaid-i-Azam Muhammad Ali Jinnah's Addresses to the Iqbal Day Meetings on March 26, 1940, March 2, 1941 and December 9, 1943

(xviii) Pirzada, Sharif-ud-Din (1970) (Ed.): *Foundation of Pakistan*, pp.336-337

(xix) Hussein, Riaz (1977): *The Politics of Iqbal*, Published by the Islamic Book Service, Lahore, Pakistan, (First Edition), pp. 1-49

(xx) *Bang-i-Dara*, op.cit.

The Pakistan Plan and the Role of Iqbal

Explanatory Notes

1. Sir Rabindranath Tagore (1861-1941) - Indian poet, philosopher and educator. However, his literary field extended beyond poetry to novels, dramas and short stories. He wrote in his mother tongue, Bengali, as well as in English. He won the Nobel Prize in literature in 1913 and Knighthood in 1915. His main interest was to combine the best in the cultures of the East and the West and create a supra-national culture. To this end he established a boys' school, Shantiniketan, and later added a university to it, called Visvabharati. He was primarily an exponent of Bengali literature and Hindu culture and civilization, and, thus had no appeal to Muslims in general.

2. Sheikh Ahmad Sirhindi Mujaddid Alf-i-Thani (1564-1624) - He was a very famous Islamic scholar and Sufi His main contribution to Islam is the repudiation of the philosophy of *Wahdat-al-Wujud* of Ibn-al-Arabi and re-establishment of the supremacy of the *Shariah*. He also fought against the un-Islamic practices of the Mughal court of the times of Akbar and Jahangir. He repeatedly warned the two emperors of their errors and un-Islamic actions for which he was imprisoned by Jahangir in the Gwalior Fort for a considerably long time. For these reasons he got the popular title of *Mujaddid Alf Thani* or "Renovator of the Second Millennium."

3. Ahmad Shah Abdali (1722-1772) - He was the founder of the State of Afghanistan and ruler of an empire which stretched, for a time, from Oxus, across Baluchistan to the Indian Ocean and from Khurasan into Kashmir, the Punjab and Sind. He was one of the generals of Nadir Shah, and on the latter's assassination in 1747, was elected the king of Aghanistan by his tribe (Abdal), which he later renamed Durran. He had several military encounters with the Sikhs, Marathas, as well as with the decadent Mughal Empire of that time. At the Initiative of Shah Waliullah he fought a fierce battle against the Marathas on January 4, 1761 at Panipat, north of Delhi. This battle was decisive in crushing the Maratha supremacy and prepared the ground for their subsequent defeat at the hands of the British in a series of Maratha wars. Thus, Ahmad Shah Abdali was instrumental in greatly weakening the Marathas who were great enemies of the Muslims at that time.

4. Siraj-ud-Daula (1729-1757) - Ruler of Bengal under the nominal suzerainty of the Mughal Emperor of India. He had several military encounters with the East India Company, the last one of which was the famous battle of Plassey on June 23, 1757 in which he was defeated, primarily due to the treachery of his Hibdu minister, and Mir Jafar, his principal general. Siraj-ud-Daula fled up country to Rajmahal, where he was captured and martyred on July 2, 1757 by Mir Jafar's son Miran. This battle and the role of traitors is famous in Indian history as well as In Iqbal' s works, especially in *Javid Namah*.

5. Bania - This is a class of Hindu small merchants, ususally engaged in grocery business and loan sharking. In the Indian sub-continent the term represents a petty minded niggardly person and is used as a stereotype for Hindus.

6. Mawlvis and 'Ulemas - Muslim religious scholars. The term is used mainly for scholars specializing in *Fiqh* or Islamic jurisprudence.

7. *Sanghatan* and *Shudhi* - They literally mean communal consolidation and purification respectively. However, in the Indian sub-continent the terms apply to a Hindu movement started in the early twentieth century in which Hindus started to "purify and consolidate" the Hindu society by forcibly converting the poor and uneducated Muslims, usually in villages and small towns to Hinduism. This action is still continuing ire India and is supported by the erroneous argument that these people were originally Hindus and had been forcibly converted to Islam by Muslims and so should be brought back to the Hindu fold where they belong.

8. John Bright Belt (or Belat)

9. Lala Lajpat Rai (1865-1928) - He was an Indian Hindu leader of extreme Hindu views. He was a lawyer and entered politics very soon in his career. He helped to found the chain of Dayanand Anglo-Vedic (D.A.V.) colleges in Lahore and other cities. He was deported in 1907 to Mandalay for anti-British activities. Later he spent some time in the United States of America during World War I, where he wrote: "The U.S.A. : A Hindu's Impression" in 1916. In this book he devoted some attention to the social problems of that country, especially the problems of negroes, whom he considered the untouchables of U.S.A. He was president of the Congress Party in 1920, when the Congress launched the non-cooperation movement. He was a member of the Legislative Assembly in which he moved a resolution for the boycott of the Simon

The Pakistan Plan and the Role of Iqbal

Commission on Indian Constitution reforms. He led this movement and suffered injuries and ultimately death as a result of police action during one such demonstration in Lahore.

10. Abdul Haleem Sharar (1860-1926) - He was born in Lucknow (India). He was a great novelist, Historian and poet. He got his education in Calcutta (India). He was a working journalist. He had also written an editorial in the favour of Muslims homeland for the Muslims of India.

11. Jamal-ud-Din Afghani (1839-97) - He was a Muslim scholar and activist whose thinking had much influence on Iqbal's thought. Afghani endeavoured to make Islam a cementing force to free the Muslim society from intellectual and socio-political domination of the West. He believed in pan-Islamism ans supra-national character of Islamic society. At the same time he realized the potential of Western science and technology in the material progress of the Muslim world. Consequently, he worked hard to persuade Muslim countries, especially Afghanistan and Iran to acquire proficiency in them. Unfortunately, he did not succeed.

12. Abdul Qadir Bilgrami

13. Hasrat Mohani (1878-1951) - He was born in Mohan (India) and got his education in Aligrah. His name was Syed Fazl-ul-Hasan. He was a syed poet and Muslim freedom fighter of sub-continent. He worked for a free home land of Muslims of India. he was a member of Muslim League.

14. Mawlana Muhammad Ali Jawhar (1828-1931) - He was a poet, journalist and a great Muslim leader of sub-continent. He was born in Rampur, bother of Mawlana Shaukat Ali Khan and son of Bi amma. He received his education in Allahabad and Oxford.

15. Sir Sultan Muhammad Shah Agha Khan III (1877-1957) - He was the fourth Imam or spiritual leader of the Nizari Ismaili sect of the Shiite Muslims. He was well educated in Islamic learning as well as in secular education of the East and the West. He applied himself to temporal as well as spiritual welfare of the Ismailies. In addition, he played a very important role in the politics of the Muslims of the Indian sub-continent of his time. He participated in or headed several Muslim delegation, and organizations, including the Muslim delegations to the three Round Table Conferences (1930-32) in London. He was also president of the All-India

Understanding Iqbal's Philosophy

Muslim League in his early years. He initiated the fund raising for up grading of the Muhammedan Anglo-Oriental College at Aligarh to the university status, which was granted in 1920.

16. Adul Qadir Badauni (1540-1615) - He was a great historian of Akbar's time. He had written some famous of his time. Selection of historians was his remarkable of his time.

17. Murtaza Ahmad Maikash (1904-1954) - He was a journalist born in Jallandar. He joined Khilafat Movement. He worked in *Zamindar*, *Inqilab* and *Ahsan*. He had written a history of nations in two volumes.

18. Chaudhry Rahmat Ali (1893-1957) - He was born in Hoshiarpur. He studied at Jallandar and Lahore. He was the student of Cambridge when he met Iqbal. He also had a Pakistan scheme, which was quite different from Iqbal's Pakistan Scheme.

19. Rajindra Prashad (1881-1960) - He was the first President of India. He joined All India Congress in 1920 and elected four times as a president of All India Congress. He was also against Pakistan.

20. Pandit Jawaharlal Nehru (1889-1964) - He was a very prominent Congress leader and the first prime minister of Independent India. He was born abd brought up in a rich, aristocratic and orthodox Brahman family. He was Instructed by English governors and tutors and got formal education at Harrow, Cambridge and subsequently at Inner Temple In London, England during the period 1905-12. This aristocratic background remained with him all his life and was reflected in his personal and political dealings. His intransigence in his dealings with Muslims and with Pakistan after independence are reflections of the same. During his stay in England he was greatly influenced by Fabian socialism, the Irish Home Rule movement and the Women's Suffrage movement. Though he claimed to be ultra-secular his personal life as well as writings show very marked anti-Islam and anti-Muslim bias. His *Autobiography* and *Glimpses of World History*, published in the early nineteen thirties amply prove this. He also observed all Hindu rituals in his personal life. However, whenever he was questioned on these by the press he said that those practices were part of the Indian culture and customs and had nothing to do with Hindu religious rites. Incidentally, this is the Hindu way in India. In subtle as well as not so subtle ways they force Indian

The Pakistan Plan and the Role of Iqbal

Muslims to observe Hindu religious rituals under the pretext that they are Indian customs, and not Hindu religious rituals.

21. Professor Waris Mir. He was a famous journalist *writer*, professor and head of the department of journalism in the University of Punjab. Died 9th July 1987.

22. Mawlana Abul Kalam Azad (1888-1958) - He was a prominent Indian statesman. He descended from an old Muslim family of Delhi, which had produced several pious persons and men of affairs. His father settled in Calcutta. He was educated exclusively in Islamic theology and oriental learning. He was an internationally famous scholar of Islam and a literary man. In these fields he gained reputation through his journal, *Al-Hilal*, his Urdu writings and his encyclopedic commentary of the Holy Qur'an in spite of this background his opposition to the Pakistan movement and adherence to the Congress ideology of secular nationalism are enigmatic. He became the Congress president several times, including the long period of 1940-46, when he conducted negotiations with several political missions sent by the British government to negotiate India's independence. It was a very clever move of the Congress to elect a prominent Muslim religious scholar as the Congress president at a time when the Muslims were struggling for the separate Islamic State of Pakistan and were arguing that the Congress was representing the Hindus and not the Indian nation. Only he could explain this enigma. A remark in the Collier's *Encyclopedia* is strange but supports what has been said above. It says, "Azad was a Muslim who supported Hindu idealism". Hindu idealism is clearly a *mushrik* idealism and aims at complete supremacy of their system and complete annihilation or Muslims from India. The long chain of events in India since independence and the unending Hindu-Muslim riots, with heavy loss of Muslim property and life bears eloquent testimony to this.

23. Mawlana Hussein Ahmad Madani (1878-1957) - He was another enigmatic personality of his times. He was a prominent alim (religious scholar) of Islam in India in the twentieth century and was the Principal of the famous seminary, known as Darul Ulum at Deoband, India. He was a staunch believer in and supporter of the ideology of Indian secular nationalism propounded by the Congress. Iqbal has expressed the following opinion about him:

Understanding Iqbal's Philosophy

عجم هنوز نداند رموزِ دیں ورنہ
ز دیو بند حسین احمد ایں چہ بوالعجبی است!
سرود بر سرِ منبر کہ ملّت از وطن است
چہ بے خبر و مقامِ محمدؐ عربی است!
بمصطفیٰ برساں خویش را کہ دیں ہمہ اوست
اگر بہ او نہ رسیدی تمام بولہبی است!

Ajam (the non-Arab world) still knows not the secrets of the Deen
Hussein Ahmad from Deoband, how grossly strange it is
Orchestration at the pulpit that the nation (Millat is based on the country!
How ignorant is he of the stand of Muhammad of Arabia
To Mutafa convey thyself, as he is the complete deen
If thou doth not reach him it is all infidelity (Bu Lahabi)
(Iqbal, Dr. Sir Muhammad (1938) - *Armaghan-i-Hijaz*. Published Javid Iqbal, First Edition (1938), p. 278.)

24. Mawlana Shaukat Ali (d.1938) - He was a leader of Khilafat Movement. A many time he was arrested by the British Government. He worked as a secretary a Sir Agha Khan. As a elder brother of Mawlana Muhammad Ali he took part in the freedom of sub-continent. He took part in political for forty years.

Chapter 11

IQBAL AND COMMUNISM[1]

The paper contradicts the misconception that Iqbal was a supporter of communism. Iqbal viewed the rise of communism as an adversary of capitalism, colonialism and feudalism, which supplement each other. Iqbal was convinced that after mankind had experienced both the extremes of economic administration, i.e. capitalism and communism; human societies would appreciate the virtues of the middle path of Islam and would gravitate towards it.

During Iqbal's life some people had attempted to create the impression of Iqbal's leanings towards communism, basing their arguments on some verses in favour of communism and its ideology. An Indian communist, Shamsuddin Hasan, commenting in the *Zamindar* of June 23, 1923 on the arrest of Professor Comrade Ghulam Hasan and his communist co-workers had said, "If supporting Bolshevik thought is a crime our country's greatest poet, Sir Muhammad Iqbal cannot escape legal action, because the Bolshevik system of government is the essence of its political philosophy and Karl Marx' philosophy is commonly callerd socialism and communism. In these circumstances even a person of average intelligence will see by a careful study of Sir Muhammad Iqbal's *Khizr-i-Rah* (The Journey's Guide) and *Payam-i-Mashriq* (The Message of the East) that Iqbal is not only a communist but communism's high priest". (i)

Immediately on publication of this articles, i.e. the very next day Iqbal explained his principles in the daily *Zamindar* as follows:

"I am a Muslim and believe, on the basis of logical reasoning, that the Holy Qur'an has offered the best cure for the economic maladies of human societies. No doubt the power of capitalism is a curse if it exceeds the limits of the happy mean: But its complete elimination is not the right way for freeing the world from its evils as the Bolshevik's propose. To keep its power within reasonable limits the Holy Qur'an has prescribed the law of inheritance, prohibition of usury and the system of *Zakat*[2] etc. and, considering human nature, this is the only practical system. Russian

Understanding Iqbal's Philosophy

Bolshevism is a strong reaction against the selfish and short sighted capitalism of Europe. But in fact the European capitalism and the Russain Bolshevism are two extremes. The happy middle path is what the Holy Qur'an has shown to us and to which I have alluded above. The equitable *Shariah*[3] aims at protecting one class from the economic domination of the other, and in my belief, the path chosen by the Holy Prophet is the one best suited for thus purpose.

"Islam does not exclude the power of capital from its economic system, but on account of its deep concern for human nature, maintains it and prescribes for us an economic system practicing which would not allow its power ever to transgress reasonable limits. I am sorry at the Muslims' indifference towards studying the economic side of Islam, otherwise they would have appreciated the great blessing of Islam in this particular respect. I believe the allusion to this blessing in" [ ]"[4], because the individuals of a nation cannot feet mutually fraternal relationship without equality among themselves in all respects, and this equality cannot be attained without establishing a social system aimed at containing the powers of capitalism within reasonable limits. Europe today is engulfed in troubles and tribulations by ignoring this. I sincerely wish that all nations of mankind frame laws in their respective countries aimed at restraining the power of capitalism within reasonable limits, thereby leading to the creation of the above equality. Also, I am sure that the Russian nation itself, experiencing the shortcomings of its own present system, will be obliged to incline towards a system whose basic principles will be either purely or approximately Islamic. In the present century, however, laudiable the economic ideals of Russians may be their practical program cannot win any Muslim's sympathy. The Muslims of India and other countries, who are very easily swayed by western thought, by the study of Europe's political economy, should make a deep study of the Holy Qur'an's political economy. I am convinced that they will find the solution of their economic problem in this book. The Muslim members of the Lahore's Labour Union should pay special attention to this. I have genuine sympathies with their aims and objectives but I hope that they will not adopt a course of action or ideology which will be contrary to the teachings of the Holy Qur'an."(ii)

This clarifies the following points:

1. Iqbal did not accept anything except Islam as an article of faith or philosophy of life and the Holy Qur'an is the source and centre of all his thoughts.

Iqbal and Communism

2. Iqbal considers unbriedled capitalism as an anathema for the whole world.

3. He rejects the use of Bolshevik system as a panacea for the evil effects of capitalism.

4. He considers the Islamic laws of inheritance, prohibition of usuary and institution of *zakat* as very close to human nature for effective protection against capitalism.

5. Iqbal considers the Russian Bolshevism to be a forceful reaction aganist the Europe's selfish and shortsighted capitalism. Still he considrs capitalism and Bolshevism as extremes, with the golden mean being the teachings of the Holy Qur'an.

6. Islam does not exclude capital's power from the economic system. To Iqbal, it is impossible to establish real fraternity between the individuals of a nation without economic equality. To achieve this equality is the social system is imperative which would aim at containement of the forces of capitalism within reasonable bounds.

7. Iqbal expresses his ardent desire that all human nations frame laws within their repective countries which would aim at establishing the aforesaid equality by containment of the forces of capitalism within reasonable bounds.

8. Iqbal also predicts that "I am convinced that the Russian nation also, after experiencing the failures of their present system, will be complelled to incline towards a system whose basic principles will be purely or approximately Islamic".

9. Iqbal clearly says that "in the present conditions, however laudabe the Russian's economic ideals may be, their practical program cannot win any Muslim's sympathy".

10. The Muslims of India (Pakistan and India) as well as other countries, who are very easily swayed by Western thought, after studying Europe's political economy, should make a deep study of the Holy Qur'an's political economy. I am convinced that they would find the solution of their problems in this book.

Understanding Iqbal's Philosophy

The purpose of the above explanations was to clarify Iqbal's views about capitalism and communism with the help of his own statements, which leaves no doubt about his thoughts concerning these two systems.

The question now remains as to why Iqbal lauded communism, Marx and Lenin so much. There are three basic reasons which follow:

1. The first reason is psychological and political. The Indian sub-continent as well as Islamic countries were under the capitalistic colonial system. The colonial system appeared invincible, and its defeat and destruction alone could free the Islamic world. When the defeat and destruction of this centuries-old caplitalistic colonial system started at the hands Marx and Lenin it naturally attracted the sympathy of Iqbal, who had been perturbed by capitalism's colonial system, in that they had dealt an effective blow to this very huge monster of despotism, who was parading in the cloak of democracy, and had demolished the spell of its invincibility.

2. The second reason was that the invitable result of the defeat and destruction of capitalism would not only be the freedom of the Islamic world from colonialism but that of the entire world from slavery.

3. Iqbal was convinced that, resulting from the defeat and destruction of capitalism, Islam also would rise as an economic power together with communism, and that when the human race would have experienced the two extremes of individual ownership in capitalism and collective ownership in communism it would appreciate the closeness of Islam's middle path approach to human nature, and would be inclined to accept it. He believed in the rise of Islam with its economic system and their universal acceptance of it in the wake of the destruction of capitalism and disgust with communism. To him the creation of Pakistan was inevitable for this experiment in Islamic economics and was necessary, in Iqbal's view, to show the world and "old spectacle".

This was the background in which Iqbal, while cautiously illuminating and praising the affirmative and positive aspects of the communist experiment, persuaded Muslims to benefit from it, also pointed out its negative aspects and warned them to guard themselves against their ill effects.

Iqbal and Communism

A basic principle must be remebered that no system either deserves complete rejection or uncritical acceptance in its entirety. Human nature loves extremism. It strays about between extremes instead of adopting the mean. It was fascinated once by the Western system and then by communism. Very few people accept the positive aspects of both, considering them the lost heitage of the *Mumin* (believer in Islam), and discard the negative aspects on account of their ill effects. Iqbal commended the feeling of human compassion in communism, Marx and Lenin, and accepted their struggle for destroying the idol of capitalism. What appealed most to Iqbal was the elixir that communism proved to be for the cancer of the concept of national organization on the basis of colour, language and race in the capitalist system, and that it created, in Europe, the new concept of ideological nationhood. Islam itself shapes its nationhood on the ideology of *Tauheed* (monotheism). This concordance in thought between the two produced a soft corner for communism in Iqbal's conscience. In other words Iqbal viewed with pleasure the successes of communism against capitalism as the ground preparation for Islamic renaissance. At the very outset of the communist experiment he predicted the arrival of the period when the meaning of the phrase[5] would be revealed, i.e. between the two extremes of the communistic and capitalistic systems, the human race will benefit from the concept of the humanism of Islam. That is why Iqbal says:

"O Muslim dive into the depths" of the Qur'an, so that God may reward thee with renovation of character (iii)

The late Justice S.A. Rahman writes in his English book "Iqbal and Socialism" (iv):

"It is now evident that Iqbal praised communism in a limited sense and for a limited purpose, while viewing it in a broader sense and for broader purposes he regarded it as deleterious and harmful to the human race, and pointed to the Holy Qur'an as the only cure for social ills. We should view Iqbal's sympathies with communism and his appreciation for Karl Marx and Lenin in the light of these facts. Whereas Iqbal has often praised the positive aspects of communism and has said:

'The author of *Das Kapital* is the descendant of Khalil[6]
That prophet not blessed with divine revelation brought by Jibrael

There is some truth concealed in his false line of thought

Understanding Iqbal's Philosophy

His heart seems to be a believer but infidel is his thought

The creed of that apostle devoid of the perceptions of the Truth
Is based on equality of materialistic life (not spiritual Truth)

When fraternal feelings are established in the human heart
Their roots are also established in the heart and not in water and earth". (v)

In "The Satan's Advisory Council" the third advisor of Satan says about Marx:

"That Moses without *Tajalli*[7] that Christ without cross
He is not a prophet, but keeps the Book for specious appearance

How can I explain what that pagain's eye will be
To the East and West nations on the Day of Judgement[8]

No worse human nature's mischief can there be
Than that the slaves have toppled the master's tent.[9] (vi)

Iqbal has written these and similar verses in praise of Karl Marx and Lenin. This is a tribute of approbation from him as well as a pointer to the fact that, in spite of attaining the climax of intellectual thought, establishing a rationalist system and writing a book aiming at curing human ills and misery, Marx is a Moses without divine guidance and is a Christ who was not crucified in a divine cause. While these verses exhibit extreme approbation for Marx on the one hand they also expose his deprivation from prophetic revelation and his lack of vision in spiritual values and ecstacy Marx has been called a materialistic prophet, i.e. one who was devoid of the exhilarating and life-giving revelations brought by Jibreel. Marx presumed materialistic equality to the panacea for human ailments. The Iqbal says that the roots of his (Marx's) imagination have not penetrated the depths of his heart but are only floating in the baser existence, and though his sympathy for mankind may give the impression of a believer's heart, his insight, being deprived of divine revelation, the system produced by him through the innovations of his intellect is not beneficial. Being deprived of the divine revelation it is no more than the gleanings of an infidel mind. Consequently, Iqbal has said that the problem would not be sloved by the proletarieat's control of government. On the contrary the bourgeoisie would parade in the cloak of the proletariate, because the real revolution is more a change of the intrinsic feelings of the heart than that of the material resources and conditions, and so

> "The transfer of political power to the proletariate will make no difference
> The ways of the proletariate are the same as those of the bourgeoisie
> It may be the majesty of kingship or the fun of democracy
> If religion is separated from politics the latter becomes mere tyranny". (vii)

In these verses Iqbal has rejected the concept of communism that the establishment of a proletarian society is the solution of all problems. Iqbal rejects the very basic hypothesis of Karl Marx's book *Das Kapital* in the following verses:

> "The world does not like tricks and guiles
> Of science and with not their contests
>
> This age does not like ancient thoughts,
> From core of hearts their show detests.
>
> O wise economist the books you write
> Are quite devoid of useful aim
>
> The have twisted lines with orders strange
> No warmth for labour though they claim.
>
> The idol houses of the West
> Their schools and churches wide:
>
> The ravage caused for greed of wealth
> Their wily wit attempts to hide". (viii)

So, to Iqbal communism is nothing but "wily wits" which attempt to hide the ravages caused by greed for wealth.

In "The Satan's Advisory Council",(ix) where Satan and his advisors have been made to praise communism and Karl Marx himself does not consider communism as a danger to his Satanic system (capitalism-colonialism). This means that the communism whose praises the Satan's advisors celebrate, in the Satan's opinion, has lasted its utility and importance. Actually, through Satan and his Advisors Iqbal, by comparing communism and Islam, wants to make it clear that the creed of, the human race of the future would be Islam and not communism, and that Islam and not communism would lead the world opinion. This will be so, because if capitalism is the extreme of individualism, communism is the other extreme of anti-individualsim, communism is the other extreme of anti-individividualism and supports collectivism. Justice and fairplay is always in the middle path between two extremes and that is Islam. Hence, Islam is a rising power of the future and it has to shoulder the responsibility of the leadership of mankind. In other words Iqbal pleads for Islam's acceptance after rejection of communism. So, Satan rejects communism as a danger to his Satanic system, and considers Islam and not communism is a challenge to his system as shown below:

"The collars to whom the Nature has torn
The logic of Mazdak[10] to them can't.

How can frighten me the socialist lads,
Since long jobless, confused and loafing fads

From that nation but I feel a threat grave,
Whose heart yet holds embers of crave.

A few of them I espy in this nation yet,
At dawn who make *wuzu*'[11] with tear drops yet.

He knows on whom hidden times are bright
That Islam not Mazdak is the future's fright. (x)

As far as the capitalist system is concerned it is evident from the Iqbal's political works that he was against capitalism and considered it contrary to Islam. He was pleased with communism because it had annihilated the tyranny of capitalism. However, in spite of all its goodness he considered communism harmful and destructive for mankind. He believed that Russia itself would eventually relinquish this system and would come close to the basic economic concepts of Islam. The fast retreat of China and Russia from communism and Marxism is a step towards the first stage of Iqbal's prediction. A conflagration of the buried sparks in Muslim Turkistan will not be surprising, and Russia, being faced with a new commotion may move towards a system which will be Islamic or very close to it.

Epilogue

Western colonization of Asian and African countries, which included the Muslim world was no exception to the usual process of slow but sure intellectual death of the colonized people. Iqbal was quick to realize this and focussed his entire genius on counteracting this influence. Western political, economic and social norms started capturing the imagination of the Muslim youth who were being exposed to the ideology of the West through Western education. Materialism and capitalism were the very foundations of this thought, Islamic thought and Qur'anic teachings were being slowly but surely effeced, partly by the efforts of the colonizers and partly by our own indifference. The deleterious effects of this change were being felt by the conquered Muslim nations, when communism appeared as an adversary of capitalism after World War II it had great appeal to Muslims. Iqbal brought home to the Muslim intelligentsia that both these systems were man-made and equally harmful and that Islam was the correct system. This has been amply shown in the foregoing. Iqbal went farther than codemning the above systems. He explained at great length the blessings of a system based on divine revelation as compared with man-made systems. His works are replete with this theme. However special attention is invited to the following passages in *Javid Namah*:

Firmament of Mercury: Glimpses of the souls of Jamaluddin Afghani and Saeed Haleem Pasha

Religion and Territorial Loyalties

Communism and Imperialism

Saeed Haleem Pasha:

East and West

Afghani

Basic Principles of the Quranic World

Understanding Iqbal's Philosophy

Vicegerency of Adam

Kingdom of God

The Earth is the Possession of God

Saeed Haleem Pasha.

The Message of Afghani to the Russian People

The Splendour of the Brotherhood of Hijaz depends upon the Haram (Kaba)

Its status is different, its system is different". (xi)

References

(i) Khurshid, Abdussalam, *Sarguzasht-i-Iqbal*, Iqbal Academy 1977, Lahore.

(ii) *Zamindar*, Lahore, June 24, 1923

(iii) Iqbal, Sir Muhammad (1936)' *Zarb-i-Kaleem*. Published by Munira Banu Begum at the Kapoor Arts Printing Works, Lahore. (Second Impression 1941, p. 138

(iv) Rahman, S.A. *Iqbal and Socialism*.

(v) Iqbal, Dr. Sir Muhammad (1932), *Javid Nama*. Published by Dr. Javid Iqbal Printed at Sheikh Ghulam Ali & Sons, Lahore, Seventh Impression (1970), p. 69

(vi) Iqbal, Dr. Sir Muhammad (1938) *Armaghan-i-Hijaz*. Published by Dr. Javid Iqbal. Printed at the Kapur Art Printing Works, Lahore First Edition (1941), p. 218

(vii) Iqbal, Dr. Sir Muhammad (1935), *Bal-i-Jibreel*. Published by Dr. Javid Iqbal at the Maktab-i-Jamia, Delhi, India (Second Edition 1941), p. 62

(viii) *Zarb-i-Kaleem,* op. cit.

(ix) Shah, Syed Akbar Ali (1938), *The Rod of Moses*. Versified English Translation of Iqbal's *Zarb-i-Kaleem*. Published by the Iqbal Academy Pakistan at the Himayat-i-Islam Press, Lahore, Pakistan, p. 87

(x) Kabir, Q.A. (1983), *Armaghan-i-Hijaz*. Versified English Translation of Iqbal's *Armaghan-i-Hijaz*. Published by the lqbal Academy Pakistan, Printed at the Himayat-i-Islam Press, Lahore, Pakistan, p. 133

(xii) Iqbal, Dr. Sir Muhammad (1924), *Bang-i-Dara*. Published by Sheikh Mubarak Ali, Lahore,
   Third Edition (1930), p. 119

Understanding Iqbal's Philosophy

Explanatory Notes

1. This paper was first published by Dr. Waheed Ishrat in the Urdu daily *Nawa-i-Waqt* of Lahore for April 21 1987 in response to a letter from Mr. Zia-ul-Haque Maiman of Sindh. In that letter Mr. Maiman had stated that some books were being published in the Sindhi language in which Iqbal, on the basis of his revolutionary poetry, was being shown as a communist as well as a cherisher of communism. As the Sindhi - knowing public did not have adequate direct access to Iqbal's thought and philosophy a clarification of his stand on communism was sought. This English translation is intended to convey Iqbal's views on communism to the English-knowing people in general and to English-knowing Muslims in particular, so that the misunderstanding created by the supporters of communism in the type of publications above referred may be removed.

(2) A system in Islamic economics in which a tax is levied on the property of a person in excess of prescribed limits. The proceeds of this tax are used exclusively for the financial support of the indigent.

(3) The divine system of Islamic jurisprudence.

(4) The Holy Qur'an iii.: 103 (part), which means "And He joined your hearts in love, so that by His Grace you become brethren". See The Holy Qur'an : Text, Translation and Commentary by Abdullah Yusuf Ali, New York, p. 149

(5) See The Holy Qur'an ii ; 219

The secret concealed in "Spend what is surplus and
May perhaps be revealed in this age".

(6) Hadhrat Ibrahim whose title is Khalilullah, the Friend of God.
This is an allusion to the fact that Karl Marx was a member of the Jewish community (Bani Israil)

(7) Appearance of God or His Powers as was witnessed by Musa on Mount Sinai.

(8) It will bring doom to those who believe in his economic system in contravention of the clear message of the Holy Qur'an by which all mankind will be judged on the Day of Judgement.

Iqbal and Communism

(9) This degree of freedom of the down-trodden people would be completely unacceptable to the Satanic system and its flage bearers.

(10) Mazdak was a Persian thinker of the sixth century and lived during the reign of the famous Persian king Anushervan (531-578). This most prominent feature of Mazdak's philosophy was communism, albeit rudimentary. He preached the equality of man and based his concept of equality on the equality of wealth. He said that the concept of individual property was the creation of demons hostile to God, with the purpose of turning God's Universe into a land of perpetual misery. For details see:

Iqbal, Muhammad (1908), *The Development of Metaphysics in Persia*. Published by Bazm-i-Iqbal, Lahore, Pakistan, Third reprint (1946): pp. 16-17.

(11) Ablution

Chapter 12

SOME RARE RESEMBLANCES BETWEEN FIRDAUSI AND IQBAL

The factors which I see shared by Firdausi and Iqbal are obviously three. First is the interest of both Firdausi and Iqbal in the basic and immutable attributes of the human personality. Both specifically stress development of personality, and, in their verse and philosophy, long to find and evolve such a magnificent character which would have the ability to influence the course of history. While Firdausi develops the character of some confirmed truthful or saintly person in his stories. Iqbal seeks the character, in the form of the confirmed truthful person or the Believing Man, who may bring to truth the dream of Islamic renaissance in the present age by motivating Muslims to action. In the words of Iqbal this is the person who has cognizance of his *Khudi*, and is singular, unique and distinguished in character and disposition. In Firdausi the search for such a person is in his unconscious or sub-conscious self and low-keyed. When, in his stories, he draws a word picture of such characters, their courage, high ideals, and uniqueness, entering his reader, find expression in his desires and longings. Such longing becomes a means of remodeling his character by a process of slow search for his ideals, and waking up his desire for adopting them in his character becomes instrumental in renovated character. In this way Firdausi imperceptibly continues creating immutable impressions on his reader's character.

By raising this individuality, uniqueness and singularity of the individual Iqbal has molded it into active effort, and has expressed in his verse the philosophy of *Khudi* in a very fine and philosophical style, in *Asrar-i-Khudi* (The Secrets of the Self), which he has himself organized in the structure of a Man in his own personality. In Firdausi the knowledge of acquiring these basic and immutable attributes of human personality was in the historical perspective. He views his favorite personality in the light of historical events and the deeds of the characters who lived in the past. In this way his entire cogitation of thought and presentation of personality moves from the past into the past. Still the suppressed longing is discernible that in addition to mere story-telling Firdausi may be desirous of molding some character in the future under the influence of these live and illustrious characters of history. This can be understood by visualizing

Some Rare Resemblances Between Firdausi and Iqbal

that while watching a drama, reading a historical novel or story, or listening to the details of some battle, sometimes. you start feeling that your are a character of that drama, story or battle rather than merely its reader. I vividly remember that, reading about the tragedy of Karbala whenever I read the details of the tents on the banks of the Euphrates, and visualized the showers of arrows and the skills of swordsmanship, I started feeling that I was also a character in combat with the powers of Yazid who had appeared as Hadhrat Hur among the companions of Hadhrat Husain. The details of the wars of crusades and the echoes of the old folk-tales certainly appear in us after repeatedly reading or listening to them. Hence, the object of Firdausi in writing the *Shahnamah* was certainly to preserve the history of his region. But history is preserved only so that the coming generations may be able to walk in the foot-steps of their ancestors, and see marks of their goals clearly. In Firdausi's art of history writing also we see a window towards the future in the journey towards the past. Still, in order to distinguish Firdausi more clearly from Iqbal we have to admit that in the search for the basic and immutable attributes of personality he had a deeper insight in history than that of Iqbal.

In contrast with this Iqbal's insight is the same basic and immutable attributes of personality was inclined to be futuristic. As in Firdausi there is a window open to the future in his art of history and traditionalism, in Iqbal also the secret of the past is spelled out in his recognition of the personality of the Holy Prophet as the climax of the basic and immutable attributes of personality, and obtains the qualification of these attributes only from his elegant personality. But with his futuristic insight, going beyond movement from the past into the past, and moving from the past into the future, he associates the expression of these basic and immutable attributes with the future. He desires that this, human self, human *Khudi* and human ego also may be persnalized in his own self -with respect to these basic and immutable attributes. He also desires that *Khudi* in its structure and organization may achieve perfection in its evolution of these attributes. To Iqbal the climax of human *Khudi* is the absorption of one's own attributes in one's self. Iqbal's insight with its slant on the future, wants to see the appearance of these attributes in the possibilities of the future, while to Firdausi the same attributes constitute a more prominent quality of the past with reference to history.

In any case the interest of both in the basic and immutable attributes of human personality is certainly a dynamic relationship. Both considered heroism as a nature of the characters carved by them. Firdausi sees this heroism in Rustum, Suhrab, Nausherwan, Ardshir, and other Iranian kings, while Iqbal finds all the aspects of human greatness in the personality of the Holy Prophet. As Iqbal has written in his *Lectures*:

> "The prophet's return is creative. He returns to insert himself into the sweep of time with a view to control the forces of history, and thereby to create a fresh world of ideals. For the mystic the repose of 'unitary experience' is something final; for the prophet it is the awakening, within him, of world-shaking psychological forces, calculated to completely transform the human world".(i)

Hence, the heroism of Iqbal considers the stage of affirmation of *Khudi* to be appropriate in the future, and instead of becoming a part of the history of the past is the architect of the history of the future. Thus, the expansion of heroism is in the past in Firdausi and in the present and the future in Iqbal.

While persons like Rustum and Suhrab represent the heroism of Firdausi the heroism of Iqbal constitutes the glad tidings of Pakistan in the form of Quaid-i-Azam Muhammad Ali Jinnah. We do not know the forms in which the heroism of Iqbal, which establishes *Khudi*, will appear in the future. In this way the canvas of Iqbal is vaster than that of Firdausi's view of history. However, the priorities of Firdausi constitute a part of the intellectual frame work of Iqbal. The manner of Firdausi's insight has also helped in the development of Iqbal's style, and has provided the intellectual material for unlocking the secrets of human *Khudi*. In *Bal-i-Jibril* (The Wings of Jibreel) Iqbal derives the meaning of preservation of *Khudi* from a verse of Firdausi alone, and including Firdausi's verse in his poem acknowledges his greatness. Iqbal says:

خودی کو نہ دے سیم و زر کے عوض

نہیں شعلہ دیتے شرر کے عوض

یہ کہتا ہے فردوسیٔ دیدہ ور

عجم جس کے سرمے سے روشن بصر

"ز بہر درم تند و بد خو مباش

تو باید کہ باشی درم گو مباش"

Some Rare Resemblances Between Firdausi and Iqbal

"*Khudi* in exchange for wealth surrender not
The flame with the spark is exchanged not

Says this Firdausi of discerning insight
With whose collyrium Ajam has got eyesight

Do not be rash and bad tempered for wealth
Be what you want to be, be not lover of wealth."(ii)

Iqbal considers Firdausi as one with discerning insight and, admitting his greatness, says that the Ajam's eye has attained insight with Firdausi's enlightening verse. In Iqbal's view Firdausi is a poet who could have been an extremely distinguished poet of any language, as Anvari had said that Firdausi was the Lord of literature and he was his ordinary servant. When Anvari who is unequaled in *qasidah* and a poet greater than whom has seldom been produced in Persian verse, accepts the superiority of Firdausi no one else can dare to gainsay that Allamah Ibn al-Aishar, about the end of his book *Mithl al-Sa'ir* (iii) comparing Firdausi with Arabian poets has said:

"The Arabic language, in spite of its vastness and rich vocabulary, cannot produce a book equal to *Shahnamah*, and really this book is the Qur'an of Ajam." (iv)

Scholars have called the *Mathnavi* of Maulana Rumi also the "Qur'an in the Persian language". Just as the literary grandeur, together with the miracle of thought and wisdom, elevates the intellectuality of the *Mathnavi*, in Firdausi also the description of events has been so miraculously achieved as to make the *Shahnamah* also an incomparable book. The Persian language has many eminent poets who are famous for their purity of language, diction, eloquence and rhetoric as well as grandeur and glory of style. In addition to Firdausi and Rumi it has poets like Anvari, Sa'adi, Hafiz, Urfi, Bedil, Hakim Sinai, Umar Khayyam, Jami, Nizami Ganjavi, Fariduddin Attar, Qa'ani, Ibn Yamin, Abu Talib Kalim, Fughani Shirazi, Faizi, Naziri, Talib Amuli, Ghalib and Mirza Sa'ib, which no other language of the world can boast of. It will be as free from exaggeration to assert that verse has reached its climax in the Persian language as it will be to say that the Arabs are unparallel in rhetoric. Regarding the beauty of diction perhaps the Persian language is ahead of all other languages of the world in sweetness. In the miracle of diction

Understanding Iqbal's Philosophy

Firdausi shines like the sun and the moon on the horizon of literature, and as some poet has rightly said:

در شعر سه تن پیمبر اند
هر چند که لا نبی بعدی
ابیات و قصیده و غزل را
فردوسی و انوری و سعدی

"In verse three men are prophetic
Though "there is no prophet after me"

In *bait, qasidah* and *ghazal*
Firdausi, Anvari and sa'di"

In the field of *bait*, Firdausi has elevated the Persian verse to its highest level of being the last word, Iqbal also acknowledges the high stature of Firdausi. Dr. Muhammad Riaz writes in his book *Iqbal awr Farsi Shu'ara* (Iqbal and Persian Poets) (v):

"Iqbal went to Afghanistan for a few days in October, November 1933, where he was the guest of the Government of Afghanistan and the memories of this trip are preserved in his whole *Mathnavi*, called *Musafir* (The Traveler) and some poems of *Bal-i-Jibreel* (The Wings of Jibril). During the pilgrimage to the mausoleum of Sultan Mahmud in Ghazni Iqbal reminded of the grandeur and glory of Mahmud in the ruins of Ghazni. In passing he was also reminded of the eulogists of his court, which included Firdausi. In his imaginary journey into the past, peeping into the window of history Iqbal says:

نکته سنج طوس را دیدم به بزم
لشکر محمود را دیدم به رزم

دولت محمود را زیبا عروس
از حنابندان و دانای طوس

Some Rare Resemblances Between Firdausi and Iqbal

"The sage of Tus in the assembly I saw
The army of Mahmud in the battle I saw

The bride suitable for the Mahmud's empire
Among its companions the sage of Tus I saw." (vi)

The sage of Tus means Firdausi.

Thus, in Iqbal's eyes Firdausi was a high - ranking sagacious intellectual of Tus. His literature bestowed fame on the Iranian civilization and his *Shahnamah* rewarded Ajam with eternal life. He, thus earned the title of the "Messenger of Verse". But the grandeur of Firdausi is not restricted to literary delicacy. He offers the philosophical explanation of the rise and fall of mankind in his verse in the form of history. Thus, through historical facts he points out the objective principles which lead one nation to grandeur and the other to perdition and disgrace. Though Firdausi has not enumerated these principles clearly we can ourselves extract them from his works by study of his verse. Actually, as you know, to Iqbal history in its capacity of being among the sources of human knowledge is one of the signs of God. The Holy Qur'an calls history as the signs of God. History is not a mere gramophone record of events but in Iqbal's view is an organic entity and a living reality and according to the Holy Qur'an is the fountainhead of knowledge. Iqbal has recognized the worlds of nature and history in addition to that of religious experience. This is so because the world of history is based on intellect and experience. In the background of these events in the course of human experience, with reference to other human beings, bestows the perception of the movements existing behind the curtain of their deeds. And Man, using the continuous flow of these experiences and with the help of induction, gerneralizing from the parts to the whole, frames rules for the continuation and connection in the current of human character. In this way we discover a new world of knowledge from the world of history. Though human history reflects the collective behavior of people it also informs us of the perceptible and imperceptible psychological forms and behaviors of the characters which arise from the stage of history. Thus, through history we learn about Man's journey from individual to society and from individualism to social orders. History informs us of the structure and the principles of the annihilation of civilizations and cultures. The insight which the Holy Qur'an has attempted to bestow on us from the events of the 'Ad, the Thamud, Bani Israel and other similar nations is connected with the same battle ground of rise and fall. Its basic teaching is that nations and *Ummah* are judged both from the individual as well as the collective points of view. History attests that nations are punished for their evil deeds in this world while the special day of judgment is fixed for the individual.

Through history the individual informs us of the variations of his experiences during his moving from individualism to collectivism. Man is the object of history. Thus, the knowledge which the objective of history wants to impart to us is experimental and scientific on account of being based on conscious comprehension, and being the bearer of universal and global results in its teachings. From its individual examples through generalization and extraction of global principles history makes it a science established on inductive principles. Its knowledge is adjudged reliable like other human experiences or other hypotheses. The Holy Qur'an has established the basic principle of historical criticism that, as a class of knowledge, history is based on our being sure of the correctness of the events of which its material is constituted. In this way in our subjective psychological states collectivity is created from objectivity and individuality with reference to events, and *Khudi*, losing its secrets, tends to move towards *Bekhudi*.

Firdausi also has protected history from the encroachment of time. From the inductive generalization of the conscious comprehension we derive from the history of the Iranian monarchs, their rise and fall, their likes and dislikes, their wars and initiatives of peace, can help us in framing objective principles for the rise and fall of nations. We can identify the collective psychology and objective behaviors of the Iranian people from the subjective behavior of people, and their individual conditions and events included in the magnificent story of the *Shahnamah*. Thus, this *Shahnamah*, spread over sixty thousand verses, together with its beauty and delicacy of expression, is a vast source for conscious comprehension of individual as well as collective human behavior. The historical narration of Firdausi converts history itself into a living organism or living reality, and the current and continuity of expression, and the interlinking of events gives to a unit in the whole process. Thus, in the language of Firdausi the history of the Iranian people is molded into a living and lasting action, where people are felt to be breathing, talking, busy in archery and swordsmanship like living people. The uniqueness of Firdausi's expression has molded the climaxes of communication into the final argument. Through this history itself becomes a part of knowledge and experience in our sub-conscience. The philosophy of history communicated to us by Iqbal clearly appears in the expression of Firdausi.

Some Rare Resemblances Between Firdausi and Iqbal

Firdausi has completely carried through Iqbal's second principle of history. According to Mawlana Shibli Nu'mani he has made use of all historical material, and has closely examined all the historical details, assembled together the historical continuity of the details of events, and verified the correctness of events so that historians may not be able to challenge the their rationality of these events. Excepting the description of some super-human, but not super-natural events the truth of historical facts has been never compromised. On the other hand the later histories also confirmed the rationality of Firdausi's knowledge of history. Thus, the common thought of history being the source of knowledge and the truth of historical facts is also common between Firdausi and Iqbal, and an intellectual similarity exists between both in the philosophy of history.

Even in the matter of subjective psychological foundation of immutability and basic attributes of human "self" or *Khudi* there is concordance between Firdausi and Iqbal from the similarity of their views to the experience of conscious comprehension of history. The *Bekhudi* towards which the *Khudi* of Iqbal moves, is also present in Firdausi from the collective behavior of different characters. But this collectivity is restricted in the scenario of the past in Firdausi, while Iqbal's futuristic view turns it towards the future, and wants to see it molded in the form of the human personality's social and cultural possibilities in the shape of a new collectivity, new society, and a new State. This revolution in Iqbal's philosophy of history was derived from his concept of prophethood, which he expressed in the form of the difference in the manner of the spiritual experience of a Sufi and a prophet. Mawlana Abd al-Quddus of Gangoh had said, "Muhammad of Arabia ascended the highest Heaven and returned. I swear by God that if I had reached that point, I should never have returned". Iqbal says that the *Sufi* does not like to come out of the pleasure which he acquires from the Unity with God in the climax of his spiritual experience, because for the *Sufi* the pleasure of Unity itself is the climax, but the prophet's return is creative. The latter comes back from this event to return to the current of time and then create a new world with the conquest and prestige of the powers which shape the world of history. Therefore, the prophet's spiritual vision is revolutionary in the sense that he re-organizes the society and the State with the purpose of new goals and objectives. Thus, this individual experience appears in a new collective form, and becomes the harbinger of glad tidings of a new social revolution for mankind. To Iqbal the Holy Qur'an, which is the treasure house of human awareness of individual as well as collective behavior with reference to the study of the physical universe, on the basis of all of its three attributes is the fountainhead of the knowledge which endows us with such knowledge and insight in every place and time through the generalizations of induction as can guide us to the shaping of our individual and collective behaviors. (vii) Here, Iqbal distinguishes himself in an entirely different direction from Firdausi and, really speaking, here Iqbal's perception attains closeness to the perception and wisdom of *Deen* of the *Mathnavi Ma'navi* of Mawlavi, and in the shaping of the different individual and collective behaviors the Indian disciple establishes relationship with the preceptor of Rum after a lapse of centuries, which we do not see anywhere in Urdu or Persian poetry after Rumi. The growth of Rumi's thought starts shining in Iqbal's thought and the comprehension of the wisdom of the Holy Qur'an which Rumi has shown in his *Mathnavi* is expressed in the verse and philosophy of Iqbal. The Egyptian scholar, Dr. Abd al-Wahhab 'Azzam has said, "If Jalaluddin Rumi is resurrected today he will be none other than Iqbal. The Jalal of the thirteenth century and the Iqbal of the twentieth century should be considered one and the same".(viii)

In my view Iqbal is the perfection of the thought of Rumi, and the extension of the traditions of Rumi's wisdom. He is the re-appearance of Rumi in the present age. (ix) The preceptor's comprehension of the *Deen* appeared in such a manner in the disciple as to bring out the wisdom of the Holy Qur'an in his complete philosophical system. Iqbal, following in the footsteps of Hadhrat Mujaddid, discovered new facets in the relationship of Man and God from the wisdom of Islam, and presented the concept of human self or *Khudi*, and in *Rumuz-i-Bekhudi* elevated it to such social level as provides a revolutionary basis for the Islamic State, which eliminates the distinction of the master and the slave, which makes all the citizens of the State embodiments of justice and virtue, where people are busy in the task of immortality and progress of their State, and the State provides opportunities for the structuring of their gifted potentialities, instead of making him its victim. To Iqbal the individual and the State are not inimical to each other but provide the material for each other's structuring and progress. Actually, European philosophers, like Camus, Fichte and Sartre are bent on proving the individual and the State to be each other's enemies. The very foundations of Sartre's "realism" are based on the other man's life being hell. (x) The origins of the concept of oppression of mankind instead of that of fraternity of mankind can be traced back to the same philosophers, and all the bloodshed rampant in the world at this time has resulted from the same Western civilization. This state of affairs is based on the Christian concept that Man is a sinner since eternity. As opposed to this Islam says that Man is innocent in nature, and

Some Rare Resemblances Between Firdausi and Iqbal

is born on the nature of God. It is his parents, society or environment which push him into the mire of sin. Here I want to say parenthetically that the Europe's propaganda is afoot that the bloodshed in the world in the name of religion has reached far greater dimensions than that due to any other cause. Contradicting this I would assert that the bloodshed perpetrated by Europe's racial glorification, greed for wealth, and secular nationalism over centuries and recently in World War II was so great that the bloodshed in the name of religion is not even a hundredth part of it. The smoke of Europe's racism is still rising from Nagasaki and Hiroshima. In the name of trade, and because of imperialism, and their racial glorification European nations have perpetrated tumult and oppression all over the world. The smell of human blood is still coming from Cyprus, Kashmir, Palestine, and the Persian Gulf. Who has planted time bombs at the strategically sensitive cites in the Islamic world? Why do not these wolves of the West who raise slogans of democracy, freedom, human rights and human fraternity arrange to obtain the right of self-determination by referendum? The reality is that in the words of Iqbal, talking about the League of Nations:

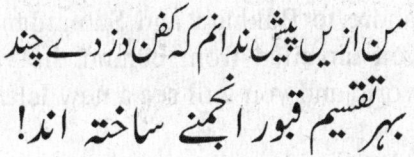

"I do not know more than this that some shroud-thieves
For dividing graves among themselves have established an assembly." (xi)

These Europeans, Hindus and Jews unite together to destroy every dream of Muslims for renaissance. However, the irony is that though the long and deep-sleeping Chinese have awaken the unfortunate Muslims are scattered about like the sheep of Hadhrat 'Isa and the leadership for drawing them into line is still non-existent in the Islamic world. However, Iqbal is not disappointed with his currently desolate world, as a little rain will certainly convert this fertile soil into fields of tulips and roses.

As I have stated above the insight of Firdausi was historical and that of Iqbal futuristic. Firdausi attempted at establishing the correctness and reliability of the past and Iqbal was aiming at the future. Firdausi was commissioned to bring out the national and Islamic traditions of Iran and Iqbal has been designated to bring out our national traditions in the present times and in the future. Thus, the continuation of the grandeur of our

Understanding Iqbal's Philosophy

.traditions lies between Firdausi and Iqbal. Firdausi's tradition has illustrious heroes like Rustum and Suhrab and Iqbal's tradition gave birth to glorious heroes like Quaid-i-Azam in the Indian sub-continent. However, the universe of the possibilities of Iqbal is much vaster than that of Firdausi, as the sky will produce many revolutions, and possibilities will appear in many forms. The system of life identified by Iqbal for the present age on the basis of the wisdom of Islam is still behind a curtain. Its dawn has not yet appeared:

عالمِ نو ہے ابھی پردہء تقدیر میں
میری نگاہوں میں ہے اس کی سحر بے حجاب

"The new world still behind destiny's curtain is
Its dawn standing unveiled before my eyes is." (xii)

In viewing the following verses of Iqbal if you draw a line on the world map from the bank of the Nile to the land of Kashghar and draw another line from Lahore to Bukhara and Samarqand Iqbal's new world will appear before you unveiled from behind the veil of destiny in the form of the Islamic world and you will see a new Islamic federation on the world map:

اک ولولہ تازہ دیا میں نے دلوں کو
لاہور سے تا خاکِ بخارا و سمرقند!

"I have conferred anew enthusiasm on hearts
From Lahore to lands of Bukhara and Samarqand."

ایک ہوں مسلماں حرم کی پاسبانی کے لئے
نیل کے ساحل سے لے کر تا بخاکِ کاشغر

"Muslims should unite for defense of the Haram
From banks of the Nile to the land of Kashghar."

طہرانِ ہو اگر عالمِ مشرق کا جنیوا
شاید کرہءِ ارض کی تقدیر بدل جائے

Some Rare Resemblances Between Firdausi and Iqbal

"If Tehran becomes Geneva of the Eastern world
It may change the destiny of the whole world." (xiii)

The current of restlessness created by the Islamic revolution in Afghanistan is casting its influence on Kashmir also. Iqbal had said this also that when Islamic movements would be mounted in Central Asia revolution would flex its muscle in Kashmir also. The prophecies of Iqbal are bound to come true that Kashmir would become independent and Tehran would become the Geneva of the Eastern world, and it may become the center of the entire united Islamic world. The storm of self-cognizance is appearing in the entire Islamic world. The bold and forceful current of Islam's materialization will rise from this very world, and the abodes of the Western and Communist crocodiles would be destroyed by it:

From the same ocean rises that bold and forceful current destroys and annihilates the abodes of the crocodiles Iqbal had charged us with the commission of acquiring clean conscienced enlightenment and to protect ourselves from the age old maladies of imperialism, and subjugation to *Mullas* and *Pirs*, to form cultural, civilizational, social, and democratic institutions in the Islamic world in the light of the spirit of Islam, and in their respective countries shape these institutions so that they reflect the clear spirit of Islam in addition to modernism. In the present circumstances Iqbal fixed this destiny for Muslims:

"For the present every Muslim nation must sink into her own deeper self, temporarily focus her vision on herself alone, until all are strong and powerful to form a living family of republics."

When the land spread over the tract from the Nile to the land of Kashghar and from the Nile to Lahore and from Lahore to Samarqand and Bukhara,, acquiring the form of a brotherhood of Islamic democracies, will rise as a new power it will convert the world into the cradle of civilization and peace, and the Islamic world, arriving at its goal of renaissance will organize a new history for the progress and welfare of mankind. This dream of Iqbal is restlessly, though slowly, advancing for its realization, and the whole Islamic world should adjudge this as its goal and destiny. Iqbal had made *Ijtihad* and reconstruction of religious thought in Islam compulsory for the establishment of this very brotherhood or federation of Islamic democracies, so that Islam, as a system of life may fulfill the role of the leadership of mankind after the demise of materialistic capitalism and communism, which his far reaching insight had visualized and expressed in 1933 in his poem "Masjid-i-Qartabah" (The Mosque of Cordova). In this way Islam will again perform its divinely endowed task of bearing fruit for the human civilization.

I admit that this paper has become slightly long. In addition to the immutable basic attributes for the shaping of human character, and after the similarity between Firdausi and Iqbal on history, another similarity existing between them is the structure of philosophical terminology in the world of verse. Though this subject requires a complete separate dissertation I shall briefly state, that Persian had no concept of philosophical terminology. This is so because the Persian language was first under subjugation of *Qasidah* Persian poetry was a lifeless body till the component of *Tasawwuf* entered it. Actually, poetry is the name for the expression of feelings. Feelings did not exist at all before the advent of *Tasawwuf*. *Qasidah* was the name of eulogism and flattery. *Mathnavi* was narration of events, and *Ghazal* was restricted to the description of the beloved's physical beauty. Sufic thoughts were first expressed in Persian verse by Hazrat Sultan Abu Sa'eed Ab al-Khair, who was a contemporary of Bu Ali Sina. Philosophy also entered into Persian poetry together with *Tasawwuf*. In the words of Mawlana Shibli Nu'mani philosophy entered poetry through *Tasawwuf*. Necessity and pre-determinism, absolute existence *Wahdat-al-Wujud*, extinction and survival started in Persian under the influence of *Tasawwuf*. Those un-acquainted with insight were ignorant of miracles and other fields of knowledge connected with insight. They sought support from philosophy, and this led to the preponderance of philosophy in the Persian language, especially poetry. At the same time Bu Ali Sina also tried to work on philosophy. However, he was compelled to use Arabic terminology in Persian philosophy, but the command of Firdausi over language was so great that in his sixty thousand verses there was not even a trace of Arabic words. In the beginning of his *Shahnamah* Firdausi has used philosophical terminology with reference to the genesis of the creation and the existence of components so beautifully as could be a source of pride or the Persian language. Terms like 'sarmayah', 'maddah' 'gauhar-i-tawanai' 'ba wujud', 'unsur', 'aaraam', 'sukun', 'fana', 'taghayyur', 'harakat', 'tark-i-bil-iradah' and numerous other terms of philosophy were coined. Firdausi not only coined these philosophical terms but with reference to these terms he also included philosophical subjects in the *Shahnamah*. In the present age Iqbal found the scope of Urdu restricted for explanation of his intellectual and ideological subjects and communication of his message. The secret of choosing Persian for expression of his thoughts was the presence of these terms in Persian in

Some Rare Resemblances Between Firdausi and Iqbal

their full meaning, which was his object. In addition to other eminent Persian poets Firdausi also provided Iqbal with a vast treasure of philosophical terminology for the dissemination of his thoughts in Persian. It is the achievement of only Firdausi and other similar poets that they produced a great thinker and revolutionist like Iqbal. The scope of Persian also would have been restricted for the dissemination of his thoughts like that of Urdu if masters of philosophical language like Firdausi and other similar thinkers had not existed.

The three intellectual resemblances described above between Iqbal and Firdausi are: (i) description of the immutable and basic attributes of Man and heroism; (ii) importance of history in the thought and expression of both; and (iii) the philosophical tone and coining of philosophical terminology in verse by both, which created depth and elegance in their theses, expression and style. History dominated the insight of Firdausi, while Iqbal's futuristic insight was the architect of the future with which he sought the appearance of his hero in the future, presented Islam in the form of a system of life and saw the dream of the renaissance of Islam. This was the distinguished personality of Iqbal on the basis of which His Eminence Ali Khaminai called him the "Shining Star of the East", Ali Shariati considered him as parallel to Hadhrat Ali, and on account of Iqbal's publicizing the interpretation of the Holy Prophet's Constitution Malik al-Shuara_Bahar attributed the-present age to Iqbal:

قرنِ حاضر خاصئہ اقبال گشت

"The present age became the characteristic of Iqbal." (xiv)

References

(i) Iqbal, Muhammad (1930), *The Reconstruction of Religious Thought in Islam*. Published by Javid Iqbal at Shaikh Muhammad Ashraf, Lahore, Pakistan. Reprinted 1982, vi + 205 pp.

(ii) Iqbal, Muhammad (1935), *Bal-i-Jibril*. Published by Javid Iqbal, at the Maktabah-i-Jamiah, Delhi, India, Second Edition (1941), 224 pp.

(iii) Ibn al-Aishar - *Mathl al-Sa'ir* In. Allamah Shibli Nu'mani's Shair al-Ajam. Published by Dar-al-Musannifin, Azamgarh, India (1940), Vol. 1,

(iv) Shibli Nu'mani - Shair al-Ajam. Published by Daral Musannifin, Azamgarh, India

(v) Riaz, Muhammad (1977), *Iqbal our Farsi Shu'ara* (In Urdu). Published by the Iqbal Academy, Lahore, Pakistan at the Ibrahimsons Printers, Lahore, Pakistan.

(vi) Iqbal, Muhammad (1936), *Mathnavi Musafir* (In Persian). Published by Munira.Banu Begam at The Taj Company, Rawalpindi. Pakistan (1972), 44 pp.

(vii) Iqbal, Javid, *Shazrat-i-Fikr-i-Iqbal*". Translation by Iftikhar Ahmad Siddiqui, Lahore.

(viii) Akhtar, Saleem (1978), *Iqbal Mamduh-i-Alam*. Published by Majlis-i-Taraqqi-i-Adab, Lahore, Pakistan.

(ix) Ishrat, Waheed (1988), "*Falsafah-i-Iqbal kay Ma'akhaz O Masadir*. (in Iqbaliyat (Urdu), Iqbal Academy, Vol.---- No. ---, January 1988)

(x) Ishrat, Waheed, Sean Paul Sartre In: *Wujudiat*. Compiled by Javid Iqbal Nadim.

(xi) Iqbal, Muhammad (1923), *Payam-i-Mashriq* (In Persian). Published by Javid Iqbal at the Pakistan Times Press, Lahore, Pakistan. Thirteenth. Reprint (1971) xiv + 264 pp.

Some Rare Resemblances Between Firdausi and Iqbal

(xii) Iqbal, Muhammad (1936), *Zarb-i-Kaleem* (In Urdu). Published by Munira Banu Begam at the Maktabah-i-Jamiah, Delhi, India, Second Edition (1941). 182 pp.

(xiii) Iqbal, Muhammad (1924), *Bang-i-Dara* (In Urdu and Persian). Published by Shaikh Mubarak Ali at the Matbah-i-Karimi, Lahore (then), India. Second Edition (1930) xvi + 336 pp.

(xiv) Irfani, Khwajah (1957), *Iqbal Iranion kee Nazar main*. Malik al-Shuara Bahar's Eulogy at the time of Iqbal's death. Published by the Iqbal Academy, Lahore, Pakistan.

Understanding Iqbal's Philosophy

Explanatory Notes

1. Ajam - The non-Arab world, especially Iran.

2. Bait – Distich, verse.

3. Bekhudi - See *Khudi*. Merging of the individual's *Khudi* with the *Khudi* of the Muslim *Ummah*.

4. Deen - Literally, it means "path" and in English "religion" is very close to it. However, the correct meaning of *Deen* in Islam is "The path or the way of life in accordance with the Law of God", and is used in that sense by the Holy Qur'an, e.g. in 12:76. Iqbal has also used it in the same meaning.

5. Ghazal - A poem in which the last words of the two hemistichs of the first verse rhyme and in all the subsequent verses the last verse of the second hemistich rhymes with the last word of the second hemistich of the first verse. There are usually thirteen verses or less and the last verse has the pen name of the poet. It may contain one or several subjects.

6. Ijtihad - The effort of a jurist to determine the right course of action in new situations in the light of the sources of the Islamic Law.

7. Khudi - The realization by Man of his highest status in the creation of God in his capacity as God's vicegerent.

8. Mathnavi - A poem in rhyming distichs, common in Persian, Turkish and Urdu. It is usually long and is used to describe a story or discuss a subject.

9. Mullah - A religious scholar in Islam. It is also used in the derogatory sense for the half-baked religious scholars who harm religion very much.

10. Pir - A preceptor. In *Tasawwuf* the term is used for the person who trains his followers (*Murids*) in the rites of the order to which they belong.

11. Qasidah - A poem in praise of some one, usually a high ranking person. Eulogy. Laudatory poem.

Some Rare Resemblances Between Firdausi and Iqbal

12. Sufi, Sufism. Tasawwuf - *Sufism* or *Tasawwuf* is Islamic mysticism. It is a system of mainly heterodox mystical groups within Islam. It advocates meditation and contentment as a means of attaining rapturous comprehension of the spiritual world and the Essence of God. It is divided into several orders, which differ slightly in the details of their practices. In some orders some form music and dancing is used to attain ecstasy. Earlier Sufism was not accepted by orthodox schools of Islam. However, the work of reformers, like Imam al-Ghazali purified it of its admixture with the Greek and pre-Islamic Persian thought after which it became acceptable to all Muslims. Since then the system has been progressively purified and improved by several sufis. Sufism has played a very important role in the spread of Islam. A sufi is a person who practices sufism.

13. Ummah - The followers of a prophet. A nation established on some ideology instead of the usual geographic regions. An ideological nation.

14. Wahdat-al-Wujud - The ideology that all creation is the Essence of the Creator (God) in different forms. A branch of the system says that the real existence is only one, i.e. God and the creation is only a figment of human imagination.

Understanding Iqbal's Philosophy

Biographical Notes

1. Hakim Auhad al-Din Muhammad Anvari (d. 1191) - He was an eminent Persian poet and had special expertise in *Qasidah*. In spite of this he has written profusely against arrogance of kings and the opulent and against flattery. Iqbal has acknowledged Anvari's greatness in his works and has used Anvari's verses or hemistichs in his poems.

2. Alfred Camus (1913-60) - He was a French writer born in Algeria. His favorite field was 'Man's lonely and absurd condition in an irrational universe'. He won the Nobel Prize (1957) for his philosophical work *The Rebel* (1951).

3. Ab al-Qasim Tusi Firdausi (d. ca. 1027) - He was a famous poet of Iran. He wrote only one book, called *Shahnamah which* has made him immortal in Persian literature. This book is a combination of historical facts and folklore and is an epic of Iran.

4. Hur - He was a contemporary of Hadhrat Imam Husain. In the famous battle of Karbala he came with the army of Yazid, but the injustice and oppression of the whole episode dawned on him later, resulting from the horrible conditions prevailing in the battlefield. Consequently he deserted Yazid's army with thirty followers and was martyred fighting on the side of Hadhrat Imam Husain.

5. Hadhrat Imam Husain (ca. 626-80) - He was the grandson of the Holy Prophet. He stands out as the shining star of the galaxy of personages who sacrificed everything, including life, in the defense of Islamic values. Iqbal had very high respect for him which is spread throughout his works.

6. Quaid-i-Azam Muhammad Ali Jinnah (1876-1948) - He is the greatest Muslim leader of the present age. He fought against Hindus and the British at the time of the independence of the Indian sub-continent for safeguarding the Muslims' right of self-determination. He organized the scattered Muslims of the Indian sub-continent in the short period of about ten years (1937-47) and infused in them, the strength to face the combined power of the British and Hindus, which resulted in the establishment of Pakistan. He worked in close cooperation with Iqbal and, as the founder of Pakistan, was the one who brought Iqbal's ideology of Pakistan to real life.

Some Rare Resemblances Between Firdausi and Iqbal

7. Sultan Mahmud Ghaznavi (969-1030) - He is a famous Turkish king and enthusiast of Islam. His efforts at the eradication of idolatry from the Indian sub-continent, especially at the temple of Somnath are famous. Iqbal has shown him great respect in his works.

8. Abd Ali Husain Ibn Abd Allah Husain Ibn Ali Ibn Sina (980-1037) - He is perhaps the most eminent Muslim philosopher, thinker and scientist. Iqbal has paid high tribute to him for his knowledge but has preferred Rumi over him in the field of search for the Truth. He is very much respected by intellectuals of the West also.

9. Yazid - He was the son of Hadhrat Amir Muawiyya and succeeded him as *Khalifah*. He made himself infamous by the horrible battle of Karbala against Hadhrat Imam Husain, who is well known in Islamic history.

Chapter 13

STUDY OF IQBALICS IN PAKISTAN

Introduction

The eminent British critic, Sir Herbert Reid, had said about the Sage of the *Ummah*, Iqbal in 1921:

"At present when our local poets, sitting in the company of their informal friends, following in the foot-steps of Keats, are testing their talent on mundane objects like dogs, cats and other similar subjects, a poem has been written in Lahore which, we have been told, has created a revolutionary storm in the thinking of the Muslim youth".

Though innumerable eminent Eastern and Western intellectuals have sought to benefit from the grandeur of Iqbal's thought and art this extract from Herbert Reid has the distinction of clarifying the basic goal of Iqbal's thought and works in the course of presenting a beautiful summary of the nineteenth century literature of the East and the West. The greatest achievement of Iqbal, in making elegant imagination and thought the subject of his works, was to create a storm in the thinking of the Muslim youth, so as to enable them to struggle for retrieval of their past glory, and to make them change their present condition so as to strive for a bright future. When Iqbal made "I am pulling the unbridled she-camel towards the line" the object of his incessant labors his desire was to stir the Muslim *Ummah* again to make it vibrant and active by showing it a glimpse of its past, so that it may attain its objective of retrieval of its past glory. Consequently, he used his works and philosophy as the "trumpet of Israfil" and created the ardent longing and desire universally in the Muslim world for independence, freedom, and re-shaping of their cultural and social life. Hence, the establishment of Pakistan, the starting of renaissance movements in different Islamic countries, war against imperialism, efforts at unity and *Ijtihad*, and adoption of Islam as a system of life are the fruits of the same thought of Iqbal. That is how the thoughts and ideologies of Iqbal disseminated among the people and drew the attention of the intellectuals towards him. These intellectuals themselves performed valuable service for analysis and explanation as well as dissemination of Iqbal's thought. Thus, much work has been done on the different aspects of Iqbal during his own life as well as after his death. The purpose of this paper is a brief survey and review of this work.

The efforts in this direction have been grouped into four categories which are briefly described below:

1. Biographical Works

More than fifty books have been written in different languages on the life and events of Iqbal, of which those in Urdu are about thirty. Some well-known books are listed below:

i. *Zinda Rud* (The Flowing Stream) (3 volumes) by Justice (r) Javid Iqbal. This book is authored by Iqbal's own son and is the most authentic publication on the biography of Iqbal. Its Persian translation prepared by the eminent Iranian translator Dr. Shahin Dukht Muqaddam Safyari has been published in four volumes by the Iqbal Academy Pakistan. Dr. Zahoor Ahmad Azhar has translated it into Arabic, a Russian translation is under preparation from the Persian one, and Begam Nasira Javid Iqbal is translating it into English. Still no translation except that in Persian has yet been published.

ii. *Zikr-i-Iqbal* (The Story of Iqbal) has been written by Mawlana Abd ul-Majeed Salik.

iii. Mawlana's son, Abd us-Salam Khurshid wrote the biography of Iqbal, entitled *Sarguzasht-i-Iqbal* (The Biography of Iqbal) in 1977.

iv. *Fikr-i-Iqbal* (The Thought of Iqbal) by Dr. Khalifah Abd-ul-Hakim is a reliable book on the life and thought of Iqbal.

v. *Dana-i-Raz* (The Knower of Secrets) Syed Nazir Niazi.

vi. *Seerat-i-Iqbal* (The Biography of Iqbal) by Dr. Tahir Faruqui.

vii. *Iqbal-i-Kamil* (The Perfect Iqbal) by Abd us-Salam Nadvi.

viii. *Nuqoosh-i-Iqbal* (The Portrait of Iqbal) by Mawlana Abul-Hasan Nadvi

ix. *Rava-i-Iqbal* (The Dreams of Iqbal) which is the Arabic translation of No. viii.

x. *Ruh-i-Iqbal* (The Spirit of Iqbal) by Dr. Yusuf Hussain Khan

xi. *Iqbal* by Maulavi Ahmad Deen. This is the first book on Iqbal's biography which has been revised recently by Mushfiq Khwajah.

xii. *A Voice from the East* by Nawwab Zulfiqar Ali Khan is also one of the first books.

xiii. Recently the first volume of Professor Dr. Iftikhar Ahmad Siddiqui's book *Uruj-i-Iqbal* (The Rise of Iqbal) has appeared which has been published by the Bazm-i-Iqbal, Lahore. After *Zinda Rud* this is the most important book on Iqbal's biography. The biographical books are not restricted to Iqbal's life story but also contain his thoughts and ideologies.

xiv-xix. *Iqbal Duroon-i-Khanah* (Iqbal within the Family), *Iqbal kee Pahlee Bivi* (Iqbal's First Wife), *Iqbal awr Bhopal* (Iqbal and Bhopal), *Iqbal awr Hyderabad* (Iqbal and Hyderabad), *Iqbal kee Ibtedai Zindagi* (Iqbal's Early Life), and *Iqbal as I Knew Him* by Doris Ahmad should also be counted as biographical works.

xx. *Iqbal awr Bhopal* - (Iqbal and Bhopal) - Several books by Master Akhtar, in India, have been published under this name

xxi. *Iqbal awr Anjuman-i-Himayat-i-Islam* (Iqbal and Anjuman-i-Himayat-i-Islam) by Haneef Shahid

xxii. *Iqbal Aiwan-i-Assembly Main* (Iqbal in the Assembly House) by Professor Haq Nawaz

xxiii. *Siyahat-i-Iqbal* (The Travels of Iqbal) by Hamzah Faruqi

xxiv. *Hayat-i-Iqbal kay Chand Makhfi Goshay* (Some Hidden Aspects of Iqbal's Life)

Study of Iqbalics in Pakistan

Nos. xx-xxiv illustrate his life stories.

In addition, several books give Iqbal's biography in parts. If all of them are counted they would add up to more or less eighty biographical books. Several other books have been compiled among which *Iqbal: the Poet Philosopher of Pakistan* by Hafeez Malik is well-known. Books like *Iqbal ba-haisiyat Siyasatdan* (Iqbal as a Statesman) and *Safarnamah-i-Iqbal* (Travelogue of Iqbal) also throw light on his life.

2. Translations of Iqbal's Works

The other important work on Iqbal is that of translations. These translations are not restricted to the regional and national languages of Pakistan but are also available in foreign languages. The Pakistani languages into which these translations have been made include Punjabi, Sindhi, Baluchi, Barohi, Pushtu, Kashmiri, Balti, Saraiki, and Gujrati. Translations of Iqbal's works and *Lectures* were made into the Bengali language also when East Pakistan was a part of Pakistan. The books of Iqbal have also been translated at the international level. These languages include English, Urdu, Arabic, Persian, French, Spanish, Swahili, Russian, German, Finnish, Italian, Turkish, Indonesian, and Chinese. Translation of his works into Japanese also is in progress. This translation work is expanding continuously. The majority of the translators into English and regional languages is Pakistani, while foreigners are translating into other languages. Along with these translations the Iqbal Academy Pakistan has finalized a plan for simplifying the Persian works of Iqbal. The project of *Payam-i-Mashriq* (The Message of the East) is in press. Together with translations work on commentaries of Iqbal's Persian and Urdu works also has been done. Mawlana Ghulam Rasool Mehr and Professor Yusuf Saleem Chishti have written commentaries on Iqbal's works, while Arif Batalavi has written the commentary of the Urdu book *Bang-i-Dara*. Mawlana Ghulam Rasul Mehr's commentaries are condensed and meant for general students, while those of Professor Yusuf Saleem Chishti are intellectual, deep and detailed. In the field of simplification Naseem Amrohavi has done valuable work in *Farhang-i-Iqbal* in two volumes, which has been published by Izhar ul-Hasan Rizvi of Lahore. The meanings of some terms in this book are controversial and are the products of Naseem Amrohavi's own far-reaching intellect. Still, ignoring these few instances, on the whole, this work is very useful and a great help in comprehension of Iqbal's works. This book covers two large volumes and includes the complete glossary of the Urdu and Persian works of Iqbal.

Understanding Iqbal's Philosophy

This can be considered useful for both the teachers and students and is very helpful in comprehension of Iqbal. The *Matalib-i-Iqbal* by Maqbool Anvar Daudi is also a glossary of this type which is certainly helpful for general students. Among the indexes of Iqbal's works *Kashf-i-Abyat* (Explanation of Verses) by Dr. Muhammad Riaz and Dr. Siddique Shibli; *Joo-i-Sheer* (The Canal of Milk) by Daud Askari and *Kaleed-i-Iqbal Urdu* (The Key to Iqbal's Urdu Works) are useful, while the *Kaleed-i-Iqbal Farisi* (The Key to Iqbal's Persian Works) is under publication. Together with simplification of Iqbal's poetic works similar work on his *Lectures* has also been done. Syed Nazir Niazi prepared the first complete translation of Iqbal's *Lectures* which has been published by Bazm-i-Iqbal. This translation is difficult and intricate, and the profusion of Arabic terminology has rendered it heavy reading. Shahzad Ahmad has recently completed the translation of *Lectures*, while I have also started its translation since 1984. The translation of three lectures has been completed, and work on the rest is in progress. In addition, the *Lectures* have been translated into Sindhi, Punjabi, and Pushtu also. Translations have been made at the international level into Arabic, Turkish, Persian and Spanish languages also. The Department of Iqbaliyat of the Iqbal Open University has done very valuable work with the name of *Tas'heel-i-Khutbat-i-Iqbal* (Simplification of *Lectures* of Iqbal). Cooperators in this work include Professor Dr. C.A. Qadir, Dr. Muhammad Ma'ruf, Abd al-Hamid Kamali, Professor Rahim Bakhsh Shaheen, Dr. Muhammad Riaz, Dr. Absar Ahmad and Professor Niaz Irfan. This book is certainly an important step towards the simplification of Iqbal's *Lectures* in spite of being full of errors. In the same way several papers of Iqbal have been translated. For example *Millat-i-Baiza per Eik Imrani Nazar* (A Social View on the Muslim Millat) has been translated by Mawlana Zafar Ali Khan, *Iqbal ka Tasawwur-i-Zaman* (Iqbal's Concept of Time) has been translated by Dr. Tahsin Firaqi, *Allamah's Letters to Quaid-i-Azam* has been translated by Abd ul-Rahman Saeed and later with some additions by Professor Jahangir Alam. Translation work is so comprehensive that a separate paper is needed for its review.

3. Research Work

A good deal of research work has also been done on the life and works of Iqbal. As an example, with reference to his biography a great deal of research material has been unearthed about the difference in the date of his birth. Different people have worked on Iqbal's stay in Europe. Dr. Saeed Akhtar Durrani wrote a book named, *Iqbal Europe Main* (Iqbal

Study of Iqbalics in Pakistan

in Europe). Several new matters have appeared by study of Hyderabad Archives. Numerous matters have come to notice through the study of *Iqbal kee Pahli Bivi* and *Iqbal Durun-i-Khanah*. *Iqbal kee Ibtidai Zindagi* by. Dr. Sultan Mahmud contains all the information which relates to the very early life of Iqbal. *Hayat-i-Iqbal kay Makhfi Goshay* is also a book which has been written by Hamzah Faruqui with the help of the daily paper *Inqilab*. The *Mazlum Iqbal* and Amin Zubairi's book *Iqbal kay Khad o Khal* are the books which bring out some new aspects of Iqbal in spite of being opposed to him. In the *Khad o Khal-i-Iqbal* some things are not only vulgar but reflect the extremely low mentality of the author and some show him to be down right short-sighted.

4. Compilation Works

A great amount of compilation work has been done on Iqbal after the establishment of Pakistan. This work is described below:

I. Discovery of the Letters of Iqbal. The most important letters of Iqbal are those which he wrote to Quaid-i-Azam Muhammad Ali Jinnah. Muhammad Jahangir Alam discovered some more letters, which he translated and published. Last year Sabir Kaluravi found another letter which was published in *Iqbal Review*. Last year the Idarah-i-Saqafat-i-Islamiyah (The Institute of Islamic Culture) discovered and published some letters to Abd al-Aziz Malvadah. Before this Shaikh Ata Ullah, Lateef Ahmad Sherwani, Syed Nazir Niazi and Dr. Rafi ul-Deen Hashmi discovered many letters and published them. Muhammad Ali Qureshi, B.A. Dar and Atiya Begum also compiled some letters. In the same way letters to Mawlana Garami (?) have been compiled. Sabir Kaluravi compiled an index with the name of *Isharia Makateeb-i-Iqbal* (Index to Iqbal's Letters). Dr. Jameel Jalibi delivered a special Iqbal Memorial Lecture on the "Letters of Iqbal" in the Department of Philosophy of the Punjab University which has been published in the journal *Iqbaliyat*. Abdullah Quraishi has published *Makateeb-i-Iqbal ka Tauzeehi Mutala'ah* (The Detailed Study of Iqbal's Letters). Syed Muzaffar Barni in India has done important work in publishing *Kulliyat-i-Makateeb-i-Iqbal* (Complete Letters of Iqbal) in 4 vols.

II. The other important work in the field of compilation is the compilation of Iqbal's works. Four collections, viz. *Navadir-i-Iqbal* (The Rare Works of Iqbal) by Abd al-Ghaffar Shakeel; *Rakht-i-Safar*

Understanding Iqbal's Philosophy

(The Journey's Chattel) by Muhammad Anwar Harith; *Sarud-i-Raftah* (Music of the Past) by Mawlana Ghulam Rasool Mehr and *Baqiyat-i-Iqbal* (The Remaining Works of Iqbal) by Abdullah Quraishi have been published which comprise the works rejected by Iqbal and not included in the *Kulliyat-i-Iqbal*. The *Baqiyat* compiled by Abdullah Quraishi later inlcudes the remaining books.(?) Sabir Kaluravi, writing his Ph.D. thesis on the same subject of *Baqiyat* has collected numerous Urdu and Persian works. In India also Gian Chand Jain has compiled Iqbal's works under the name of *Iqbal ka Ibtidai Mutalaah* (A Preliminary Study of Iqbal) in which he has described the year and occasion of some poems.

III. In compilation the work of Professor Muhammad Sa'eed Shaikh on *Lectures* also would be considered memorable. After much research he has very assiduously prepared the footnotes for Iqbal's *Lectures* in English. Perhaps Iqbal had delivered these lectures orally. Consequently, he refers to different books and authors but the references are incomplete. Professor Muhammad Sa'eed has collected and provided these references. Thus, all these references have become authentic. Professor Sa'eed Ahmad Shaikh is doing similar work on Iqbal's Ph.D. thesis also. In this way Professor Sa'eed Ahmad Shaikh has made several other discoveries about. He has shown how Iqbal used to obtain new books from Europe for updating his knowledge and used to provide rationality for Islamic beliefs and concepts in the light of these books after analyzing them with his far-reaching intellect. Still it would not have been inappropriate to acknowledge the benefits derived by him from Syed Nazir Niazi where applicable, because the original work on the *Lectures* is of the latter.

IV. The fourth important work in compilation is the discovery of some new papers of Iqbal, which have been published by some scholars with the necessary notes. The English book *Speeches, Statements and Writings of Iqbal* by Latif Ahmad Shirwani contains numerous statements, speeches and papers of Iqbal. Similarly, his book *Harf-i-Iqbal* (The Word of Iqbal) contains some of Iqbal's Urdu papers and the translations of some papers in English. Numerous papers and writings of Iqbal have been included in *Guftar-i-Iqbal* (The Talks of Iqbal) by Muhammad Rafique; *Auraq-i-Gum Gashtah* (The Lost Pages) by Dr. Rahim Bakhsh Shaheen and *Anvaar-i-Iqbal* (The Splendor of Iqbal) by B.A. Dar.

Study of Iqbalics in Pakistan

Dr. Tahsin Firaqi has discovered a paper of Iqbal on the concept of time, and a paper on Bedil, which presents the comparative study of Bedil and Bergson by Iqbal. Sabir Kaluravi has compiled the first three chapters with foot-notes in connection with the history of *Tasawwuf*, which has been published by Maktabai-Tamer-i-Insaniyat. Dr. Muzaffar Abbas has also published *Millat-i-Baiza per Imrani Nazar* together with the English text by Iqbal, which had been published earlier in *Tasaneef-i-Iqbal ka Tauzeehi Mutalaah* (The Detailed Study of Iqbal's Publications) by Dr. Rafi-al-Deen Hashmi. Still the text and translation together have been published in English for the first time.

V. The Iqbal Academy Pakistan has also recently prepared another plan for compilation under which all the works of Iqbal will be published in the form of "Complete Works". The purpose of this compilation plan is to provide the workers on Iqbal with basic foundation material, so that the specialists of Iqbalics may get all the material in one place. The first level of work in this connection comprises compilation of Iqbal's books. Dr. Rafi-al-Deen Hashmi is compiling these books. All books, journals, papers, M.A. and Ph.D. theses, and papers in newspapers and journals published on Iqbal will be included in all their details. All the prose works of Iqbal in Urdu will be included in the volume to be named *Kulliyat-i-Nasariyat-i-Iqbal* (The Complete Prose Works of Iqbal). This volume will include papers, statements, speeches, whether in Urdu or translations (?). In the same way another volume will contain all the publications, papers, speeches, statements and miscellaneous material (?) authored by Iqbal. Thus these two books of complete works in Urdu and English will contain all the publications of Iqbal in Urdu and English respectively. The third collection will be *Kulliyat-i-Makateeb-i-Iqbal* (The Complete Collection of Letters of Iqbal), which will contain all the available letters of Iqbal, with indices. The Academy has already published, the *Kulliyat-i-Iqbal* (Urdu)" and *Kulliyat-i-Iqbal* (Farsi). After careful correction of the text, the calligraphy of the Persian book has been done by an eminent calligrapher of Iran, and that of the Urdu book by the admirable calligrapher, Jameel Quraishi.

VI. Annual Publication of Works on Iqbal - On joining the Iqbal Academy Dr. Waheed Ishrat prepared the plan for compilation of the papers on Iqbal separately by years. So far *Iqbal 84*, *Iqbal 85* and

Understanding Iqbal's Philosophy

Iqbal 86 have been published. This series will include all material since 1938.

After this introductory statement we now turn to our real subject. Altogether more than three thousand books have been written on Iqbal, while a very conservative estimate places the number of papers written on Iqbal during the same period as exceeding even ten thousands. In addition to the above mentioned biographical, compilation, analytical, and research work on Iqbal work of two kinds has been done on him at the level of thought. On the one hand work of important nature has been done on his verse. This includes the qualities of his works, their rare and wonderful virtues from poetical perspectives, the subjects and objects of similes, allusions, metaphors, and allegories, terminology and the sound effects of his writings, as well as the weaknesses of his writings, according to the views of some critics. This means that in all this work the art of Iqbal has been tested on the basis of different standards of language and expression, and many different inferences have been deduced from it. In short, it can be said that the perfection of Iqbal in the art of poetry has been acknowledged in these books, and it has been admitted that Iqbal has endowed Urdu as well as Persian poetry with valuable treasures of literature, similes, metaphors, allusions, and excellence of rare and wonderful virtues. This thought has been expressed with full confidence about Urdu poetry, while the distinction of Iqbal in the Persian language is conversion of the tradition of the monarchical manner of Persian language into revolutionary tendencies, and including in Persian verse the new diction, similes and metaphors of revolution. The music of revolution pervades through his entire Persian poetry. This is the reason why, in the war against imperialism the revolutionaries of Iran did not obtain inspiration and leadership from Hafiz, Sa'di and Naziri but from the ecstasy of the revolutionary songs of Iqbal. Still this aspect of Iqbal's Persian poetry has to be further researched. Another work on this aspect of Urdu and Persian is the search for the sources of Iqbal's verse in Urdu and Persian.

Out of the books written on Iqbal at the intellectual level those which pertain only to his poetry or those which highlight the intellectual and sound effects also contain numerous important books which have made public appearance with reference to his intellectual thought aspects. As it would not be possible to encompass all of them in this paper even some important book may be missed. However, efforts have been made to include all such books. The following subjects have been discussed in the books written on him at the intellectual level.

Study of Iqbalics in Pakistan

1. Iqbal's System of Thought

Effort has been made in these books, written on Iqbal at the intellectual level, to present the system of his thought. The basis of his metaphysical thinking has been given and his philosophy of *Khudi* has been explained. An important book among them is the one titled *Iqbal ka Zehni Irtiqa* (Iqbal's Intellectual Evolution) by Dr. Ghulam Husain Zulfiqar. This book presents the intellectual evolution of Iqbal stage by stage from birth till secondary education, from the period of porfessorship to his stay in Europe, and then from his return and stay in Lahore till his death. The beauty of this book is its presentation of Iqbal as possessing an intellect striving towards evolution, which is not solidified in theories, and which is not reactionary, but which appears as promoting expansion of the above in the light of new knowledge and discoveries. This book gives us a graph of intellectual evolution from which Iqbal appears to us as acquiring new knowledge and carving and polishing his concepts and theories all the time. Actually this book is the story of Iqbal's intellect, as to how an Iqbal nurtured in the Western education emerges as a missionary of Islamic renaissance, and correlates his past, present and future with that of the Islamic *Millat*. This book takes us even beyond the intellectual discipline, through which Iqbal labored to elevate himself to his high status. Sa'eed Ahmad has beautifully presented his study of the comparison between Iqbal and Mawlana Mawdudi in his book *Nava-i-Mashriq* (The Song of the East). Though two more books have been written on this subject, in this book the importance of Iqbal and Mawlana Mawdudi has been highlighted by presenting them as exponents of Islamic thought. Actually, this book contains two papers of Mawlana Mawdudi also about Iqbal. This book owes its importance to the presence of Iqbal's influence in Mawlana Mawdudi's struggle in the field of organization of Islamic thought. In fact the starting of the movement on coming from Deccan to the Punjab was also the result of Iqbal's persuasion. To a large extent Mawlana Mawdudi organized his struggle up to the concept of establishing a modern Islamic State was also created through inspiration from Iqbal. The movement of Mawlana Mawdudi can be considered as the culmination of the intellectual movement of Iqbal. Still its practical shaping was the creation of the keen mind of Mawlana himself. Perhaps if Iqbal had been alive the movement of Mawlana Mawdudi would have been more productive, both intellectually as well as practically, and would have produced more effective results. Iqbal was against the distinction between secular and religious lives. Iqbal did not consider Islam as merely a system of beliefs

Understanding Iqbal's Philosophy

and rites, but looked upon it as a complete system of life, and was desirous of the organization of an Islamic democracy in the ideological environment existing in the world today. These same three points are the essence of Iqbal's political and religious ideology. He considered *Ijtihad* as inescapable for it. An analysis of Mawlana Mawdudi's thought will reveal these very four points to be the essence of his entire thought and struggle. Mawlana Mawdudi advanced Iqbal's thought. Undoubtedly he succeeded in this but his reactionary philosophy and absence of political insight harmed Iqbal's movement to some extent. However, the movement of Mawlana Mawdudi can be considered to be the extension of Iqbal's thought.

Three books by Professor Dr. Syed Abdullah in the field of Iqbal's thought are fairly important. These are *Maqasid-i-Iqbal* (The Goals of Iqbal), *Masael-i-Iqbal* (The Problems of Iqbal), and *Mutala'ah-i-Iqbal: Chand Nae Rukh* (The Study of Iqbal: Some New Aspects). In *Maqasid-i-Iqbal* Dr. Syed Abdullah adjudges retrieval to be the central point of Iqbal's thought. In this book of seven chapters the author considers all the poetry, literature, thought and philosophy of Iqbal to be aiming at the retrieval of the glory of the past or the age of Islam. In this context in the first three chapters, considering the attitude of Iqbal against the West as an external attack of the time, the author brings out the evils of the West in the light of Iqbal's works. In the fourth chapter he analyses the three internal enemies of the Islamic unity, viz. sectarianism, racism and a 'Ajami influence, and brings out Iqbal's concept of "I am the nation. In the fifth chapter he describes the remedy for the malady of the components of the *Millat* in the light of Iqbal's thought. In the next chapter the author points out that Iqbal's thought is a continuation of the practical traditions of Muslims. Iqbal is not a thinker isolated from the past, but has his roots inseparably fixed in the past. The most important chapter of the book is *Iqbal and Science* in which the author has analyzed a new aspect of the intellectual and scientific trend in the thought of Iqbal, and has highlighted Iqbal's interest in science, showing how, in Iqbal's view, the scientific concepts of Muslims have inspired modern scientific concepts and the science perpetuated by the Holy Qur'an among Muslims by persuading them to the study of the tangible universe and nature is nothing but science. But the Muslims, being caught in the clutches of Greek deduction, brought about their downfall by arresting their advances in science. In *Mutala'ah-i-Iqbal kay Chand Nai Rukh* the author has done very important work on Iqbal at the level of thought. He has written an important paper on 'Iqbal and Alberuni', especially about the concept of both about history. In the same way in the paper "Ibn Khaldun and Iqbal" he has enhanced the importance of history. These papers point to the same importance of history which Iqbal has asserted about it as a source of knowledge based on the arguments derived from the Holy Qur'an. He has shown that Alberuni and Ibn Khaldun in the past had adopted the same direction of thought as Iqbal by accepting the importance of history as stressed by the Holy Qur'an. Some other important papers are: "Iqbal kay Kalam Main Haram ka Tasawwur" (The Concept of Haram in the Works of Iqbal); "Iqbal ka Mard-i-Yaqeen" (Iqbal's Brave Believer); "Islami Fiqh kee Tadween-i-Nau" (The re-organization of Islamic *Fiqh*); "Iqbal our Sufi: Ikhtilaf awr Itefaq kee Kahani" (Iqbal and Sufi: A Tale of Agreement and Disagreement). Still this book is not written on any one subject but is a collection of separate papers. Though all these papers are important and thought provoking but the somewhat reduce the over all value of the book.

Several collections of different papers written on Iqbalics have also been published. Examples are: two collections of the papers published in *Iqbal Review* in Urdu and English, titled *Sahifah-i-Iqbal* (The Book of Iqbal) compiled by Yunus Javid; *Majmuah Maqalat* (Collection of Essays) by Professor Sa'eed A. Shaikh; *Iqbal: The Poet Philosopher of Pakistan* by Hafeez Malik; *Mutala'ah-i-Iqbal* (Study of Iqbal) by Gauhar Naushahi. A few others are: Ghulam Dastgir Rashid's collections and *Iqbal ba Kamal* (The Perfect Iqbal) by Asghar Ali. Indeed there is no limit to such essays for which reason they have not been reviewed here.

Recently Professor Dr. Aslam Ansari's Book, *Iqbal and Afreen* (Iqbal: Creator of an Age) has been published. According to Justice (r) Javid Iqbal this book discusses all those facets of Iqbal and his poetry which are related to the great literary traditions of the East as well as to our present and future. The book analyzes the reality of the influence of Iqbal on our collective life at the cultural, intellectual, political, and literary levels and points out the intrinsic components of the "New Times" constructed by Iqbal. The learned author, discussing the *Reconstruction of Religious Thought in Islam* in the Islamic perspectives, says that after the stalemate of centuries this book has acquired the status of such a revolutionary agitation and turning of the way as can help us in getting the comprehension of the social needs of Islam in the present-day world. In the author's view Iqbal's *Lectures* is an extension of the traditions of Shah Waliullah Muhaddith of Delhi and Mawlana Shibli Nu'mani in new style.

Understanding Iqbal's Philosophy

In the learned author's view by a deep study of Iqbal's 'Mathnavi, *Rumuz-i-Bekhudi* (The Enigmas of Selflessness) and the last three chapters of *Lectures* the conclusion will automatically appear that the acquisition, comprehension, or cognizance of the Self, in Iqbal's opinion, has the status of the starting point of the collective renaissance of Muslims.

Aziz Ahmad's book *Iqbal: Eik Nai Tashkeel* (Iqbal: A New Re-structuring) is very important among some thought provoking books written on Iqbal. Its peculiarity is the oceanic nature of its subjects. Still, being spread over innumerable subjects the book could not do justice even to one of them. The book presents Iqbal's poetry and intellectual development with reference to Iqbal's patriotism, Islamic poetry, revolutionary poetry and his concept of art. The part dealing with Iqbal's revolutionary poetry and his concept of art is fairly important, because it has specially highlighted Iqbal's revolutionary poetry and has brought out the significance of Iqbal's different symbols, like fire fly, eagle, tulip etc.

The book *The Islamic Culture in Iqbal's View* by the eminent scholar of the Institute of Islamic Research, Mazharuddin Siddiqui is a short but excellent book on Iqbal's thought and ideology. Sultan Zubairi has also translated this book in Urdu. In my opinion this book should be counted among the few excellent books written on Iqbal's philosophy and thought. This is so because this book discusses the subjects of the fifth and sixth chapters of the *Lectures*, in which Iqbal has expressed his opinion of the Holy Qur'an being contradictory to Greek philosophy, as well as his opinions on *Ijtihad* and *Tasawwuf*. It has been explained in this book as to how the legislation of Islamic laws can be effected in the present age in the light of Iqbal's thought and as to how the spirit of the Holy Qur'an contradicts Greek philosophy. The learned author, following this attitude of *Ijtihad*, and examining the new present-day concepts in the light of Islam, has elucidated the democratic features of the Islamic State, and has strengthened Iqbal's rationale for Islamic democracy for the new Islamic welfare democratic state. Under the influence of Iqbal's concept of *Ijtihad* he has also deemed necessary the re-organization of *Fiqh* according to the requirements and conditions of the present age. Indeed this book is the confirmation of Iqbal's thought in the light of Islamic thought and wisdom and is a good effort connected with the tradition of purely Islamic thinking, which reminds us of the deep comprehension of Iqbal's thought. This book points out the new directions for Islamic legislation in the present-day world.

Study of Iqbalics in Pakistan

The book of Aijaz al-Haq Quddusi, *Iqbal awr Ulamah-i-Pak o Hind* (Iqbal and Religious Scholars of Pakistan and India), published by the Iqbal Academy is a piece of good research. This book clearly brings out the environment in which Iqbal was born and the heritage he received from the religious scholars of the Indian sub-continent. The excellence of Iqbal lies in not being suspended in a vacuum but, in spite of his innovative nature, is not only aware of his heritage of thought and knowledge but, accepting their good aspects and viewing them with critical eyes, he moves forward. All work conducted in the Indian sub-continent on the comprehension of the Holy Qur'an as well as analysis and illustration of Islamic knowledge was known to Iqbal from which he fully benefited. This book of Aijaz al-Huq Quddusi is important from the point of view of giving us a good understanding of Iqbal's familiarity in different ways with the traditions of the thought of the religious scholars. The book contains accounts of all the religious scholars from the advent of Islam in the sub-continent to the scholars contemporary with Iqbal, with whom he was familiar at the intellectual, scholarly and notional level. This book disproves the notion that Iqbal did not respect religious scholars. Iqbal was very fond of learned people. He was against only the fanatic and inert type of *Mullahs*.

Islami Tasawwuf awr Iqbal (Islamic Tasawwuf and Iqbal) is the Ph.D. thesis of Dr. Abu Sa'eed Nuruddin. The author has taken great pains to present Iqbal's concept of *Tasawwuf*. He has shown that Iqbal was not against the philosophy of *Tasawwuf*. On the other hand Iqbal's 'Mathnavi' *Asrar-i-Khudi* (The Secrets of Self) was a protest against only those components of *Tasawwuf* which had crept into it by the upheavals of time and which, by nurturing asceticism among Muslims, had made them enamored of autocracy and abdication of the world, which in turn had deprived them of the movement and activism needed for the conquest and administration of the world. Iqbal believed in a *Tasawwuf* which, purifying the Self of the Muslim, brings him out as an exemplary person who performs the function of the leadership of nations, and which gives birth to a creative character. The book of Dr. Abul Laith Siddiqui *Iqbal awr Maslak-i-Tasawwuf* (Iqbal and the Creed of Tasawwuf) and the book of Dr. Farman Fatehpuri *Iqbal awr Tasawwuf* (Iqbal and Tasawwuf) also bring out the same concepts of Iqbal. Iqbal's own book, *Tareekh-i-Tasawwuf* (The History of Tasawwuf), which has been compiled and published by Sabir Kaluravi exhibits the same thoughts of Iqbal.

Understanding Iqbal's Philosophy

In my opinion an important and reliable book on Iqbal is *Fikr-i-Iqbal* (Iqbal's Thought) by Dr. Khalifah Abd ul-Hakim, which is very comprehensive. This book contains a critical review of the concepts of Iqbal together with his intellectual development. A complete review of this book is not possible here. However, it appears that perhaps the author himself has not understood Iqbal adequately. For example in the three chapters on communism, democracy and intellect Dr. Abd-al-Hakim has not adequately explained the problem. Iqbal has never opposed democracy. Not to talk of abandoning democracy Iqbal has never supported autocratic dictators or kings. I have discussed this matter fully in my book *Jamhuriat Pakistan Main* (Democracy in Pakistan). How can Iqbal, who confers the right of *Ijtihad* on the elected parliament, accept dictators? Iqbal had some admissible objections against democracy, which he has pointed out in his works. Iqbal wanted to remove these objections or shortcomings of democracy with his concepts of spiritual democracy or social democracy, while the statements of Dr. Abd-al-Hakim give the impression that Iqbal was against democracy itself. In the same way Iqbal indicates his inclination towards experimenting with communism as a new concept. In opposition to the racism as well as the racial and national imperialism of the West, Iqbal talks about studying the humanism, and the economic betterment of the poor and deprived classes of humanity conceived by communism and finding their proximity to Islam, and persuades Muslims towards the philosophy of "Qul il-Afv" of the Holy Qur'an. On the other hand Dr. Abd-al-Hakim gives the impression that Iqbal had some soft corner for communism. In the same way Dr. Abd-al-Hakim has not adequately understood Iqbal's criticism of Intellect. Iqbal talks about limitations on Intellect, barring which he cannot be accused of being against intellect when he himself accepts an organic relationship between *Wahi* and Intellect. In respect of all these three concepts of Iqbal *Fikr-i-Iqbal* is the victim of confusion, though on the whole this is a good book on Iqbal.

2. Studies in Psychology

Only nominal volume of work has been done on Iqbal with reference to psychology. Only the small book by Dr. Ishtiaq Husain Quraishi *Iqbal kay Nafsiyati Manabay* (The Psychological Sources of Iqbal) and Dr. Saleem Akhtar's book, *Iqbal ka Nafsiyati Mutala'ah* (Study of Iqbal with Reference to Psychology) have been published. Dr. Saleem Akhtar, with reference to the influence of Iqbal's family and personal affairs in the shaping of his thought and art, has exposed the rare truth that the grandeur which Iqbal has achieved in his art cannot wane. Iqbal may be presented as an angel or his personal weaknesses may be exaggerated Iqbal will remain what he is. His greatness lies in his being a man.

3. Political Philosophy of Iqbal

Three very good books have been published on the political philosophy of Iqbal. One is the *Iqbal ka Siyasi Karnamah* (The Political Achievement of Iqbal) by Muhammad Ahmad Khan. The second book is *Iqbal awr Siyasat-i-Milli* (Iqbal and Politics of the Millat) by Rais Ahmad Jafari and the third one is the book of Dr. Parveen Shaukat, titled *The Political Philosophy of Iqbal. Iqbal Ba-haisiyat Mufakkir-i-Pakistan* (Iqbal as the Thinker of Pakistan) by Dr. Abd ul-Hameed also encompasses Iqbal's political thought. In the same way *Iqbal kay Akhiri Do Sal* (The Last Two Years of Iqbal) presents the political thoughts and ideologies of Iqbal. The author of this book is Dr. Ashiq Husain Batalavi. *Iqbal ka Siyasi Karnamah* is important in this respect, as it presents Iqbal's political views in great detail. It has also been stated in this book that Chaudhry Rahmat Ali himself had heard the word, "Pakistan" from Iqbal in 1931 at the time of the Round Table Conference, and Iqbal had explained to him how this word was formed, which was coined by Iqbal using English characters. This means that in the view of Muhammad Ahmad Khan the word "Pakistan" had not been invented by Chaudhry Rahmat Ali but was coined by Iqbal himself. Iqbal's "Separate Electorates", "Two Nations Theory", and acquisition of Pakistan under them have been described very beautifully in detail. In *Iqbal awr Siyasat-i-Milli,* Rais Ahmad Jafari has very well explained Iqbal's ideological and political war for renaissance of the *Millat* in the Indian sub-continent and at the world level. The book has complete information on the fronts and the mode of Iqbal's fight at them. Dr. Parveen Shaukat also has presented Iqbal's political thought very beautifully in the perspective of the politics of the Indo-Pakistan sub-continent. Recently, Syed Noor Muhammad Qadiri has made good research in his book *Iqbal ka Akhiri Ma'rikah* (Iqbal's Last Battlefield). Explaining the insistence of Iqbal on Islamic nationhood and the background of "Millat az watan ast" (Secular nationhood), and analyzing the strong reaction of Iqbal against the school of thought of Mawlana Husain Ahmad Madani he has said that the new ideology presented by Iqbal in his paper "Jughrafiai Hudud awr Musalman" (Geographic Boundaries and Muslims) and his response to the paper on *Taloot* was that a nation is not created by geographical boundaries but on ideology. It has also been explained in this book that even after Iqbal's appeal and particularly after his death the group of Husain Ahmad Madani remained firm in the ideology of the Congress, which led to his and his companions' expulsion from the Muslim League. According to Noor Muhammad Qadiri the war of Husain Ahmad Madani as neither intellectual nor ideological but was motivated by the basic ingredient of the greed of the Congress. In this last struggle Iqbal blasted the very foundations of the Congress as a result of which the two-nation theory finally rewarded with clear victory.

4. Allamah Iqbal's Persian Poetry

With reference to Iqbal's Persian poetry some important books are: *Iqbal kee Parsi Shairi kay Ma'khaz* (The Sources of Iqbal's Persian Poetry) by Dr. Wazeer al-Hasan; *Iqbal awr Parsi Shuara* (Iqbal and Persian Poets) by Dr. Muhammad Riaz; the recently published book of Rafique Khawar titled, *Iqbal ka Farsi Kalam* (The Persian Works of Iqbal); and the book of Professor Muhammad Munawwar titled, *Iqbal kee Farsi Ghazal* (The Persian Ghazal of Iqbal). In the same way the book of Dr. Muhammad Akram, *Iqbal dar Rah-i-Mawlavi* (Iqbal on the Path of Mawlavi) and the book of Dr. Muhammad Riaz titled, *Javid Namah: Tauzih o Tahqiq* (Javid Namah: Explanation and Research) are useful books which show that Iqbal adopted Persian poetry for special purposes. One was that the expanse of his works could not be contained in the Urdu language. Secondly communication of ideas was relatively simpler in Persian than in Urdu. Thirdly, in Iqbal's opinion Persian had great importance as the refined and cultural language of Muslims after Arabic, and was understood in Afghanistan, Iran, and the Indian sub-continent. That meant that the greater part of the Islamic *Millat* knew Persian. This very region was the audience of Iqbal. Later the revolutions in Iran and Afghanistan attested to the truth of Iqbal's judgment. All these four or five books are comprised of the significance of Iqbal's Persian works and communication of the deep cultural and civilizational relationships of Iqbal with the Persian language.

5. Iqbal as an Exegete

Professor Muhammad Munawwar had a special status as an exponent of Iqbal's expertise in exegesis. Among his books published on Iqbal to date in Urdu and Persian are: *Meezan-i-Iqbal* (The Rhyme of Iqbal), *Burhan-i-Iqbal* (The Reasoning of Iqbal), *Iqan-i-Iqbal* (The Faith of Iqbal), and *Iqbal kee Farsi Ghazal* (The Persian Ghazal of Iqbal). He has written three books in English also. They are: *Iqbal: The Poet-Philosopher of Islam*, *Iqbal and Qur'anic Wisdom*, and *Dimensions of Iqbal*. Professor Muhammad Munawwar was highly enamored by Iqbal. His style is explanatory and analytical. This greatly helps in comprehension of Iqbal's basic thoughts. In the field of Iqbal's faith his paper "Iqbal ka Tasawwur-i-Taqdeer" (Iqbal's Concept of Destiny) is the most important, in which he writes under comprehension of Iqbal's concept of destiny that in the view of Iqbal destiny is the name of selecting or choosing among the open options. Man is not tied down to any pre-determined destiny, but he carves out his destiny every moment by selecting and choosing from open options. This book of the Professor is the most important from the intellectual point of view. Its other extremely thought provoking papers are: "Iqbal awr Brahimi Nazar" (Iqbal and Ibrahim's Insight), "Iqbal awr Taleem-i-Adamiyat" (Iqbal and Education of Man), "Iqbal ka Tasawwur-i-Millat" (Iqbal's Concept of Nation), "Iqbal awr Marg-i-Majazi" (Iqbal and Common Death), "Faqr-i-Iqbal" (The Faqr of Iqbal). "Meezan-i-Iqbal" is a literary and artistic survey of Iqbal. In this book the meaning and balance of '*Ajam* in Iqbal's works is extremely important. In Iqbal's view '*Ajam* is not Iran but un-Islamic and non-Quranic ideas are '*Ajami* concepts. *Burhan-i-Iqbal* really tells us that the fountainhead of Iqbal's thought is the Holy Qur'an. Subjects like "Qur'ani Tasawwur" (The Qur'anic Concept), "Tareekh-i-Iqbal ka Mard-i-Yaqeen" (Iqbal's Believer in Iqbal's Concept of History), "Iqbal awr Ijtihad" (Iqbal and Ijtihad), "Jahan-i-Iqbal, Jahan-i-Qur'an" (Iqbal's Universe, Qur'an's Universe) all show that the center and axis of Iqbal's thought was the Holy Qur'an. There is also a research work of Dr. Ghulam Mustapha Khan, titled *Iqbal awr Qur'an* (Iqbal and Qur'an). By placing the Qur'anic verses side by side with the Urdu and Persian verses of Iqbal he has proved that the works of Iqbal are nothing but the literary miracle of the Holy Qur'an. Professor Munawwar's book, *Iqbal and Quranic Wisdom* also basically manifests the same thing, and his book, "Iqbal: Poet-Philosopher of Islam" is really comprised of the English translations of the papers in *Iqan-i-Iqbal* and *Meezan-i-Iqbal* At the intellectual level *Dimensions of Iqbal* is an attested book of the author. In spite of all this we cannot agree with his thought that Iqbal was against democracy. However, the assertion of the Professor that by using *Ijtihad* in democracy we should bring it closer to the ideals of our lives so as to reach the goal of Iqbal.

6. Educational Philosophy of Iqbal

Some important books exist on the educational philosophy of Iqbal also. Among them *Iqbal awr mas'alah-i-Taleem* (Iqbal and the Education Problem) by Muhammad Ahmad Khan, *Iqbal ba-hasiyyat Mufakkir-i-Ta'leem* (Iqbal as an Educational Thinker) by Professor Bakhtiar Siddiqui, *Iqbal's Educational Philosophy* by Khwajah Ghulam-al-Saiyyidain, *Iqbal and Education* by Mian Muhammad Tufail are all important. Iqbal attached much importance to the education of Muslims. He has himself written on the problems of education, and on education of children and Muslim women. All these books contain Iqbal's concepts on an important problem. The book of Khwajah Ghulam-al-Saiyyidain in English and that of Professor Bakhtiar Husain Siddiqui in Urdu on this subject are important. Professor Siddiqui has very beautifully highlighted Iqbal's ideological designs in connection with his aims of education, and has brought out the salient features of Iqbal's philosophy in their comparative study with that of Western educational philosophers, and has explained the high ideological and practical advantages of the former. The books of Mian Muhammad Tufail and Muhammad Ahmad Khan are books of the same kind in the field of education, and show us the way for profiting from Iqbal in the field of compilation of an education system for the Islamic welfare state. Muhammad Ahmad Khan has particularly presented Iqbal as a thinker and preceptor of education and a critic of the aimless present day education. He has very beautifully shown Iqbal's aims of education.

7. Iqbal as a Parliamentarian

Iqbal Aiwan-i-Assembly Main (Iqbal in the Assembly House), the new book of Professor Haq Nawaz is singular because of being the first book which presents Iqbal as a parliamentarian. It shows that as a member of the Assembly Iqbal was very effective in performing his task of addressing the intellectual and applied problems of Muslims in general, and those of the Punjab Muslims in particular during the period March 5, 1927 and March 7, 1930. The study of this book brings out the anguish to Iqbal caused by the dangers facing the political, cultural and civilizational existence of the Muslims of the Indian sub-continent and their timely solution.

Seerat-i-Iqbal (The Biography of Iqbal) and *Iqbal awr Muhabbat-i-Rasool* (Iqbal and Love for the Holy Prophet) the two books of Dr. Muhammad Tahir Faruqui are singularly important. Dr. Muhammad Tahir Faruqui was a true lover of Iqbal. In his *Seerat-i-Iqbal* he has presented Iqbal as a thinking movement and eternal Iqbal, and in *Iqbal aur Muhabbat-i-Rasool* he has assembled all the evidence in support of the love of Iqbal for the Holy prophet. In the view of Dr. Faruqui this love of Iqbal was not the common place love, but was the love which exhibited the unity of thought and the singleness of Faith and Belief for Iqbal, which cast the character of Iqbal in a thinker's mold and made him the leader of Muslims in the intellectual and political fields in the twentieth and twenty-first centuries. To Tahir Faruqui this is the beneficence of Iqbal's love for the Holy Prophet's love.

Iqbal: Eik Mutala'ah (Iqbal: A Study) is the second book of Dr. Ghulam Husain Zulfiqar. Though this book is a collection of different papers of his, all of them open up the different layers of Iqbal's thought with great thinking and planning. Among these papers "Kishwar-i-Punjab awr Iqbal" (The Land of Punjab and Iqbal) "Iqbal kay Imrani Tasawwurat" (The Social Concepts of Iqbal) are important. Innumerable collections of papers have been compiled on the intellectual and emotional relationship of Iqbal with prominent personages, like Jamaluddin Afghani, Kamal Ataturk, Akbar Allahabadi, and Zafar Ali Khan. Still I cannot overlook the collection compiled by Dr. Syed Abdullah titled, *Muta'aliqat-i-Khutbat-i-Iqbal* (Concerning the Lectures of Iqbal). All these papers refer to the *Lectures* of Iqbal. Among them the extremely deep ones are: *Iqbal awr Zehni Tajrubah* (Iqbal and Intellectual Experience) by Abd ul-Hafeez Kardar, *Iqbal ka Junoobi Hind ka Safar* (Iqbal's Travels in South India) by Dr. Abdullah Chaghatai, *Elam'-i-Khutubat-i-Iqbal* (The Herald of Iqbal's *Lectures*) by Dr. Ghulam Husain Zulfiqar, *Tasawwur-i-Taqdeer* (The Concept of Destiny) by Professor Muhammad Munawwar, *Iqbal ka Tasawwur-i-Baqa-i-Dwam* (Iqbal's Concept of Eternal Existence) by Chaudhry Muzaffar Husain, *Khutbat Main Hukama-i-Islam kay Havalay* (References to the Intellectuals of Islam in *Lectures*), by Dr. Amcenullah Watheer, and Dr. Syed Abdullah's own papers *Iqbal awr Razi* (Iqbal and Razi) and *Iqbal awr Shabistari* (Iqbal and Shabistari). Thus, this book is a very important help in comprehension of *Lectures*. In the same way *Muntakhab Maqalat-i-Urdu awr Angrezi* (Selected Papers in Urdu and English) by Dr. Waheed Quraishi are very important. Among them the papers of Abd ul-Hameed Kamali titled, "Spengler, Iqbal awr mas'alah-i-Taqdeer" (Spengler, Iqbal and the Problem of Destiny), and "Jinnah awr Iqbal" (Jinnah and Iqbal) and Dr. Wazir Agha's "Iqbal awr Spengler" (Iqbal and

Understanding Iqbal's Philosophy

Spengler) are the papers which cannot be overlooked in any circumstances. The Bazm-i-Iqbal is publishing the Urdu and English papers of Abd-al-Hameed Kamali which I have compiled. Whoever has read the papers of Mr. Kamali will testify to his being an eminent and great scholar of Iqbalics. The series of his papers on time and space published in Iqbaliyat is one of great importance. In the book compiled by me titled; *Zaman o Makan* (Time and Space) published by Sang-i-Meel Publishers these papers have been published along with other papers of Iqbal.

Talking of Spengler it is appropriate to point out the importance of the paper of Dr. Wazir Agha on this contemporary thinker of Iqbal. The book of Dr. Wazeer Agha entitled *Tasawwurat-i-Ishq o Khirad* (Concepts of Love and Intellect) is among the very serious books in Iqbalics. Dr. Wazeer Agha has described the importance of Intellect and Love in Iqbal's thought in the highlight of the background of the European and Islamic concepts of Iqbal. Dr. Wazeer Agha writes that with Iqbal the situation arose in which the invincible speed of Love conferred the rank of night enlightening insect on the simple insect. But the heart of Iqbal after passing through the times of search was rewarded with such a radiance which can be described appropriately only by the word "awareness". Awareness is neither Love nor Intellect, though it has the effulgence provided by Love as well as the perception provided by Intellect. Awareness is another name for alertness, Essence or the perception of the Essence. This is a stage where the distinction between Love and Intellect disappears and the subject starts breathing at the creative level of the universe. Iqbal has used the word *Khudi* for this state of awareness, which is appropriate in every respect. Explaining in detail the attitudes of both *Sufis* and rationalists about Intellect and Love Dr. Wazeer Agha has explained very well this perplexity of Iqbal that he was aware of the limitations of both Intellect and Love and, combining both in his concept of awareness or *Khudi*, he tried to highlight man's creative character so that he may subdue the expanse of the Self and the universe.

The book of Professor Fateh Muhammad Malik, Iqbal: *Fikr o Amal* (Iqbal: Thought and Action) occupies a special place in Iqbalics. Fateh Muhammad Malik explains, with reference to the democratic and revolutionary concepts of Iqbal, how Iqbal's thought changed into movement and action the inactive society caught in the clutches of colonialism. Professor Malik's method is analytical and his philosophy is thought - provoking. According to Professor Fateh Muhammad Allamah

Study of Iqbalics in Pakistan

Iqbal saw the dream of Pakistan and Quaid-i-Azam, with the complete cooperation of the Indian sub-continent's Muslims, changed this dream into a solid reality. Hence, the people who look upon Pakistan separate from the sayings of Iqbal and Quaid-i-Azam commit the mistake of denying the basic concept of Pakistan. Fateh Muhammad Malik has correlated the concept of Pakistan with Iqbal's system of thought, and has rightly pronounced the verdict that the continuance and progress of Pakistan depends upon the true and honest efforts at bringing Iqbal's thought and message to life. He wants to see Iqbal's thought enforced in the political, economic, civilizational and cultural life of Pakistan, because this alone is the defensive rampart of Pakistan. Adjudging politics as the real motivation of the 'progressives' Professor Fateh Muhammad Malik has highlighted it in his works. Professor Malik maintains the study of Iqbal to be the fountainhead of knowledge as well as a daily duty for activism, which has a live and organic relationship with our renaissance. The subjects on which the Professor has expressed his ideas are: "Iqbal: Knower of the Secret(?)", "Iqbal: Confirmation of Prophethood and Pakistan", "Iqbal and the Land of Pakistan", "Pakistan and the Difficulties of La Ilaha", "Iqbal and our Cultural Organization", "Iqbal and Our Literary Re-organization", "Iqbal the Land of Pakistan and the Mosque of Qartabah". The whole attitude reveals a creative and thought-provoking attitude. The whole book exhibits a creative and thought-provoking attitude.

For comprehension of Iqbal at the intellectual level S.M. Umar Faruque, who has recently passed away in Rawalpindi, has made very hard efforts in his book *Tawaseen-i-Iqbal*. He has described some basic concepts of Iqbal in 2 volumes 1 and 2. This book contains the footsteps for a serious effort to comprehend Iqbal's attitude towards Plato, Nietzsche, Hallaj and Splenger, the *Ijtihad* of Turks, Iqbal's concepts of the universe and homeland, state, woman and some other basic principles. He presents very serious subjects with philosophical insight. In spite of all this his book is so full of protractions, and repetitions that sometimes the concepts do not appear rightly.

8. Iqbal as an Artist

Several books bring out the thought and art of Iqbal at the artistic level. The books which are serious efforts in this direction are: *Shair-i-Iqbal* (The Verse of Iqbal), *Nafaesi-Iqbal* (The Beauties of Iqbal), and *Talmihat-i-Iqbal* (Allusions of Iqbal) by Abid Ali Abid;

Understanding Iqbal's Philosophy

Tashbihat-i-Iqbal (The Similes of Iqbal) by Nazir Ahmad Khan; a short book titled "Iqbal kay Mushabbah Beh awr Musta'ar Ash'aar) by Dr. Sa'ad Ullah Kaleem; Mutala'ah-i-Talmihat-o-Isharat-i-Iqbal" (The Study of Iqbal's Allusions, Similes and Metaphors) by Dr. Akbar Husain Quraishi and *Auzan-i-Iqbal* (Meters of Iqbal) by Abul Athar Hafeez Siddiqui. The very names of these books show that the aim of their authors is to show the beauties of Iqbal's verse. All these books are proof of Iqbal's complete grasp of the art of versification. Together with allusions to the Holy Qur'an, *Hadith*, philosophy and history, Akbar Husain Quraishi has spread out the works of Western and Eastern poets and some other special persons and has described Iqbal's attitudes in the light of these. Still I think that in this respect Syed Abid Ali's *Talmihat-i-Iqbal* has retained its unique excellence.

9. Iqbal and Aesthetics

The book of Dr. Nazeer Ahmad Khan, titled, *Iqbal awr Jamaliat* (Iqbal and Aesthetics) is the one single book which is worth reading with reference to this subject. No other book exists on this subject. The book starts with *Khudi* and *Wahdat al-Wujud* and subjectivity and objectivity have been measured on the scale of Objective Beauty and Subjective Beauty. Dr. Nazeer has based the aesthetic concepts of Iqbal on the theory of dynamism of Beauty. In the second part of the book the aesthetic taste present in Iqbal's works has been highlighted with reference to the essence and purpose of art, art and nature, blind following, slavery and *Ijtihad*. Dr. Naseer Ahmad Nasir has also compiled the index of Iqbal's works which has not yet been published. This book is the display of Dr. Nasir's maturity in Iqbalics.

10. Books Hostile to Iqbal

There are also three books about Iqbal which are irritably hostile. These are: *Khad o Khal-i-Iqbal.* (The Features of Iqbal), and *Allamah Iqbal kay Qadiyani Bhateejay* (Allamah Iqbal's Qadiyani Nephews) by Muhammad Ameen Zuberi, *Mazloom Iqbal* (The Oppressed Iqbal) by Shaikh Aijaz Ahmad and *Iqbal' Ek Sha'er* (Iqbal a Poet) by Saleem Ahmad. Muhammad Ameen Zuberi has been the literary assistant to the ruler of Bhopal, Sultan Jahan Begum. Earlier he had smeared the character of Mawlana Shibli Nu'mani by writing *Hayat-i-Ma'ashiqa* (The Life of Love). This book obviously belongs to the category of character smearing, because instead of talking about some intellectual aspect, petty incidents have been used to draw wilful inferences. In the same way the author of

Study of Iqbalics in Pakistan

Mazloom Iqbal, Shaikh Aijaz Ahmad has attacked the household of Iqbal with reference to Qadianism, and has said that Iqbal adopted opposition to Qadianies on account of being coaxed by Ahrars. This assertion is absolutely wrong. Iqbal himself, in view of the wire-pulling of Qadianies against Muslims, their considering the Muslims beyond the pale of Islam, their efforts at converting Kashmir, Baluchistan, and the Punjab into Qadiani provinces and of sabotaging the establishment of Pakistan, demanded that they be classed as a minority and called Qadiyaniat 'infidelity with the Holy Prophet'. In the third book, *Iqbal, A Poet* the author has adjudged the poetry of Iqbal as the poetry of Mochi Darwazah. He has said that Iqbal was afraid of every healthy woman (?), was probably suffering from some venereal disease, and that Iqbal's poetry was the one established on the negative foundation of escape from death. Vulgar sarcasm has been cast also at Iqbal's poetic character "Ssaheen". In reality the author of this book has been nurtured by the Lucknow school of poetry and suffers from a special kind of prejudice, which is specially directed against Urdu and speakers of Urdu (?). To him it is inappropriate to be such an eminent poet for a person with a different language (?). Consequently, that is the reason why even while accepting Iqbal to be an eminent poet he did not lose any opportunity to play tricks with him. With reference to the smearing of Iqbal's character Munshi Abd ul-Rahman Khan has published a book in which he has described all such classes and groups who have ideological and intellectual enmity with Iqbal. This group includes some who are victims of linguistic prejudice and some are confirmed communists. Dr. Manzur Ahmad has adequately examined in his book the three classes against Iqbal. Analyzing the attitude of Saleem Ahmad about Iqbal Dr. Manzur Ahmad writes, "I do not have the slightest hesitation in saying that Saleem Ahmad is devoid of even the slightest professional capability required for this art". The learned critic has objected to the lack of knowledge of Saleem Ahmad about the private life of Iqbal, and in spite of this lack he has drawn a sensational inference on his own, i.e. Iqbal was afraid of natural sex. At the same time he admits this to be his own conjecture for which he has no proof. This is not conjecture but deliberate accusation. According to Dr. Manzur Ahmad, Saleem Ahmad has knowingly tried to demolish Iqbal's personality in *Iqbal, Aik Sha'er.*

11. Miscellaneous

The late B.A. Dar does not need any introduction in the field of Iqbalics. Together with the English translations of some important books

Understanding Iqbal's Philosophy

of he has also collected some rarities of in his book titled, *Anwar-i-Iqbal* (The Splendors of Iqbal). In the same way he has compiled Iqbal's English letters also. However, his real work on Iqbal has appeared in two books. His one important book is *Iqbal and Post-Kantian Voluntarism* and the other is *A Study of Iqbal's Philosophy*. In the first book, recording the results of the very high level intellectual comparative study of Iqbal with Kant, Fichte, Schopenhauer, Milton, Goethe, Bergson, Nietzsche, James Ward, Carlyle, Browning, Bernard Shaw, McDougal, and W. James has highlighted the fact that though Iqbal has certainly benefited from them he did not follow any one of these philosophers. On the other hand, sifting the truths from their study, Iqbal has compiled the results of his own inventive genius. The late author was also given the Iqbal Award for this book. In spite of this he has committed some errors also, as if the entire philosophy of Iqbal is the gleaning from these Western philosophers. Probably a keener comprehension of this subject was expected from the capability of B.A. Dar. Due to the absence of the background of philosophy B.A. Dar was instrumental in giving birth to ambiguities with reference to Iqbal. His second book, *A Study in Iqbal's Philosophy* is comprised the comprehensions of Iqbal on the individual and society. B.A. Dar has played an important role in this book in the comprehension of the concepts of Iqbal. A book in Urdu also with the name of *Maqalat-i-Dar* (The Essays of Dar) is under publication by the Iqbal Academy. In the same way his English essays have also been collected. B.A. Dar has also remained the Director of the Iqbal Academy and has labored hard in the presentation of Iqbal's ideology. Another good book of his titled, *Iqbal's Philosophy of Society* manifests Iqbal's social philosophy with reference to *Rumuz-i-Bekhudi*. The intellectual debate which B.A. Dar has conducted with Ali Abbas Jalalpuri with reference to the theology of Iqbal also attests to his thorough comprehension of Iqbal.

The book of Syed Ali Abbas Jalalpuri titled *The Theology of Iqbal* has the status of an intellectual critique of Iqbal. Actually it would not be out place to say that this is the one single book which is a critique of Iqbal at the intellectual level. Ali Abbas Jalalpuri has taken the stand in this book that Iqbal was not a philosopher but a theologian. A philosopher is the master of the natural gift of thoughts and a theologian presents intellectual rationale for his beliefs with the help of philosophy and logic. He presents the logical and intellectual explanations of only the pre-settled beliefs. If this difference between a theologian and a philosopher is accepted perhaps nobody can claim to be called a philosopher. This is so because not a single individual in the world possesses naturally created abstract thought and not every philosopher renunciates his right to his basic beliefs. Alberuni says even about Socrates, Plato and Aristotle that they were believers in the religion of Hadhrat Musa and the paths of their thought join those of the beliefs and ideologies of their predecessors. Kant, and Descartes also could not be freed from the metaphysics of Christian concepts. Hence, Iqbal can be called a theologian also in a restricted sense, but with reference to the dynamic concept of the universe and the philosophy of *Khudi* he can be adjudged a philosopher also. According to Ali Abbas Jalalpuri Iqbal believed in the Syriac concept of God with reference to the transcendental nature of God and the Syriac concept, i.e. 'God is beyond the universe and also encompasses the universe at the same time'. In spite of all this I consider it inappropriate to bracket Iqbal in any one concept of God in the transcendental or Syriac thought. This is so because in Iqbal's own concepts there is the negation of the Syriac concepts. Separate from the Syriac or Semitic concepts Iqbal accepted the Islamic concept of God in which He is 'an Absolute, Creator, Absolutely Perfect, Eternal in Self Entity', who is our personal God as well as beyond this universe, and this universe is one possibility out of His many possibilities. Hence the assertion of Ali Abbas Jalalpuri that Iqbal did not reconstruct the religious thought in Islam by presenting the Syriac ideology in pursuance of the path of Bergson and Alexander, but has conferred a scientific form on the same Syriac concept of *Wahdat-al-Wujud*, (against which he fought a holy war all his life), is based on the complete lack of comprehension of Iqbal's concept of God. Iqbal did not accept Transcendentalism or Semitism in their entirety but confirmed the correctness of the Holy Qur'an's concept of God, which has in itself the basic essence of both the concepts of Transcendentalism and Semitism. According to this concept God is a Perfect, Most Perfect, Omnipotent, Eternal in His Essence, Pure and Transcendental Essence, who created the universe from absolute non-existence. His creativity is based on continuous development and evolution(?). So Iqbal called the natural universe such an explanation of the creative dynamism of the Real *Ana*, which is done from the human point of view in the present stage of Man's evolution, whose expanse cannot be comprehended, and in which Nature is a live and consistently expanding Organic Unity which cannot be bounded from outside. It has only internal boundary, if any. Iqbal's concept has been produced by a judicious balance of the concepts of transcendentalism and Syriacism. Compared with Transcendentalism and Syriacism Iqbal had greater interest with the Qur'anic concept of God than the former. According to the Qur'anic concept God is a God who is live and an effective Creative Power for the universe. He is not isolated from His people but has close connection with them. Therefore, Ali Abbas Jalalpuri's assertion of Iqbal being under the influence of Syriac concept of God is not very acceptable. Iqbal did not accept the concepts of *Wahdat-al-Wujud*, because in them we do not rise above the stage of Existence, while in *Wahdat-al-Shuhud* the status of Essence rises above Existence. Hence, to call Iqbal as afraid of Intellect, only believer in Intuitional Romanticism and an enemy of Intellect is not his correct comprehension. When Iqbal shows an organic relationship between Intuition and thought he himself accepts the importance of Intellect. If Intellect is viewed in a broad perspective it will be realized that *Wahi* encompasses both Intellect and Knowledge. The Absolute Intellect (Hazrat Jibrail) is the *Wahi*, which sees things in their complete perspective and Gestalt, while Intellect sees only partial truth in its parts. Iqbal has explained this very difference in his concepts of Intellect and Intuition. Iqbal has not rejected Intellect *per se*. Consequently Iqbal first started the movement for the Intellect, the need for the expansion of which was stressed by Ali Abbas. In Iqbal adjudging the study of history and nature as the foundation of religion and knowledge, and in giving importance to the world of the perceptible, or in more clear terms the world of science, the same concepts of Iqbal are contained. These are that with the search of thought and Intuition's organic relationships we should search for a new theory of knowledge. Therefore, Ali Abbas Jalalpuri has made some basic errors and confusions the foundation for his thought, and he could not understand the spirit of the philosophy of Iqbal on account of being the victim of some strong errors.

In my view the most authentic book on Iqbal is *The Metaphysics of Iqbal* by Dr. Ishrat Hasan Enver, which is his Ph.D. thesis. His supervisor was Dr. Zafar al-Hasan. Dr. Shams al-Deen Siddiqui has translated it into Urdu. This shortest book contains extremely important discussions at the intellectual level. "Introduction", "Method of Intuition", "The Self", "The Material World", "The Absolute Entity or God" are its five chapters. In fact all these four concepts are the spirit of Iqbal's philosophy. According to Dr. Ishrat Hasan Enver Iqbal's thought passed through two stages, viz., pre-Intuitional and Intuitional. In the first stage he follows that traditional way of thought which has close relationship with "All is He" or *Wahdat-al-Wujud's* concepts, which had strong appeal for the shattered and shaking Muslim society of the times. But his trip to Europe gave Iqbal new ambitions and a new strength to his determination. A political reaction developed in him. Now he started stressing activism, and unveiling of the Essence instead of contrition, inaction and stalemate. He got strength in his thoughts from Bergson, Nietzsche and McTaggart, and in this way he started giving fundamental importance to Essence or the reality of *Khudi*. He claimed to have knowledge of God, *Khudi*, independence of *Khudi* and eternity, i.e. eternity of the soul and started confirmation of the Reality and all its related rationale. Dr. Ishrat Hasan Enver has also clarified the dynamic philosophy of Iqbal. According to him the most coherent effort in an effective way at creating concordance between religion and philosophy in Islam has been done only by Iqbal in the twentieth century. A collection of the essays of Dr. Ishrat Hasan Enver titled, *Iqbal awr Mashriq o Maghrib kay Mufakkir* (Iqbal and the Thinkers of the East and West) has been recently published. Let me state that in this book Dr. Ishrat Hasan Enver has appeared as the best interpreter and commentator of Iqbal's philosophy, who has himself been a serious student of philosophy. I give great importance to his work in the field of Iqbal's thought.

A serious effort by Dr. Khalid Mas'ud, Editor of *Islamic Studies* on Iqbal's concept of *Ijtihad* has come to my notice. He had read a paper on this subject at the Columbia University in 1977. This book is the expansion of the same. *Islam and Social Changes* has remained the special subject of Dr. Khalid Mas'ud, He has analyzed the interest of Iqbal in *Ijtihad* after analyzing the efforts of *Fatawah-i-Alamgir* (The Religious Edicts of Alamgir) in the Mughal period, and the works of Shah Waliullah and Shah Ismail Shaheed in the period of downfall, those of Jamal ul-Din Afghani, Sir Syed Ahmad Khan, Saeed Haleem Pasha, Zia Gokalp, and Aghni Daiman (?) in the present age. He has also tested the Iqbal's concepts of *Ijtihad* as a dynamic concept in Islam, as well as on free opinion and right of legislation. He has used some *Ijtihad* of Iqbal as argument after studying his conditions and sources of *Ijtihad*, the Holy Qur'an, *Hadith* and *Ijma*. He has described Iqbal's *Ijtihads* about the woman's right for the annulment of marriage, *Khilafat* and legislative assembly, and has pointed out that Iqbal himself wanted a new determination, in the new world, for the old tools of *Ijtihad* so that we may succeed in shaping our social and economic life according to the requirements of the present day world and in the light of the new explanations of the Holy Qur'an and *Hadith*. To Iqbal *Ijtihad* is the name of complete authority in the field of law-making. Hence, Iqbal has used *Ijtihad* in the sense of absolute *Ijtihad* alone. According to Dr. Khalid Mas'ud Iqbal, examining the sources of *Ijtihad*, finds dynamism and the

Understanding Iqbal's Philosophy

principle of movement as a common factor among them, which takes society towards progress and betterment in every age. According to him, applying the concept and ideology of *Ijtihad*, Iqbal took out the society from stalemate and led it to the path of progress, and he searched for its foundations inside and not outside the traditions of Islam.

In the field of Iqbalics the book of Dr. Absar Ahmad, titled, *The Concept of Self and Self Identity in Contemporary Western Philosophy* is also very important. This book is not exclusively on Iqbal but is a separate creation on the subject of Self. However, it is very effective in comprehension of the philosophical foundations of the concept of *Khudi*. Two books of Dr. Muhammad Mar'uf on Dr. Iqbal are available. One book *Iqbal's Philosophy of Religion* is his Ph.D. thesis. This book also revolves round Iqbal's *Lectures*. This book encompasses subjects like theoretical, ideologies about religion, psychological concepts, arguments for verification of religion, the potential of religious experience for experimental verification and the intrinsic value of religion. In reality this book describes the concepts of Iqbal about verification of religion and religious experience as a foundation for knowledge, and shows the intellectual factors of religious experience. I give a special place to this book and Dr. Mar'uf's new book, *Iqbal and His Contemporary Western Religious Thought* among serious and intellectual books in Iqbalics. This book presents on an intellectual level the goals of Iqbal in religion and his impressionability to Western philosophers and their philosophical movements. It belies the hypothesis that Iqbal's thought does not possess any entity of its own, and is nothing more than a rehash of ideas of other people. Dr. Mar'uf has conducted a thought-provoking discussion of the fundamental hypotheses of these Western movements and Iqbal's criticism of them. These discussions include Hegelianism, English metaphysics, American absolutism, concept of individualism and collectivism, the Anglo-American concepts on the place of the philosophy of *Ruh* in their metaphysics, ethical atheism and metaphysics, their concepts of Neo-Kantianism and religion based on nature, capacity for inferences and the philosophical movements connected with them, or history and realism and analytical study of social philosophers. Presenting these discussions with reference to the study of Iqbal the reality has been disclosed that Iqbal is aware of his contemporary movements, but this awareness does not constitute an argument for thinking that he also gleaned verbatim from these movements. On the contrary, presenting his own analysis of these movements in his *Lectures* and verse and describing their misleading and weak aspects Iqbal has presented his own unique thinking.

Study of Iqbalics in Pakistan

The book of Dr. Muhammad Rafi ul-Deen titled, *Hikmat-i-Iqbal* (The Wisdom of Iqbal) is also counted among the reliable books in Iqbalics. Basically, this book is the expansion and explanation of Iqbal's philosophy of *Khudi* with reference to its reality and its relationship with important contemporary subjects and departments of knowledge like creation, philosophy of history, the Holy Prophet, Intellect, vision of nature, science, worship, ethical philosophy, art, revolution, *Tauheed*, socialism and political philosophy. The book of Manzur Ahmad Abbasi is also very important on the subject of *Khudi*. With reference to the concept of Iqbal about socialism two small papers by Justice S.A. Rahman and A.K. Barohi are very important. Muhammad Hanif Ramay has compiled the writings of Professor Khwajah Muhammad Zakariyya, Professor Muhammad Uthman, and Dr. Khalifah Abd ul-Hakim, under the name of *Iqbal awr Socialism* (Iqbal and Socialism). He has also compiled the papers of Safdar Mir under the name of *Iqbal, Socialism awr Maududiat* (Iqbal, Socialism and Mauduism). Only S.A. Rahman has presented Iqbal's thoughts on this subject in a balanced manner, that Iqbal stressed the importance of studying socialism so that the Islamic economic concepts may be applied to the solution of the present day problems of the human race. Otherwise Iqbal had no interest in Russian, Chinese or Marxist socialism. With reference to Iqbal's ethical philosophy the book of Professor Sa'eed Ahmad, published by the Institute of Islamic Culture, is also a serious academic effort in the study of Iqbal's philosophy, as to how the ethical ideology of Iqbal has appeared from his concept of *Khudi*. Professor Muhammad Uthman has written three or four important books on Iqbal. These are: *Hayat-i-Iqbal ka Jazbati Daur* (The Intuitional Period of Iqbal's Life), *Iqbal awr Ta'meer-i-Pakistan* (Iqbal and Establishment of Pakistan), and *Asrar-o-Rumuz per aik Nazar* (A View on Asrar-o-Ramooz) which was published later as *Iqbal ka Tasawwur-i-Khudi* (Iqbal's Concept of Khudi). Still his most important book with reference to *Lectures* has been published under the tile of *Fikr-i-Islami kee Tashkeel-i-Nau* (The Re-organization of Islamic Thought). Really, Professor Muhammad Uthman has made an analytical and explanatory study of *Lectures* in this book and in his own words the book can be called *Tasheel-i-Khutbat* (Simplification of *Lectures*). But the lack of philosophical background has rendered this study incomplete and has failed to convey to him the deeper subjects of the *Lectures*. With reference to *Lectures* of Iqbal the book of Mawlana Sa'eed Ahmad Akbarabadi, *Khutbat-i-Iqbal per aik Nazar* (A View on the *Lectures* of Iqbal) is also very important. The book is short but important. In spite of

Understanding Iqbal's Philosophy

being connected with the conventional school of theology Mawlana has exhibited comprehension of the fact that the *Lectures* has laid the foundation of a new theology. Contradicting the objections of some religious circles he writes, "The *Lectures* is a serious and meaningful academic effort of Iqbal, and its importance cannot be reduced only by calling it an effort at promoting intellect and enlightenment of thought. Actually these *Lectures* constitute the theology of the present age, the need for which has been felt by the people with insight since long. It cannot be denied that this theology is far superior, more stable and enlightening to Faith and insight than the old theology. Iqbal is talking from a level where the conflict and friction between Intellect and *Wahi* is out of question". The book of Dr. Muhammad Razi ul-Deen Siddiqui *Iqbal ka Tasawwur-i-Zaman-o-Makan* (Iqbal's Concept of Time and Space) is a beautiful book. This book of Dr. Muhammad Razi ul-Deen Siddiqui has two English and seven Urdu essays, which are: "Iqbal and the Problem of Freewill", "Iqbal's Concept of a Muslim" "Iqbal Huzur-i-Bari Main" (Iqbal in Audience with God), "Maut-o-Hayat Kalam-i-Iqbal Main" (Life and Death in the Works of Iqbal), "Mathnavi 'Asrar-i-Khudi ka Tajziyah" "(The Analysis of the Mathnavi 'Asrar-i-Khudi'), "Qaumon ka Urooj-o-Zawal" (The Rise and Fall of Nations), "Iqbal awr Jazbah-i-Azadi" (Iqbal and the Feeling of Independence), and "Mazhab awr Science Iqbal kee Nazar Main" (Religion and Science in the View of Iqbal). Most important of these is "Iqbal ka Tasawwur-i-Zaman-o-Makan". Being an excellent scholar of philosophy and science Dr. Muhammad Razi ul-Deen Siddiqui has a special status. He has viewed Iqbal's concept of time and space philosophically and scientifically. According to Dr. Siddiqui Iqbal sees a kind of spiritualism in the science of Physics also, and adjudges research and investigation into the universe as an act of worship. According to Iqbal the Muslim thinkers, revolted against the Greek concept of a static universe and presented the concept of an evolving, vibrant and dynamic universe. In Iqbal's view time and space is one condition out of the different conditions of life. Iqbal agrees with the concept of time and space presented by the theory of relativity. He agrees with the explanation of relativity presented by Whitehead, i.e. Nature is not a static entity existing in a static vacuum, but is the sum total of the events which have in them the property of continuous flow. Time and space both are relative and real, and time has more basic reality of the two. Though time and space both are present in all things their mutual relationship is similar to that of the body and intellect. The real time is a special kind of creative dynamism, which cannot be conceived to be continuous or divisible into the past, present and future but time is purely and continuously running.

Iqbal has three or four positions by which he is known at the intellectual level. After the downfall of religion in the West the thought was finding acceptance even among the the Eastern people that religion was some thing decayed and anachronistic which could not keep pace with new concepts. Secondly, it was thought that as the foundation of religion was on blind faith, it militated against use of intellectual rationale for religious beliefs and concepts, and so there was no such thing as intellectual rationale for religious beliefs and concepts. Talking about the possibilities of religion in his *Lectures* Iqbal emphasized religion as an inescapable need for the human race. Introducing the concept of organic relationship between Intuition and thought he enunciated the hypothesis of religious experience being capable of being experienced and understood, and adjudged this experience to be also capable of communication like other scientific experiences, and as being real.

In this way Iqbal proved to be a great and strong champion of religion in the present age. He also challenged the materialism of the West and declared the materialistic basis of the universe fallacious with reference to the concepts of destructibility and mutability of matter and its conversion from the tangible to the intangible form on the basis of modern Physics. From this he adjudged the universe to be of spiritual origin. Then he presented the dynamic concepts of the Holy Qur'an in contradiction of the static concepts of the Greeks. Iqbal supported the concept of renaissance of nations and civilizations on the basis of the Islamic concept of life after death, and proved Spengler's theory of the death of civilizations and cultures after going through childhood, youth and being the victim of old age as false. Declaring this concept false Iqbal argued that the Islamic concept of life after death is a proof for resurrection of nations after death. Hence, just as the dry grass becomes green again after rain, old cultures also are resurrected with the infusion of new thoughts and ideologies. Iqbal deduced the revival and renaissance of Islamic civilization from this.

Enhancing the importance of history and nature with reference to the Holy Qur'an, Iqbal talked about tangible sciences such as study and observation of the natural universe and adjudged science as the heritage of Muslims. In Iqbal's view Islam presented the concepts of dynamism in contradiction of the static concepts of the Greeks. Consequently, he spawned the idea of dynamism and activism among Muslims so that they could reach their goal of renaissance and revival. Through the study of history and nature Iqbal nurtured among Muslims inclination for studying science and technology, so that they could capture the sources of power and energy. Iqbal bestowed self respect on Man with the concept of *Khudi*, raised him above angels in rank and taught every Muslim to acquire the perception and knowledge of his self. In "Seeing oneself in one's own light" Iqbal made it incumbent on the individual to see his essence through himself, in "Seeing oneself in the light of others" he made it incumbent on Man to see himself by diving through the vast expanse of history, and in "Seeing himself in the light of God" he made it obligatory for Man to see himself with reference to the Will and Pleasure of God.

Iqbal taught Muslims the lesson of rising above race and color, sect and cast, and of merging into one *Ummah* and one *Millat*, and instructed them to unite into a single unit from the banks of the Nile to the land of Kashghar. Above all, by enriching the Muslims of Southern Asia with the concept of Pakistan he gave them the leadership of a personage like the Quaid-i-Azam, who was the practical expression of Iqbal's *Mard-i-Mumin* (The Brave Believer) and concept of *Khudi*, and whose politics, based on truth, defeated the lies of the Congress. Thus, Iqbal was the savior of the Muslims of Southern Asia and a tune of revolution for all Muslims.

Iqbal's ideology and thoughts appeared in several persons after his age. His political concepts and ideologies provided a leadership in the person of Quaid-i-Azam who founded an Islamic State in the north-western India. The latter was a living example of Iqbal's concept of *Khudi*. This practical representation of Iqbal's *Mard-i-Mumin*, who had the eagle's heart, succeeded in dispersing the Hindu-British-Nationalist Muslim alliance.

Quaid-i-Azam was a living master-piece of Iqbal's political ideology. Iqbal did not conceive Islam as a sum total of some beliefs but wanted to witness it as a system of life among the Muslims of Southern Asia. This very thought of his was at the back of the establishment of Pakistan. The attitude of Iqbal in presentation of Islam as a system of life through *Ijtihad* in the re-organization of Islamic *Fiqh*, found its way into Mawlana Syed Ab-al-A'ala Maududi. Iqbal was not a mere spiritual support for Mawlana Mawdudi but was also the architect of Mawlana Mawdudi's thoughts. Iqbal's ideology of enforcing Islam as a system of life through Islamic democracy and effective Islamic system appeared in

Study of Iqbalics in Pakistan

Mawlana Mawdudi. Islam's revival and renovation, his stress on economic concepts together with the revolt against the age-old and dead conventionalism of the past appeared in the person of Ghulam Ahmad Parvez. Though Ghulam Ahmad Parvez deviated from the golden mean and, in the end adopted the path of revolt from Iqbal himself, with reference to the history of *Tasawwuf*, Iqbal's attitude of stressing the importance of religion, disgust with dead conventionalism, and reasoning from the new science and technology made appearance in him. The influences of the revolutionism of Iqbal, his disgust with the West and cogitation with reverting to our origin appeared in Ali Shariati. Consequently In *Ma wa Iqbal* (We and Iqbal) Dr. Ali Shariati called Iqbal "Ali Numa" (Like Hazarat Ali, or One Pointing to Hadhrat Ali). Heralding the Iranian revolution he called Iqbal to be his preceptor and leader. The present leaders of Iranian revolution have also called Iqbal their leader. In the same the Afghans drew strength and power from Iqbal in their struggle against Russian imperialism, and during their fighting on all fronts kept Iqbal's works near and dear to themselves. The thoughts of Dr. Fazl al-Rahman and Justice (r) Javid Iqbal have been very deeply influenced by Iqbal's concept of *Ijtihad* and his philosophy of acquisition of strength respectively. I am voluntarily disregarding Iqbal's influence on poetry, because it is very well known that neither prose nor poetry could escape the influence of Iqbal during the last fifty years and will not be able to do so in the next fifty years.

Though much work has been done on Iqbal in other languages of the world I have restricted myself to the study of the work in Pakistan since 1947 as that was my assignment. Indeed Iqbal is echoing all over the world in the form of the music of hope and revolution.